The Diaries of
GEORGE WASHINGTON
Volume I
1748–65

ASSISTANT EDITORS

Beverly H. Runge, Frederick Hall Schmidt,
and Philander D. Chase

George H. Reese, CONSULTING EDITOR

Joan Paterson Kerr, PICTURE EDITOR

THE DIARIES OF
GEORGE
WASHINGTON

VOLUME I

1748-65

DONALD JACKSON, *EDITOR*

DOROTHY TWOHIG, *ASSOCIATE EDITOR*

UNIVERSITY PRESS OF VIRGINIA

CHARLOTTESVILLE

This edition has been prepared by the staff of
The Papers of George Washington,
sponsored by
The Mount Vernon Ladies' Association of the Union
and the University of Virginia.

THE UNIVERSITY PRESS OF VIRGINIA

Copyright © 1976 by the Rector and Visitors
of the University of Virginia

First published 1976

Frontispiece: George Washington, by Charles Willson Peale.
(Washington and Lee University, Washington-Custis-Lee Collection)

Library of Congress Cataloging in Publication Data

Washington, George, Pres. U.S., 1732–1799.
  The diaries of George Washington.

  Bibliography: p. 349
  Includes index.
  1. Washington, George, Pres. U.S., 1732–1799.
I. Jackson, Donald Dean, 1919–   II. Twohig, Dorothy. III. Title.
E312.8 1976   973.4'1'0924 [B]   75–41365   ISBN 0–8139–0643–1 (v. 1)

Printed in the United States of America

Administrative Board

Contents

Maps

Illustrations

Illustrations

Illustrations

Acknowledgments

The editors' first obligation is to the sponsors and agencies whose financial support and enthusiastic backing made our work possible. The cosponsors of *The Papers of George Washington* are the Mount Vernon Ladies' Association of the Union and the University of Virginia. Our principal governmental support has come from the National Endowment for the Humanities, with strong additional funding from the National Historical Publications and Records Commission. An annual grant from the William Stamps Farish Fund has been most appreciated.

Of the many colleagues at the University of Virginia who assisted in the formation and encouragement of *The Papers of George Washington,* the editors are particularly indebted to former president of the University, Edgar F. Shannon, Jr., and his special assistant Francis L. Berkeley, Jr. All the many others who gave us assistance with the countless details of planning, financing, and day-to-day operation are perhaps best represented by one person, Charles L. Flanders of the Office of the Associate Provost for Research at the University of Virginia.

We are grateful for the interest and encouragement of the Regent of the Mount Vernon Ladies' Association of the Union, and of her predecessor, the late Mrs. Francis F. Bierne. The editors also owe a debt of gratitude to the Mount Vernon staff, especially Charles C. Wall, resident director; John A. Castellani, librarian; Frank E. Morse, librarian emeritus; Robert B. Fisher, horticulturist, and Christine Meadows, curator.

For assistance in research on Washington's diaries, we would like to thank the staff of the Manuscript Division, Library of Congress, the research staff of the Colonial Williamsburg Foundation, and members of the Virginia Division of Parks. The Alderman Library at the University of Virginia has housed our editorial offices and its staff has graciously and efficiently performed all the library services essential to an editorial project.

The reproduction of Washington's diaries in these volumes has been made possible by the cooperation of the following repositories and individuals who own the original manuscript material: the Library of Congress, Columbia University Libraries, the Detroit Public Library, Mount Vernon, John K. Paulding, the Historical Society of Pennsylvania, the Virginia Historical Society, and the Public Record Office, London.

Our typographic consultant for general design is P. J. Conkwright, of Princeton, N.J.

The editors acknowledge with appreciation the industry and competence of the following members of the research and clerical staff who over a period of several years were directly involved in the laborious task of transcribing and checking the Washington diaries: Lynne Crane, Dana K. Levy, Patricia Waddell, Corinne Poole, Jessie Shelar, Kathleen Howard, Patricia De Berry, Roger Lund, Barbara Morris, Cynthia S. Miller, Christine Hughes, Nancy Morris, and Karen Whitehill.

Introduction

This edition of the Washington diaries has been prepared by the staff of *The Papers of George Washington,* an enterprise jointly sponsored by the Mount Vernon Ladies' Association of the Union and the University of Virginia. The future labors of the staff will be devoted to the vast body of letters, military records, financial accounts, and other documents that comprise one of the nation's finest historical treasures. In the introductory pages that follow, the editors present their own views of the nature of the diaries, something of their history, and a brief discussion of the present edition.

Washington as a Diarist

The diaries of George Washington are not those of a literary diarist in the conventional sense. No one holding the long-prevailing view of Washington as pragmatic and lusterless, a self-made farmer and soldier-statesman, would expect him to commit to paper the kind of personal testament that we associate with notable diarists. Even when familiarity modifies our view of the man, and we find him warmer and more intense than we knew, given to wry humor and sometimes towering rage—even then we do not find in these pages what we have come to expect of a diary.

But let us not be unfair to a man who had his own definition of a diary: "Where & How my Time is Spent." The phrase runs the whole record through. He accounts for his time because, like his lands, his time is a usable resource. It can be tallied and its usefulness appraised. Perhaps it was more than mere convenience that caused Washington to set down his earliest diary entries in interleaved copies of an almanac, for an almanac, too, is an accounting of time.

That his diaries were important to him there is no doubt. When in the spring of 1787 he journeyed to the Constitutional Convention in Philadelphia and discovered that he would be away from Mount Vernon many weeks, he wrote home for the diary he had accidentally left behind. "It will be found, I presume, on my writing table," he said. "Put it under a good strong paper cover, sealed up as a letter" (GW to George A. Washington, 27 May 1787, CSmH).

We can be unfair to Washington in another way by calling this collection of diaries uneven, mixed, or erratic. That is not his fault but ours, for it is we—his biographers, editors, and archivists —who have brought these items together since his death and given them a common label. It would surprise Washington as often as it does his readers to find between the same boards his "where and how" diaries, weather records, agricultural notations, tours of the North and South during his presidency, together with such documents as a travel journal published in 1754 under the title, *The Journal of Major George Washington, Sent by the Hon. Robert Dinwiddie, Esq; . . . Commander in Chief of Virginia, to the Commandant of the French Forces on Ohio* (Williamsburg, 1754).

Even when his preoccupation with other matters reduces Washington to a mere chronicling of dinner guests, the record is noteworthy, although at times the reader may feel he has got hold of an eighteenth-century guest book rather than a diary. What a diarist chooses to set down, and what not to bother with after a busy day, can be worthy of scrutiny: the number of "respectable ladies" who constantly turned out to pay Washington homage during his southern tour in 1791, tallied so precisely that one suspects Washington of counting heads; his passion for fruits and flowers and the resulting diary notes that very nearly constitute a synopsis of eighteenth-century horticulture; his daily horseback rides, necessary to any large-scale Virginia farmer but clearly a ritual with him; his notices of the dalliance, both planned and impromptu, of his male and female foxhounds—a vital record if canine bloodlines were to be kept pure.

The Washington of the diaries is not the Washington who penned hundreds of letters to neighbors dealing for farm produce and to foreign potentates attending to the affairs of the eighteenth-century world. He is not on guard here, for he seems unaware that any other eyes will see, or need to see, what he is writing.

"At home all day. About five oclock poor Patcy Custis Died Suddenly," runs the complete entry for 19 June 1773. Good enough for his purposes; it was what happened on that day. His curt entry would serve to remind him of his devotion to his ill-fated stepdaughter, dead in her teens after a life made wretched by epilepsy. The place for sorrow was in communications to friends, not in the unresponsive pages of a memorandum book, and so it was to Burwell Bassett that he wrote of his grief for the "Sweet Innocent Girl" who had entered into "a more happy, & peaceful abode than any she has met with in the afflicted Path she hitherto has trod" (20 June 1773, WRITINGS, 3:138).

Reading these diaries from beginning to end can become a tedious exercise, though rewarding. Sampling them in brief sessions can become an equally rewarding way to probe the depths, those uneven depths, of a man who has come to personify the spirit of America in his time. John C. Fitzpatrick realized this essential value of the diaries in the 1920s when he undertook to issue the first compilation, the edition which the present one is intended to supersede. Writing to a committee of the Mount Vernon Ladies' Association of the Union in 1924, he said: "Now that I have read every word of these Diaries, from the earliest to the last one, it is impossible to consider them in any other light than that of a most marvelous record. It is absolutely impossible for anyone to arrive at a true understanding or comprehension of George Washington without reading this Diary record."

The Worlds of Washington

As he rode about Mount Vernon on his daily inspection trips, Washington could turn his eyes frequently to the shipping traffic on the Potomac, his principal link with the great outside world. Vessels with such names as the *Fair American,* the *Betsy,* and the *Charming Polly* plied the river, some trading with the ports of Virginia and Maryland and some bound for far more distant anchorages in North America, the West Indies, or Europe. Most of the schooners, brigs, and ships that Washington watched come upriver were bound for Alexandria's docks and warehouses, and often their cargoes included goods for him: fine clothing and fabrics, bridles and saddles, books and surveying instruments, tools and nails, delicate chinaware and jewelry, fruits and spices, and great wines from France and the Madeiras. Outward bound, they carried the tobacco—and in later years the wheat or flour—that were sent to pay for his imports.

Now and then his commercial representatives in London, Robert Cary & Co., would err and place his shipment aboard a vessel bound for another Virginia river, such as the Rappahannock, and he must endure not only the inconvenience of further transportation but also the risk of loss. On one occasion he warned the Cary company never to ship by any vessel not bound for the Potomac, for when a recent cargo via the Rappahannock finally reached him, he found "The Porter entirely Drank out" (10 Aug. 1760, DLC:GW).

Moving along the growing network of roads that ran from New England to Georgia were more goods and the all-important packets of letters and newspapers that kept Washington in touch with an expanding nation in a restless world. Besides the English journals that came to him, he regularly read American newspapers and periodicals from Boston, New York, Philadelphia, Baltimore, Annapolis, and Williamsburg.

There was little isolation from the world at any time during his life. His diary for 1751–52 relates a voyage to Barbados when he was nineteen, with his dying half brother Lawrence. The next two accounts concern the early phases of the French and Indian War, the momentous struggle for control of the North American continent in which he commanded a Virginia regiment. By the 1760s, when Washington's diaries resume, young George III was on the British throne, and the American colonists were beginning to feel an ominous sense of discontent that during the 1770s grew into rebellion and placed Washington in command of a revolutionary army.

After the War of Independence, Washington never again fought on a field of battle, but military matters and political affairs of national and international import continued to engage his attention. In 1787 he journeyed to Philadelphia for the Constitutional Convention, which he chaired. During his two terms as president of the new nation there were no wars, but serious diplomatic problems arose with Great Britain, France, and Spain in 1793 and 1794. Even in retirement near the end of his life, Washington could not escape the turmoil among nations. When in 1798 relations with France deteriorated to the point that a sea war was developing, old General Washington was placed at the head of a nominal land force that never took the field.

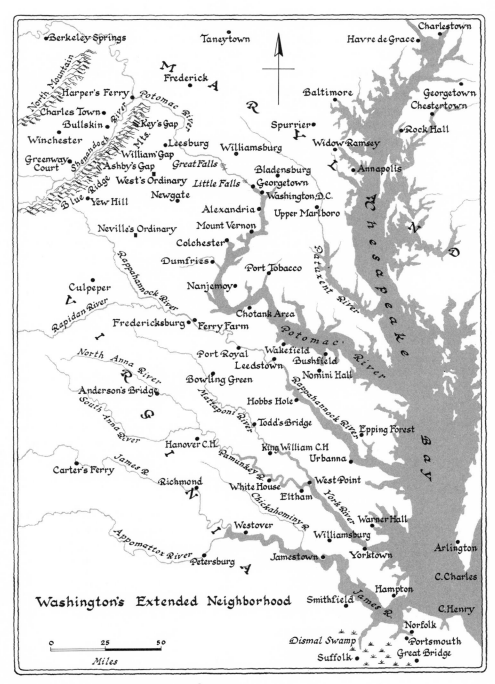

Washington's Extended Neighborhood

In such a world, Washington felt happiest within a much smaller region bounded on the south by the James River and on the north by the Potomac. This was his neighborhood, somewhat extended, a world of very different responsibilities and pleasures that is best revealed in his diaries.

At the heart of this world lay Mount Vernon, the Potomac River plantation that Washington's father Augustine had established in the 1730s on an old family patent and which his half brother Lawrence had inherited and built up before his death in 1752. It was to Mount Vernon that young Colonel Washington came when, in 1758, his involvement in the French and Indian War was finished, for the plantation was now his home, Lawrence's widow having leased it to him four years earlier. It would become permanently his by right of inheritance when she died in 1761. In the meantime, Washington settled at Mount Vernon, thinking that his military career had ended forever. He was prepared for country living, a bit of politics, and plenty of riding to the hounds. The good life truly began for him in January 1759 with his marriage to Martha Dandridge Custis, a sensible young widow with a handsome dowry and two small children nicknamed Patsy and Jacky.

Washington was passionately devoted to Mount Vernon, eagerly extending its borders during the next three decades with numerous purchases of surrounding lands and striving constantly to improve its buildings, fields, and furnishings. But he did not neglect his immediate neighbors in Fairfax County nor did they disregard him. He became a vestryman of the local parish, a magistrate of the county court, a trustee of Alexandria, and one of Fairfax's two burgesses in Virginia's legislature, a position that he held from 1765 to 1775. In the course of carrying out the duties of those offices and of conducting the daily business of his plantation, he came to know well a host of local merchants, craftsmen, farmers, and planters. One of the most notable was George Mason of Gunston Hall, with whom Washington traded horticultural specimens and with whom he sometimes disagreed politically.

But Washington's closest ties, both of friendship and personal interest, were with the Fairfax family, members of the British aristocracy, whose principal American seat was at Belvoir only a few miles down the Potomac from Mount Vernon. There until 1773 lived George William Fairfax, member of the governor's

Council and collector of customs for the South Potomac Naval District. His influence was derived from his father's cousin, Thomas Fairfax, sixth Baron Fairfax of Cameron, proprietor of all the land between the Potomac and the Rappahannock rivers from their mouths to their headwaters, the area that was known as the Northern Neck of Virginia in Washington's time. Lord Fairfax had the exclusive power to grant lands in the Northern Neck and the right to collect annual quitrents of two shillings per one hundred acres on lands that he granted, privileges that he retained until the Revolution.

The proprietor's home was a hunting lodge called Greenway Court, located west of the Blue Ridge Mountains in Frederick County. It too was an area that Washington knew well, for as a youth he surveyed dozens of Lord Fairfax's grants in the Shenan-

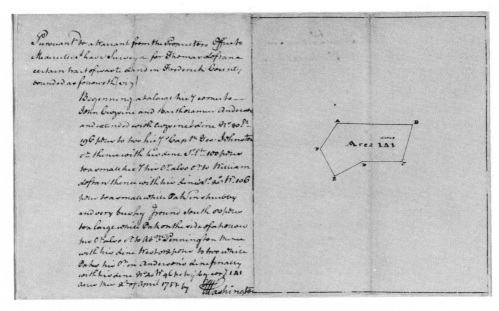

Washington made this survey of land in Frederick County, Va., for Thomas Loftan in 1751. (Smithsonian Institution photo no. 49445)

doah Valley and the valleys beyond. He himself acquired lands along Bullskin Run, a tributary of the Shenandoah River, lands which he retained until his death. During the French and Indian War he was charged for a while with the defense of this region, and for seven years before he was elected a burgess from Fairfax, the freeholders of Frederick sent him to Williamsburg as one of their representatives. In the 1770s and 1780s two of Washington's three younger brothers, Samuel and Charles, also found opportunities west of the Blue Ridge, settling on lands of their own within a few miles of Bullskin.

At the other end of the Northern Neck, south and east of Mount Vernon, lay another part of Washington's extended neighborhood, a region of concern to him mainly because of family ties. Westmoreland County, stretching for about forty miles along the Potomac, was the first home of the Washington family in the New World. There lived Washington's half brother Augustine and his favorite younger brother, Jack, and it was there, on the bank of Pope's Creek, that Washington was born. Farther up the Potomac, about halfway between Westmoreland County and Mount Vernon, was the Chotank area, part of Stafford County until 1776 and then of King George County. In that locality lived a number of Washingtons: brother Sam until 1770, and many distant cousins, some of whom Washington had known from his childhood. Several miles west of Chotank, at Fredericksburg on the south bank of the Rappahannock, was the home of Fielding Lewis, husband of Washington's sister Betty, and before 1780, the home of brother Charles. Across the river from Fredericksburg was the Ferry Farm, where Washington lived as a boy and where his mother, Mary Ball Washington, resided until old age obliged her in 1771 to retire to a house in the town, there to spend the last eighteen years of her life.

At the southern extremity of Washington's extended neighborhood was the provincial capital of Williamsburg and near it, on the York and Pamunkey rivers, were the principal lands of the Custis family and the homes of their relations, the Dandridges and the Bassetts. For Washington this was an area to which he came to fulfill his duties as a burgess, to settle accounts with merchants, and to see that the affairs of his Custis stepchildren were properly managed. But it was also the place in which he attended the theater and balls, dined with men of note, and began to move into the role of an American leader, which eventually took him away from his beloved neighborhood again. Indeed, the network of interconnecting regions between the Potomac and the James that made up that neighborhood helped to develop in Washington that broad feeling of kinship and responsibility for men of differing experience and outlook which enabled him to enter the larger world beyond with ease.

But seldom was his home on the Potomac far from his thoughts, and never did he fail to return there when he could, for it was at Mount Vernon that all his worlds came together. From both inside and outside his extended neighborhood came a galaxy of people from all walks of life to visit him. Some were friends and relatives who came for a holiday, to play cards, to ride to the hounds, or to shoot ducks. Others came on business, to discuss politics and land transactions, to deal in wheat, flour, fish, and other commodities, to bring their mares for breeding, to call at his mill and, in the last years, at his distillery, or sometimes just to ask for help in solving their problems.

After the Revolution he wrote his mother, who had suggested that she might wish to move to Mount Vernon, that "in truth it may be compared to a well resorted tavern, as scarcely any strangers who are going from north to south, or from south to north, do not spend a day or two at it. . . . What with the sitting up of Company; the noise and bustle of servants, and many other things you would not be able to enjoy that calmness and serenity of mind, which . . . you ought now to prefer" (15 Feb. 1787, DLC:GW).

With this endless flow of friends, neighbors, and the idly curious coming to his home, Washington must have thought it an unusual day indeed when on 30 June 1785, at a time when he truly believed that he was done with service to his country, he wrote in his diary that he "dined with only Mrs. Washington which I believe is the first instance of it since my retirement from public life."

Washington and the New Agriculture

No theme appears more frequently in the writings of Washington than his love for the land—more precisely, his own land. From the ordered beauty of the mansion house grounds to the muddiest fields on Bullskin plantation in the Shenandoah Valley, his estate and those who inhabited it were his constant concern. The diaries are a monument to that concern.

In his letters he referred often, as an expression of this devotion and its resulting contentment, to an Old Testament passage. After the Revolution, when he had returned to Mount Vernon, he wrote the marquis de Lafayette 1 Feb. 1784: "At length my Dear Marquis I am become a private citizen on the banks of the Potomac, & under the shadow of my own Vine & my own Fig-tree" (DLC:GW). On the occasion of another joyous homecoming after his two terms as president, the phrase came back to him. He wrote to Oliver Wolcott, Jr., 15 May 1797, that if he ever were to see distant friends again, "it must be under my own Vine and Fig tree as I do not think it probable that I shall go beyond the radius of 20 miles from them" (DLC:GW).[1]

Maintaining the mansion house and its grounds, which required constant attention from carpenters and gardeners, was in part a diversion; farming, on the other hand, was a profession in which he took immense pride. "I shall begrudge no reasonable expence that will contribute to the improvement & neatness of my Farms," he wrote manager William Pearce on 6 Oct. 1793, "for nothing pleases me better than to see them in good order, and every thing trim, handsome, & thriving about them; nor nothing hurts me more than to find them otherwise" (NBLiHi).

The surviving diaries which deal with agriculture begin in 1760, a year sometimes used to denote the beginning of a new agriculture in England. It was also the year of the ascension of George III, a monarch so fond of farming that he maintained experimental plots at Windsor and submitted articles for publication under the name of his farm overseer. The influence of English agriculture on Washington and others in this country—Jefferson included—was indeed great.

Before the agricultural revolution in England, farmers there

[1] "And Judah and Israel dwelt safely, every man under his vine and under his fig tree," 1 Kings 4:25. For similar passages, see 2 Kings 18:31, and Micah 4:4. The allusion occurs at least eleven times in GW's letters of 1796 and 1797, written to such old comrades as Charles Cotesworth Pinckney, Rufus King, Charles Vaughan, and Lafayette. To the earl of Buchan he wrote 4 July 1797: "Be these things however as they may, as my glass is nearly run, I shall endeavour in the shade of my Vine & Fig tree to view things in the 'Calm light of mild Philosophy'" (DLC:GW).

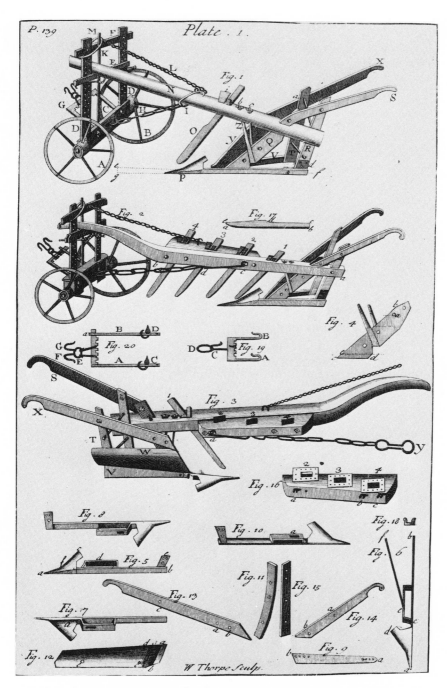

Jethro Tull's *Horse-Hoeing Husbandry*, London, 1733, influenced Washington's early attempts at scientific farming. (Beinecke Rare Book and Manuscript Library, Yale University)

had relied upon a three-year crop rotation: winter grain, a spring crop, and a year of fallow. The revolution brought forage crops, roots, and "artificial," or nonnative, grassses, an entire new system of cultivation pioneered by Jethro Tull. Tull mistakenly believed that plants were fed by tiny particles of soil and that the secret of good farming was to keep the soil well pulverized so the roots might take up the particles. To accomplish this he devised "horse-hoeing," or deep plowing, with crops drilled in rows so that the cultivating implements could pass between them. Although his theory about soil particles was wrong, his cultivating practices marked the beginning of mechanization. But the science of agriculture was changing rapidly. In 1760 Washington was a practitioner of Tull's horse-hoeing husbandry. At his death in 1799 he was devoted to the more sophisticated experiments and writings of Arthur Young and practiced a seven-year rotation.

The period extending from his return after the Revolution until his death was a time of intensive scientific agriculture for Washington. He was faced with the prospect of rebuilding his very large farms after the years of neglect they had suffered while he was the commanding general. He also faced the realization, with many of his fellow Virginians, that soil exhaustion and the evils of a one-crop agriculture were, together with slavery, edging them toward disaster. A general agricultural depression in the United States added to the problem. Washington wrote to George William Fairfax 10 Nov. 1785 that he never rode to his plantations "without seeing something which makes me regret having [continued] so long in the ruinous mode of farming which we are in" (DLC:GW).

At this point, Arthur Young (1741–1820) came into Washington's life. The English agriculturist had read a letter which Washington had written extolling the virtues of manure.[2] Young then began a correspondence which was to last for many years, saying he thought it possible that Washington was as good a farmer as he was a general. Sending the first four volumes of his *Annals of Agriculture* (1784–1808), Young also offered to obtain grain seeds, farm implements, and other items for Washington.

[2] GW had asked George William Fairfax 30 June 1785 to help him find a farm manager in England who knew how to plow, sow, mow, hedge, ditch "& above all, Midas like, one who can convert every thing he touches into manure, as the first transmutation towards Gold" (DLC:GW).

On 6 Aug. 1786 Washington sent him a grateful response. "Agriculture has ever been amongst the most favourite amusements of my life, though I never possessed much skill in the art, and nine years' total inattention to it, has added nothing to a knowledge which is best understood from practice; but with the means you have been so obliging as to furnish me, I shall return to it (though rather late in the day) with hope & confidence" (PPRF). Washington asked Young to send him two plows with extra shares and coulters and the best varieties of cabbage, turnip, sainfoin, winter vetch, and ryegrass seeds, as well as any other grasses which might seem valuable.

One of Washington's great preoccupations, during his whole

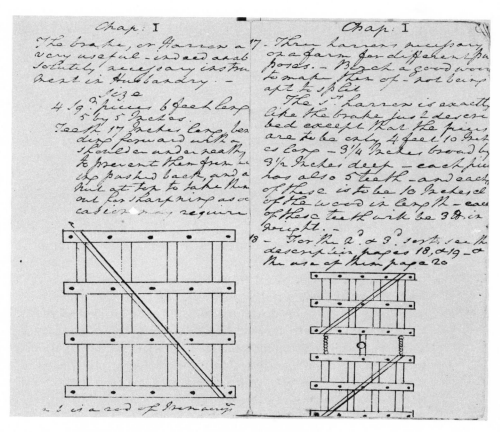

A drag harrow, sketched by Washington from a contemporary work on agriculture. (Library of Congress)

career in agriculture, was finding the right crops for the soil, climate, and practical needs of his Mount Vernon establishment. His determination to throw off the bondage of single-crop farming seemed at times almost too dogged. The number of field crops he raised, attempted to raise, or at least experimented with on a small scale is well above sixty. In a set of "Notes & Observations" he kept for 1785–86 (DLC:GW) he mentions planting barley, clover, corn, carrots, cabbage, flax, millet, oats, orchard grass, peas, potatoes, pumpkins, rye, spelt, turnips, timothy, and wheat.

His experience with tobacco typifies the change in his thinking. Early in the diaries it is his all-important cash crop—the shipment he sends to England every year to exchange for goods he cannot obtain in America. When he drastically reduced his tobacco production he became, in the terminology of the day, no longer a planter but a farmer. One English observer wrote that Washington had no land left which would bring in a good crop of tobacco without appropriating woodland badly needed as a source of firewood for his family and slaves. Also, it required more manure to raise tobacco than his farms could produce (PARKINSON, 2:423–24). By 1766 he was saying that he raised no tobacco at all except at his dower plantations on the York River, and in 1768 he repeated this assertion. He said he raised no tobacco at all on the Potomac.

He could never give up tobacco entirely, however; it was still being raised in 1790 on the Mount Vernon farms. George Augustine Washington's farm report for 20 Aug. reveals that for the preceding week twenty man-days were spent at Muddy Hole in weeding, topping, and suckering tobacco, and similar work was being done at Dogue Run, River Farm, and Union Farm.

Washington raised alfalfa from 1760 to 1795, then gave it up in favor of chicory. He tried the horsebean, as did Jefferson, but it could not thrive in the hot Virginia summers. He tried buckwheat with enthusiasm, both as a feed for livestock and as a green manure, and finally concluded that it depleted as much as it enriched the soil. He raised burnet, sainfoin, ryegrass, hop clover, tick trefoil, guinea grass, hemp, Jerusalem artichoke, Siberian melilot, field peas, and potatoes. He kept on with flax even after Arthur Young had chided him for wasting his time and lands on it; it was essential for his spinning and weaving operations. He even hoped to give up most of his corn crop late in life and buy what he needed, because the hard substratum of clay on his farms made it difficult to till the crop properly without serious erosion. He needed corn because he believed that his slaves did not thrive as well on wheat as on cornmeal, and because he was fond of it himself. "General Washington had so habituated himself to eating the Indian corn bread, that I know some instances of tavern-keepers having to send several miles for it, for his breakfast" (PARKINSON, 2:632).

Experimentation with all these many crops was one of Washington's chief delights as a farmer. He tried drill culture instead of broadcasting the seed; he varied the distance between rows; he planted potatoes and peas between the corn rows. He tried different rates of seeding, carefully noting them in his diaries and other memoranda. In Sept. 1764 he sowed oats on the Dogue Run farm to see if it could endure the winter as his wheat did. Apparently the crop failed. Learning of his interest in experimental agriculture, admirers at home and abroad were eager to assist him. If tabulated, Washington's experiments in agronomy might not appear too different from those of agronomists in the twentieth century.

His experiments with manures extended to animal dung, marl, green crops plowed under, and in at least one instance mud from the Potomac River bottom. In Oct. 1785 he borrowed a scow from Col. George Gilpin to use in collecting mud "to try the efficacy of it as a manure" (GW to Gilpin, 29 Oct. 1785, ViMtV).

The growing shortage of timber with which to make rail fences caused him to turn to live hedges for fencing. He tried honey locust, Lombardy poplar, cedar, and some of the hundreds of species of thorned trees and shrubs. His plan was to start such fences with the fast-growing willows and poplars (which he then thought would turn back any farm animal but a hog), while the slower cedars and locusts were coming up to thicken the hedge. He told manager William Pearce 22 Nov. 1795 that nothing concerning his farms—even the crops—made him so solicitous as his desire to get all his fields enclosed with hedge fences. And the following year, when his crop of honey locust died, he lamented to Pearce that "it would seem I think as if I never should get forward in my plan of hedging" (22 May 1796, NBLiHi). By then he had become resigned to the fact that no live hedge would turn back a hog, but that any tree which would tolerate close planting

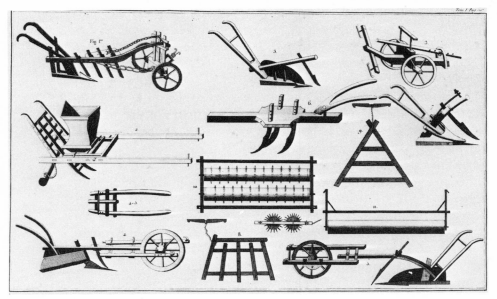

Cultivating tools from an eighteenth-century work, *La Nouvelle Maison rustique*, Paris, 1798. (Mount Vernon Ladies' Association of the Union)

could be used to fence in other livestock. Another decade was to pass before Lewis and Clark would send back to Jefferson specimens of the Osage orange, *Maclura pomifera,* from the West —one of the most successful of all hedge plants in restraining livestock. Except hogs, of course.

Improved cropping calls for improved machinery, as Washington knew, and he shared Jefferson's interest in the mechanical aspects of agriculture. The two men visited the farm of Samuel Powel, near Philadelphia, in 1791 to see the operation of a new threshing machine. It was a primitive device harvesting only six bushels an hour "fit for the miller," but Powel felt that a larger unit might produce 100 to 130 bushels a day (ANNALS, 17 [1792], 206–8). Five years later Jefferson built a similar thresher, and Washington was enthusiastic about it. He wrote Jefferson 6 July 1796: "If you can bring a moveable threshing Machine, constructed upon simple principles to perfection, it will be among the most valuable institutions in this Country" (DLC: Jefferson

Papers). When the farms of the Mount Vernon estate were inventoried in 1800, the listing for the River Farm included one threshing machine, probably a stationary one (ViMtV).[3]

Like most farmers through the ages, Washington was most fascinated by the plow and its potential for advancing agriculture. He ordered a Rotheram patent plow from England 6 Mar. 1765, instructing the firm of Crosbies & Trafford that it ought to be made extremely light, "as our Lands are not so stiff as yours nor our Horses so strong" (DLC:GW). The Rotheram, dating from 1730, was a swing plow of compact design, lighter of frame and with a better moldboard than earlier designs. Made in Rotheram, Yorkshire, it had a coulter and plowshare of iron and a breast covered with iron plate. Farmers in England and Scotland liked its light draft and low cost of manufacture.

Years later, at Washington's request, Arthur Young sent two plows with extra shares and coulters, capable of a nine-inch furrow from four to eight inches deep—depending upon the friability of the soil. Young thought it should be drawn by two stout oxen or horses (Young to GW, 2 Feb. 1787, DLC:GW). By 1788 Washington had found another model he liked so well that he told Thomas Snowden 3 Oct., "I mean to get into the use of them *generally*" (DLC:GW). In the end, however, it was the old reliable Rotheram which pleased him most. He told Benjamin Latrobe in 1796 that he preferred it over all other plows but had found replacement parts impossible to get (LATROBE, 60–61).

Livestock was another vital interest of Washington's, though it is not as apparent—either in the diaries or the letters—as his preoccupation with crops. He was fully aware of the breeding required to prosper with livestock and equally aware of the shortcomings of American farmers in that regard. "The fact is," he wrote Arthur Young 18 June 1792, "we have, in a manner, everything to learn that respects neat & profitable husbandry" (DLC: GW). And to Sir John Sinclair he said 20 Oct. 1792, "we have been so little in the habit of attending either to the breed or improvement of our Stock" (British Museum: Add. Ms. 5757).

---

[3] Other equipment at River Farm was less sophisticated: 8 plows, 10 harrows, 3 ox carts, a horse cart, 20 weeding hoes, 8 axes, 2 mortising axes, 6 mattocks, 2 spades, 3 shovels, 8 rakes with iron teeth, 3 mauling wedges, a pair of steelyards, and a flax rake. Among the more complicated implements at Dogue Run were Dutch fans, double moldboard plows, cultivators, wheat and corn drills, and a machine for gathering clover seed (ViMtV).

His own self-confessed failures in husbandry were due more to his long absences from home than to a lack of good intentions; his letters to his farm managers are filled with exhortations about the care, culling, and breeding of his stock—especially sheep and swine. "At Shearing time . . . let there be a thorough culling out, of all the old, and indifferent sheep from the flocks, that they may be disposed of, & thereby save me the mortification of hearing every week of their death!" he wrote William Pearce 6 April 1794 (NBLiHi).

Washington customarily culled his flock of unthrifty lambs, wethers, and ewes and took care to withhold from market the ram lambs with the best conformation and most wool. He wrote Sir John Sinclair 15 Mar. 1793 that he normally raised from 600 to 1,000 head of sheep and that if he could always be at home to attend to their management he could produce five pounds of wool from each animal and from eighteen to twenty-two pounds of mutton per quarter. He attributed this success in part to the choice of good rams from English stock which he occasionally could obtain, "notwithstanding your prohibitary Laws, or customs" (DLC:GW). The best wool he produced was, he thought, equal to the finest Kentish wool.

Cattle were raised both to serve as oxen and to provide meat. At a time when most Virginians kept cattle in open pens the year around, Washington housed his in sheds from November until May, instructing his managers that they were to be well fed and carefully watered, the ice being regularly broken in cold weather to give them access to clean water. When 300 head of cattle brought him only 30 calves, he decided that "old and debilitated bulls" must be to blame. Despite the rarity of imported stock, some did find its way to America. Washington told manager James Anderson 8 Jan. 1797 to see if he could buy a bull from Henry Gough of Baltimore, even if the price was high. "I should not stand so much upon the price, provided the breed is to be depended upon" (DLC:GW).

Of milk and butter production we learn little from his papers, although he expressed to Pearce 2 Nov. 1794 a desire to get into the dairy business—thinking it might be profitable because of his proximity to Alexandria, Georgetown, and the Federal City (NBLiHi). He sometimes supplemented his own butter production by purchases.

G. Washington

A

COMPLEAT BODY

OF

HUSBANDRY.

CONTAINING

Rules for performing, in the moſt profitable
Manner, the whole Buſineſs of the Farmer and
Country Gentleman,

IN

Cultivating, Planting and *Stocking* of Land;

In judging of the ſeveral Kinds of *Seeds,* and of *Manures* ; and
in the Management of *Arable* and *Paſture Grounds :*

TOGETHER WITH

The moſt approved Methods of Practice in the ſeveral
Branches of HUSBANDRY,

From ſowing the SEED, to getting in the CROP ; and in Breeding
and Preſerving CATTLE, and Curing their DISEASES.

To which is annexed,

The whole Management of the ORCHARD, the
BREWHOUSE, and the DAIRY.

Compiled from the Original Papers of the late
THOMAS HALE, Eſq;

And enlarged by many new and uſeful Communications on
Practical Subjects,

From the Collections of Col. STEVENSON, Mr. RANDOLPH,
Mr. HAWKINS, Mr. STOREY, Mr. OSBORNE, the Reverend
Mr. TURNER, and others.

A WORK founded on Experience ; and calculated for general Benefit ;
conſiſting chiefly of Improvements made by modern Practitioners in
Farming ; and containing many valuable and uſeful Diſcoveries, never
before publiſhed.

ILLUSTRATED WITH

A great Number of CUTS, containing Figures of the Inſtruments of
Huſbandry ; of uſeful and poiſonous Plants, and various other Subjects,
engraved from Original Drawings.

Publiſhed by his Majeſty's Royal Licence and Authority.

VOL. I.

THE SECOND EDITION.

LONDON:

Printed for THO. OSBORNE, in Gray's-Inn;
THO. TRYE, near Gray's-Inn Gate Holbourn; and
S. CROWDER and Co. on London-Bridge. MDCCLVIII.

Washington's own copy of Thomas Hale's *Compleat Body of Husbandry*, London,
1758. (Boston Athenaeum)

His swine ran loose in fenced woodlands until it was time to select the best for fattening in pens. They rooted and shoved their way through his hedges and eluded any attempt to count them. In listing his livestock on the various farms he could only say, in effect, "plus an uncertain number of hogs." He once directed his manager to put a dozen young shoats in a sty and keep an exact account of the cost of raising them for a year. Later he brought up the possibility of raising hogs in pens from birth, at least experimentally. But, as most of his swine must always run at large, he insisted that none be brought from the woodlands to be fattened until they reached sufficient size and age. "I had rather have a little good, than much bad, Porke," he told Anthony Whitting 4 Nov. 1792 (DLC:GW).

The records speak little about poultry. The weekly reports from Washington's manager faithfully record the number of chickens, ducks, and geese on each farm, but the flocks were not large. At a time when wildfowl was abundant, no extensive work with domestic fowls was necessary.

A few days before his death in Dec. 1799, Washington was hard at work on a plan for his future farming operations. He drew up a scheme for each of the farms at Mount Vernon, setting forth in minute detail such matters as crop rotation, the handling of pasture lands and meadows, and use of manures (including the systematic penning of cattle and sheep on regularly shifted temporary enclosures to fertilize the land). His instructions for the River Farm, written 10 Dec. 1799, closed with a characteristic statement: "There is one thing however I cannot forbear to add, and in strong terms; it is, that whenever I order a thing to be done, it must be done; or a reason given at the *time,* or as soon as the impracticability is discovered, why it cannot; which will produce a countermand, or change." Any other course of action was disagreeable to him, he said, "having been accustomed all my life to more regularity, and punctuality, and *know* that nothing but system and method is required to accomplish all reasonable requests" (DLC:GW).

Four days later he was dead, and system and method began to disappear from the farms of Mount Vernon. It would be more than fifty years before the mansion house, eventually bereft of most outlying farmland, was restored to beauty and order. Meanwhile, time and neglect diminished much of what Washington had longed to improve and preserve.

Introduction

In 1834 a writer from Fairfax County, signing himself "F," wrote a letter to the editor of the *Farmers' Register*. He had recently ridden across the farms. "Any, curious to mark the operation of time upon human affairs, would find much for contemplation by riding through the extensive domains of the late General Washington. A more widespread and perfect agricultural ruin could not be imagined; yet the monuments of the great mind that once ruled, are seen throughout. The ruins of capacious barns, and long extended hedges, seem proudly to boast that their master looked to the future" (1:552).

The Weather Watch

Washington's preoccupation with the weather was clearly an extension of his needs and interests as a farmer. He was not a scientific observer, as was Jefferson, and his weather records are

This recording thermometer now at Mount Vernon is similar to those used by Washington.

irregular in scope and content. In editing the diaries for the 1925 edition, Fitzpatrick abandoned the weather record midway in his first volume except when it could not be sorted from other matters recorded, calling the weather entries "unessential" (DIARIES, 1:288n). Our view is that because we cannot and should not attempt to predict the use which readers will be making of the diaries, the weather material should remain. Records for the study of eighteenth-century meteorology are not so plentiful that Washington's may be ignored.

It is difficult to separate him from the weather because so much Washington lore is weather-connected. Seasick days during a stormy voyage to Barbados; the cruel winters at Valley Forge and Morristown; the dust and mud of carriage roads during a lifetime of travel; and, at least in the minds of his family and friends, the probability that an ill-advised horseback ride in a December storm contributed to his death.

His instruments for recording the weather were few, but one in particular is notable. His prized weather vane has survived the changing winds and still serves atop the cupola at Mount Vernon. The vane is in the shape of a dove of peace, the copper body bound with iron strips and the bill with olive branch fashioned from a piece of iron. The bird is forty inches long, and the wing from tip to tip measures thirty-five inches. The vane was made in Philadelphia, by Joseph Rakestraw, in July or Aug. 1787, and was sent immediately to Mount Vernon. Washington wrote his nephew George Augustine Washington, 12 Aug. 1787, that the bill of the dove was to be painted black and the olive branch green. This color scheme is no longer maintained today, the vane having been covered with gold leaf to deter corrosion of the copper body.

Washington made no attempt to measure barometric pressure (though he mentions "falling weather" now and then), and his references to humidity are subjective assessments, not readings from an instrument. Aside from the weather vane, his only known weather instrument was the thermometer. Writing to farm manager William Pearce, from Philadelphia 22 Dec. 1793, he said, "And as it is not only satisfactory, but may be of real utility to know the state of the weather as to heat & cold, but drought or moisture, prefix, as usual, at the head of every weeks report a meteorological account of these. The Thermomiter which is at Mount Vernon will enable you to do the first" (NBLiHi).

Introduction

Two barometer-thermometers now at Mount Vernon, one in Washington's study and the other in the central hall of the mansion, are connected with Washington by family tradition only. A third instrument is probably one mentioned in an inventory of his effects not long after his death. While the inventory accords it a place in the Washingtons' bedroom, where it hangs today in restored form, it may have been located originally in the east hall outside the study. It is a registering thermometer designed to record high and low temperatures for the day, and bears the name of Joseph Gatty, a New York instrument maker.

One of Washington's comments about temperature leads to the speculation that at least some of his readings were made inside the mansion house. "Thermometer at 52 in the Morning & 59 at Noon," he writes in the diary on 7 Dec. 1785, "but removing it afterwards out of the room where the fire was, into the East Entry leading in to my Study, this circumstance with the encrease of the cold fell the Mercury to 42." Meteorologists might charge that Washington was ill advised if not actually foolish for recording indoor readings, and certainly such readings would be of little use today in studying eighteenth-century weather. And ill advised he may have been, by Dr. James Jurin, secretary of the Royal Society of London. Publishing a set of recommendations for keeping a meteorological register, Jurin advocated placing the thermometer "in a room which faces the north, where there is very seldom if ever any fire in the fireplace" (Royal Society, *Philosophical Transactions*, 32 [1723], 425).

In Europe, Jurin's fellow scientists objected to this recommendation, but in English-speaking countries the practice continued through the end of the century. New York and Philadelphia scientists carried on a debate about the practice of thermometer location, and at least one Philadelphia record carries one column for indoor and another for outdoor readings. Jefferson, however, was not a disciple of Jurin. When he discovered that his thermometer in the northeast portico was being affected by an unknown source of heat, perhaps a mound of earth, he changed its location and rejected eighteen months of readings in his weather record (weather diary, MHi; transcript, ViU). For a brief discussion of early views on the correct location of the thermometer, see MIDDLETON (1), 208–13.

Washington's temperature records begin Jan. 1785. It may never be possible to determine which readings were made indoors

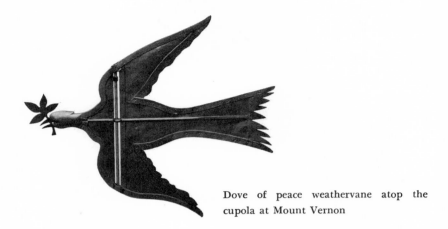

Dove of peace weathervane atop the
cupola at Mount Vernon

and which outdoors, although there are hints in the records
themselves. In 1785, during a period when he was recording
three readings daily—morning, noon, and sunset—there is very
little variation in the day's temperature from reading to reading.
For example, on 19 Jan. he records a reading of 48° Fahrenheit
in the morning, 48° at noon, and 48° at sunset. On occasion there
seems to be a discrepancy between his temperatures and what he
says the weather is doing. He wrote on 26 May that the weather
was warm until about 5:00 P.M. when clouds and high wind
brought about a marked change in the temperature of the air.
Yet his three readings for the day are 65°, 68°, and 67°.

Some of his extremely cold readings may indicate that the
thermometer was outdoors. He wrote on 5 Feb. 1788 of weather
so cold that the mercury did not rise out of the bulb of the thermometer all day. But he was writing about one of the coldest
days of the century, when near Philadelphia the temperature
registered −17° F.

If he was not scientifically accurate, he was at least persistent.
See his entry for 30 April 1785 when, unable to record the
weather personally because of a trip to Richmond, he had put
Mrs. Washington in charge of the thermometer. "Mercury (by
Mrs. W's acct.) in the Morning at 68—at Noon 69 and at Night
62." Even on great occasions in his life, the weather was on his
mind. On 9 Mar. 1797 he left Philadelphia for the last time, after
a lifetime of public service in which he longed always to return

to Mount Vernon. "Wind changed to No. Wt. blew very hard & turned very cold," he wrote in his diary. "Mer. at 28. Left Phila. on my return to Mt. Vernon—dined at Chester & lodged at Wilmington."

History of the Diary Manuscripts

Except for special occasions, such as his mission to the French commandant and his voyage to Barbados, Washington apparently kept no daily record until 1760. Even then, his dairy-keeping was erratic until 1768, when he settled down to a program that he was to continue faithfully until he became commander in chief in 1775.

Washington kept no diary during most of the Revolution. The rigor of his activities would have made it difficult to do so, and the full record of the period which accumulated in his official letterbooks and general orders rendered the custom less necessary. He tried to resume his old habit in 1781, but it was not until he had resigned his command and returned home that he became a confirmed diarist again.

It seems likely that diaries were kept for the presidential years 1789–97, and the fact that so few have survived is particularly vexing to historians. "The Journal of the Proceedings of the President (1793–97)," a daily account of Washington's official activities and correspondence, written in the first person but kept by his secretaries, will be published later. An entry for 16 April 1789, recounting his departure from Mount Vernon to assume office, appears only in SPARKS, 1:441–42. The entry for 23 April 1789, remarking on the enthusiasm with which the public received him, is from IRVING, 4:511. So at least we know that Jared Sparks and Washington Irving had access to material indicating that Washington began his presidency with a determination to continue the record. Diaries are extant for the period covering his tours of the northern and southern states and a brief one kept during the Whisky Rebellion of 1794. Apart from an unrewarding record for 1795, all else is lost for the presidential years.

The earliest diaries were kept in notebooks of various sizes and shapes, but when Washington began in earnest to make daily entries he chose to make them in interleaved copies of the *Vir-*

ginia Almanack, a Williamsburg publication. By the end of the Revolution he had grown accustomed to the blank memorandum books used in the army, and he adopted a similar notebook for his civilian record. By 1795 he had gone back to his interleaved almanacs.

As Fitzpatrick observes, ruled paper was not available to Washington, and he obtained regularly spaced lines by using a ruled guide-sheet beneath his writing paper. "This practice gives us evidence of his failing vision, as the diaries, after the Presidency, show frequent examples of his pen running off the outer edge of the small diary page, and whole words, written on the ruled guide-sheet beneath, escaped notice of not being on the diary page itself" (DIARIES, 1:x).

Upon Washington's death in 1799, most of his papers still in his hands became the property of his nephew Bushrod Washington, an associate justice of the U.S. Supreme Court. We shall have more to say about the fate of these invaluable documents in the Introduction to Volume I of *The Papers of George Washington.*

Destruction and dispersal of the papers began very early when Mrs. Washington reportedly burned all the correspondence she had exchanged with Washington during his lifetime—overlooking only two letters, we believe. There followed long years of careless handling by Bushrod, biographer John Marshall, and editor Jared Sparks. Indeed, what is most important in the story of Washington's papers is not such natural processes as fire, flood, mildew, and the tendency of paper to fall into dust. Rather, there has been an overabundance of stewardship by misguided caretakers, persons who thought they knew what was important and what was trivial, what should be saved and what given away to friends and autograph collectors.

The editor who laments the disappearance of so many Washington diaries can only sink into despondency upon learning that Bushrod gave many away. To diplomat Christopher Hughes, in 1825, he gave the 1797 diary and a sheaf of Washington's notes on agriculture; Hughes dispersed these among his friends in the United States and Europe. Two years later, Bushrod gave the diaries for 1795 and 1798 to Margaret and Robert Adams, of Philadelphia. Then he presented the 1767 diary to Dr. James W. Wallace, of Warrenton. These and certain other diaries once in

October 1799

19. Morning quite clear with a
small breeze from the s° E —
Mer. at 43 — a great circle round
the Sun about Noon which cont'd for
hours. & towards night it began
to Cover much — Mer 55 at Night

20. Morning very heavy — Wind
Southerly & Mer at 54 — a strug
gle all day between the Sun &
the Clouds — but no Rain yet
Mer 62 at Night. — Doct. Stuart
wife & three daughters — and
young Dav.d McCarty came to
Dinner & stayed all Night

21. Morning clear — wind Southerly
Mer at 60 — the forepart of the day
Variable — the latter part clear
Warm & pleasant — Mer at 64

22. Clear, with the Wind at N.W.
and Mer at 58. in the Morning
fresh wind all day from the
Same quarter. — Mer 50 at Night
M.r Liston (British Minister)
& Lady came to dinner — as did
young M.r McCarty. —

23. Morning clear & calm — Mer
at 42 — Clear all day wind com=
ing out from the N West but not
fresh — Mer 49 at Night. —
M.r Herbert — M.r & M.rs Patton —
M.r   M.r Gilman came
to dinner — the last stayed all
Night.

*This leaf from the Diary of General Washington was given
to me by Mr Sparks the editor of his correspondence on the
22.d February 1832 the centenary of his birth*   Robert Gilmor

Editor Jared Sparks gave away this page from a Washington diary in 1832. (Historical Society of Pennsylvania, Dreer Collection)

private hands have been preserved; others apparently have not.

Jared Sparks's turn to mishandle the papers came in 1827, when he persuaded Bushrod to let him take large quantities to Boston, where he was to prepare his twelve-volume edition, *The Writings of George Washington* (Boston, 1837). Sparks decided that carefully excising a Washington signature from a document, and sending it to a friend, did not really damage the manuscript as a piece of history; that a page torn from a Washington diary, or an entire Washington letter, could safely be given away if he, Sparks, judged it to be of no historical value. It was Sparks who cut Washington's draft of his first inaugural address into small pieces and so thoroughly disseminated this document of more than sixty pages that the efforts of several collectors have failed to reassemble more than a third of it. Even after he had supposedly returned all the papers to the Washington family, Sparks retained a supply to distribute. He was still mailing out snippets in 1861.

The pillage stopped in 1834 when the Washington family sold the basic collection to the U.S. government. This corpus, together with a later, smaller sale, forms the basis of the principal Washington archive at the Library of Congress. Other acquisitions have been made throughout the years.

In the following list, the present location of all known diaries and diary fragments is shown. The Regents' Numbers are numbers assigned by Fitzpatrick in the 1920s and used since as a cataloguing device. The diaries without Regents' Numbers were not published by Fitzpatrick, nor were several to which he assigned numbers but could not locate. His number 54, which he believed to have been kept but did not locate, is partially represented by the next diary in the series.

Date	*Regents' Number*	*Location*
11 Mar. 1747–13 April 1748	1	Library of Congress
28 Sept. 1751–4 Feb. 1752	2	Library of Congress
31 Oct. 1753–11 Jan. 1754	3	Public Record Office, London
31 Mar.–27 June 1754	4	Printed version [see p. 167]

Date	Regents' Number	Location
1 Jan.–11 April 1760	5	Library of Congress
1 Jan.–22 May 1760	6	Library of Congress
24 May–22 Oct. 1761	7	Library of Congress
1 Jan.–31 Dec. 1762	—	Library of Congress (on deposit)
2 Mar.–18 Nov. 1763	8	Library of Congress
29 Mar.–18 Oct. 1764	9	Library of Congress
1 Jan.–13 Nov. 1765	10	Library of Congress
12–31 May 1765	—	Hist. Soc. of Pa.
14 Jan.–29 Oct. 1766	11	Library of Congress
1 Feb.–20 Nov. 1767	12	Library of Congress
21 Nov.–31 Dec. 1767	13	Missing or not kept
1 Jan.–31 Dec. 1768	14	Library of Congress
1 Jan.–31 Dec. 1769	15	Library of Congress
1 Jan.–31 Dec. 1770	16	Library of Congress
1 Jan.–31 Dec. 1771	17	Library of Congress
1 Jan.–31 Dec. 1772	18	Library of Congress
1 Jan.–31 Dec. 1773	19	Library of Congress
1 Jan.–31 Dec. 1774	20	Library of Congress
1 Jan.–19 June 1775	21	Library of Congress
1 Jan.–4 June 1780	—	Library of Congress
1 May–5 Nov. 1781	22 & 23	Library of Congress
1 Sept.–4 Oct. 1784	24	Library of Congress
12 Oct.–31 Dec. 1784	25	Missing or not kept
1 Jan.–16 May 1785	26	Library of Congress
17 May–26 Sept. 1785	27	Library of Congress
27 Sept. 1785–16 Jan. 1786	28	Library of Congress
17 Jan.–30 April 1786	29	Library of Congress
1 May–26 July 1786	30	Library of Congress
27 July–18 Oct. 1786	31	Library of Congress
19 Oct. 1786–30 Mar. 1787	32	Library of Congress
30 Mar.–27 Oct. 1787	33	Library of Congress
11 May–15 Nov. 1787	34	Library of Congress
28 Oct. 1787–17 April 1788	35	Library of Congress
17 April–31 July 1788	36	Library of Congress
1 Aug. 1788–2 Feb. 1789	37	Library of Congress
3 Feb.–30 Sept. 1789	38	Missing or not kept (but see p. xli)

Date	Regents' Number	Location
16 April 1789	—	Printed fragment, SPARKS
23 April 1789	—	Printed fragment, IRVING
1 Oct. 1789–11 Mar. 1790	39	Detroit Public Library
12 Mar. 1790–1 June 1791	40–43	Virginia Historical Society
2 June–4 July 1791	44	Library of Congress
5 July–31 Dec. 1791	45	Missing or not kept
1792, 1793, 1 Jan.–29 Sept. 1794	46–48	Missing or not kept
30 Sept.–20 Oct. 1794	49	Library of Congress
21 Oct.–31 Dec. 1794	50	Missing or not kept
1 Jan.–13 April 1795	51	Missing or not kept
14 Apr.–24 Dec. 1795	52	Columbia University
22–31 Dec. 1795	53	Missing or not kept
1796	54	Missing
1 Jan.–21 June 1796	—	Historical Society of Pennsylvania
1 Jan.–31 Dec. 1797	55	Mount Vernon
1 Jan.–31 Dec. 1798	56	Columbia University
1 Jan.–21 Jan. 1799	—	Historical Society of Pennsylvania
22 Jan.–9 Feb. 1799	—	Historical Society of Pennsylvania
10 Feb.–13 Dec. 1799	57	Library of Congress
13–23 Oct. 1799	—	Historical Society of Pennsylvania

Previous Editions

During most of the nineteenth century, publication of Washington diaries was sporadic and limited. Sparks used extracts from certain diaries in an appendix to his second volume of *Writings,* edited as to grammar and spelling in the usual Sparks manner. Benson J. Lossing edited and published two small editions at mid-century, *Diary of Washington from the First Day of October, 1789, to the Tenth Day of March, 1790* (New York, 1858), and *The Diary of George Washington from 1789 to 1791* (New York, 1860). Another edition of the latter, published in Richmond in 1861, included Washington's 1753–54 journal of his mission to the French.

A quarter century after Lossing's editions, two men found that each had been preparing more extensive collections of the diaries, unknown to one another. Their work marked the beginning of a series of events that would culminate in the publication of the first comprehensive edition in 1925.

Dr. Joseph Meredith Toner (1825–1896), a physician, writer, and collector, began the practice of medicine in Washington, D.C., in 1855 and later became president of the American Medical Association. His practice was nearly overshadowed by two hobbies, the collecting of books and ephemera in the field of medicine and the study of George Washington. By 1888 he had employed a copyist to begin transcribing Washington's diaries (at seven cents per hundred words) and had begun to approach publishers. A rejection letter of 31 May 1888 from Houghton Mifflin Co. explains that a particular Washington diary probably would not be suitable for publication because it was available in other forms (DLC: Toner Collection). But Toner did achieve publication of a pamphlet entitled *George Washington's Rules of Civility and Decent Behavior* (Washington, D.C., 1888).

A. C. McClurg & Co. rejected a diary manuscript in a letter of 15 Feb. 1889, explaining that it would not be a profitable venture (DLC: Toner Collection); but the doctor's determination to go ahead was becoming known. At this point his work came to the attention of Worthington Chauncey Ford (1858–1941), an archivist and a historical editor who was preparing the first multivolume edition of Washington's papers in more than half a century. Apprehensive that he and Toner were duplicating work, he asked for an appointment in a letter of 23 Jan. 1889, seeking a consultation for their "mutual advantage" (DLC: Toner Collection).

If the two men did confer at this time, Ford must have explained that he already had in press the first volume of his *Writings of George Washington* (New York, 1889–93) and that the first two volumes would contain the diaries of 1747/48, 1753–

54, and 1754 with extracts from later diaries through 1774. The entire work would contain fourteen volumes.

Toner was determined to proceed despite this competition from an industrious man more than thirty years younger than he. On 9 June 1890 the publishing house of Joel Munsell's Sons, in Albany, N.Y., accepted a manuscript from Toner, offering him terms which required him to advance $200 for publication costs. By 23 June the publisher was planning to issue an entire set of diaries in volumes of about 500 pages each. And by 3 Dec. Toner was receiving galley proof of the 1747/48 journal (DLC: Toner Collection).

The Munsell firm published three works for Toner, the diaries of 1747/48, 1753–54, and 1754, the first two issued in 1892 and the third the following year. Even before these books appeared in print, however, it had become apparent to Munsell's that the venture was unprofitable. Toner began to solicit other publishers, writing 27 May 1891 to C. L. Webster & Co., of New York, offering about 3,000 pages of foolscap transcriptions with footnotes. The file contains a similar letter, undated, to Harper & Brothers, of New York (DLC: Toner Collection, letters sent, 1849–96). No replies have survived. Except for an annotated abstract of the 1774 diary, covering Washington's attendance at the First Continental Congress, which appeared in the *Annual Report* for 1892 of the American Historical Association, Toner published no more of the diaries upon which he and his copyist, Mary Stevens Beall, had labored for so many years.

There remains in the Library of Congress, however, the complete and carefully made transcript, valuable now because it was written at a time when the manuscripts were in a somewhat more readable condition. Toner's copious notes are useful mainly as an incentive to further research, for he gave no sources for the thousands of annotations that he made.

Diary publication during the ensuing three decades was sporadic. Archer B. Hulbert produced *Washington and the West: Being George Washington's Diary of September, 1784* (New York, 1905). In the same year, Worthington C. Ford returned to the scene with extracts from the diaries of 1785 and 1786 in *Publications of the Colonial Society of Massachusetts*. That society was to issue his remaining work on the 1786 diary in its publications of 1915 and 1917.

Introduction

The Regent and Vice-Regents of the Mount Vernon Ladies' Association of the Union began to move toward a comprehensive edition in 1914, unaware that shortages and other pressures of World War I would soon bring disappointing delays. Some of the impetus for the Regents' campaign for publication came from Charles Sprague Sargent (1841–1927), director of the Arnold Arboretum at Harvard University. As counsel to the Association since 1901 on horticultural matters, he began in 1914 to make annual visits to Mount Vernon. Because the diaries are so rich in horticultural lore, he studied them thoroughly. Apparently as a result of his first visit to the mansion house and grounds, he suggested to Regent Harriet Clayton Comegys that her Association ought to sponsor a complete edition. The following discussion of ensuing events is based upon correspondence and reports in the Regents' files at Mount Vernon.

A diary committee was formed in 1915, consisting of Vice-Regents Harriet L. Huntress of New Hampshire and Alice M. Longfellow of Massachusetts. By the end of the year they were seeking an editor. The Regent had suggested Owen Wister, "who writes so well about Washington and understands him so well." Others considered included Clarence H. Brigham, librarian of the American Antiquarian Society, and Mark Howe, editor of the *Harvard Alumni Bulletin.*

There was an obvious choice, of course, and the committee soon got around to him. Worthington C. Ford was invited to assume the task and at first declined, suggesting instead Professors Max Farrand of Yale, Sidney Fiske Kimball of Smith College, or William MacDonald of Brown University. But when the diary committee submitted its annual report for 1916, it declared that Ford himself had at last agreed to edit the diaries. Having served for several years as chief of the manuscripts division at the Library of Congress, Ford was now in his seventh year as editor of publications for the Massachusetts Historical Society. (For an excellent memoir of Ford's vast career as an editor and historian, see BUTTERFIELD [2].)

Printer's copy for the text of the diaries was nearly ready in March 1917, Ford told Miss Huntress. He said the annotation was "well in hand." In November he again reported the work going well but voiced a complaint familiar to anyone who has attempted to edit the diaries: the myriad names of persons to be identified. "To name generation after generation the same is an evil habit," he wrote.

By now the United States was at war with Germany, and normal routines were interrupted. Ford, however, reported in April 1918 that he was still forging ahead and thought he would be ready for the printer "on the return of peace." Peace came, but new trials developed. On 5 May 1919 he wrote Miss Huntress, "Judging from the current prices of printing and the situation of the book market, which is entirely unsatisfactory, I should recommend the postponement of the publication for another year." Besides, he was planning a trip to England and would not be available to read galleys. What he did not say was that his optimism about the completion of his editorial chores was utterly unjustified. He was not nearly ready for the printer.

By May 1921 the diary committee was reporting to the council of the Association that Ford's work was nearing completion but that a printers' strike as well as high production costs would delay publication. In Feb. 1923 Ford seemed to realize that he was never going to finish his work. He wrote the diary committee, the chairman of which was then Annie B. Jennings of Connecticut, that he wanted to be relieved of his assignment because of illness.

When John C. Fitzpatrick (1876–1941) entered the scene, he was on the staff of the manuscripts division of the Library of Congress. He had been a journalist until joining the library staff soon after the appointment in 1897 of his uncle-in-law, John Russell Young, as librarian of Congress. Since then he had become a respected curator, responsible for a number of calendars and guides issued by the library. Two of these dealt with Washington: calendars of his correspondence with the Continental Congress (1906) and with his officers of the Continental Army (1915). Fitzpatrick also had produced a facsimile edition of Washington's expense account while commander in chief (Boston, 1917) and was a frequent contributor of historical articles to the *Daughters of the American Revolution Magazine*.

Fitzpatrick's work was known to Fairfax Harrison (1869–1938), a Virginia railroad magnate, writer, and patron of many historical projects. Harrison had begun a movement to publish the Washington diaries privately, edited by Fitzpatrick, when he learned that the Mount Vernon Ladies' Association of the Union had revived its hope of sponsoring an "official" edition. The plan for a privately sponsored edition was dropped, and on 22 May 1923 Fitzpatrick was told by Eleanor Tyrell, secretary of the Regent, that he had been chosen to edit the Regents' own edition.

As his later thirty-nine volumes of the *Writings of George Washington* would attest, Fitzpatrick was a prodigious worker. Because of his energy and perhaps some previous work on the diaries for Harrison, and aided by materials from Toner and Ford, he was able to advise the council 20 June 1924 that he had completed his editorial work on the manuscript. All that remained was to find a publisher (Houghton Mifflin was to become the majority choice, but the presses of Harvard and Yale were still under discussion) and to settle on the costs of production and distribution.

The four-volume edition, *The Diaries of George Washington, 1748–1799,* came off the press in Oct. 1925. Houghton Mifflin had agreed on a mutual sharing of the costs, the Association to pay for composition and plates, the publisher to assume the expense of printing, paper, binding, and advertising. There were three printings in the fall of 1925. The publisher reported sales to 1 April 1926 of 3,096 copies. From their royalties, the Ladies paid Fitzpatrick $1,500 for his editorial work and an additional $350 for preparing the index.

The Present Edition

Although in a generic sense the diaries in this edition are part of Washington's "papers," they are published separately from the forthcoming series, *The Papers of George Washington.* This decision seems fitting because the diaries span Washington's entire career in relatively few volumes and are thus a complete work in themselves. There are lamentable gaps, but the reader may savor the man's words and works as they evolved from the day he set out as a boy of sixteen, to survey for Lord Fairfax, until that day before his death when, always conscious of the weather, he wrote a final entry: "Mer[cury] at 28 at Night."

Another persuasive reason to issue the diaries before the *Papers* has been the time required to assemble, from repositories and private owners all over the world, the letters and documents that will comprise the main series. While these thousands of manuscripts were being located, catalogued, and transcribed by some members of our staff, others proceeded with the editorial work on the diaries. The fact that as these diaries go to press we are still receiving substantial numbers of manuscripts for inclusion in the *Papers* provides further justification for our decision.

The present text of the diaries varies but slightly from that of the 1925 edition. Fitzpatrick missed the 1762 diary (not a significant one) and a few other fragments. His reading of the tattered manuscripts often differs from ours. He did some rearranging, and he omitted much of the weather data. But in general his transcription of the diaries is substantially the same as ours.

What differs is the editing. The re-editing of a historical document is much like the cleaning of an old and well-loved painting. The design, the basic theme, remains unchanged; but the colors brighten and reveal forgotten nuances of brushstroke and pigment. Occasionally, figures emerge from the background that have long been concealed, and suddenly new meanings are there; new interpretations are possible.

Succeeding generations of editors have always gone about their work in ways that differ from those of their predecessors, hoping that in the process they are improving upon the craft. They have an inevitable advantage in the vast quantity of historical research turned out by every generation of historians. Many of our manuscript sources, as well as large numbers of printed books used in our work, were unavailable to earlier editors. Washington's diaries present a peculiar problem to the modern editor in that some of the daily entries are long, detailed, and informative; others are perfunctory and, to be frank, often dull. This has brought about a variation in the length and nature of our annotation that is not accidental. When Washington feels talkative, we let him talk. When he grows laconic and uninformative, we feel a greater urge to let the reader know what is going on. Yet we must avoid the temptation to overshadow his brief entries with extended editorial statements better left for our edition of the *Papers*.

The principal aims of the editorial staff have been these:

a. To present the most accurate text possible (an editor's first important task).

b. To identify all persons and to connect them to Washington and his activities when possible. In this we have often failed.

Preparing these short biographical statements about obscure eighteenth-century figures has proved to be the most difficult part of the editorial process. The urge to follow the example of Dr. Toner has been great. In his notes on the Washington diaries he identifies one Private John Doe simply as "a soldier." Our system, however, is to remain silent if we have no useful biographical information to offer. People and places have generally been identified at first appearance in the diaries. Washington commonly refers to individuals only by surname. In cases where the person has been previously identified the full name will be found in the index.

c. To edit fully his various travel narratives, such as the voyage to Barbados in 1751, the mission to the French in 1753, the trip to Ohio and Kanawha rivers in 1770, and his two presidential tours.

d. To maintain a running account of his activities in and around Williamsburg while serving in the Virginia House of Burgesses.

e. To clarify for the reader Washington's many dealings in land and especially to keep abreast of his farming operations on his five Mount Vernon farms, his Bullskin plantation in the Shenandoah Valley, and the dower plantations on the York.

f. To identify all plant materials at first mention, whether field crops or horticultural specimens, and to discuss them if appropriate.

g. To cover his presence at the Virginia Convention of 1774 and the Continental Congresses of 1774 and 1775.

h. To make those persons around Washington, including the family and friends he loved and the neighbors he saw so frequently, come alive. And, we must add, to do the same for him.

Editorial Procedures and Symbols

Transcription of the diaries has remained as faithful as possible to the original manuscript. Because of the nature of GW's diary entries, absolute consistency in punctuation has been virtually impossible. Where feasible, the punctuation has generally been retained as written. However, in cases where sentences are separated by dashes, a common device in the eighteenth century, the dash has been changed to a period and the following word capitalized. Dashes which appear after periods have been dropped. Periods have been inserted at points which are clearly the ends of sentences. In many of the diaries, particularly those dealing with planting and the weather, entries consist of phrases separated by dashes rather than sentences. Generally if the phrase appears to stand alone, a period has been substituted for the dash.

Spelling of all words is retained as it appears in manuscript. Errors in spelling of geographic locations and proper names have been corrected in notes or in brackets only if the spelling in the text makes the word incomprehensible. Washington occasionally, especially in the diaries, placed above an incorrectly written word a symbol sometimes resembling a tilde, sometimes an infinity sign, to indicate an error in orthography. When this device is used the editors have silently corrected the word.

The ampersand has been retained. The thorn has been transcribed as "th." The symbol for per has been written out. When a tilde is used to indicate either a double letter or missing letters, the correction has been made silently or the word has been transcribed as an abbreviation. Capitalization is retained as it appears in the manuscript; if the writer's intention is not clear, modern usage is followed.

Contractions and abbreviations are retained as written; a period is inserted after abbreviations. When an apostrophe has been used in contractions it is retained. Superscripts have been lowered, and if the word is an abbreviation a period has been added. When the meaning of an abbreviation is not obvious, it has been expanded in square brackets: H[unting] C[reek]; so[uther]ly.

Other editorial insertions or corrections in the text also appear in square brackets. Missing dates are supplied in square brackets in diary entries. Angle brackets ($<$ $>$) are used to indicate mutilated material. If it is clear from the context what word or words are missing, or missing material has been filled in from other sources, the words are inserted between the angle brackets.

A space left blank by Washington in the manuscript of the diaries is indicated by a bracketed gap in the text. In cases where Washington has crossed out words or phrases, the deletions have not been noted. If a deletion contains substantive material it appears in a footnote. Words inadvertently repeated or repeated at the bottom of a page of manuscript have been dropped.

Introduction

If the intended location of marginal notations is clear, they have been inserted in the proper place without comment; otherwise, insertions appear in footnotes.

In cases where the date is repeated for several entries on the same day, the repetitive date has been omitted and the succeeding entries have been paragraphed.

Because Washington used the blank pages of the *Virginia Almanack* or occasionally small notebooks to keep his diaries, lack of space sometimes forced him to make entries and memoranda out of order in the volume. The correct position of such entries is often open to question, and the editors have not always agreed with earlier editors of the diaries on this matter. Such divergence of opinion, however, has not been annotated.

Bibliographical references are cited by one or two words, usually the author's last name, in small capitals. If two or more works by authors with the same surname have been used, numbers are assigned: HARRISON [2]. Full publication information is included in the bibliography for each volume. The symbols used to identify repositories in the footnotes precede the bibliography.

Surveying notes and dated memoranda kept in diary form have not been included in this edition of Washington's diaries, although the information contained in them has often been used in annotation.

The Diaries of
GEORGE WASHINGTON
Volume I
1748–65

Surveying for Lord Fairfax

11 March–13 April 1748

EDITORIAL NOTE. During the spring of 1748 GW undertook a journey that introduced him for the first time to an area which was to play an important part in his career. In March of that year he had an opportunity to join a party engaged by Lord Fairfax[1] to survey his properties on the South Branch of the Potomac River. Fairfax was the proprietor of the Northern Neck of Virginia, which encompassed the area between the Potomac and Rappahannock rivers from the Chesapeake Bay to the headwaters of the two rivers. The grant for the proprietorship of the Northern Neck was originally made in 1649 by the exiled Charles II to John Culpeper, first Baron Culpeper of Thoreaway, and others as a reward for their support. No effort was made to implement the grant during the period of Cromwell's rule, but it was revived in 1660 when Charles II returned to England. The Culpeper interest in the proprietary passed to Lord Culpeper's son Thomas and to other relatives. By 1662 there was evident opposition in Virginia to the grant because of its interference with headright grants made by the colony. But by 1689, Thomas, Lord Culpeper, after serving for a time as governor of Virginia, had obtained a crown renewal of the grant and had secured the rights of all the

---

[1] Thomas Fairfax, sixth Baron Fairfax of Cameron (1693–1781), was born at Leeds Castle, County Kent, and educated at Oriel College, Oxford. Somewhat of a recluse and misogynist, he led a quiet life at Leeds Castle until about 1733, when an awakening interest in his inheritance in America interrupted his fox hunting and horse breeding. In 1735 he went to Virginia to protect his estate against attack by the colonial legislature. Successful in his efforts, he returned to England in 1737, but in 1747 settled permanently in Virginia and for the rest of his life engaged in the development of the proprietorship. In 1752 he established Greenway Court, his permanent residence in the Shenandoah Valley, where he lived the life of a country gentleman and participated actively in the affairs of his domain. He served as a justice of the peace in all the counties created in the proprietorship and as a county lieutenant in the Virginia militia. Although he probably leaned somewhat to the British side during the Revolution, his activities were carefully neutral and he was in no way molested by the Patriots. He died at Greenway Court in 1781.

The Fairfax coat of arms. (Trustees of the British Museum)

Thomas Fairfax, sixth Baron Fairfax of Cameron, an early influence on the young Washington. (Alexandria-Washington Lodge No. 22, A.F. & A.M., Alexandria, Va.)

proprietors except those of other members of the Culpeper family. Upon his death in 1689 the Northern Neck proprietorship was left to his wife and his only legitimate child, Catherine.

In 1690 Catherine married Thomas Fairfax, fifth Baron Fairfax of Cameron, bringing the Northern Neck into the possession of the Fairfax family. The deaths of the fifth baron in 1710 and of Lady Culpeper in 1719 left Thomas Fairfax, sixth Baron Fairfax, the sole proprietor of the Northern Neck.[2] By the time Lord Fairfax had settled in Virginia in 1745, there had been extensive occupation of his lands, with ensuing uneasiness on the part of the settlers concerning the validity of their claims and a desire on the part of Lord Fairfax to confirm title to his property in the area. In 1746 the western boundary of the proprietary had been surveyed, under conditions of great difficulty, and with the confirmation of the boundary the settlers began to request valid grants from the proprietor.[3] By 1747 surveyors for Fairfax were active

[2] For the involved history of the Northern Neck proprietary, see FREEMAN, 1:447–525; BROWN, 26–66; HARRISON [2]; DICKINSON [2], 1–30.

[3] For a description of the hardships endured by the surveyors of the 1746 boundary, see BROWN, 104–8; LEWIS. Members of the expedition included Col. William Fairfax and George William Fairfax, William Beverley, Col. Lunsford Lomax, Peter Hedgeman, Peter Jefferson, Joshua Fry, and James Genn.

An early map of the Northern Neck of Virginia. (Map Division, Library of Congress)

in the area of the Rappahannock, the Shenandoah, and the South Branch of the Potomac.

GW's association with the powerful Fairfax family grew out of the marriage of his half brother Lawrence, owner of Mount Vernon, to Ann Fairfax, daughter of Col. William Fairfax.[4] When-

---

[4] William Fairfax (1691–1757) was born in Toulston, Yorkshire, Eng., the son of Henry and Anna Harrison Fairfax. He was a first cousin of Lord Fairfax. As a young man William served briefly in the British army and held a royal appointment in the Bahamas. While he was stationed there he married Sarah Walker, daughter of Maj. Thomas Walker of the British army. In 1725 he received an appointment as collector of customs at Salem and Marblehead and moved to Massachusetts. Sarah died in 1731 and he then married Deborah Clarke of Salem. In 1734 Lord Fairfax's perennial dissatisfaction with his land agents in Virginia led him to offer the post to his cousin, who accepted and moved to Virginia in the same year. He subsequently built Belvoir about 1741 on the banks of the Potomac near Mount Vernon.

ever possible GW escaped from the austerity of his mother's home at Ferry Farm to the pleasant plantation life of his brother's house. While he was staying with Lawrence at Mount Vernon, GW was a frequent visitor at Belvoir, the beautiful estate of William Fairfax some four miles from Mount Vernon. He soon became an intimate of the family and formed in particular a warm friendship with George William Fairfax,[5] Colonel Fairfax's son. It was natural, therefore, when George William was sent as Lord Fairfax's agent on a surveying trip, that GW should be asked to accompany him.

It is uncertain when GW's interest in surveying as a career began. For a time in 1746 he had considered the possibility of going to sea, but the determined opposition of his mother and her family had compelled him to seek a career closer to home.[6] Surveying in eighteenth-century Virginia promised a respectable and lucra-

[5] George William Fairfax (1724–1787) was born at Providence in the Bahamas, the son of William and Sarah Walker Fairfax, was educated in England, and returned in 1746 to America to join his father in Virginia. He frequently acted as estate agent for Lord Fairfax. He served as a burgess from Frederick County 1748–49 and 1752–55, was a colonel in the Frederick militia 1755–56, and a member of the council in 1768. In 1759 he inherited Toulston Manor in Yorkshire from his uncle. After his father's death he was owner of Belvoir. In 1773 the Fairfaxes went to England and never returned to Virginia. During the years they lived at Belvoir they were among GW's closest friends, and after they went to England he took on the management of their Virginia estate. His admiration for George William's wife, the lovely and vivacious Sally Cary Fairfax, has given rise to persistent legends of romantic infatuation.

[6] At first GW's mother appeared to favor his ambition to go to sea, but she soon wavered. "I am afraid Mrs. Washington will not keep up to her first resolution. She seems to intimate a dislike to George's going to Sea & says several Persons have told her it's a very bad Scheme. She offers several trifling objections. . . . I find that one word against his going has more weight than ten for it" (Robert Jackson to Lawrence Washington, 18 Sept. 1746, NjMoNP: Smith Collection). In Dec. 1746 Mary Ball Washington requested advice from her brother in England, Joseph Ball. His reply of 19 May 1747 lent effective support to his sister's campaign to keep her son at home: "I understand you are advised, and have some Thoughts of putting your son George to sea. I think he had better be put apprentice to a Tinker; for a Common Sailor before the Mast, has by no means the Common Liberty of the Subject; for they will press him from a Ship where he has 50 shillings a month and make him take Three and twenty; and cut him and staple him and use him like a Negro, or rather, like a Dog. And as for any Considerable Preferment in the Navy, it is not to be expected, there are always so many Gaping for it here, who have Interest, and he has none" (DLC: Joseph Ball Papers).

tive career to a young man without a large estate. As early as Aug.
1745, in his "School Exercise Book," GW had made notes on
"Surveying or Measuring of Land," including examples of plats
with fields, trees, and streams.[7] It is probable that he received
some instruction in surveying, possibly from James Genn,[8] before
the journey over the mountains, but in any case the chance to
acquire practical experience under the supervision of a skilled
surveyor was not to be missed. On 11 Mar. 1748, with George
William Fairfax and the rest of the surveying party, he set out
for the South Branch of the Potomac. The group was led by
experienced surveyor James Genn, with Henry Ashby and Richard Taylor as chainmen, Robert Ashby as marker, and William
Lindsey as pilot.

GW's journal of the trip was kept in a small notebook measuring 6 × 3¼ inches. Together with the entries for the "Journey
over the Mountains," GW kept in this book accounts of the
group's surveying activities for the period. Because of changes in
the terrain, most of the surveying entries are now meaningless
and will be omitted from the diary.[9] However, in each case the
name of the person for whom the survey was made will be
noted. Also contained in the notebook, but obviously dating from
a somewhat later period, are random notes and memoranda,
copies of correspondence, and even one poem. This material will
be considered in the chronological series of the *Papers*.

[7] DLC:GW.

[8] James Genn was a prominent surveyor of Prince William County. His
home was on the Falmouth Road near present-day Catlett. In 1746 he had assisted in the survey of the boundaries of the Northern Neck and in 1747 had
surveyed Lord Fairfax's boundaries on the South Branch and on the Greenway Court manor. He was also an extensive landowner in Orange County; on
21 July 1748 he was issued grants in that area by Lord Fairfax for 1,080 acres
(Northern Neck Deeds and Grants, Book G, 93–95, Vi Microfilm).

[9] On the recorded grants based on these surveys James Genn's name appears as the surveyor (see Northern Neck Deeds and Grants, Book G, Vi
Microfilm).

A Journal of my Journey over the Mountains began Fryday the 11th. of March 1747/8

[March]

Fryday March 11th. 1747/8.   Began my Journey in Company with George Fairfax Esqr.; we travell'd this day 40 Miles to Mr. George Neavels in Prince William County.

The two dates used by GW are explained by the difference between New Style and Old Style dating. Until 1752 England, Ireland, and the colonies followed the Julian Calendar (Old Style). Under England's interpretation of the Julian Calendar the new year began on 25 Mar. Because the year under the Julian Calendar was 365 days 6 hours, by the sixteenth century a considerable surplus had accumulated, moving the vernal equinox from 21 to 11 Mar. The error was corrected in 1582 by the Gregorian Calendar (New Style), adopted by most European countries. By 1752, when Great Britain adopted the Gregorian Calendar, the displacement was 11 days.

George Neville (Neavil) (d. 1774), a planter and land speculator, had settled on Cedar Run, then in Prince William County (now in Fauquier County), as early as 1730. Although Neville was not licensed to keep an ordinary until 1759, the location of his house at the juncture of the Carolina Road and a branch of the Dumfries Road made it a convenient stopping place for travelers. As early as 1743, Neville had acquired a tract of 181 acres in Prince William and had also made extensive purchases of land in Frederick County. In 1750 GW was engaged to survey for him some 400 acres of "Waste & ungranted Land" in Frederick belonging to the Fairfax proprietary and adjoining George William Fairfax's property (warrant for survey, 13 Oct. 1750, DLC:GW; survey, 30 Oct. 1750, owned by Mr. Sol Feinstone, Washington Crossing, Pa.). The deed to Neville from Lord Fairfax is dated 20 Nov. 1750 (Mr. Sol Feinstone).

Saturday March 12th.   This Morning Mr. James Genn the surveyor came to us. We travel'd over the Blue Ridge to Capt. Ashbys on Shannondoa River. Nothing remarkable happen'd.

John Ashby (1707–1797) was a member of a prominent frontier family. His father, Thomas Ashby, had settled in Stafford County in 1710 and moved to what is now Fauquier County before 1748. In 1741 John Ashby married Jean Combs of Maryland and moved with his father to the banks of the Shenandoah, where the Ashby Tract lay along the river just below the mouth of Howell's Run. He was widely known as an Indian fighter, serving as captain in the 2d Virginia Rangers which from 1752 to 1754 maintained headquarters at Fort Ashby at the juncture of the Potomac River and Patterson's Creek. In 1752 he was elected to the Frederick Parish vestry. After Braddock's Defeat in July 1755 Ashby carried news of the disaster to Williamsburg. He participated in the Battle of Point Pleasant in 1774 and shortly after went

[6]

George William Fairfax, painted by an unknown artist after his return to England in 1773. (Mrs. Charles Baird, Jr.)

to Kentucky, where he spent several years locating and improving a grant of 2,000 acres he had received from Virginia for his services in the Indian wars. He died in Virginia in 1797.

Sunday March 13.   Rode to his Lordships Quarter about 4 Miles higher up the River we went through most beautiful Groves of Sugar Trees & spent the best part of the Day in admiring the Trees & richness of the Land.

It has usually been suggested that the party proceeded on 13 Mar. to Fairfax's land across the Shenandoah—the area known as Greenway Court (FREEMAN, 1:212–13; WRITINGS, 1:6). It is more likely that GW was referring to land owned by Lord Fairfax on the east side of the river in the vicinity of Howell's Run (see DICKINSON [1], 48–55).

Monday 14th.   We sent our Baggage to Capt. Hites (near Frederick Town) went ourselves down the River about 16 Miles to Capt. Isaac Penningtons (the Land exceeding Rich & Fertile all the way produces abundance of Grain Hemp Tobacco &c.) in order to Lay of some Lands on Cates Marsh & Long Marsh.

Jost Hite (d. 1760) was born in Strasbourg, Alsace, and emigrated to America about 1710, settling first in the vicinity of Kingston, N.Y. About 1716 he moved to Pennsylvania and in 1731 purchased a tract of nearly 40,000 acres from John and Isaac Van Meter in what soon became Frederick County, Va. In 1732 he moved to his Virginia lands with 16 other families of settlers. He was a member of the first Frederick Parish vestry. Hite was one of the leading

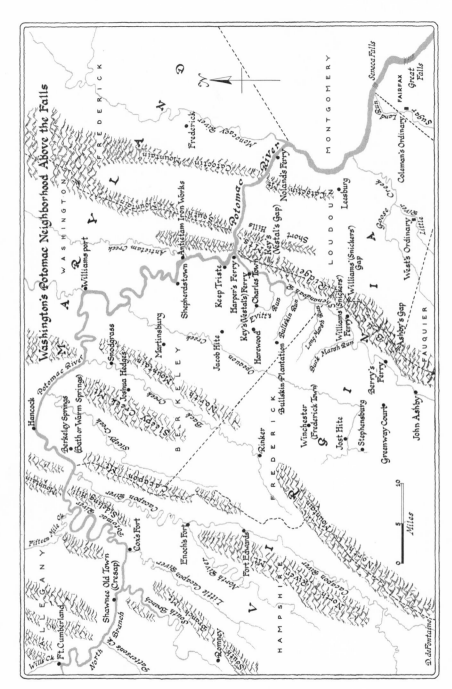

Washington's Potomac Neighborhood above the Falls

Map Key: The Formation of Counties
in the Upper Potomac Region,
1738–89

Virginia		
Frederick	from Orange	1738
Fairfax	from Prince William	1742
Hampshire	from Frederick and	
	Augusta	1752
Loudoun	from Fairfax	1757
Fauquier	from Prince William	1759
Berkeley	from Frederick	1772
Maryland		
Frederick	from Prince George's	1748
Montgomery	from Frederick	1776
Washington	from Frederick	1776
Allegany	from Washington	1789

land speculators and developers in Frederick, eventually settling families on a tract amounting to 94,000 acres. His land purchases involved him in a dispute with Lord Fairfax over ownership of his grants. The case continued in the courts for 50 years and was settled in Hite's favor in 1786, 26 years after his death.

Frederick Town is now Winchester, Va.

Isaac Pennington came to the Shenandoah Valley, probably from New Jersey, about 1734 and settled a tract of some 600 acres on the south bank of Buck Marsh Run, near present-day Berryville, Va. He was a member of the first grand jury empaneled in Frederick County in May 1744 (CARTMELL, 23). In 1750 GW surveyed a tract of land for him in Frederick County (survey for Pennington, 23 Oct. 1750, NN: George Washington Newspaper and Catalogue Clippings Box). Pennington sold his holdings in Frederick County, including most of the site of Berryville, to Gabriel Jones of Augusta County and John Hite of Frederick County in 1754 and moved to South Carolina in the fall of that year (CHAPPELEAR, 17–18).

Tuesday 15th.   We set out early with Intent to Run round the sd. Land but being taken in a Rain & it Increasing very fast obliged us to return. It clearing about one oClock & our time being too Precious to Loose we a second time ventured out & Worked hard till Night & then returnd to Penningtons we got our Suppers & was Lighted in to a Room & I not being so good a Woodsman as the rest of my Company striped my self very orderly

Greenway Court, Lord Fairfax's western seat of operation, as depicted in Woodrow Wilson, *George Washington*, New York, 1897. (University of Virginia Library)

& went in to the Bed as they call'd it when to my Surprize I found it to be nothing but a Little Straw—Matted together without Sheets or any thing else but only one Thread Bear blanket with double its Weight of Vermin such as Lice Fleas &c. I was glad to get up (as soon as the Light was carried from us) & put on my Cloths & Lay as my Companions. Had we not have been very tired, I am sure we should not have slep'd much that night. I made a Promise not to Sleep so from that time forward chusing rather to sleep in the open Air before a fire as will Appear hereafter.

On this day the party surveyed a tract of land for George William Fairfax on Cates Marsh and Long Marsh, the "names of small streams which flow from the foothill of North mountain to the Shenandoah river and have along their course considerable meadow or marshy land" (TONER [1], 26).

Wednesday 16th.   We set out early & finish'd about one oClock & then Travell'd up to Frederick Town where our Baggage came

[10]

Young Washington, the surveyor. (American Antiquarian Society)

to us. We cleaned ourselves (to get Rid of the Game we had catched the Night before) & took a Review of the Town & then return'd to our Lodgings where we had a good Dinner prepar'd for us Wine & Rum Punch in Plenty & a good Feather Bed with clean Sheets which was a very agreeable regale.

Thursday 17th.   Rain'd till Ten oClock & then clearing we reached as far as Major Campbells one of there Burgesses about 25 Miles from Town. Nothing Remarkable this day nor Night but that we had a Tolerable good Bed [to] lay on.

Andrew Campbell, who lived northwest of Winchester, was one of Frederick County's most prominent residents. He served as one of the county's first justices, as a member of the House of Burgesses from Frederick in 1745–47, and as the third sheriff of the county. On 2 Jan. 1744 the Frederick County court licensed Campbell and several other residents to keep ordinaries "at their respective houses" and to "furnish lodgings and food and Liquors at prices fixed by the court" (CARTMELL, 21). Campbell appears to have had a puritanical interest in preserving decorum in Frederick County. The long list of charges laid by him against various citizens range from breaking the Sabbath to "raising a riot" (see NORRIS [1], 83, 85). Retribution finally overtook him. He had served as a vestryman for Frederick Parish since 1745 but in the latter part of the decade charges were laid against him for collecting and appropriating for himself the funds collected for the use of the parish. That there was indeed chicanery afoot in the management of the parish finances is indicated in legislation passed by the House of Burgesses in Feb. 1752. "An Act for dissolving the Vestry of Frederick parish, in Frederick county" charged that the Frederick vestry had collected £1,570 on pretense of building churches in the parish and had "misapplied or converted the same to their own use, and refuse to render any account . . . to the great impoverishment of the people" (HENING, 6:258–60). Campbell eventually "had to run away to Carolina" (MEADE [2]).

Fryday 18th. We Travell'd up about 35 Miles to Thomas Barwicks on Potomack where we found the River so excessively high by Reason of the Great Rains that had fallen up about the Allegany Mountains as they told us which was then bringing down the melted Snow & that it would not be fordable for severall Days it was then above Six foot Higher than usual & was Rising. We agreed to stay till Monday. We this day call'd to see the Fam'd Warm Springs. We camped out in the field this Night. Nothing Remarkable happen'd till sunday the 20th.

Thomas Barwick (Berwick?) was settled in Frederick County as early as 1744 and served as a juror in the county court in February of that year (CARTMELL, 23).
   Warm Springs is now Bath, or Berkeley Springs, Morgan County, W.Va.

Sunday 20th. Finding the River not much abated we in the Evening Swam our horses over & carried them to Charles Polks in Maryland for Pasturage till the next Morning.

Charles Polk had land under cultivation in the area as early as 1748 (NORRIS [1], 68).

Monday 21st. We went over in a Canoe & Travell'd up Maryland side all the Day in a Continued Rain to Collo. Cresaps right against the Mouth of the South Branch about 40 Miles from Polks I believe the Worst Road that ever was trod by Man or Beast.

Thomas Cresap (1694–1790) was born at Skipton, Yorkshire, Eng., and emigrated to America about 1719, settling first in Maryland and later moving to the area of present-day Wrightsville, Pa. There he became a leader of the Maryland forces in the boundary dispute between Maryland and Pennsylvania, 1730–36. His Pennsylvania establishment was burned by Pennsylvanians in 1736, and he moved to the vicinity of Shawnee Old Town (now Oldtown, Md.), where he built a fortified trading post at the crossroads of a series of trails much traveled by Indians and whites. By 1749, when he was one of the organizers of the Ohio Company, Cresap was widely known throughout the frontier as a trader and land speculator, and Shawnee Old Town had become one of the leading frontier trading posts. Cresap acted as a surveyor and agent for the Ohio Company and helped lay out the company's road from Wills Creek to the Monongahela. He supported the Patriot cause during the American Revolution, in which his more famous son Michael played a leading role on the frontier.

Tuesday 22d. Continued Rain and the Freshes kept us at Cresaps.

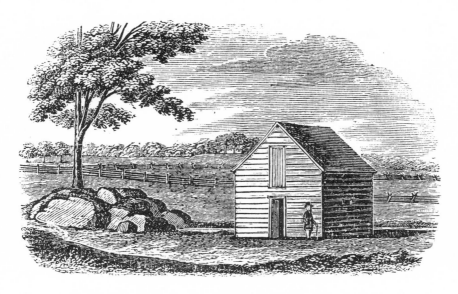

A hut near Berryville, Va., thought to have been used by Washington while surveying for Lord Fairfax. From Henry Howe, *Historical Collections of Virginia*, Charleston, S.C., 1845. (Sterling Memorial Library, Yale University)

Wednesday 23d.   Rain'd till about two oClock & Clear'd when we were agreeably surpris'd at the sight of thirty odd Indians coming from War with only one Scalp. We had some Liquor with us of which we gave them Part it elevating there Spirits put them in the Humour of Dauncing of whom we had a War Daunce. There Manner of Dauncing is as follows Viz. They clear a Large Circle & make a great Fire in the Middle then seats themselves around it the Speaker makes a grand Speech telling them in what Manner they are to Daunce after he has finish'd the best Dauncer Jumps up as one awaked out of a Sleep & Runs & Jumps about the Ring in a most comicle Manner he is followd by the Rest then begins there Musicians to Play the Musick is a Pot half of Water with a Deerskin Streched over it as tight as it can & a goard with some Shott in it to Rattle & a Piece of an horses Tail tied to it to make it look fine the one keeps Rattling and the other Drumming all the While the others is Dauncing.

Washington's drafting instruments, *Century Magazine*, May 1890. (University of Virginia Library)

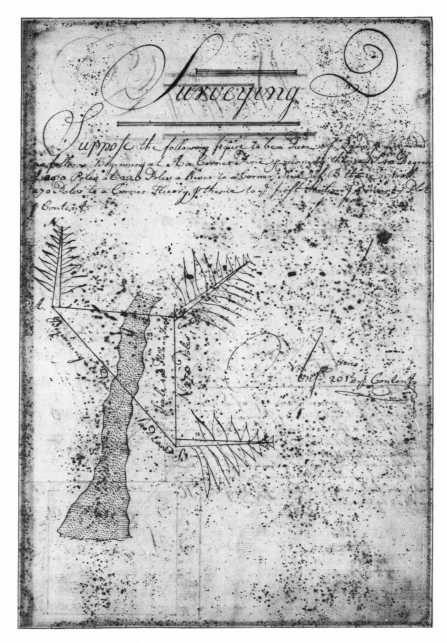

Among his papers in the Library of Congress is this page from the young Washington's copybook of 1745.

Fryday 25th. 1748.   Nothing Remarkable on thursday but only being with the Indians all day so shall slip it. This day left Cresaps & went up to the Mouth of Patersons Creek & there swum our Horses over got over ourselves in a Canoe & travel'd up the following Part of the Day to Abram Johnstones 15 miles from the Mouth where we camped.

Patterson's Creek flows into the Potomac about 12 miles below Cumberland, Md. It rises in Hampshire County, W.Va.

Abram Johnson received a deed to 309 acres on Patterson's Creek on 26 Oct. 1748 (Northern Neck Deeds and Grants, Book G, 141, Vi Microfilm).

Saterday 26. Travelld up the Creek to Solomon Hedges Esqr. one of his Majestys Justices of the Peace for the County of Frederick where we camped. When we came to Supper there was neither a Cloth upon the Table nor a Knife to eat with but as good luck would have it we had Knives of [our] own.

Solomon Hedges. usually called Squire Hedges, a justice of the peace for Frederick County, was a member of a Quaker family from Maryland who were early settlers in Frederick. Hedges was living in the county as early as 1744, when he served on the first grand jury for Frederick in May of that year.

Sunday 27th.   Travell'd over to the South Branch (attended with the Esqr.) to Henry Vanmetriss in order to go about Intended Work of Lots.

The Van Meter family was among the earliest settlers in the Shenandoah Valley. John Van Meter, a New York state Indian trader who carried on an extensive trade among the Delaware Indians, visited Virginia about 1725. With his encouragement his sons Isaac and John obtained extensive grants of land on the South Branch of the Potomac and in the lower Shenandoah Valley in 1730 and brought in a number of settlers. It was their sale of a portion of their lands to Jost Hite in 1731 which precipitated the latter's legal entanglements with Lord Fairfax. Henry Van Meter, who died about 1759, was a son of Isaac and a nephew of John. He received a deed for 405 acres on the South Branch on 7 June 1749 (Northern Neck Deeds and Grants, Book G, 187, Vi Microfilm). For an account of the Van Meter family, see *W.Va. Hist. Mag.*, 2, no. 2 (April 1902), 5–18.

Monday 28th.   Travell'd up the Branch about 30 Miles to Mr. James Rutlidge's Horse Jockey & about 70 Miles from the Mouth.

Tuesday 29th.   This Morning went out & Survey'd five Hundred Acres of Land & went down to one Michael Stumps on the So. Fork of the Branch. On our way Shot two Wild Turkies.

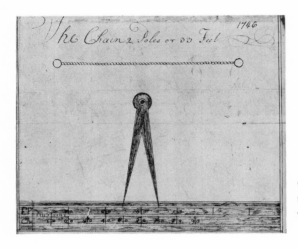

Chain, compass, and scale drawn by the young Washington. (Cornell University)

On 29 Mar. the party surveyed a tract of land for James Rutledge (surveying notes, DLC:GW). Rutledge acquired 500 acres in Frederick County in May 1748 (Northern Neck Deeds and Grants, Book G, 56, Vi Microfilm). He was presumably a member of the family that had settled on the South Branch as early as 1734 or 1735.

Michael Stump, Sr. (1709–1768), received a grant for Lot No. 3, on the South Fork of the South Branch of the Potomac, on 8 Sept. 1749 (Northern Neck Deeds and Grants, Book G, 227, Vi Microfilm).

Wednesday 30th. This Morning began our Intended Business of Laying of Lots. We began at the Boundary Line of the Northern 10 Miles above Stumps & run of two Lots & returnd to Stumps.

On this day the party surveyed tracts for Peter Reid, Anthony Regar, Harmon Shoker, and Elias Cellars (surveying notes, DLC:GW).

Thursday 31st. Early this Morning one of our Men went out with the Gun & soon Returnd with two Wild Turkies. We then went to our Business. Run of three Lots & returnd to our Camping place at Stumps.

[April]

Fryday April the 1st. 1748. This Morning Shot twice at Wild Turkies but killd none. Run of three Lots & returnd to Camp.

Saterday April 2d. Last Night was a blowing & Rainy night. Our Straw catch'd a Fire that we were laying upon & was luckily Pre-

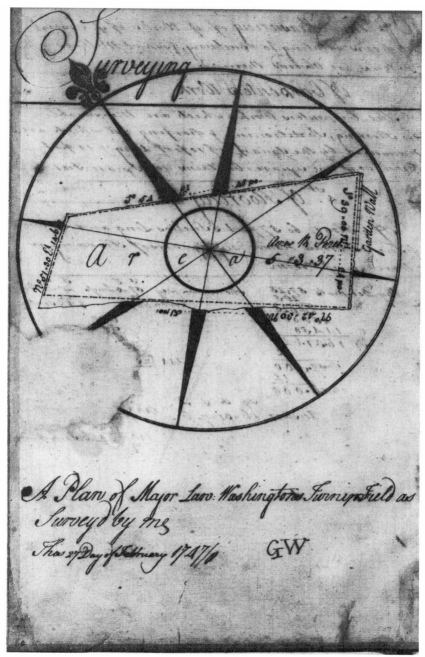

An early Washington survey done for his half brother Lawrence. (Library of Congress)

serv'd by one of our Mens awaking when it was in a ⟨   ⟩ We run of four Lots this day which Reached below Stumps.

From 2 to 5 April the party surveyed tracts for Michael Calb. Liveron (?), Leonard Nass, Michael Stump, James Simpson, Philip Moore, the Widow Wolf, Henry Shepler, and Jeremiah Osborne (surveying notes, DLC:GW).

Sunday 3d.   Last Night was a much more blostering night than the former. We had our Tent Carried Quite of with the Wind and was obliged to Lie the Latter part of the Night without covering. There came several Persons to see us this day one of our Men Shot a Wild Turkie.

Monday 4th.   This morning Mr. Fairfax left us with Intent to go down to the Mouth of the Branch. We did two Lots & was

David Rittenhouse of Philadelphia made this surveying compass for Washington. (Smithsonian Institution photo no. P65774)

attended by a great Company of People Men Women & Children that attended us through the Woods as we went shewing there Antick tricks. I really think they seem to be as Ignorant a Set of People as the Indians. They would never speak English but when spoken to they speak all Dutch. This day our Tent was blown down by the Violentness of the Wind.

Fairfax borrowed 5s. from GW before he left (miscellaneous accounts, entry for 5 April 1748, DLC:GW).

Tuesday 5th.   We went out & did 4 Lots. We were attended by the same Company of People that we had the day before.

Wednesday 6th.   Last Night was so Intolerably smoaky that we were obliged all hands to leave the Tent to the Mercy of the Wind and Fire this day was attended by our aforesd. Company untill about 12 oClock when we finish'd we travell'd down the Branch to Henry Vanmetris's. On our Journey was catch'd in a very heavy Rain. We got under a Straw House untill the Worst of it was over & then continued our Journy.

Thursday 7th.   Rain'd Successively all Last Night. This Morning one of our men Killed a Wild Turky that weight 20 Pounds. We went & Surveyd 15 Hundred Acres of Land & Returnd to Vanmetris's about 1 oClock. About two I heard that Mr. Fairfax was come up & at 1 Peter Casseys about 2 Miles of in the same Old Field. I then took my Horse & went up to see him. We eat our Dinners & Walked down to Vanmetris's. We stayed about two Hours & Walked back again and slept in Casseys House which was the first Night I had slept in a House since I came to the Branch.

Peter Casey acquired 356 acres of land on the South Branch on 14 Aug. 1749 (Northern Neck Deeds and Grants, Book G, 271, Vi Microfilm) .

Fryday 8th.   We breakfasted at Casseys & Rode down to Van-metris's to get all our Company together which when we had accomplished we Rode down below the Trough in order to Lay of Lots there. We laid of one this day. The Trough is couple of Ledges of Mountain Impassable running side & side together for above 7 or 8 Miles & the River down between them. You must Ride Round the back of the Mountain for to get below them. We Camped this Night in the Woods near a Wild Meadow where was a Large Stack of Hay. After we had Pitched our Tent & made a very Large Fire we pull'd out our Knapsack in order to Recruit ourselves. Every[one] was his own Cook. Our Spits was Forked Sticks our Plates was a Large Chip as for Dishes we had none.

Saterday 9th.   Set the Surveyors to work whilst Mr. Fairfax & myself stayed at the Tent our Provision being all exhausted & the Person that was to bring us a Recruit disappointing us we were obliged to go without untill we could get some from the Neighbours which was not till about 4 or 5 oClock in the Evening. We then took our Leaves of the Rest of our Company Road Down to John Colins in order to set off next Day homewards.

John Collins, a member of a pioneer Shenandoah Valley family, had settled near present-day Moorefield, Hardy County, W.Va.

George William Fairfax commissions Washington to make a survey in 1750. (Library of Congress)

A sketch of a portion of the Mount Vernon estate near the Mansion House and Little Hunting Creek, about 1747. (Library of Congress)

Sunday 10th. We took our farewell of the Branch & travelld over Hills and Mountains to 1 Coddys on Great Cacapehon about 40 Miles.

James Caudy (Coddy) owned some 98 acres of land in Frederick County. On 19 Mar. 1752 GW noted that "Pursuant to a Warrant from the Proprietors Office I have Surveyed for James Caudy of Great Cacapehon a certain tract of waste & ungranted Land on the So. Fork of Dillans commonly call'd & known by the Name of the Little Meadows" (survey for Caudy, Vi).

Monday 11th. We Travell'd from Coddys down to Frederick Town where we Reached about 12 oClock. We dined in Town and then went to Capt. Hites & Lodged.

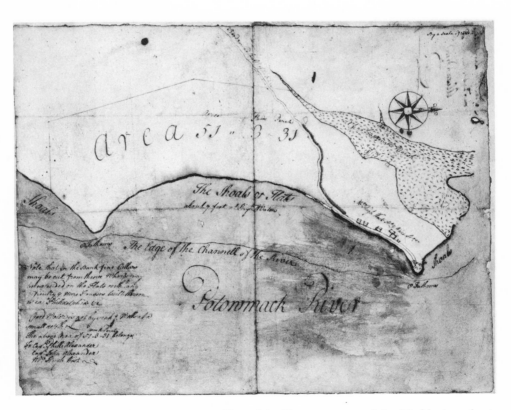

Belhaven, later to become Alexandria, Va., was surveyed by Washington about 1748. (Library of Congress)

Tuesday 12th.   We set of from Capt. Hites in order to go over Wms. Gap about 20 Miles and after Riding about 20 Miles we had 20 to go for we had lost ourselves & got up as High as Ashbys Bent. We did get over Wms. Gap that Night and as low as Wm. Wests in Fairfax County 18 Miles from the Top of the Ridge. This day see a Rattled Snake the first we had seen in all our Journey.

Williams' Gap was a pass through the Blue Ridge Mountains on a line east from Winchester. It was later known as Snickers' Gap.

Ashby's Bent, or Ashby's Gap, is a pass into the Shenandoah Valley through the Blue Ridge Mountains. It was presumably named for Thomas Ashby, father of John and Thomas Ashby, who settled in the area in the 1740s.

West's ordinary was at the junction of the Carolina Road and the Colchester Road near Bull Run, slightly east of the beginning of the Bull Run Mountains. It was operated by William West, who died between 1762 and 1765. As early as 1740 West had acquired grants of land in the area (Northern Neck Deeds and Grants, Book E, Vi Microfilm). He may have been the William West who was a brother of Hugh and John West of Alexandria, although the evidence is only conjectural (see HARRISON [1], 139, 494–95). The ordinary was operated after the Revolution under the name Lacey's and was located at the present site of Aldie, in what is now Loudoun County.

Wednesday the 13th. of April 1748.   Mr. Fairfax got safe home and I myself safe to my Brothers which concludes my Journal.

Voyage to Barbados

1751–52

EDITORIAL NOTE. GW's older half brother Lawrence had been in poor health during the decade following the British assault upon Spanish bases in the Caribbean, an encounter commonly termed the War of Jenkins' Ear. He had led a Virginia military company in the 1741 attack on Cartagena, becoming so fond of Vice Admiral Edward Vernon, naval commander of the expedition, that he later named his own home Mount Vernon. Now his lung ailment was worse, and his life had been further burdened by the deaths since 1745 of three children, Janet, Fairfax, and Mildred. In 1751 he decided to sail for Barbados in search of a healing climate, accompanied by young GW.

Barbados was a logical choice. Not only were there strong commercial ties between Virginia and the Leeward Islands, but there also were family connections. Gedney Clarke, a prominent Barbados merchant and planter, had also married into the family of William Fairfax; he was from Salem, Mass., and owned property along Goose Creek in Virginia. The Clarkes and their Barbadian friends would be the principal hosts of the two Washingtons during their stay on the island. There is no evidence that families named Washington living in the British West Indies about 1750 were related to or even acquainted with Lawrence and GW, and none is mentioned in the diary. The name appears frequently in early burial records of Barbados, and the will of a man named George Washington was proved in Barbados in 1769.[1]

To prepare themselves for the voyage, Lawrence and GW could turn to a new work by Rev. Griffith Hughes, *The Natural History of Barbados* (London, 1750). A folio volume issued serially in ten parts, it was heavily laden with botanical lore but contained enough general information to make useful reading for GW (see his comments, p. 87). He may have seen the book in the home

[1] WESSEL, 6–8. See also HOPPIN, 143–50.

Lawrence Washington, whose poor health took him and his half brother George to Barbados in the fall of 1751. (Mount Vernon Ladies' Association of the Union)

of one of the Fairfaxes, for both—Thomas, Lord Fairfax, and his cousin William—were among the thirty-three Virginia subscribers to the publication. Another subscriber was Hon. James Carter, in whose home the Washingtons stayed briefly upon their arrival in Barbados; GW may have studied the book there.

After learning that George Muse would be appointed to serve

Bridgetown, capital of Barbados, as Washington saw it and as depicted in Griffith Hughes's *The Natural History of Barbados*, London, 1750. (Beinecke Rare Book and Manuscript Library, Yale University)

in his stead as adjutant of Virginia,[2] Lawrence set sail with his brother about 28 Sept. 1751. Because the first few pages of GW's diary are missing, we cannot know for certain the date, the port of embarkation, or the vessel upon which the two took passage. Jared Sparks wrote that the ship sailed 28 Sept. J. M. Toner reported the voyage as originating in the Potomac, as did John C. Fitzpatrick and Douglas S. Freeman, none citing the source of his information.[3] We have found no primary source.

If the vessel did sail from the Potomac, it was the *Success*, Jeremiah Cranston, 40 tons, 8 men, carrying a cargo of 4,480 barrel staves, 7,627 feet of plank, 984 bushels of corn, and 31 barrels of herring. Cranston gave bond for his square-sterned sloop at the customs office of the South Potomac district either on 23 Aug. or 23 Sept.—the surviving report is not clear. If August, the delay between the date of clearing the port and leaving the river was not unusual. Washington himself remarked in later life that masters of vessels never sail on time.[4] Only one other vessel bound for Barbados, other than the *Success,* cleared any Virginia port at a time that would place it at sea on 28 Sept. For a note on the *Fredericksburg,* a sloop that might possibly have carried the Washingtons, see p. 79.

Two elements of ocean travel fascinated GW most: the daily progress as indicated in the captain's log and the variable and often violent weather. He kept his own log as part of his diary, very probably basing it upon the captain's and introducing such nautical acronyms as RMTS, reefed main topsail; DRTS, double-reefed topsail; HFS, hauled foresail. His amazement at the stormy weather seems justified. There had been severe hurricanes in the West Indies in September, resulting in heavy shipping losses. Though the heaviest losses were in the Jamaica area, merchants in the Leewards reported considerable loss in their letters to American shippers, and on 18 Oct. when GW was noting in his

[2] Lawrence Washington received half a year's pay of £75 in a warrant dated 25 Oct. 1751; the next surviving warrant of 25 Oct. 1752 is to Muse, listed then as deputy adjutant. He became adjutant after Lawrence's death in 1752 (P.R.O., C.O.5/1327, ff. 189, 248, 322).

[3] TONER [2], 5; DIARIES, 1:16n; FREEMAN, 1:248.

[4] The *Industry,* on which GW returned from Barbados, gave bond in Bridgetown on 19 Nov. and did not sail until 22 Dec. Data on the *Success* are in P.R.O., C.O.5/1445, f. 59, Naval Office Accounts.

log the occurrence of heavy seas and high winds, there was a strong earthquake in the Santo Domingo area.[5]

Biographical Data

Information on the persons mentioned by GW during his stay on the island is in most instances scant. What follows is data obtained both from standard biographical references and from documents in the Barbados Department of Archives at Black Rock. The archives have suffered much from the ravages of time and climate, and identifications are made more difficult by GW's customary use of surnames only and by his phonetic spelling of those names.

BARWICK, WILLIAM (d. 1756). A member of the colonial council and owner of Pine Plantation in St. Michaels Parish.[6]

CARTER, JAMES (d. 1753), of St. Thomas Parish.[7] Member of the council in the 1740s and chief justice of grand sessions, appointed 1749.

CHARNOCK, BENJAMIN (1698–1783), of St. James Parish—a tentative identification. At his death he left what remained of his "oppulent fortune" to a friend, Dowding Thornhill.[8] There is no surviving record of the criminal proceedings against him for "committing a rape on his servant maid."

CLARKE, GEDNEY (1711–1764). Member of the council, collector of customs at Barbados, merchant, and planter with holdings in America—including 3,000 acres on Goose Creek in northern Virginia. Clarke's sister Deborah was William Fairfax's wife and his connection with the Fairfaxes. Because of this link not only did

---

[5] For Jamaica, see *Gentleman's Mag.*, Dec. 1751, 569. For the Leewards, see Dr. Walter Tullidepth to Sir George Thomas, Antigua, 21 Sept. 1751, in SHERIDAN, 21: "We had the most violent hurricane ever known here the 8th Instant which hath done great Damadges to our buildings, and much more to our Canes." For Santo Domingo, see *Gentleman's Mag.*, Feb. 1752, 91.

[6] Barbados Department of Archives, hereafter BDA, RB6/35:180.

[7] BDA, RB6/22:309.   [8] BDA, RB6/38:20.

Washington was especially fond of the "Pine-Apple" of Barbados. From Griffith Hughes, *Barbados*, London, 1750. (Beinecke Rare Book and Manuscript Library, Yale University)

GW and Lawrence depend much upon the Clarkes, but Bryan Fairfax, son of William and a lifelong friend of GW, also spent time with the Clarkes in 1752–54. In his will, recorded 4 Sept. 1764, Clarke left property to his wife, his niece Hannah Fairfax, and his sons, Peter, Francis, and Gedney Jr. The bulk of the estate went to Gedney, including the Goose Creek lands.[9] During the 1750s Clarke dealt extensively with Henry Laurens, of South Carolina, purchasing slaves for resale in America by Laurens. Many of his letters appear in Laurens's letterbooks (ScHi), where his name is always entered as "Gidney" Clarke.

CLARKE, MARY. Gedney Clarke's wife.

CROFTAN (Crofton), CAPT. ———. The officer commanding James Fort who rented a house to the Washingtons. GW wrote his name "Crawford" twice, then corrected it. He may have been a militia officer. Although the Thirty-eighth Foot was the regiment assigned to the Leewards at this time, there are no extant records associating this unit with service on Barbados; no Captain Croftan or Crofton appears on the manuscript or printed army lists of the period in the Public Record Office, London.

FINLAY, THOMAS. A native of Scotland whose will was recorded in Barbados 27 May 1762, after his return to his Scottish estate called Balkirsty. He served as clerk of the General Assembly of Barbados in 1743–44.[10]

GASKIN, JOHN (d. 1779), of St. Michaels Parish.[11] At his death he owned the schooner *Success,* apparently not the vessel which may have transported GW to Barbados.

GRAEME, GEORGE (d. 1755), a judge and member of the General Assembly representing Christ Church Parish.[12] Brother of John Graeme.

GRAEME, JOHN (d. 1755). Onetime professor of natural philosophy and mathematics at the College of William and Mary, succeeding Joshua Fry. He had come from England in 1725 to take over the ironworks and plantation of Alexander Spotswood, an assignment in which he was not very successful. Spotswood complained that he should have known better than to commit such a venture to a mathematician. Graeme joined the college faculty Aug. 1737. Although not an experienced surveyor, he apparently

[9] BDA, RB6/17:195.

[10] BDA, RB6/30:440, and *Jl. of Barbados Museum and Hist. Soc.,* 13 (1946), 86.

[11] BDA, RB6/23:210.   [12] BDA, RL1/21:127.

was in charge of the licensing of surveyors in Virginia, a privilege assigned to the college by the crown. There is nothing in the scant record to connect him with GW before their meeting in Barbados, although GW had been surveying for Lord Fairfax and others.[13]

GRENVILLE, HENRY (1717–1784), governor of Barbados 1746–56.

HILLARY, DR. WILLIAM (1697–1763), a physician trained at Leyden and newly arrived in Barbados. He became Lawrence's doctor.

HAGGATT, OTHNIEL (d. 1761). Probably the man mentioned by GW, although Nathaniel Haggatt was living at the same time. One of the plantations on Barbados is called Haggatt Hall.

HOLBURNE, COMMODORE FRANCIS (1704–1771). Arrived in the Leewards about Sept. 1748 aboard the *Tavistock*, "a worn-out 50-gun ship," as commodore and commander in chief. He returned to England in 1752, then went to Halifax as vice admiral, July 1757, to attempt the reduction of French-held Louisbourg. French reinforcements and bad weather thwarted the plan.[14]

JENKINS, EDMUND. No new information except his first name, supplied from BDA records.

LANAHAN, DR. JOHN (1699–1762). A physician and third-generation resident of Barbados. It is not clear why he was called to attend GW during his illness with smallpox while Lawrence was being treated by Dr. Hillary, unless it was because he was a friend of the Clarkes. Gedney was executor of his estate when he died in 1769.[15]

MAYNARD, WILLIAM. Member of the General Assembly for many years, from St. Thomas Parish, and owner of Black Rock Plantation.

PATTERSON, WILLIAM. Surveyor general of customs whom Gedney Clarke succeeded in 1759.

PETRIE, CAPT. ———. Commander of Charles Fort. An officer named John Petrie appears in the army *List* for 1745 as a lieuten-

---

[13] "Journal of the Meetings of the President and Masters of William and Mary College," WMQ, 1 (1892–93), 132; BYRD, 358. For Graeme's burial in Christ Church Parish, see BDA, RL1/21:125. For the deeds to two plantations near Germanna, which Spotswood gave Graeme to induce him to move to Virginia, see Spotsylvania County Records, Deed Book A, abstracted in CROZIER [2], 97–98.
[14] DNB; VA. EXEC. JLS., 6:61, 77.   [15] SHILSTONE, 3–10.

ant in the Thirty-sixth Foot and was a major by 1746 according to the *Gentleman's Magazine,* March 1746, 165. The Barbados captain was probably a militia officer, perhaps George John Petrie, who gave a power of attorney to Jonas and John Maynard 9 June 1753 and died in Middlesex, Eng., the same year.[16]

PURCELL, JOHN. Lieutenant governor of the British Virgin Islands with headquarters in Tortola.

ROBERTS, ELIZABETH. Mary Clarke's niece, who by 1787 was the widow of Thomas Beard, according to the will of her brother William.[17]

ROBERTSON, CORNELIUS. Master of the *Fredericksburg.*

SANDARS, JOHN. Master of the *Industry.*

STEVENSON, THOMAS & SONS. Thomas Stevenson (d. 1763) owned Pool Plantation in St. Johns Parish and engaged in mercantile activities with his sons on other islands of the Leeward group.

WARREN, ROBERT. Onetime clerk of the General Assembly.

The Washingtons in Barbados

The arrival at Bridgetown, on Carlisle Bay, is not well documented because pages are missing from the diary at this point. There are no collateral data such as newspaper listings of shipping arrivals, for not a single copy of the *Barbados Gazette* for 1751 is known to exist. The first two diary entries after the Washingtons disembarked are supplied by Jared Sparks, who obviously saw them while he was preparing his edition of GW's papers. He may indeed be responsible for the fact that the originals are missing, considering his penchant for distributing sample pages from GW manuscripts.

After dining with the Clarkes and taking up temporary lodging with James Carter, the travelers confronted the matter of prime importance—Lawrence's physical condition. Then, assured by Dr. Hillary that the disease was "not so fixed but that a cure might be effectually made," they looked for a place to live.

Although they thought it extravagant at £15 a month, they chose a house owned by Captain Croftan, or Crofton, overlooking Carlisle Bay. The little house which Barbadian taxi drivers now show to tourists as the Washington home is merely the object of

[16] BDA, RB7/10:51.   [17] BDA, RB6/33:164.

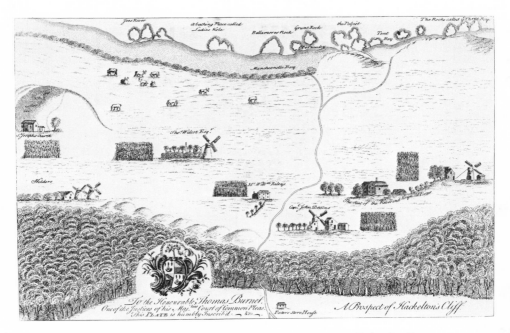

An island scene from Griffith Hughes's *Barbados*, London, 1750. (Beinecke Rare Book and Manuscript Library, Yale University)

a legend. Located on Bay Street at Chelsea Road not far from St. Ann's Garrison, it bears no resemblance to the architecture of the mid-1700s. Even if it had been standing in GW's time, it could not have survived the devastating hurricanes of 1780 and 1831, which nearly destroyed Bridgetown and brought havoc to the entire island. Some credence was given the legend when an official historic sites committee in 1910 referred to the building as Crofton's House and associated it with GW. Tourist literature still designates the place "the Washington House," but the question of its authenticity has been disposed of by local historians.[18]

The brothers had a busy social life, and those who entertained

[18] For example, [Neville Connell], "Historic Sites Re-Visited: Crofton's House," *Jl. of Barbados Museum and Hist. Soc.*, 12 (1945), 208–11.

To Her Royal Highness
The Princess of Wales
This Plate is humbly Inscrib'd
&c.

The coconut, another tropical plant seen by Washington for the first time in Barbados. From Griffith Hughes, *Barbados,* London, 1750. (Beinecke Rare Book and Manuscript Library, Yale University) them were prominent in commercial, political, and military circles. GW delighted in the novelty of his surroundings. He developed a taste for the "avagado pair," the "Pine Apple," and other tropical fruits. He indulged his emerging taste for the theater by attending a performance of George Lillo's *The London Merchant, or the History of George Barnwell,* which was also playing in Drury Lane that season. Lillo's play may have been the first stage production which GW had ever seen, other than amateur performances.

While Lawrence's health was still failing, illness struck GW. On 16 Nov. he developed smallpox and Dr. Lanahan was sent for. It may have been fortunate for GW that smallpox caught up with him in Barbados rather than in Virginia. The practice of inoculation—not vaccination—was common in Barbados but frowned upon in Virginia.[19] Rev. Griffith Hughes reported that although the island was seldom free of the disease, the practice of inoculation had lowered the death rate to a very small percentage.[20] It is conceivable that GW had been inoculated sometime before his trip to Barbados, causing his attack to be a relatively mild one. The practice of vaccination with cowpox vaccine did not begin until the end of the century.

That a kind of ennui was affecting the two brothers, as well as apprehension about Lawrence's pulmonary condition, is shown in a letter that Lawrence wrote to his father-in-law, William Fairfax: "This climate has not afforded the relief I expected from it, so that I have almost determined to try the Bermudas on my return, and, if it does not do, the dry air of Frederic. This is the finest island of the West Indies, but I own no place can please me without a change of seasons. We soon tire of the same prospect. Our bodies are too much relaxed. . . . We have no kind of bodily diversions but dancing. . . . I am obliged to ride out by the first dawn of the day, for by the time the sun is half an hour high, it is as hot as at any time of the day. The gentlemen are very polite and hospitable."[21]

It was decided that Lawrence would try Bermuda and that GW would return to Virginia. Lawrence wrote a friend from Bermuda 6 April 1752, despairing over his health and expressing the wish

[19] HENING, 8:371–74. [20] HUGHES, 39. [21] SPARKS, 2:422.

that his wife Anne would come to him—accompanied by GW.[22] As his condition worsened, however, he returned hastily to Mount Vernon and died there 26 July.

By 19 Dec. 1751 GW had booked passage out of Barbados on the *Industry*. He spent Christmas at sea, dining on beef and "Irish Goose," and settled down to an uneventful though frequently stormy homeward voyage, content to maintain a terse diary rather than a ship's log.

At the end of January the *Industry* cleared the Virginia capes and made a landfall in the lower York River. Proceeding by land to Williamsburg, GW paid a call on Gov. Robert Dinwiddie, gave him some letters, and was invited to dine. It may have been a crucial moment in GW's career, providing Dinwiddie an opportunity to evaluate the young man. The governor, only recently appointed, had lived in America for several years and may already have known the Washingtons; certainly he knew the Fairfaxes. He was no stranger to Barbados, either, having investigated customs affairs there as early as 1738 while serving as surveyor general of customs for the Southern District of America. He must have queried GW about the Gedney Clarkes and mentioned the occasions upon which he had been a guest in their home.[23]

Within a few years, disquieting differences would arise to mar GW's relationship with Dinwiddie, but the young man's immediate prospects brightened after his dinner with the governor. Later in 1752, when the colony was divided into four military districts, Dinwiddie appointed him one of the district adjutants; and in 1753, upon dispatching GW with a message to the French on the Ohio River, Dinwiddie would refer to him as "a person of distinction."

The Manuscript

The Barbados diary had deteriorated seriously before it was silked and mounted at the Library of Congress; there is evidence

[22] SPARKS, 2:422–23. Sparks dates the first letter "a few weeks after his arrival in Barbadoes" and says it is addressed to Lord Fairfax. William Fairfax seems a much likelier addressee. Sparks does not identify the recipient of the April letter; neither manuscript has been located.

[23] Writing to William Fairfax 13 July 1739, Dinwiddie mentioned frequent visits to the Clarke household, where they drank Fairfax's health (CSmH: Brock Collection).

that some of the preliminary pages were already missing when Jared Sparks used it in the early nineteenth century. Transcribing it according to conventional standards would result in a confusing array of blank spaces enclosed by brackets and many speculative footnotes. The editors feel it can best be presented in facsimile, accompanied by the gloss that follows.

Pages 38–39
Fragments of what apparently are two of the first leaves in the blank book that GW used for his diary. They are in about the same condition as they were when Toner's publisher set them in type in 1892.

Page 40
REMARKS FOR SATERDAY 28TH: Assuming this to be the first entry in GW's log and that he began the log on his first day out, we have an accurate date for the beginning of the voyage, 28 Sept. 1751. The second fragment, on the reverse side of the leaf is for 29 Sept.

Page 43
I SUPPOSE THIS TO BE A FRAGMENT: A comment in the hand of Jared Sparks, as is the date of Oct. 1751. If Sparks wrote on the first full page available to him, it is likely that the earlier pages were mutilated when he saw them about 1827.

Page 44
For the first time, GW's labels for the bottom line of data are readable, including departure, course, distance, difference of latitude, latitude, meridian distance, difference of longitude, and longitude. His indication of the mariner's term *departure* is usually mutilated but would always be a two-digit figure expressing nautical miles.

Page 71
With a landfall on the morning of [2] Nov., GW terminates his log. One or more leaves are missing at this point; presumably 2 Nov. was spent in entering Carlisle Bay and getting ashore at Bridgetown.

Page 73
The entries for 4 and 5 Nov. are from SPARKS, 2:424, and are misdated. Correct dates are 3 and 4 Nov. The Gedney Clarke town house where the Washingtons dined was on the north bank of a creek that emptied into the careenage, near the old bridge which gave the town its name (SHILSTONE, 2n).

Page 74
TUESDAY 6TH: He means the 5th. GW's use of dates is erratic during his stay on the island; he will be one day ahead of the calendar until the temporary interruption of his entries on "17th" Nov., actually the 16th. THE [S]CHOONER FREDERICKSBURG, CAPTN. ROBINSON: The square-sterned sloop *Fredericksburg*, Cornelius Robertson, 80 tons, 6 guns, 8 men, registered at Williamsburg Oct. 1750; owner John Champe & Co. Lading: 3,300 bushels of corn, 70 bushels of oats, 17,000 shingles. The vessel cleared the port of Rappahannock 2 Sept. 1751 (P.R.O., C.O.5/1444, f. 118, Naval Office Accounts). While it is possible that the Washingtons went to Barbados aboard this vessel, there are two reasons for doubt. GW probably would not have listed it so formally, includ-

ing the captain's name, if he had just debarked from it after several weeks on the "fickle & Mirciless Ocean" (p. 69). Also, it is not likely that a vessel arriving in port on 2 Oct. would be preparing to sail by 6 Oct. MRS. CLARKE & MISS ROBTS.: Mrs. Mary Clarke, wife of Gedney Clarke, and her niece Elizabeth Roberts. TO COME & SEE THE SERPTS. FIR'D: Serpents, or fireworks discharged in commemoration of Guy Fawkes Day, 5 Nov. This remark enables us to correct the dating of the diary entries made during this period.

Page 75
THE SURVEYOR GENL.: William Patterson. JUDGES FINLEY & HACKET: Thomas Finlay and Othniel Haggatt. JAMES FORT: A fortification at Holetown in St. James Parish which by 1762 mounted 23 guns and 10 swivels.

Pages 77–79
GW has extended his entry for "Fryday 9th," actually 8 Nov., to cover the following Saturday.

Page 82
MR. GRAEME . . . OF THE MASTER'S OF THE COLLEGE OF VIRGINIA: John Graeme. STRONGLY ATTACKED WITH THE SMALL POX: On 16 Nov., GW suspended his

A West Indies farmyard from Charles de Rochefort's *Histoire naturelle des Iles Antilles de l'Amérique*, Rotterdam, 1658. (Arents Collections, New York Public Library, Astor, Lenox and Tilden Foundations)

diary entries for the duration of his illness. The wording indicates that he made the 16 Nov. entry after recovering on 12 Dec.

Page 83
DECEMBER 12TH: GW's dates will square with the calendar until he assigns both Monday and Tuesday the date of 16 Dec.; then, by skipping from 19 to 21 Dec., he will again be correct. MAJR. GASKENS: John Gaskin. COLO. CHAU-NACK: Benjamin Charnock.

Page 85
GENERAL BARRACK: William Barwick. MESSRS. STEPHENSON'S MERCHT.: Thomas Stevenson & Sons. THE INDUSTRY CAPTN. JOHN SAUNDERS: The *Industry*, John Sandars, a square-sterned brig of 50 tons, 7 men, of Bristol registry and owned by Sandars. Lading: 1,230 gallons of rum. Sandars gave bond at the Barbados customs office 19 Nov. 1751 and entered the York River of Virginia 30 Jan. 1752 (P.R.O., C.O.5/1444, f. 43).

Page 86
THE GOVERNOR OF BARBADO'S: Henry Grenville.

Page 88
40 TO 70 POLLS: Both "polls" and "bolls" have been used as units of measure, but it is likely that GW neglected to cross his *t*'s and here means "potts." In the literature of the West Indies sugar industry, a pot is often used to denote a batch or boiling-down of sugar and also may mean a quantity equaling a hogshead.

Page 89
GUNIA CORN: Guinea corn, a grain sorghum. HUGHES, 254, says it was mainly used to feed slaves, each receiving from a pint to a quart a day.

Page 104
A SLOOP CALLD THE GLASGOW: The *Glasgow*, Matthew Stroud, a square-sterned sloop of 40 tons, 7 men, built in Virginia in 1750, owner Andrew Sprowle. She cleared Port Hampton 18 Oct. 1751, bound for St. Kitts (P.R.O., C.O.5/1446, f. 53).

Page 113
MOUTH OF YORK RIVER: 29 Jan. 1752. The Naval Office record showing the arrival 30 Jan. was probably made when the captain checked in with the customs officer in Yorktown the next day.

Page 115
GREAT MAIN: Reference to a cockfight in Yorktown, where GW returned after his interview with Governor Dinwiddie. Colonel Lewis is unidentified.

Page 116
MONDAY 3D: He went to Hobbs Hole, now Tappahannock. TUESDAY 4TH: Layton's ferry was on the Rappahannock about 20 miles above Tappahannock. This crossing would have placed him in Westmoreland County, not far from the old family home at Pope's Creek where his brother Augustine then lived. TONER (2), 77n, says that GW "rested there that day and night, and procuring a horse, proceeded in the morning to his mother's, near Fredericksburg. Here he tarried one night, and rode the next day to Mount Vernon." That is probably what happened, but Toner's source is not known.

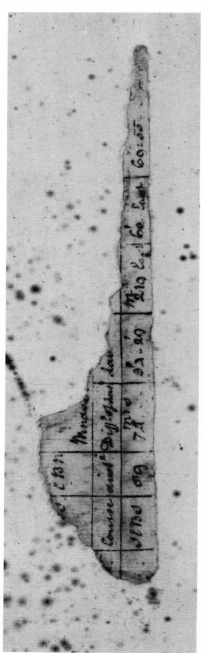

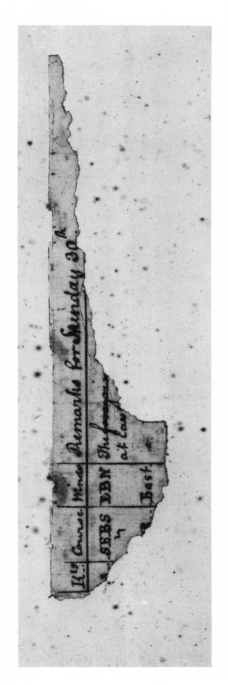
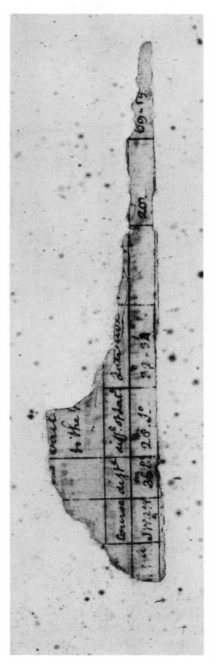

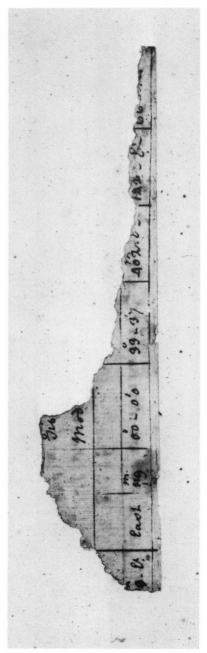

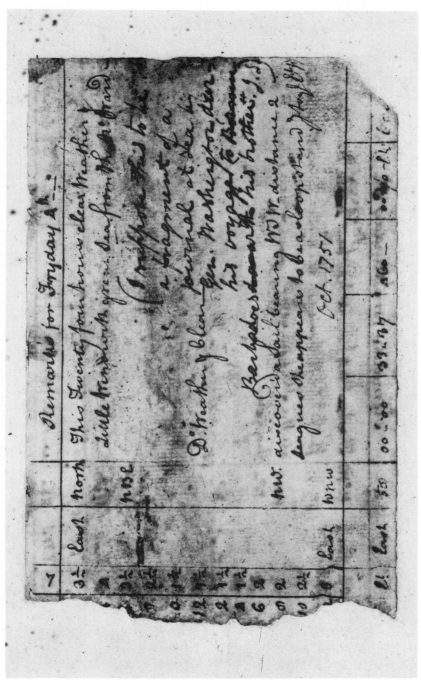

Remarks for Saturday 8th . . .

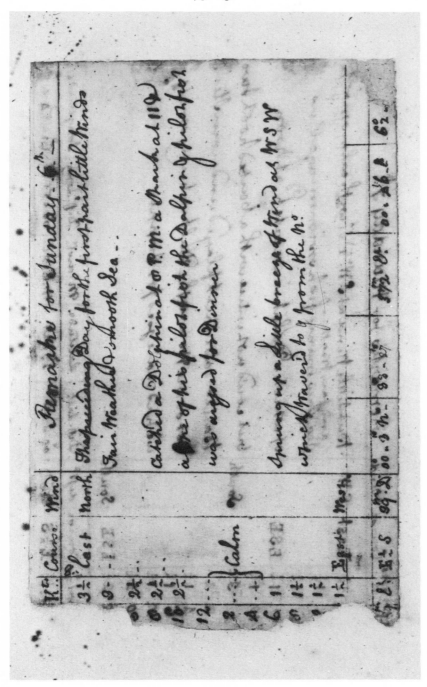

H.rs	Course	Winds	Remarks for Munday 7th &c
1½	East	S.W	but little Wing at S.W.r & S.r with calm smooth
1½			and fair weather
1¼			saw many fish morning & c.o
1½	ESE		opened a Dolphin we eaten at noon
1½			
9	South		but wind not note with a boiled North hare
2..			
1¼			Nair so obstinately play'd under our stern
1¼			or ever since the Dolphin swam
1½			
2½			we had indulged for supper
2¼	ESE	South	

	Course	dist.º	Diff. Lat.	Latitude	Mr d West	Diff.º Long	Longitude
6.8	E ½ S	26	00..56 S	33.25	611 W	02.55 W	61.52

H	Course	Knots	Remarks for Thursday &c
9	ESE	S W	Small Wind at SW with smooth sea & fair weath[er]
10			was attended by a long Dolphin even
11			aioned of ship that would not be moved by
12	ESE	S W	any bait whatever &c
2			
4			
6		WSW	
8			
10			
	ESE		
86 H	ISE	71D	00–27 S	32.60	60A E	01–19 E	60

H	Courses	Winds	Remarks for Wednesday 9th
8		ESE WSW	Fine clear Weather with moderate gale
2¼			of Wind and smooth Sea for the first part
2¼		SW	the latter was favoured with a breeze
3½			(Wind)
4			
4½			
4½			
4½		SW	
5			
6			
5½		WSW	
5½		ESE	

Course	diff:	dist.	departure	latitude	Meridian	Dist: long	Longitude
N E SES	No D	00:31 S	32:87	770: E	01:50 W	55:25

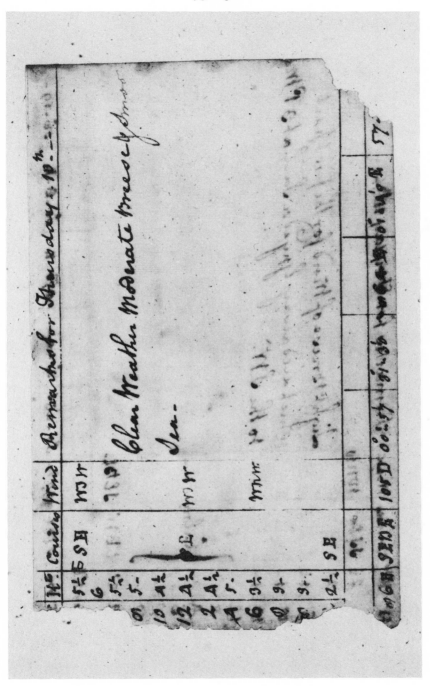

H..	Courses	Wind	Remarks for Thursday 11th —
2½	SSE	WNW	
2			Light Breezes of Wind for the first part
1½			which dies away Weigd a Sail at 9 PM
1			to the SW.
1			
12		Calm —	
2			
4			
6			
8			
10			
2¼	EBN	SEBE	

pr D			
m	SWE	272	60 · 26S	21 · 0i	070 · E	12 · 6 · B	56 · 5Q

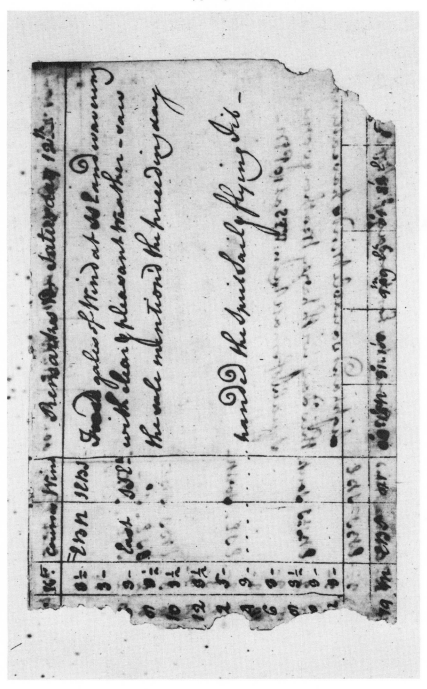

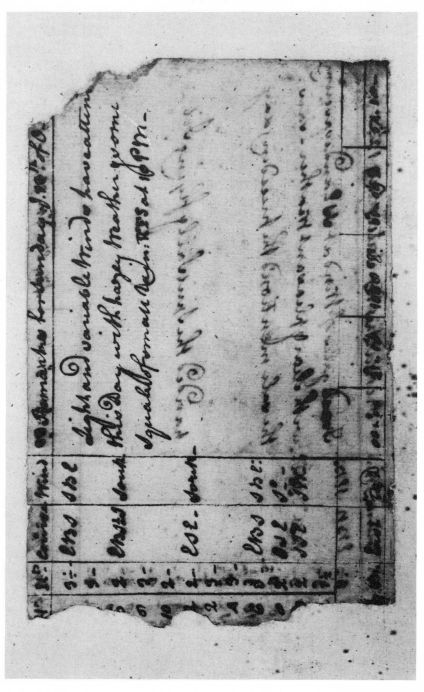

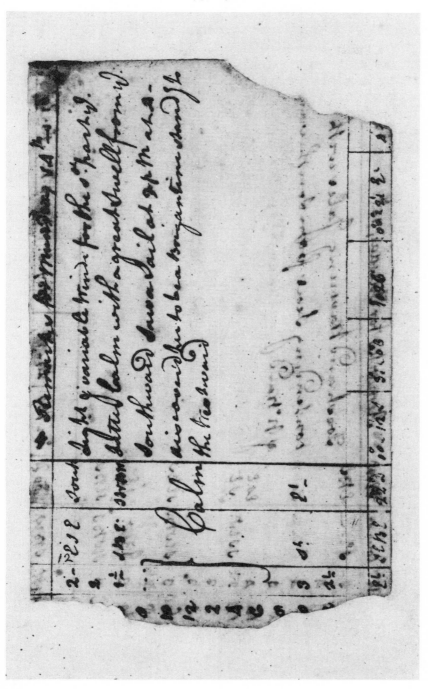

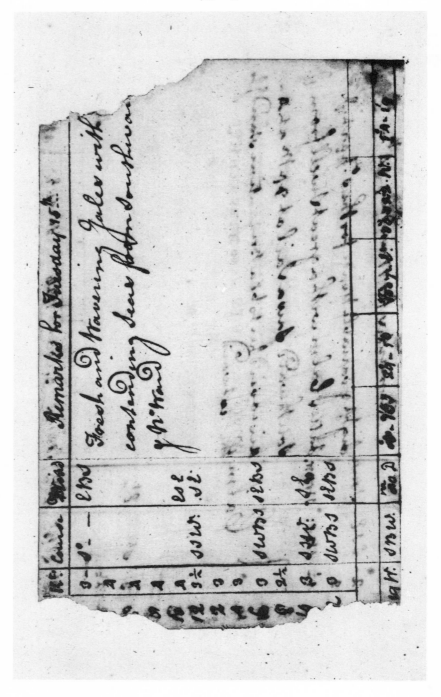

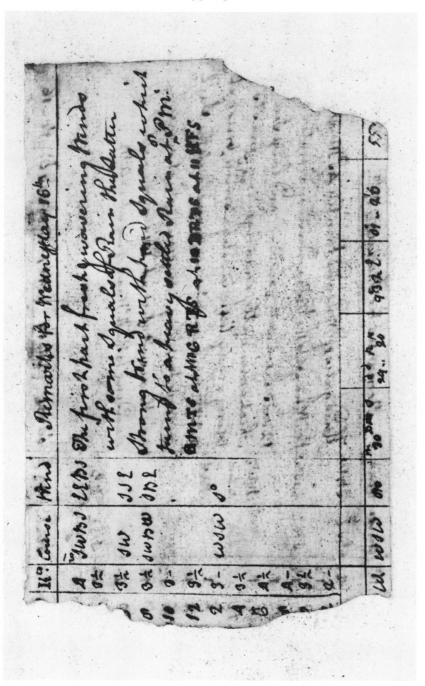

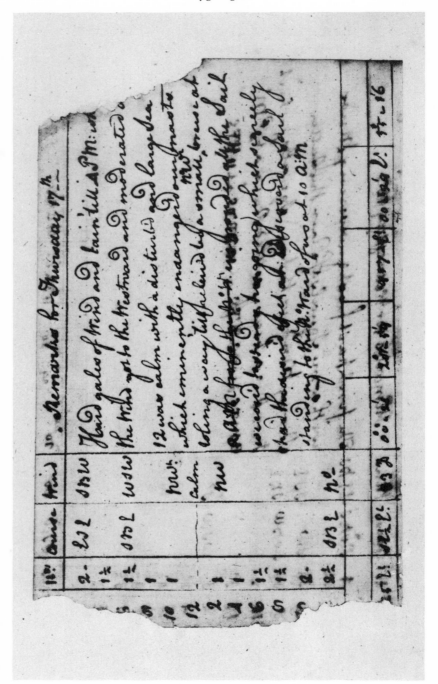

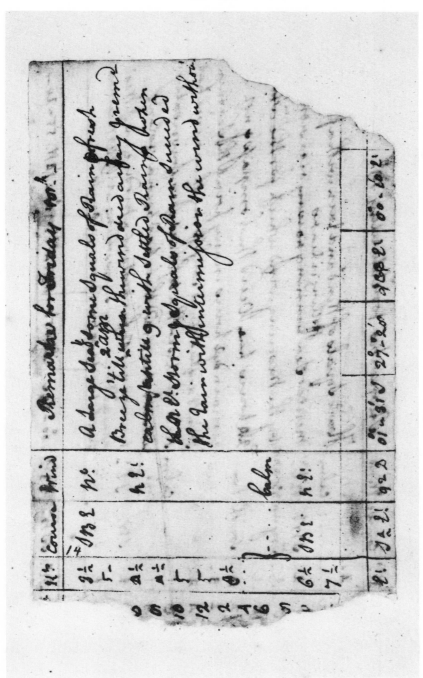

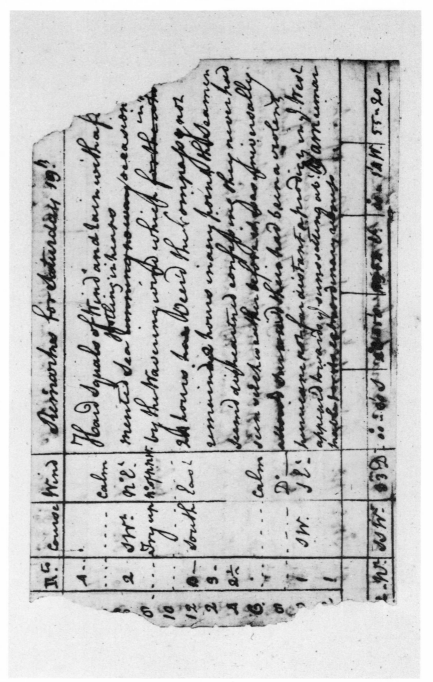

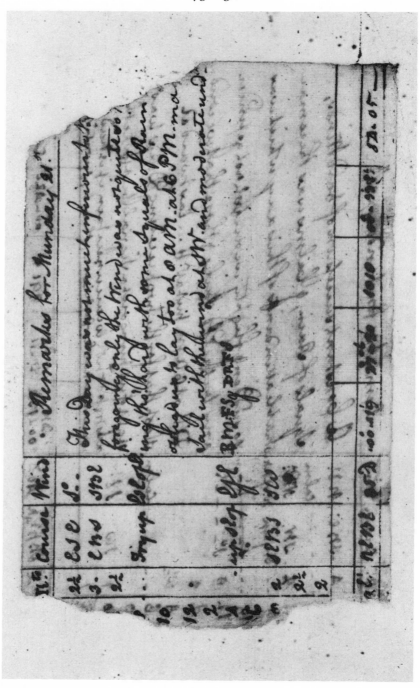

H.º	Courses	Winds	Remarks for Thursday 22.ᵈ
1½	SSE:	SW.ᵗ	Light Breez.ʸ haveing Winds with a large
2			swell, the runing Sea many ways by
2½			fits Confus.ᵈ undeschribed with hds
1½	SSE:		all hands we breifly employd in refitting
1½	South	WSW	
2		•	the Rigg.ᵍ an which had sufferd much in
1		•	the bllecum storme .
1½		•	
1		•	
		Calm	

| n E: | SSE: | SSE: | 22.D | 00 . 19 E: | 27 . 11 . 00 | 10 . 08 E: | 00 . 09 E: | S. |

Remarks for Wednesday 20th —

Calm till 9 AM with a considerable sea
the wind freshned upal last with fine
heathy regular weather wind downto—
which weather most latein up by Noon

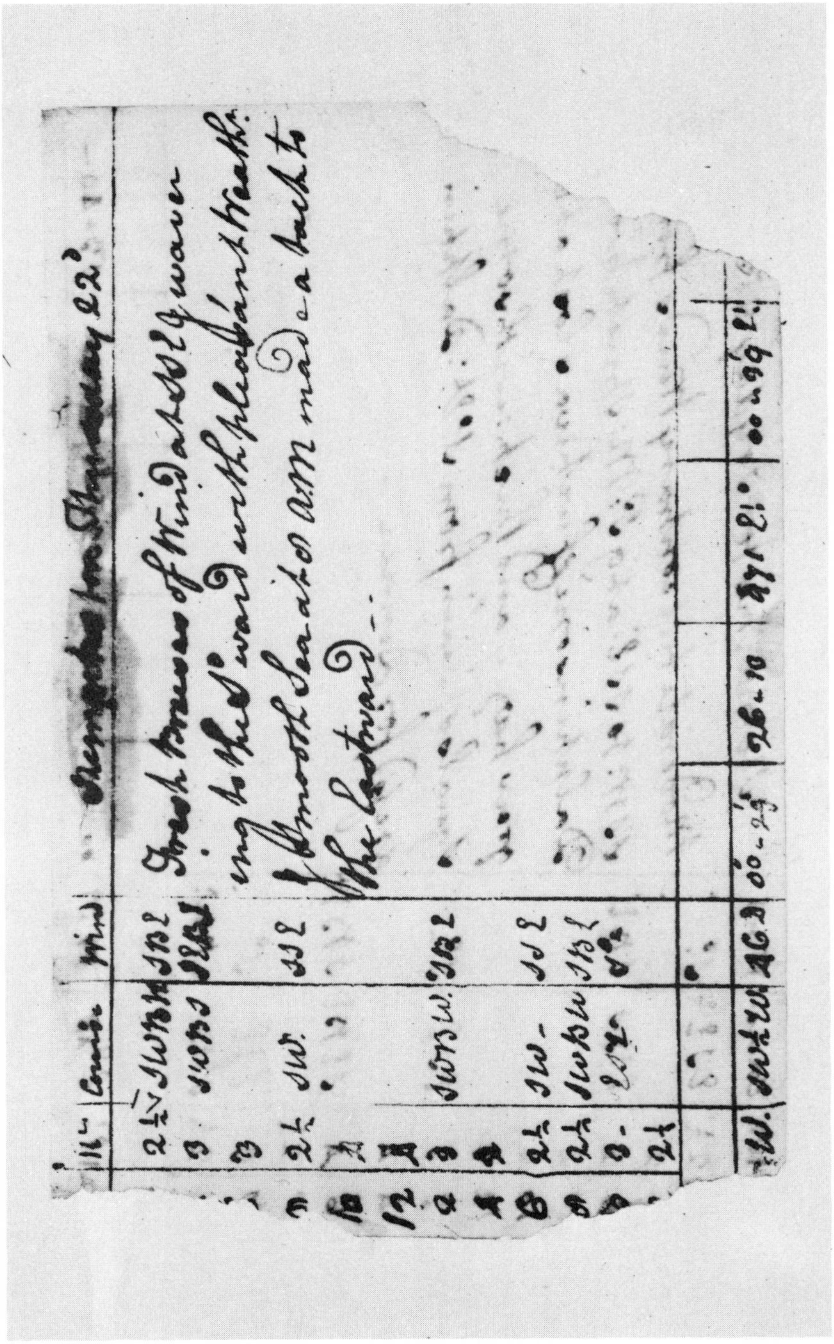

Remarks from Thursday 22d

Fresh breezes of Wind at SSE & varr-ing to the Sd ward with pleasant Weather. Smooth Sea at 10 A.M made a tack to the Eastward.

Remarks for Sunday 26th

Moderate but contrary winds f[...]
dsWt to sdE: at 9 P:M: struck hove [...]
Dolphin one of which was took [...]
grew hazey and thick, wherein [...]
Squals of Rain from SSW: Dolphin
[...]nged for Dinner —

H	Course	Wind			
2½		d°:			
2		sdEs			
2					
2					
10					
12					
3		ESE	d°-		
2					
4		NSW SdE			
4					
2½		d°:			
0		ESE			
2½		sdEsE Smw:			

| Dt: 23½N | DLt 24N | | dist[...] | 1025½ | 87.49 — |

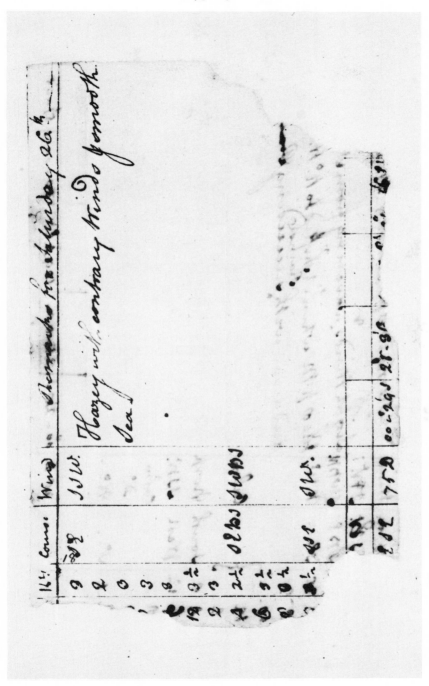

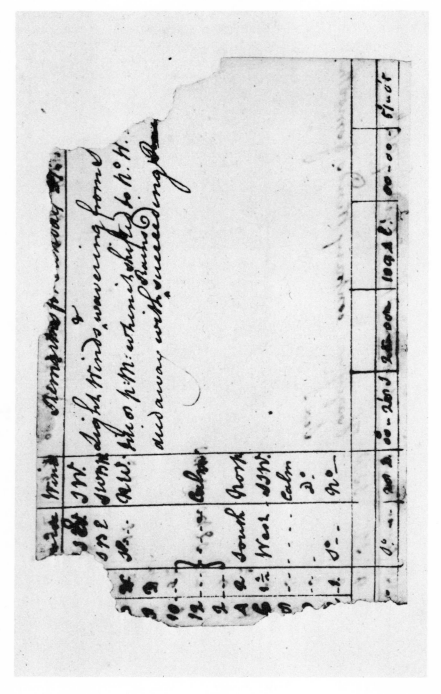

H'r	Course	Wind	Remarks for Munday 20th
	South	ENE	Fresh gale of Wind at ENE came on at noon with happy weather some rain squalls to the Eastward and moderate; at 6 a'm
		East	saw a sail to the leastward bearing
			on course, made her to be a sloop; unbent mended and set the main topsail
	ENEWt.		
	South	SWbS.	
	ESW	SE	
		SWbWSSE.	

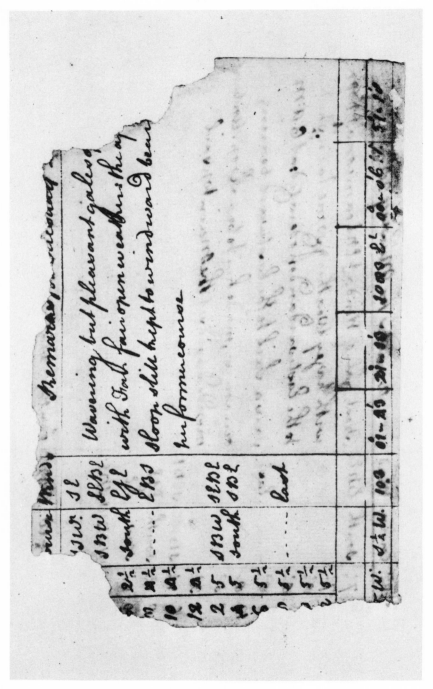

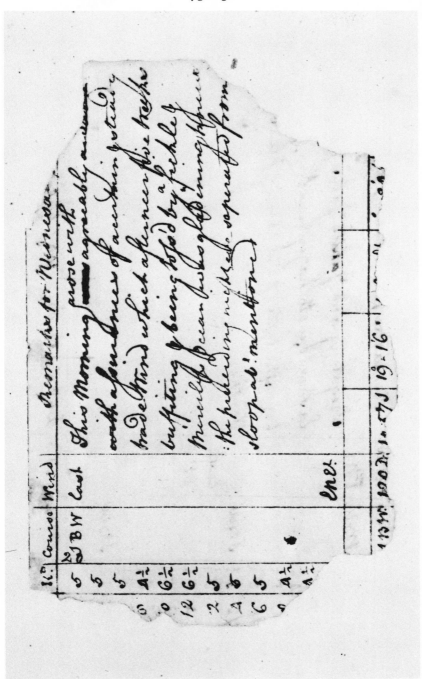

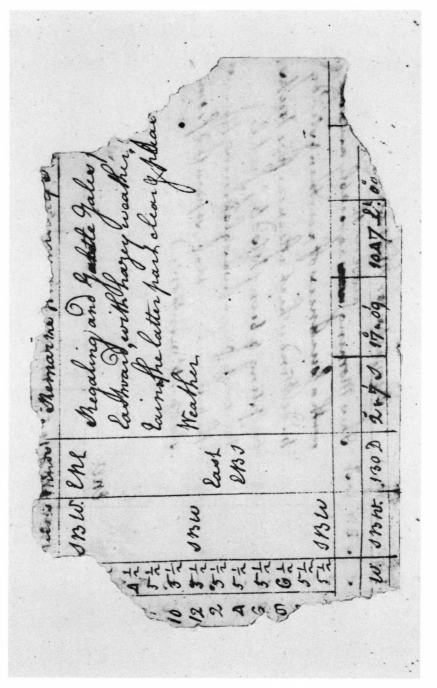

We were gre[...]

[...]arm'd with the cry of Land

[...]t 4 A:M: we gu[...]ed our [...]

[...]ith surprise and found of

[...]and plainly appearing at

[...]out 3 leagues distance whi[...]

[...] your reckonings we should

have *been* near 150 leagues to the

Windward we to[...] d by [...]

distance above mention[...] end

[...]ad we been but 3 or 4 leagues

more we should not have been

[...]ight of

the Island undoion the latitu[...]

[...]d probably not have discov[...]

[...] more in time to have gain'd

[...]and for 3 weeks or a Mo[...]

November 4th, 1751.—This morning received a card from Major Clarke, welcoming us to Barbadoes, with an invitation to breakfast and dine with him. We went,—myself with some reluctance, as the smallpox was in his family. We were received in the most kind and friendly manner by him. Mrs. Clarke was much indisposed, insomuch that we had not the pleasure of her company, but in her place officiated Miss Roberts, her niece, and an agreeable young lady. After drinking tea we were again invited to Mr. Carter's, and desired to make his house ours till we could provide lodgings agreeable to our wishes, which offer we accepted.

5th.—Early this morning came Dr. Hilary, an eminent physician recommended by Major Clarke, to pass his opinion on my brother's disorder, which he did in a favorable light, giving great assurances that it was not so fixed but that a cure might be effectually made. In the cool of the evening we rode out accompanied by Mr. Carter to seek lodgings in the country, as the Doctor advised, and were perfectly enraptured with the beautiful prospects, which every side presented to our view,—the fields of cane, corn, fruit-trees, &c. in a delightful green. We returned without accomplishing our intentions.

and was perfectly ?? ...
the beautiful prospects which
every side presented to our view
The fields of Cain, Corn, Fruit
Trees, &c in a delightful Green ...
We returned without accomplish
ing our intentions —

Tuesday 6th

          At Mr. Carter's
imploying ourselves in Writ g
Letters to be carried by the Schooner
Fredericksburg, Capt. Nr. Robin
son to Virginia, received a Card
from Majr. Clarke wherein our
companys were desired to Dinner
to morrow & myself an invitation
from Mr. Clarke & Miss Roberts to come
see the slept field being June 7. I had
the pleasure of seeing Mr. Chur h

22

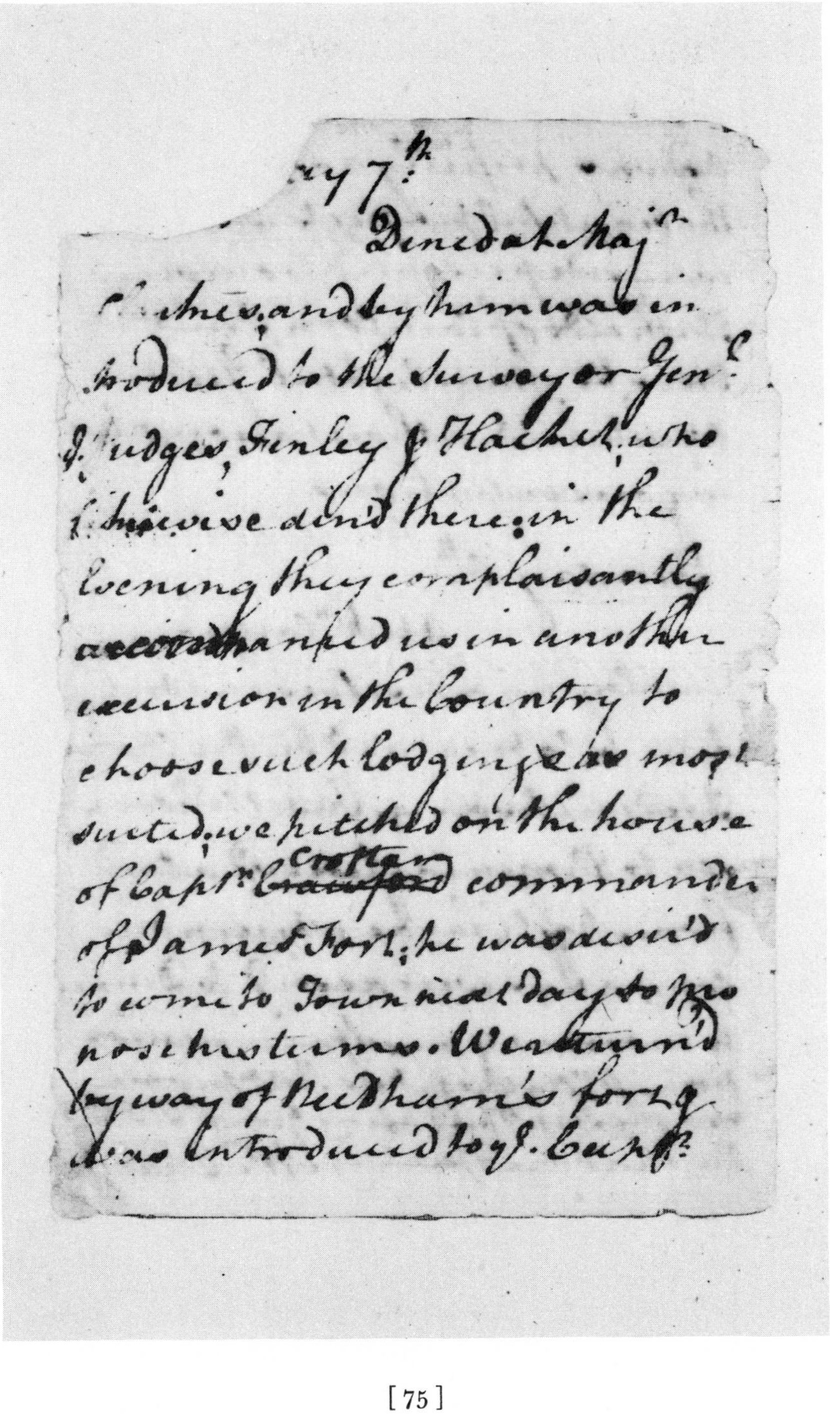

ry 7th

Dined at Majr

& ames, and by him was in

troduced to the Surveyor Genl

Judges, Finley & Hackel, who

likewise dind there in the

Evening they complaisantly

~~accom~~thanped us in another

excursion in the Country to

choose such lodgings as most

suited, we pitchd on the house

of Capt. ~~Crawford~~ (Cotton) commander

of James Fort; he was desir'd

to come to Town next day to pro

pose his terms. We return'd

by way of Beckham's fort, &

as Introduced to J. Capt.

thereof, a good Gentle
man. sup'd and others
Evening at Majr Cooke
with the Gentlemen before
mentioned

Thursday 8th.

Came Captn Crossan
crawford with his proposals
which tho extravagantly dear
my Brother was oblig'd to give
2₁₅ pr. Month is his charge
exclusive of Liquors & washing
which we find. in the Evenings
we remov'd some of our things
up and and ourselves its very
pleasantly situated pretty

23

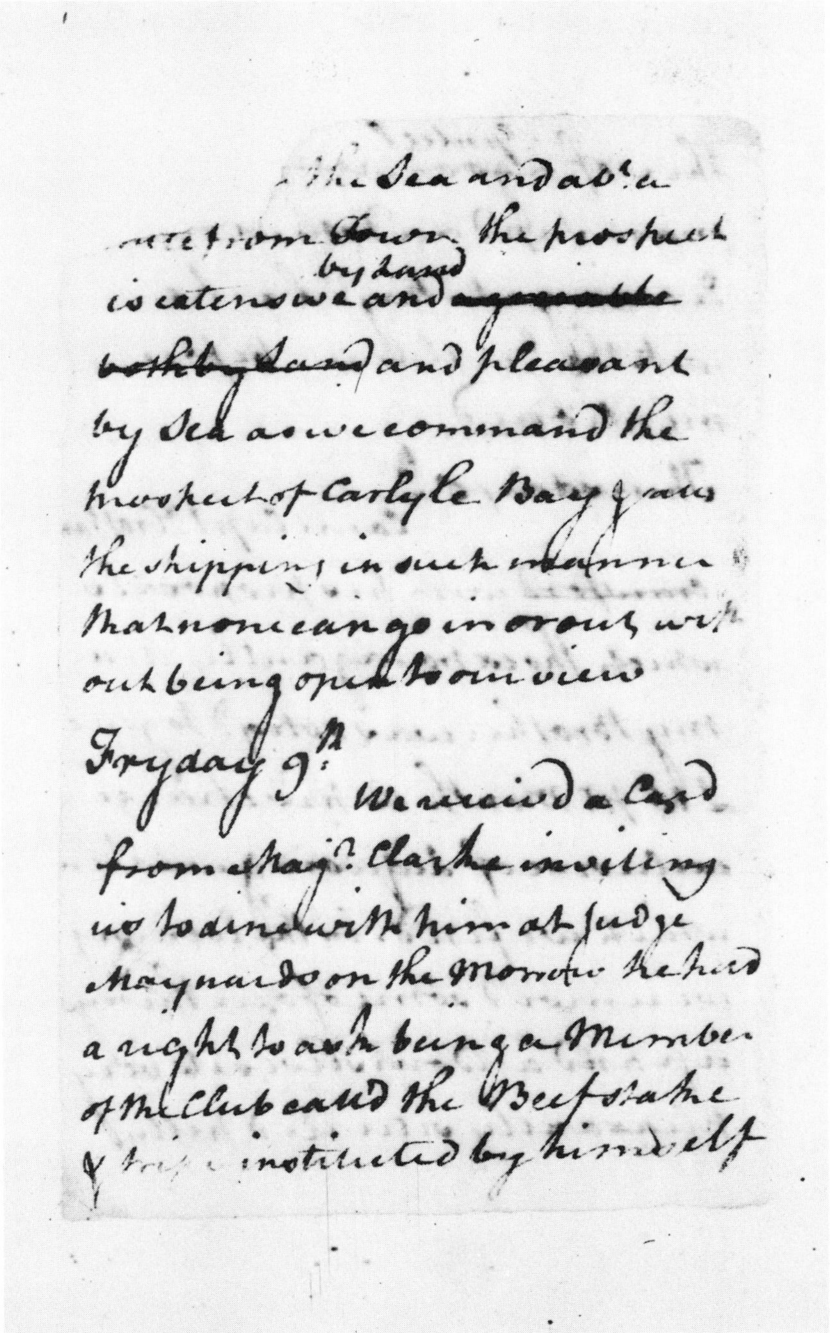

the Sea and also a
view from town the prospect
by land
is extensive and agreeable
with by land and pleasant
by Sea as we command the
prospect of Carlyle Bay & all
the shipping in such manner
that none can go in or out with
out being open to our view

Fryday 9th   We receivd a Card
from Majr Clarke inviting
us to dine with him at Judge
Maynards on the Morrow he had
a right to ask being a Member
of the Club called the Beefstake
& tripe instituted by himself

& Judges Maynard

Rob[t] Warren Efq[r] g [illegible] p[r]son &
/ the Commander of Needhams
Fort / We were Genteely received
Sat[urday] Maynard
by Judge his Lady and agreeable
entertaind by the Company, they
have a meeting every Saturday
this being Col[o] Maynards
After Dinner was the greatest
collection of Fruits I have yet
seen or on the Table there was
the Granadilla the Sappadilla
Pomgranate sweet Orange
water Lemmon forbidden Fruit
app[le] is Rubaba &c &c &c
We received invitations from
every Gentleman there gone

2.4

yᵉ Jenkins's who also
true tho not one of theᵐ

Sᵒ Mⁿ Warren desir'd Mayʳ
Clarke to shuw us the way to his
house; Mʳ Hackᵗ insisted on our
coming Saturday next to his
house being his Day to treat with
yᵉ of State y Trip but above all
the invitation of Mʳ Maynard
was the most kind and friendly
he desir'd and even insisted as
well as his Lady on our coming
to spend some Weeks with him
and promis'd nothing should be
wanting to render our
stay agreeable my Mⁿ promis'd
he would as soon as he was a
little disengaged from the Dᵒ

the altered and I ye it
was invited to Dine at
Clarkes the next Day by him
self
Sunday 11:th

Dressed on order
for Church but got to town
two late Dind at Majr Clarkes
iniss S: G:
and went to Evening Service
and returned to own Lodgings
in the Evening rewards

Munday 12:th

recevd an afternn:
Visit from Captn Petrie and
an invitation to dine with
him the next Day

25

13th

Dined at the Fort with some Ladies its pretty strongly fortifyed and mounts about 36 Guns within the fortific" but ffaciffe ballerys m'c 51

Wednesday 14:

At our Lodgings

Thursday 15

Was treated with by Mr Carter a play ticket to see the Trag of George Barnwell acted the charaktar of Barnwell and several others was said to be well perform'd there was a band of Musick adapted and regular ly conducted by Mr

Fryday 16:th

    Mr Graeme 2.
of the Masters of the College of
Virginia came to Visit us past
us at Morninger & c & c, and inv
us to dine with Judge Graeme
his Br on Sunday: dind this
Day at Maj Blathie's

Saturday 17:th   Nov?

    Was strongly atta
ed with the small Pox, sent f
Dr Lanahan whose attendance
was very constant, till my was
very and going out which wa
not till thursday the 12th of
December

26

December 12th.

went to Town visited
Majr. Clarke's Family who
so kindly occasionally to visited
me in my illness and contri
buted all they coud in regard
me the necessarys acquired
in my disorder
and dined with Messrs Gasker,
a half Br. to Wm. Clarke On Mun
day last began the Grand Jesciv,
and this Day brought on the
tryal of Coll Chauncek a Man
of oppulent fortune & infam
ous Character he was indicted
for commiting a rape on his
servant Maid and was brought
in Guilltles and saved by one

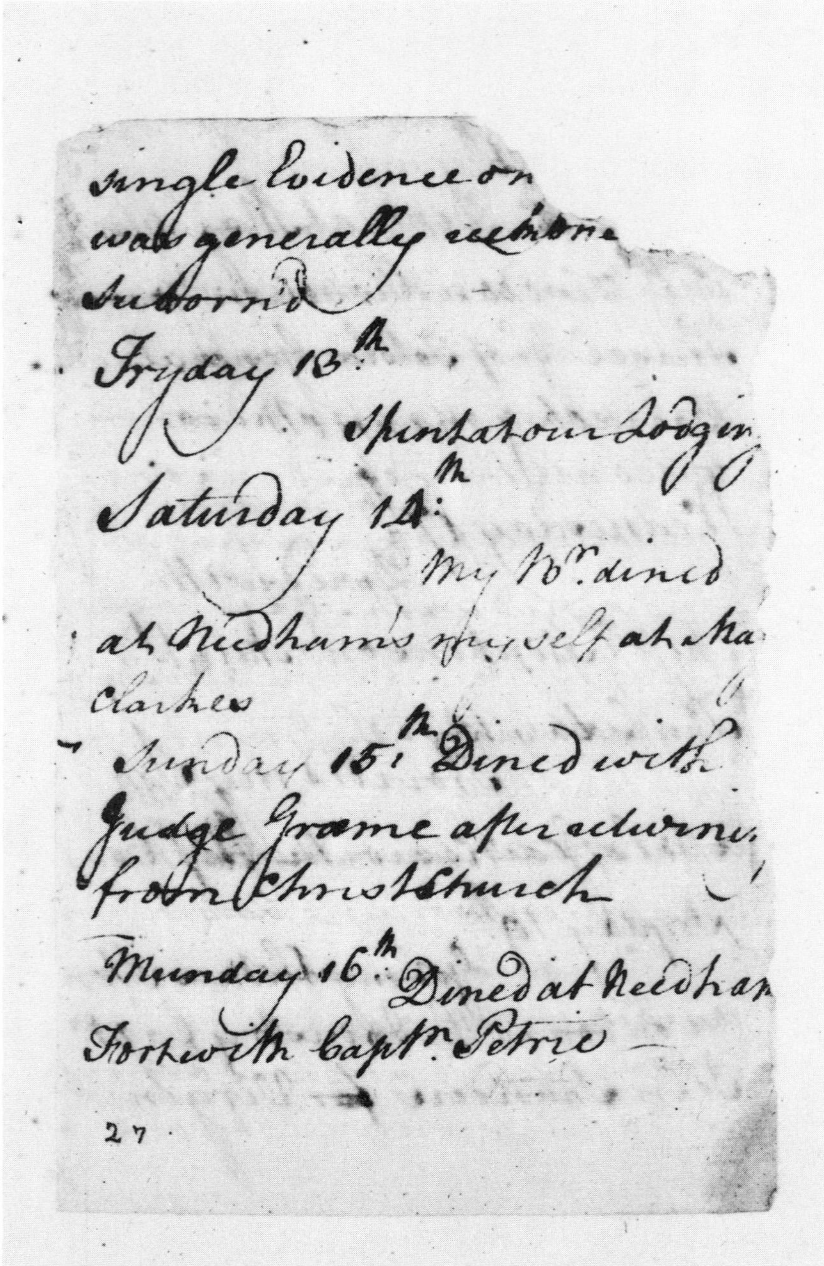

single Evidence on
was generally such one
Suborn'd

Fryday 13th

Spint at our Lodgin

Saturday 14th:

My Br. dined
at Needhams myself at Mar.
Clarkes

Sunday 15th. Dined with
Judge Grame after returning
from Christ Church

Munday 16th. Dined at Needhams
Fortwith Captn. Petrie —

27

Dined at Maj.^r Clark
with comodore Hobourn Gove.^{nr}
Pursel Govr of Jotola General
Barrack & many Others

Wednesday 17th
Dined with
Messrs Stephenson's Merch.^{ts}

Thursday 18
Provided my Sea
Store & dined with Messrs bac.^t

Fryday 19th
Got my Clothes Sto
re on board the Industry Capt.^t
John Saunders for Virginia

Saturday 21.

At my Lodgin

my Brother

Sunday 22.

Took my Leave of my Br. Maj.n Clarke &c. & Imbar. in the Industry Capt. John Saum. for Virginia waid anchor and got out of Carlile Bay ab.t 12

The Governer of Barbados seems to keep a proper State: Lives very retired and at Little expence it is said he is a Gentleman of good Sence. As he avoids the Errors of his predecessor, he gives no handl. to complaint, but at the same time by declining much familiarity is not over zealously beloved and being deprived of power to

28

... with

&c.ª ——— There is ...
regular risings in this Islan...
above another so that scarcel...
...ry part is deprived of a beautif...
Prospect both of Sea & Land and
what is contrary to the observati...
...other Countrys is that each
...ing is better than the other belo...

There are many delicious
fruits in this but as they are
particularly describ'd by the Rev.
Mr. Hughes in his Natural hist.
of the Islan... shall say nothing fur...
...an that the Pine Apple China
...ange is good the Avagado pai...
...nerally more admired tho no...
...leases my taste as do's the ...

The Earth in most parts is
...treamely rich & as black as ou...

richest Marsh ..
common produce of ea..
Canes is from 40 to 70 poles of
Sugar each poll valued at 20/ ..
of which a third is deducted for
expences unless turn sells for
2/ and upwards p: Gallon then
it is though the Sugar is near
clear — There was many acres
last year that turn'd out from
1200 to 1702 as I was inform'd by
credible auth'y tho that was iff
Ginger ? a very extraordinary fee
for the fail thereof How wonderful
such people should be in debt & not
be able to indulge themselves in
all the Luxurys as well as necessa
rys of life Yet so it happens Esttes
are of unalienated for debts indeed

29

... an Interest of ...
... Carerin an Estate
... at a full value ... Interest
... how persons coming to Estates
... two, three, and four hundred Acres
... which are the largest I can want is
... not wonderful to Me 1/3 of their
Land or nearly generally is in Car-
... Flax ... is in Young Can
... nia Corn / which ... supports
their Negros / Yams plantens
Potatos ... & and some ... pas
... waste for Stock. Their dung
... are very careful in saving &
... curious in making which they ...
... through ...
... up large heaps of ...
... a Number of Stakes drove ...
... sufficient for sixteen head of Cat...
... Stand seperately tied too which ...
... three Months together tramp...

all the trash [...] [...]
and then its fit to manu[re]
[the] ground. Provisions in Gen[l] are
very indeferent but much bette[r]
than the same quantity of past[u]-
rage would afford in Virginia
The very grass that grows amo[ng]
[their] corn is not lost but carefully
gathered for provender for their [...]

    Hospitality & a Genteel behav[iour]
is shewn to every Gentleman
Stranger by the Gentlemen Inhab[itants]
Taverns they have none, but in
their Towns, so that Travellers is
oblig'd to go to private houses.
however the Island being but ab[ou]t [...]
Miles in length & [...] in width presen[tly]
their being much infested with y[m]

    The Ladys Generally are very
agreeable but by ill custom or [...]

30

affect the Negro Healthiness of this Island

sufficiently shewn in the florid countenances of the country Gentle. and its said they live to great age where they are not intemperate they are however very unhappy in regard to there Officers Fees which are not fixed by any Law, they complain particularly of the Proovost Marshal or Shireff Genl. of the Island Patented at Home and rented at £ooo 2 p. ann. So yt every other officer is exorbitant in demanding. — There are few who may be called midling people they are either very rich or very poor. for by a law of the Island every Gentl. is obligd to keep a white person for every ten acres, capable of acting in the Malitia and consequently those persons is kept early but very

poor The Number
Barbados is compute...
Thousand ſwhich is more t...
is in Jamaica ſall the other Leeſo...
Iſlands ſthey are well diſciplin'd ...
appointed to their several Statio...
ſo that up ᵒʳ an allarm every Ma...
is at his poot in leſs than two H...
They have large Intrenchmen to
caſt up where ever its poſsible
for an Enemy to Land and may
...ſas nature has greatly aſ...
...d improperly bevaid to be one
...ire fortification —

3¹

Met with a brisk Trade
wind and pretty large Swell w.ch
made the Ship roul much and
me very sick at 2 P: M: Espy.d
a Sail in the Latitude of Marti
nica bearing down for the Island
Tuesday 24.th

A Fresh gale for
what in this part of the world is
called a fiery Breeze hurried us
pass the Leeward Islands, the Capt.n
altered his course from N.o to NW.b.

Wednesday 25.th

Christmas Day fine
clear and pleasant with moderate Sea
the continuance of the Trade which by
servation set us in the Latitude

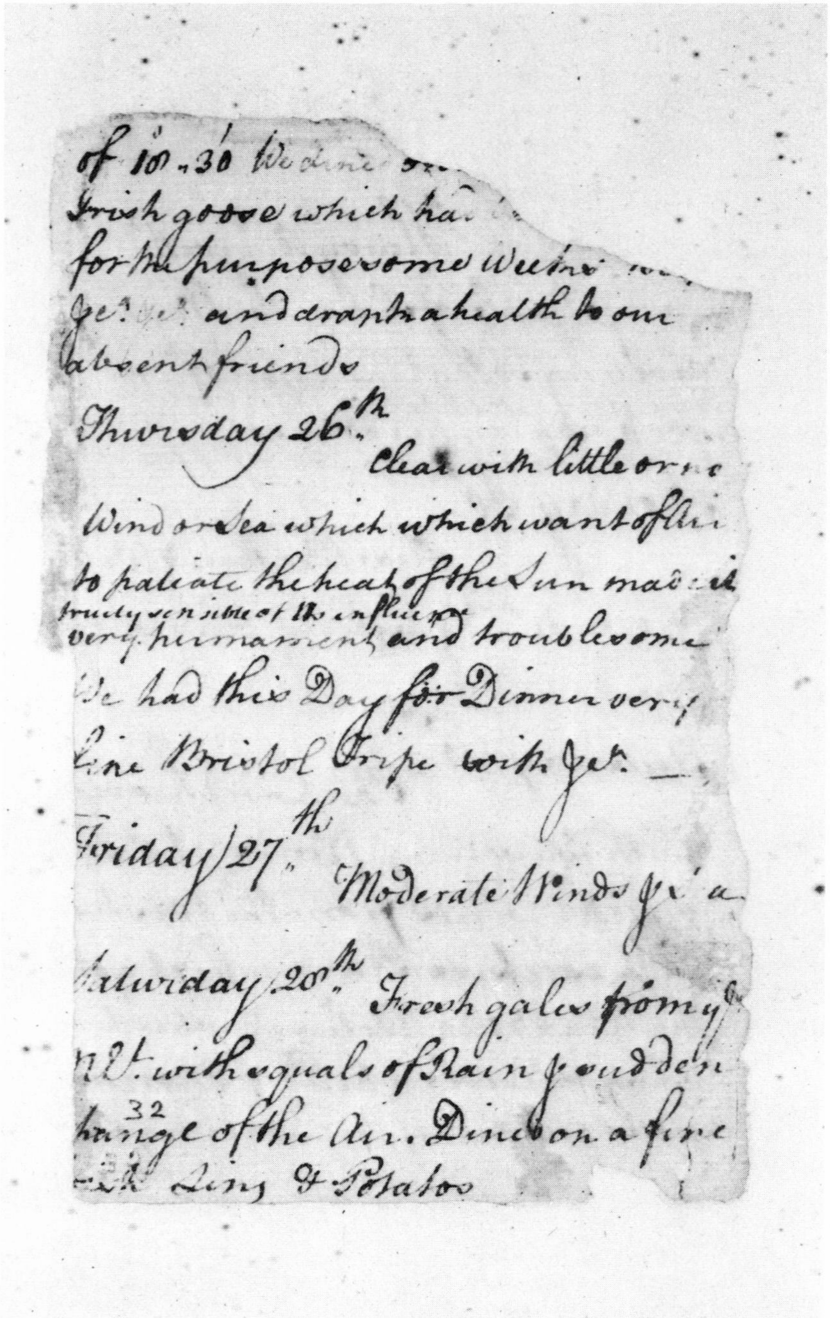

of 10°–30 We dine o...

Irish goose which ha...

for the purpose some Wedns...

Je: &c. and drank a health to our

absent friends

Thursday 26th.

Clear with little or no

Wind or Sea which which want of Air

to paliate the heat of the Sun made it

truly sensible of the influence

very hermament and troublesome

We had this Day for Dinner very

fine Bristol Tripe with Je. —

Friday /27th"

Moderate Winds Je: a.

Saturday 28th

Fresh gales from y

NW. with squals of Rain & sudden

32

change of the Air. Dined on a fine

... Ling & Potatos

Heavy Air with
many Squalls of Rain the Wind
wavering so that the Vessel often
would not lay her course

Monday 30th

Clear Weather & Wind
from N° E° & Easterly blew very
fresh

Tuesday 31

Thick and heavy
with wavering Winds at 8 PM
violent winds from the Westw
with excessive Rain which got
the N° a Et 12 and cleared which
being directly ahead & Mount
noils running prevented car

rying Sail but oblig'd
to Under the fore Sail

Wednesday January 6:— 1751
                                1752
   The Wind still continuing at N
tho.' not so violent, we made Sail
ab.' 12 and stood N.º W.B W. holeing
as near the Wind as we cou'd —

Thursday 2.ᵈ —
                      The Sea greatly
fallen & winded something aba.
the p still directly a head which
oblig'd us to keep the course we did
the Preceeding day

Fryday 3
33   In the Morning
Calm and clear, at noon the
Wind breezed up and clouded
            at 3º

rain and about 9 m

... squally with some
violent storms of Wind which
before ten oclock got to N.Wd. and
remaind there the Night with
divers hard squalls of Wind &
Rain

Saturday 4th The Wind still
at N.Wd. directly a head & Mountanous Sea we bore away N.NE
the whole day was attended with
successive Squals

Sunday 5th Wind continues at
N.W. tho much abated and clear with

The Sea greatly fa[
changed our course to
other Tack

Monday 6.th Last night the Wind
varied to the S.ward and grew calm
at 6 AM freshned and had got to
West we made another tack and
stood N.N.W. this day Warm & plea
sant

Tuesday 7.th
Wind fresh & Waver
ing with some Squals & rough
Sea

Wednesday 8.th About 2 this morn
ing the Wind died away and at
.34

.... W. and variable
.... hard Squals of Wind
.... by Observation were in
the Lattitude of 32..30 of Mard
of Bermudos,

Thursday 9th

         At 2 A:M came on
excessive hard Wind at N:Wt Rain
Lightning & some thunder the
Wind increased so violently & had
raiz'd so Mountanous a Sea that
oblig'd the handing all her Sails &
driving with bear Masts which
She did untill 2 P:M. when the
Wind had something Moderated
and Sea abated and then She

was laid too under

Stay Sail — this day
mess cripple by the Ships
Fryday 10th

This Mor.
Wind was moderate tho aa
head about 8 A:M we made saile
and stood W:S:W upon searchin
my chest discoverd I had been
robd of 16 pistoles at 2 P:M the
Wind had changed to S: Wt and
blew fresh which increasing
obliged us to Hand all but the
fore Sail, and that coud be carry
ed no longer than 12 when the
Wind was so Violent the Sea so
high with great Quantity of Rain

nder ye Sharp'd right
the Ship was laid
refd fore Sail

y 11.th The wind still
as violent as ever with many
hard Squals of Rain I had got
Somewhat more to the Westward
the Sea excessively high lay too
all day

Sunday 12.th The Wind as violent
as the preceeding day with Rain
Hail & Snow & high & Mounta
nous Sea from WNW^t Lay too
all the Last night and this day
nder Main & fore Sail

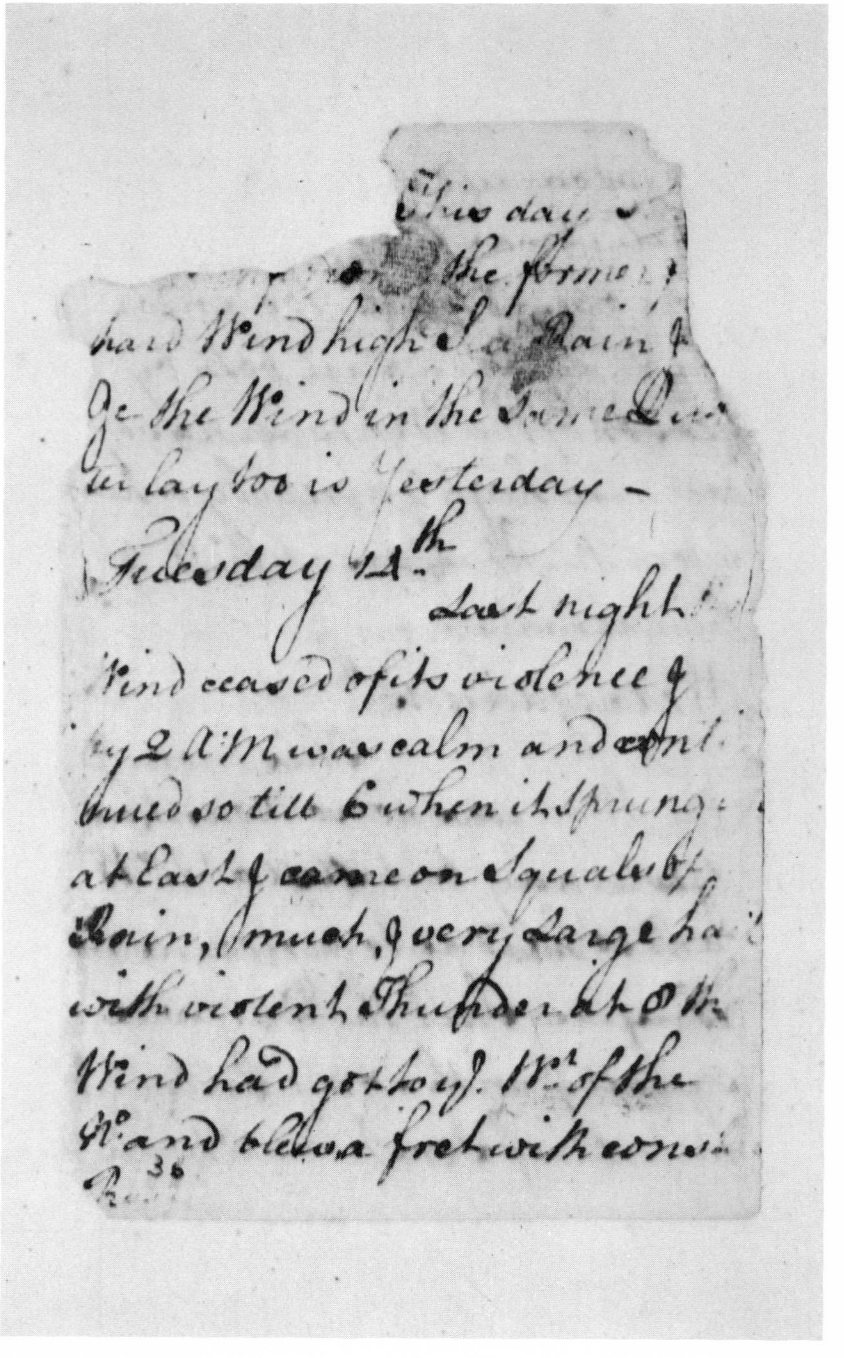

This day
the former
hard Wind high Sea Rain &
&c the Wind in the Same Qur
er lay too is Yesterday —

Tuesday 14th.
Last night
Wind ceased of its violence &
by 2 A'M was calm and con-
tinued so till 6 when it Sprung
at last & came on Squalls of
Rain, & much & very Large ha
with violent Thunder at 8 th
Wind had got to ij Wt of the
No and blew a fret with conv

e we carried
hile it was
ne oblig'd to Lay too under
he Main stay Sail both by
Reason of the Winds being so
excessive high & directly ahea
before Night it was at N°. W. &
there remaind. —

Wednesday 15th.

This morn &
the Wind was not so Violen[t] as
Yesterday but still at N°. W.
and so hard as to hinder us from
carrying Sail the Day was
squally with some Inter
mission of Sunshine which

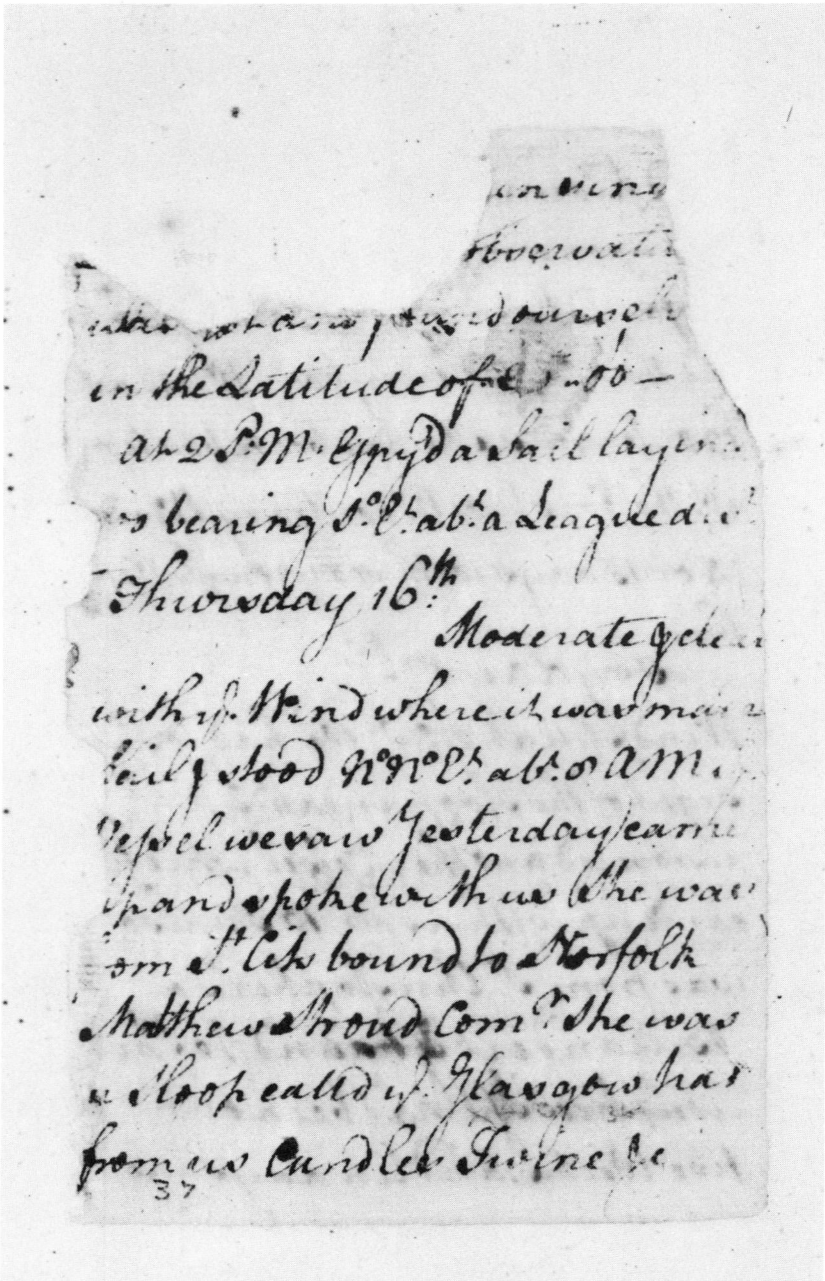

an very

observation

... ... a p... down ...

in the Latitude of ... — 00 —

at 2 P. M. espy'd a sail laying

... bearing S. E. ab.ᵗ a League d...

Thursday 16th

Moderate gale...

with y.ᵉ Wind where it was main...

tain'd stood N.º N. E.ᵗ ab.ᵗ 0 A. M...

Vessel we saw Yesterday came...

... and spoke with us she was...

... S.ᵗ kits bound to Norfolk

Matthew Stroud Com.ʳ she was

a Sloop call'd y.ᵉ Glasgow has

from us Candles Twine &c

37

d promi

s upon comy

found them to agree on a ... alike

nd that Cap. e Henry boar WNW ab:

120 Leagues she had been beating

ab: the Coast with contrary Wind

14 or 15 days with very rough Wea

ther —

    Fryday 17th

Wind still at N: W: we had lost

sight of the sloop and ab: 6 A M

discovered another Vessel which

came up with us ab: 10 She also

was from St. Christopher's a

Billander ~~she had~~ and to Phi

ladelphia ~~she~~ had been out

five Weeks and ten days ago

'y Cap.t

of Wal.

oveis another Sa.

ganing No Wt ab.t 2 Leagues
and f'close to Windward as he
cou'd whether it was if Sloop we
saw Yesterday or not it was too
far to distinguish thus Philadel
phia Man proposed keeping
Company and also of going into
Virginia if he saw no better pros
pect, the two Capt.ns mutually ag:
to alter their Course at 6 o'clock
westward

38

...rday:

...nged and a

...re on very fresh with

...other Ship was very Sociable

in keeping company being

seldom more than a 1/4 Mile diff

both steering Wes: as the day ad..

ced the Wind increased with con-

tinued Rain and by 10 P: M: was

oblig'd to hand all our Sails and

lay too under a Stay Sail until

at 11 lost sight of the Vessel.

Sunday 19th The wind had shifted

from S. to N. and blew extreame

hard with Mountainous Sea

but moderating somewhat a..

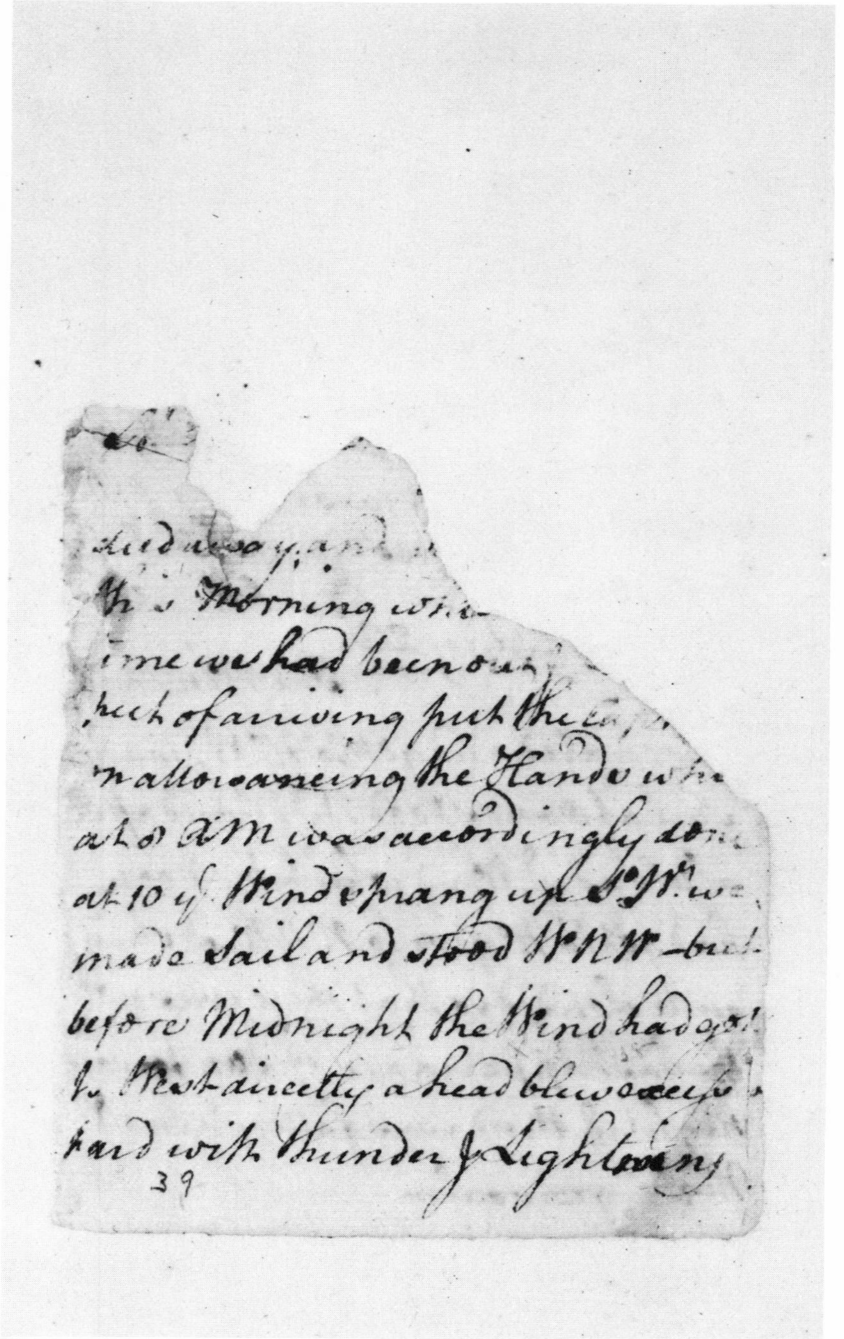

sed also yard in

th s Morning whie

ime we had been our

uch of arriving put the

n allowaneing the Hands wh

at 8 AM was accordingly don

at 10 yf Wind sprang up S S W we

made Sail and stood W N W — but

before Midnight the Wind had got

to West directly a head blew deep

hard with thunder & Lightening

39

. . . . . was . . . .
10 P.M. . . . .

. . . day 22 . . . . . . The Wind ha . . .
. . . oderated and got to N°. W°. made
Sail at 8 and stood W. S. W. and after
alterd as y°. Wind which by Noon
had got to N°. gave to WNW of. whic
quite clouded so that there was not
the least appearance of Sun toward
night y°. Wind was fallen & in y°
Night grew calm

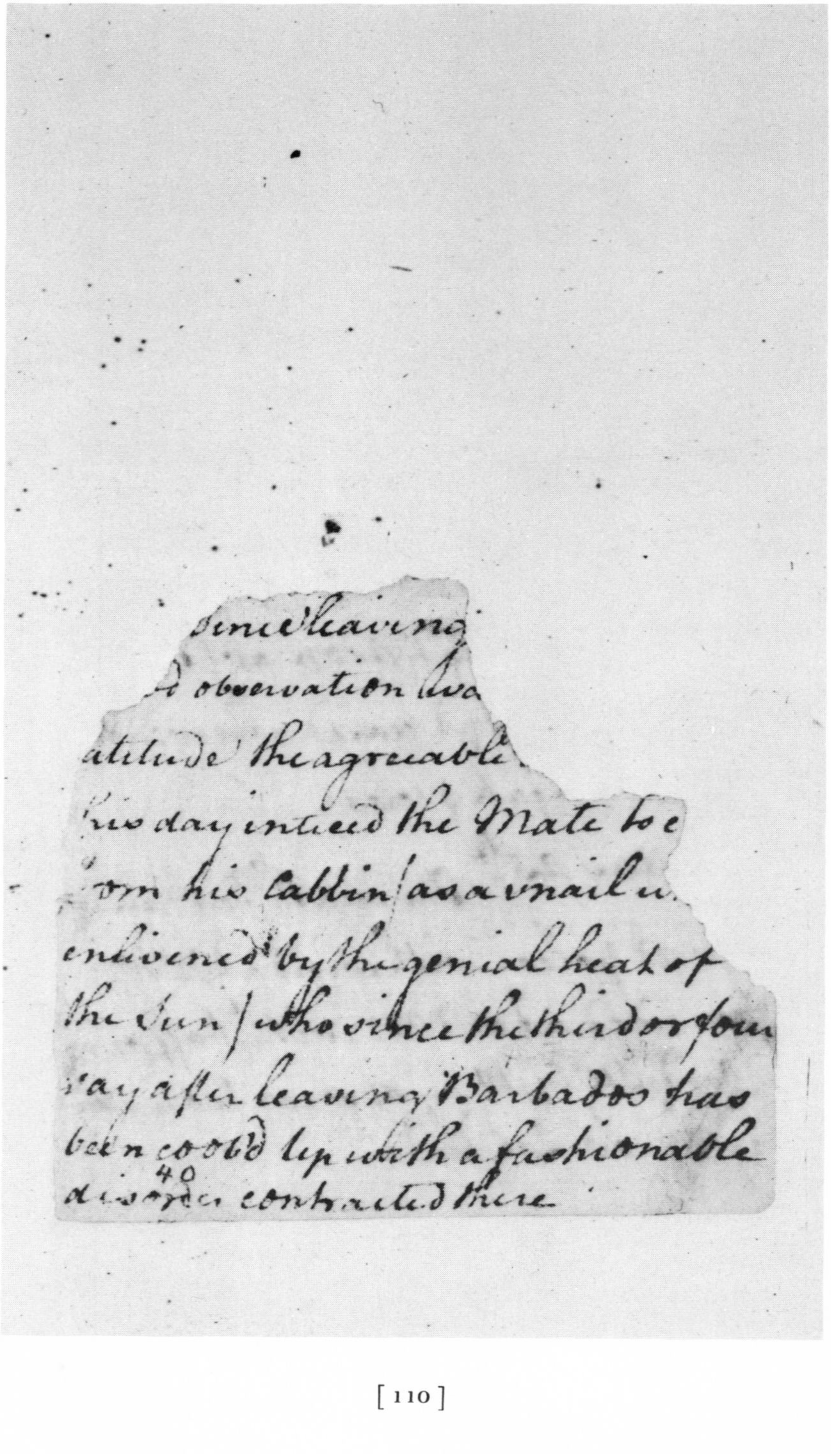

since leaving

... observation was

atitude the agreuable

his day induced the Mate to c

om his Cabbin (as a snail u...

enlivenied by the genial heat of

the Sun) who since the third or four

day after leaving Barbados has

been coold up with a fashionable

dis... 40 contracted there

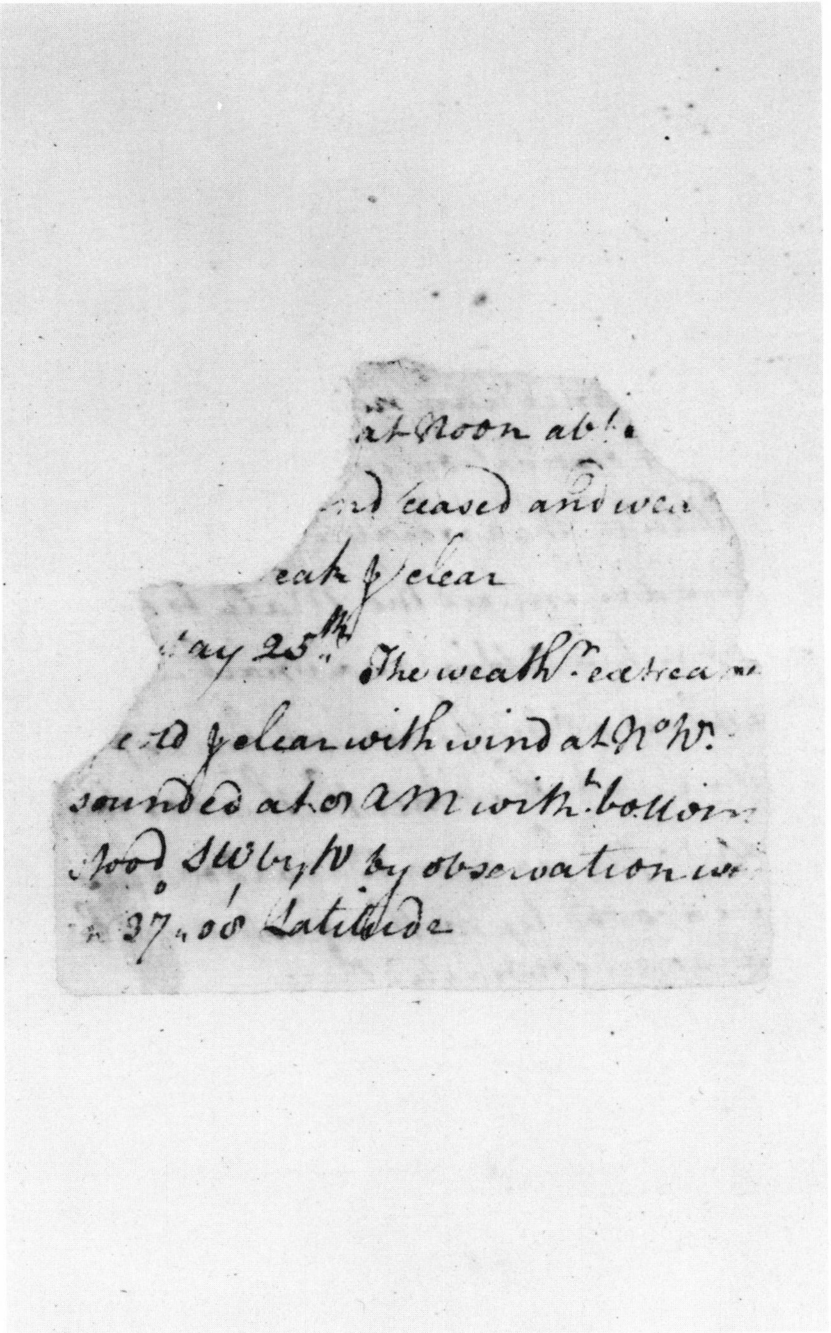

at Noon ab.[t]

nd ceased and wea

eak & clear

[M]ay 25th The weath.[r] extrea[m]

e[d] & clear with wind at N[o]°W.[r]

sounded at 10. AM with[h] bottom

Nood SWbyW by observation in

n 37.,00 Latitude

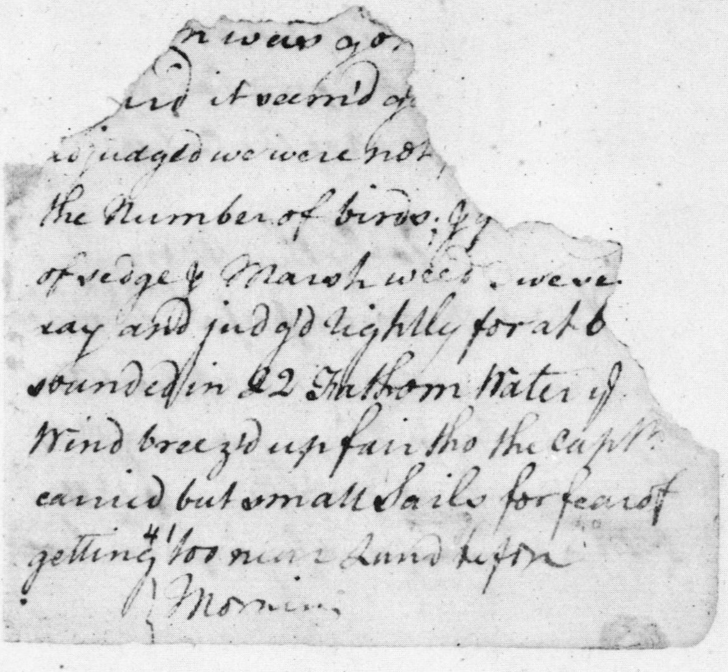

n was go
nd it seem'd of
so judged we were not,
the Number of birds, &c
of sedge & Marsh weed . we ve
ray and judg'd rightly for at 6
sounded in 22 Fathom Water if
Wind breez'd up fair tho the Capt.
carried but small Sails for fear of
getting too near Land before
Morning.

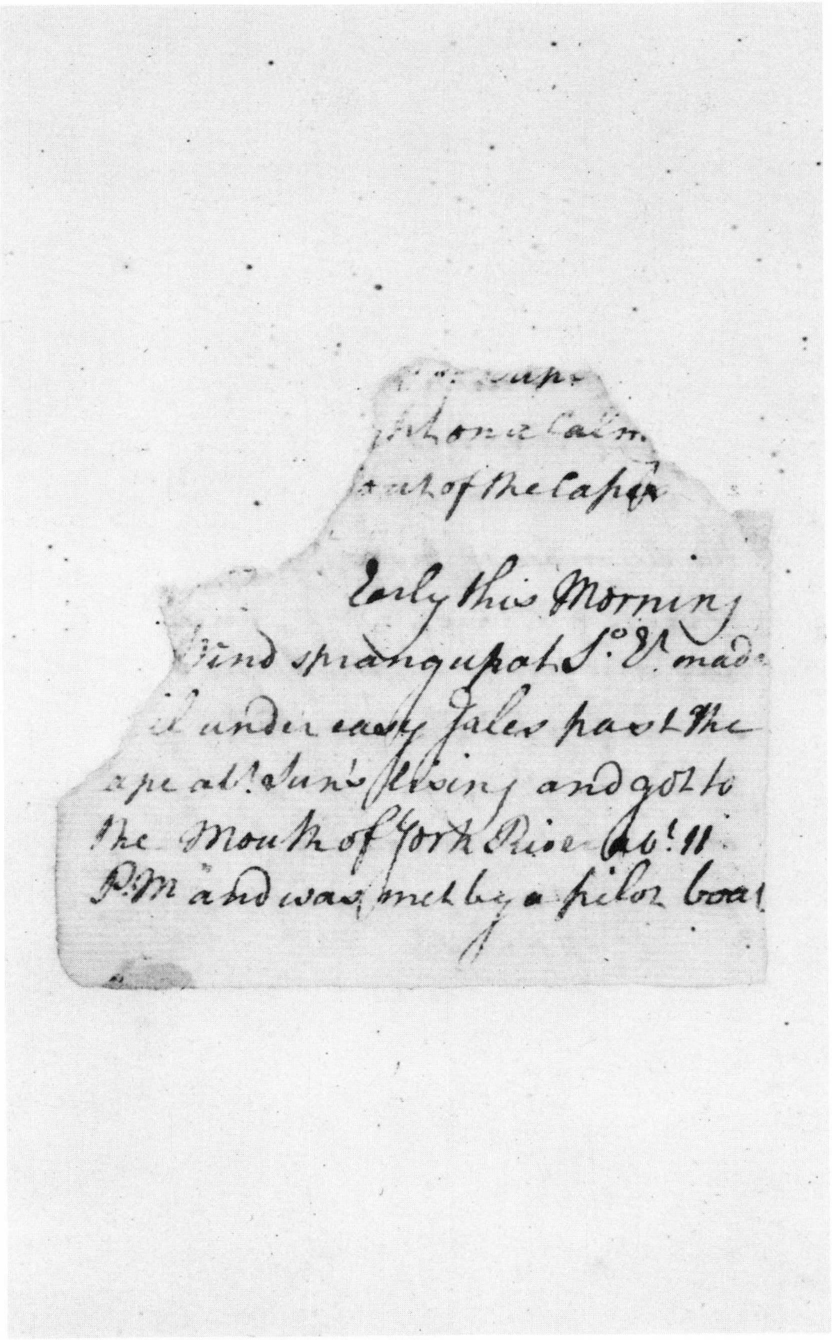

[. . . sup . . .
[. . . a Calm . . .
[. . . at of the Cape

Early this Morning [the]
Wind sprang up at S° W° made
[sai]l under easy sales past the
[C]ape abt Suns Rising and got to
the Mouth of York River Abt 11
P.M. and was met by a pilor boat

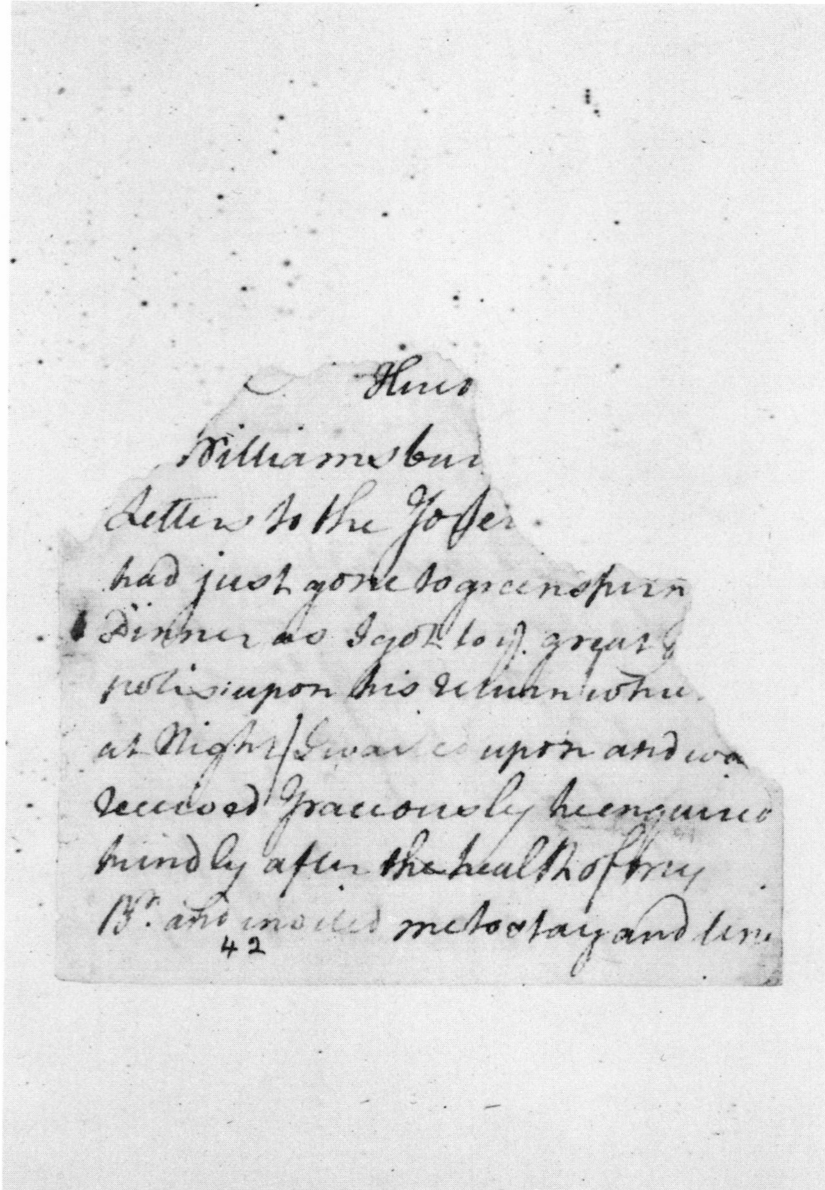

Hon.

Williamsbu[rg]

Letter to the Jose[ph]

had just gone to greenspri[ng]

Dinner as I got to it greatl[y]

polis upon his return who[m]

at Night I war es upon and wa[s]

received Graciously he enquire[d]

kindly after the health of my

B[roth]er and invited me to stay and tim[e]

42

Kings Da.

t. great Mair of
le fought in Yorktown
wen Gloucter & York for
pistoles each bottle of 100 of
... I left it with Cost. Lewis
... fore it was decided of hod
... of his Chair of this horse

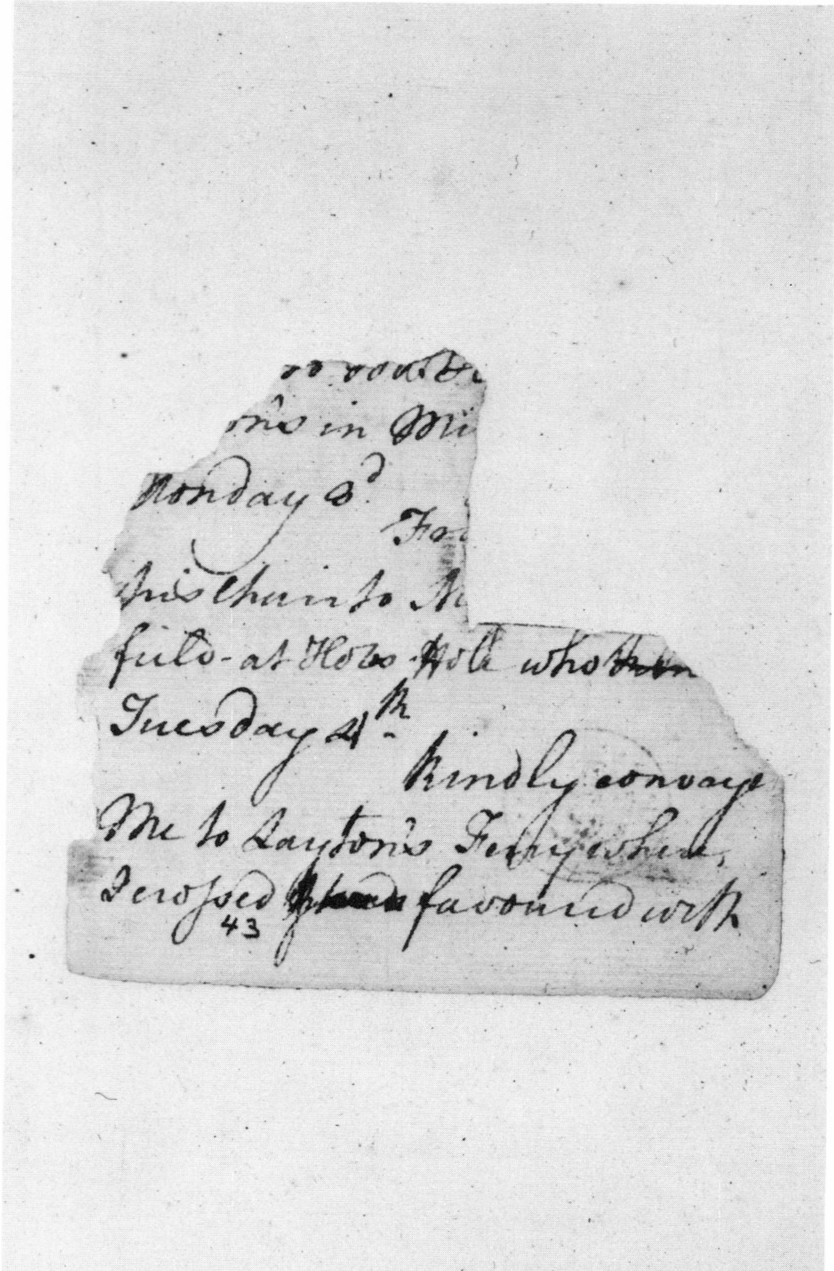
ns in Mi
Monday 3d.
Fo
his Chair to M
field at Hole Hole who
Tuesday 4th.
kindly convey
Me to Layton's
proposed favoured with
43

Journey to the French Commandant

31 October 1753–16 January 1754

EDITORIAL NOTE. In the two years between his return from Barbados and the outbreak of the French and Indian War, GW steadily advanced his position in the Virginia community. He already owned some two thousand acres of land in the Shenandoah Valley, with additional holdings at Ferry Farm and Deep Run. His half brother Lawrence's death in July 1752 brought expectations of more property.[1] In Feb. 1753, at the age of twenty-one, he was appointed adjutant of the Southern District of Virginia with the rank of major by Gov. Robert Dinwiddie.[2] His military duties were light, leaving him ample time to pursue his flourishing career as a surveyor.

[1] Under the terms of Lawrence Washington's will, his wife Ann received a life interest in Mount Vernon and half of his slaves, with the remainder of his estate left to his infant daughter Sarah. After Ann's death, Mount Vernon and other Fairfax County property would go to GW. If Sarah died childless, part of the estate would descend to her mother and part of her lands were to be divided between Augustine Washington and GW (FORD [2], 14:423–27).

[2] GW's commission is dated 13 Dec. 1752, "to be Major and Adjutant of the Militia, Horse and Foot, in the counties of Princess Anne, Norfolk, Nansemond, Isle of Wight, Southampton, Surrey, Brunswick, Prince George, Dinwiddie, Chesterfield, Amelia, and Cumberland." He took the oath 10 Feb. 1753 (CROZIER [2], 516).

Robert Dinwiddie (1693–1770) was born in Scotland and, after a brief career as a merchant, was made admiralty agent for Bermuda in 1721 and collector of the customs for the island in 1727. In 1738 he was appointed surveyor general for the southern part of America. His appointment as lieutenant governor of Virginia came in July 1751 and he arrived in the colony in November to take up his duties. Although the titular governor of Virginia at this time was William Anne Keppel, earl of Albemarle, who remained in England, the colony's executive duties were carried out by the resident lieutenant governor, a situation which also existed in several other colonies. Dinwiddie served as Virginia's governor from 1751 to Jan. 1758, when he was succeeded by Francis Fauquier. In spite of numerous conflicts with the House of Burgesses, Dinwiddie was successful in raising funds and military support for the defense of the colony during the French and Indian War. He was a strong advocate of intercolonial cooperation in matters of defense. A friend and advocate of the Ohio Company, he lent the weight of his office to expansion of the Virginia frontier into the Ohio country.

Lawrence Washington's marriage into the Fairfax family had introduced his young brother to the most influential segment of Virginia society. He was well on his way to becoming a respected member of Virginia's ruling class, and his attention was turning increasingly to public affairs. It was natural, therefore, that he should offer his services to Gov. Robert Dinwiddie when, in the fall of 1753, it became apparent that French forces from Canada were moving into the Ohio Valley and posing a threat to Virginia's ambitions in the area.

The Ohio country had attracted both British and French explorers and traders during the seventeenth and early eighteenth centuries. The ownership of the region, however, was not seriously contested until the middle years of the eighteenth century By the 1730s and 1740s the British coastal colonies had discovered the profits to be made from a vigorous trade with the Indians and the area's potential as a gateway to the West. The expeditions of the baron de Longueuil in 1739 and Pierre Joseph Céloron de Blainville in 1749 had proved to the French the strategic importance of the Ohio as a link between Canada and the Mississippi. Possession of the Ohio Valley became crucial to both powers. If the British colonies were to expand beyond the eastern seaboard, they must control the gateway to the West. If they did, France was almost certain to lose its control over Louisiana. And both coveted the immensely lucrative fur trade.

Before the early 1750s the contest between England and France

Robert Dinwiddie, governor of Virginia from 1751 to 1758. From a miniature by C. Dixon. (Colonial Williamsburg Photograph)

in America had been chiefly over control of the Indians in the region. The French claimed the Ohio Valley largely on the basis of La Salle's explorations in 1669–70. The British contended that the territory had been included in the original Virginia grant of 1609 and that their traders had established a firm foothold in the area. Furthermore, they rested their claims heavily on the concessions wrung from the Iroquois in the Treaty of Lancaster in 1744, when Maryland, Virginia, and Pennsylvania met with the chiefs of the Six Nations at Lancaster, Pa., and signed a treaty in which the Iroquois surrendered much of their land in present-day Virginia and recognized British control in the Ohio country. The Indians almost immediately disputed the treaty, however, claiming they had by no means intended to relinquish claim to so large a portion of their Virginia lands.[3]

Settlement beyond the mountains would clearly benefit British ambitions in the Ohio country. As a result the Privy Council regarded favorably a petition to the king by the newly organized Ohio Company of Virginia for a grant of more than a half-million acres in the vicinity of the Ohio Valley. The company offered the inducement of providing an impetus to the fur trade and instituting a lucrative trade with the Indians; in return the members petitioned that "two hundred Thousand Acres . . . may be granted immediately without Rights on Condition of Your Petitioners Seating at their proper expence a hundred Familys upon the Land in Seven Years the Lands to be Granted Free of Quit Rent for Ten Years on Condition of their Erecting a Fort and Maintaining a Garrison for protection of the Settlement for that time."[4] In Mar. 1749 the Privy Council recom-

[3] The Virginians contended that the Treaty of Lancaster ceded settlement rights for the area east of the Allegheny Mountains and south of the Potomac River. The Iroquois interpreted the treaty to provide for a western boundary at the Blue Ridge Mountains. For a discussion of the treaty, see MULKEARN, 400–403. The minutes of the council and the text of the treaty are in FRANKLIN, 41–79.

[4] "Petition of John Hanbury," 11 Jan. 1749, P.R.O., C.O.5./1327, ff. 26–28. The petition was presented on behalf of the company by John Hanbury and is printed in MULKEARN, 246–48. The original members of the Ohio Company included John, Capel, and Osgood Hanbury, London merchants, Thomas Cresap, William Thornton, John Carlyle, Nathaniel Chapman, Richard Lee, Thomas Lee, George William Fairfax, and Lawrence and Augustine Washington. Soon such prominent figures as Robert Dinwiddie, Robert Carter, George Mason, and Philip Ludwell Lee became members.

mended that a grant be made on terms most favorable to the company, and Gov. William Gooch was instructed to transfer to the company "Two hundred Thousand Acres of Land lying betwixt Ramanettos and Buffalo's Creek on the South Side of the River Alligane otherwise the Ohio, and betwixt the two Creeks and the Yellow Creek on the North Side of the River, to the Westward of the great Mountains within the Colony of Virginia." The grant was made by Gooch on 12 July 1749.[5]

The Ohio Company moved quickly to fulfill the terms of its grant. Wills Creek, near the present site of Cumberland, Md., was selected as the company's headquarters on the frontier, and in the winter of 1749–50 a storehouse was built on the Virginia side. In 1750 the company sent out Thomas Cresap, Hugh Parker, and other traders to locate tentative sites for settlement and commissioned Christopher Gist to make a complete survey of the area. On 11 Sept. 1750 Gist signed a contract with the company to arrange for the settlement of some one hundred fifty families on the company's Ohio lands. Gist made a second survey of the area in 1751–52.[6]

In 1752 the Ohio Company erected a second store on the right bank of Red Stone Creek, soon known as Red Stone Old Fort. Led by Governor Dinwiddie, the colony of Virginia gave vigorous support to the company's efforts. From 1 through 13 June 1752 Virginia commissioners held meetings with chiefs from the Ohio tribes at Logstown, and in return for a promise of cheaper trading goods and protection against the French, they obtained Indian consent to construction of a fort at the Forks of the Ohio and the Monongahela rivers.[7]

The French government in Canada was by no means indifferent to British advances. Since the 1720s judicious observers had been urging the establishment of French settlements on the Ohio frontier as a barrier to British encroachment.[8] As a countermove to the Treaty of Lancaster, the French in 1748 held a council with

[5] Minutes of Council Meeting, 16 Mar. 1748/49, P.R.O., C.O.5/1327, ff. 43–44; VA. EXEC. JLS., 5:295–96.

[6] The agreement is printed in MULKEARN, 172–73. For Gist's account of his activities on behalf of the Ohio Company, see GIST, 32–79.

[7] The commissioners appointed by Dinwiddie were Joshua Fry, Lunsford Lomax, and James Patton. See LOGSTOWN; BAILEY [3], 132–38. For minutes of the council, see MULKEARN, 273–84.

[8] See "Memoir on the French Colonies in America," N.Y. COL. DOCS., 10:220.

the Iroquois at the Castle of Saint Louis of Quebec, warning them against becoming English "vassals." The Indians claimed that although "the English had continually solicited them to take up the hatchet against the French, which they constantly refused to do," they had "not ceded to anyone their lands, which they hold only of Heaven." On the strength of this assurance the French proceeded to move south into the Ohio country.[9]

In June 1749 the comte de La Galissonnière, governor of New France, commissioned Céloron de Blainville to undertake an exploratory expedition down the Ohio to the Miami River and thence north to Quebec, warning Indians and English traders along the way that the French would not tolerate further British advances into the Ohio country. Céloron buried at intervals along his route a series of lead plates reiterating the claim of the French to the territory. Within the next few years a trading post was established at Logstown on the Ohio to serve as a center for the increasing number of French traders operating in the area; after the arrival of the marquis Duquesne, the new governor, in the summer of 1752, a vigorous policy of fort building was undertaken.

Early in 1753 Duquesne developed a plan to send a force of some two thousand men under the command of Pierre Paul de La Malgue, sieur de Marin, to establish an effective occupation of the Ohio frontier. An advance party, led by Charles Deschamps de Boishébert, left Montreal 1 Feb. 1753. By early May Boishébert had constructed a fort at Presque Isle portage, and by the end of the month Marin's force was ready to move south from Niagara. Using Presque Isle as a base, the French constructed a road south to a new post at Le Boeuf. By midsummer of 1753 an effective French army was operating at various sites in the Ohio country.[10]

The French had thus far been plagued with bad weather, labor troubles with their Indian workmen, lack of supplies, and dissension among the officers. They had not as yet met any opposition from the British or the Indians in the Ohio Valley. As they moved farther south, however, they confronted the pro-English Seneca chief, the Half-King, who warned them at a council at

[9] N.Y. COL. DOCS., 10:186–88.
[10] For a discussion of the French expedition, see KENT, 24–26.

Presque Isle in September that the Iroquois tribes were in treaty with the English, who had agreed not to occupy the valley. "With this belt we . . . ask you to have them cease setting up the establishments you want to make. All the tribes have always called upon us not to allow it. We have told our brothers the English to withdraw. They have done so, too." Marin dismissed the Half-King's claims contemptuously, retorting, with some truth, that he was not speaking for all the Iroquois.[11] The Indians were clearly impressed by the French advance.

English traders on the frontier had even more reason to be apprehensive. The warning delivered by one Ohio Company trader to Governor Dinwiddie was typical: "The French have already built a Fort on Lake Erie, and another is partly finished. . . . By the last account I can get the French Army consists of about fifteen hundred Souldiers besides Battoe Men. The French told the Indians their Army when collected will make up 15,000 Men, that that Part of their Army which is on their way from Mississippi have built two Forts down the Ohio, that the Country belongs to them & that they will build when they like. Now is our Time, if we manage well all the Indians may be brought to join against the French, otherwise they will join the French against the English."[12]

During the winter and spring of 1752–53, Dinwiddie and the other colonial governors were in constant correspondence concerning the French threat. In May 1753 Dinwiddie informed James Glen, governor of South Carolina, that the French from Canada had marched out a large force of regular troops and Indians to the Ohio to prevent British settlement and "to take Possession of these Lands, & to build Forts on that river, a Step not precedented in the Time of confirm'd peace."[13] On 22 May he

[11] Quoted in KENT, 49.

[12] William Trent to Dinwiddie, 11 Aug. 1753 (PHi: Ohio Company Papers, Etting Collection). As early as 1749 Céloron had ordered the English traders "to retire to their country with all their employees" (CÉLORON, 35). He complained to Gov. James Hamilton of Pennsylvania that he had been "much surprised to find traders belonging to your government in a country to which England never had any pretension. . . . Those whom I have just encountered . . . I have treated with all possible courtesy, though I had a right to regard them as interlopers and vagabonds" (Céloron to Hamilton, 6 Aug. 1749, STEVENS [2], 25–26).

[13] Dinwiddie to Glen, 23 May 1753, P.R.O., C.O.5/1327, ff. 304–5. See also Hamilton to Dinwiddie, 6 May 1753, PA. ARCH. COL. REC., 5:628–30.

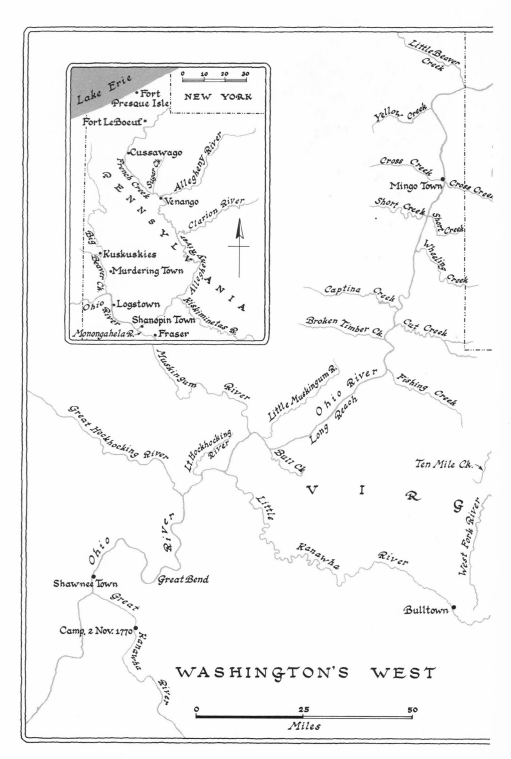

Washington's West

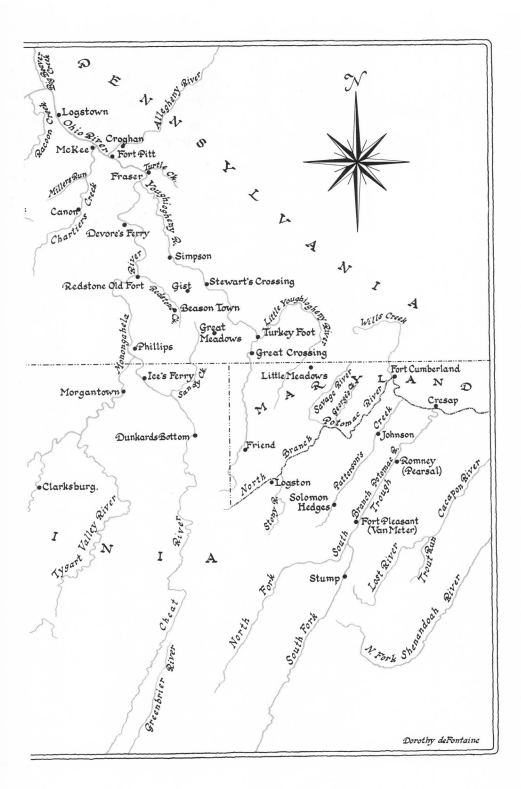

Dorothy deFontaine

wrote to James Hamilton, governor of Pennsylvania, concerning "the French Designs to settle the Ohio. I have sometime ago heard of their Robberies & Murders, & if they are allow'd a peaceable Settlemt. on the Ohio, I think the Consequence will be attend'd with the Ruin of our Trade with the Indians & also in Time will be Destruction to all our Settlemts. on the Continent . . . And We further think it wou'd be absolutely necessary, for all the Colonies to join together, in raising a proper Force to prevent the French settling on the Lands of the Ohio." [14]

On 16 June 1753 Dinwiddie wrote to the Board of Trade transmitting reports received by the colonial governors of French encroachments on the frontier. "I hope you will think it necessary to prevent the French taking Possession of the Lands on the Ohio, so Contiguous to Our Settlements, or indeed in my private Opinion they ought to be prevented making any Settlements to the Westward of Our present Possessions." [15] Dinwiddie's letter was received by the Board of Trade 11 Aug. 1753. On 18 Aug. the information was sent to the king, and on 28 Aug. the earl of Holderness, secretary of state, wrote to Dinwiddie, transmitting the crown's instructions to verify the rumors of the French invasion and, "if You shall find, that any Number of Persons, whether Indians, or Europeans, shall presume to erect any Fort or Forts within the Limits of Our Province of Virginia, . . . You are to require of Them peaceably to depart, and not to persist in such unlawfull Proceedings, & if, notwithstanding Your Admonitions, They do still endeavour to carry on any such unlawfull and unjustifiable Designs, We do herby strictly charge, & command You, to drive them off by Force of Arms." Dinwiddie received the instructions in mid-November and on 17 Nov. informed the Board of Trade that he had "sent one of the Adjutants of the Militia here, out to the Commander of the French Forces, to know their Intentions, & by what Authority they presume to invade His Majesty's Dominions in the Time of tranquil Peace; when he returns I shall transmit you an Account of his Proceedings, & the French Commander's answer." [16]

The adjutant sent by Dinwiddie was, of course, GW. An entry

[14] Dinwiddie to Hamilton, 22 May 1753, P.R.O., C.O.5/1327, ff. 306–7.
[15] P.R.O., C.O.5/1327, ff. 292–94.
[16] Holderness to Dinwiddie, 28 Aug. 1753, P.R.O., C.O.5/211, ff. 21–40; Dinwiddie to Board of Trade, 17 Nov. 1753, P.R.O., C.O.5/1328, ff. 8–9.

for 27 Oct. 1753 in the journals of the council reads: "The Governor acquainted the Board that George Washington Esqr. Adjutant General for the Southern District, had offered himself to go properly commissioned to the Commandant of the French Forces, to learn by what Authority he presumes to make Incroachments on his Majesty's Lands on the Ohio." The council approved the appointment, and a committee of the council prepared a letter to be taken to the French commandant.[17] The instructions drawn up by the committee and presented to GW by Dinwiddie read:

Whereas I have receiv'd Information of a Body of French Forces being assembled in an hostile Manner on the River Ohio, intending by force of Arms to erect certain Forts on the said River, within this Territory, & contrary to the Peace & Dignity of our Sovereign the King of Great Britain.

These are therefore to require & direct You, the said George Washington, Esqr., forthwith to repair to the Logstown on the said River

[17] VA. EXEC. JLS., 5:444–45.
The letter from Dinwiddie to the French commandant, 30 Oct. 1753, reads as follows:

"The Lands upon the River Ohio, in the Western Parts of the Colony of Virginia, are so notoriously known to be the Property of the Crown of Great Britain, that it is a Matter of equal Concern & Surprize to me, to hear that a Body of French Forces are erecting Fortresses, & making Settlements upon that River within His Majesty's Dominions.

"The many & repeated Complaints I have receiv'd of these Acts of Hostilities, lay me under the Necessity of sending, in the Name of the King my Master, the Bearer hereof, George Washington Esqr. one of the Adjutants General of the Forces of this Dominion; to complain to you of the Encroachments thus made, & of the Injuries done to the Subjects of Great Britain, in open Violation to the Laws of Nations, & the Treaties now subsisting between the two Crowns.

"If these Facts are true, & You still think fit to justify Your Proceedings; I must desire You to acquaint me by whose Authority & Instructions, You have lately marcht from Canada with an arm'd Force, & invaded the King of Great Britain's Territories, in the Manner complain'd of; That according to the Purport & Resolution of Your Answer, I may act agreeable to the Commission I am honour'd with from the King my Master.

"However Sir, in Obedience to my Instructions it becomes my Duty to require Your peacable Departure, & that You wou'd forbear prosecuting a Purpose so interruptive of the Harmony & good Understanding which His Majesty is desirous to continue & cultivate with the most Christian King.

"I perswade myself You will receive & entertain Major Washington with the Candour & Politeness natural to Your Nation; & it will give me the greatest Satisfaction, if You return him with an Answer suitable to my Wishes, for a very long & lasting Peace between Us" (P.R.O., C.O.5/1328, ff. 45–46).

Ohio; & having there inform'd Your Self where the said French Forces have posted themselves, thereupon to proceed to such Place, & being there arriv'd to present Your Credentials, together with my Letter, to the chief commanding Officer, & in the Name of His Britanic Majesty, to demand an Answer from him thereto.

On Your Arrival at the Logstown, You are to address Yourself to the Half King, to Monacatoocha & [the] other . . . Sachems of the Six Nations; acquainting them with Your Orders to visit & deliver my Letter to the French commanding Officer; & desiring the said Chiefs to appoint You a sufficient Number of their Warriors to be Your Safe-guard, as near the French as You may desire, & to wait Your further Direction.

You are diligently to enquire into the Numbers & Force of the French on the Ohio, & the adjacent Country; how they are like to be assisted from Canada; & what are the Difficulties & Conveniencies of that Comunication, & the Time requir'd for it.

You are to take care to be truly inform'd what Forts the French have erected, & where; How they are Garrison'd & appointed, & what is their Distance from each other, & from Logstown: And from the best Intelligence You can procure, You are to learn what gave Occasion to this Expedition of the French: How they are like to be supported, & what their Pretentions are.

When the French Commandant has given You the requir'd & necessary Dispatches, You are to desire of him that, agreeable to the Law of Nations, he wou'd grant You a proper Guard, to protect You as far on Your return, as You may judge for Your Safety, against any stragling Indians, or Hunters, that may be ignorant of Yr. Character, & molest You.[18]

Dinwiddie also issued the following commission to GW: "I reposing especial Trust & Confidence in the Ability, Conduct, & Fidelity, of You the said George Washington have appointed You my express Messenger; and You are hereby authoriz'd & impowered to proceed hence with all convenient & possible Dispatch, to that Part, or Place, on the River Ohio, where the French have lately erected a Fort, or Forts, or where the Commandant of the French Forces resides, in order to deliver my Letter & Message to Him; & after waiting not exceeding one Week for an Answer, You are to take Your Leave & return immediately back."[19]

At the same time the following passport was issued to GW by Dinwiddie:

[18] P.R.O., C.O.5/1328, f. 47.   [19] P.R.O., C.O.5/1328, f. 48.

Whereas I have appointed George Washington Esqr., by Commission under the Great Seal, My express Messenger to the Commandant of the French Forces on the River Ohio, & as he is charg'd with Business of great Importance to his Majesty & this Dominion.

I do hereby Command all His Majesty's Subjects, & particularly require ALL IN ALLIANCE AND AMITY WITH THE CROWN OF GREAT BRITAIN, & all OTHERS to whom this PASSPORT may come, agreeable to the Law of Nations, to be aiding & assisting as a Safeguard to the said George Washington & his Attendants . . . in his present [passage] . . . to & from the River Ohio as aforesaid.[20]

On 31 Oct. 1753 GW set out for Fredericksburg on the first stage of his journey.

The text for this diary has been taken from a copy in P.R.O., C.O. 5/1328, ff. 51–58.

[20] P.R.O., C.O.5/1328, f. 60

On Wednesday the 31st. of October 1753 I was Commission'd & appointed by the Honble. Robert Dinwiddie Esqr. Governor &ca. of Virginia

To visit & deliver a Letter to the Commandant of the French Forces on the Ohio, & set out on the intended Journey the same Day. The next I arriv'd at Fredericksburg, & engag'd Mr. Jacob Vanbraam, Interpreter,[21] & proceeded with him to Alexandria where we provided Necessaries. From thence we went to Winchester & got Baggage Horses &ca. & from there we pursued the new Road to Wills Creek,[22] where we arriv'd the 14th: of November.

Here I engag'd Mr. Gist[23] to Pilot us out, & also hired four others as Servitors (vizt.) Barnaby Currin, & John McGuier (Indian Traders) Henry Steward, & William Jenkins;[24] & in Company with those Persons I left the Inhabitants the Day following. The excessive Rains & vast Quantity of Snow that had fallen prevented our reaching Mr. Frazer's, an Indian Trader at the Mouth of Turtle Creek, on Monongehela, 'til Thursday.[25]

[21] Jacob Van Braam, born about 1729 in Bergen op Zoom, Holland, had come to America in 1752, where he solicited employment as a teacher of French (*Md. Gaz.*, 30 July 1752). In 1753 he was living in the vicinity of Fredericksburg. For his subsequent career, see entry for 2 April 1754.

[22] Now Cumberland, Md.

[23] Christopher Gist (c. 1706–1759), a prominent figure on the Virginia-Pennsylvania frontier, was born in Maryland. After early experience in surveying and exploration, he was living in northwestern North Carolina when approached in 1750 by the Ohio Company and engaged to explore the Ohio country as far as the mouth of the Scioto River. In 1751 he carried on further explorations as far south as the Great Kanawha and in 1752 represented the Ohio Company at the Logstown council. By 1753 he had settled on the frontier near the present site of Brownsville, Pa., but soon moved to a new settlement near Mount Braddock, Pa. GW later wrote concerning him: "He has had extensive dealings with the Indians, is in great esteem among them; well acquainted with their manners and customs, is indefatigable, and patient: most excellent qualities indeed, where indians are concerned! And, for his capacity, honesty and zeal, I dare venture to engage" (GW to John Robinson, 30 May 1757, DLC:GW).

[24] Barnaby Currin was a Pennsylvania trader who had been associated in the Indian trade with George Croghan. In 1750 he accompanied Gist on his explorations for the Ohio Company (GIST, 35). Toner notes that McGuire (McGuier) served as a soldier from Fairfax County in 1754 (DLC: Toner Collection). Jenkins was frequently employed by Dinwiddie as a messenger.

[25] John Fraser (Frazier), a Pennsylvania gunsmith and Indian trader, had established a trading post at Venango in the 1740s. Forced to leave by a French force that occupied the post in 1753, he resumed his trading operations at another trading post he had already established at the mouth of Turtle Creek on the Monongahela about ten miles above the present site of Pittsburgh (DONEHOO, 235–36).

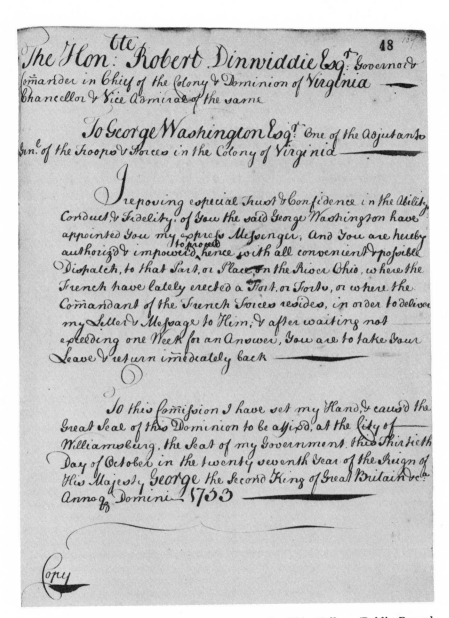

Robert Dinwiddie's orders send Washington to the Ohio Valley. (Public Record Office, London. Crown Copyright)

22d: We were inform'd here, that Expresses were sent a few Day's ago to the Traders down the River to acquaint them with the General's Death,[26] & return of Major Part of the French Army into Winter Quarters. The Waters were quite impassable, without Swimming our Horses, which oblig'd us to get the loan of a Canoe from Mr. Frazer, & to send Barnaby Currin & Henry Steward down Monongehela, with our Baggage to meet us at the Forks of Ohio, about 10 Miles to cross Allegany.

As I got down before the Canoe, I spent some Time in viewing the Rivers, & the Land in the Fork, which I think extreamly well situated for a Fort; as it has the absolute Command of both Rivers. The Land at the Point is 20 or 25 Feet above the common Surface of the Water; & a considerable Bottom of flat well timber'd Land all around it, very convenient for Building. The Rivers are each a quarter of a Mile, or more, across, & run here very nigh at Right Angles; Allegany bearing N: E: & Monongehela S: E: The former of these two is a very rapid swift running Water the other deep & still, with scarce any perceptable Fall. About two Miles from this, on the S: E: Side of the River, at the Place where the Ohio Company intended to erect a Fort; lives Singess, King of the Delawars; We call'd upon him to invite him to Council at the Logstown.[27]

As I had taken a good deal of Notice Yesterday of the Situation at the Forks; my Curiosity led me to examine this more particularly; & my Judgement [is] to think it greatly inferior, either for Defence or Advantages, especially the latter; For a Fort at the Forks wou'd be equally well situated on Ohio, & have the entire

[26] Pierre Paul de La Malgue, sieur de Marin (1692–1753), commandant of the French army on the Ohio during its advance into the Ohio country in 1753, died at Fort Le Boeuf 29 Oct. 1753. Shortly before his death the major part of the French forces were sent into winter quarters; most returned to Montreal, except for a garrison force in the frontier forts (KENT, 64).

[27] Shingas was a principal chief of the Turkey or Unalachtigo tribe of Delawares. At the time of GW's visit to the frontier, Shingas was supporting the British, but he went over to the French after Braddock's Defeat in 1755. The Ohio Company intended to erect a fort near McKee's Rocks just below the present site of Pittsburgh. Shingas was apparently living near there or at the mouth of Chartier's Creek in 1753 rather than at Shingas Old Town (now Beaver, Pa.). Logstown was located about 18 miles below the Forks of the Ohio on the north bank of the river (near present-day Ambridge, Pa.) and was one of the chief Indian trading villages in the Ohio Valley. In 1752 it had been the site of the council between the tribes and commissioners appointed by Governor Dinwiddie to ratify the Treaty of Lancaster.

Command of Monongehela, which runs up to our Settlements &
is extreamly well design'd for Water Carriage, as it is of a deep
still Nature; besides a Fort at the Fork might be built at a much
less Expence, than at the other Place. Nature has well contriv'd
the lower Place for Water Defence, but the Hill whereon it must
stand, being a quarter of a Mile in Length, & then descending
gradually on the Land Side, will render it difficult & very expensive making a sufficient Fortification there. The whole Flat upon
the Hill must be taken in, or the Side next the Descent made
extreamly high; or else the Hill cut away: otherwise the Enemy
will raise Batteries within that Distance, without being expos'd
to a single Shot from the Fort.

Singess attended us to Logstown, where we arriv'd between
Sunsetting & Dark, the 25th: Day after I left Williamsburg. We
travel'd over some extream good & bad Land to get to this Place.
As soon as I came into Town, I went to Monacatoocha [28] (as the
Half King [29] was out at his hunting Cabbin on little Bever Creek,
about 15 Miles off) & inform'd him, by John Davison Interpreter [30] that I was sent a Messenger to the French General, &
was ordered to call upon the Sachems of the Six Nations, to acquaint them with it. I gave him a String of Wampum, & a twist
of Tobacco, & desir'd him to send for the Half King; which he
promis'd to do by a Runner in the Morning, & for other Sachems.
I invited him & the other Great Men present to my Tent, where
they stay'd an Hour & return'd.

According to the best Observations I cou'd make, Mr. Gist's

[28] Monacatoocha, a pro-English Oneida chief also known as Scarouady, apparently ranking only below the Half-King in authority. He had been sent
by the Six Nations to superintend the Shawnee at Logstown.

[29] The Half-King, or Tanacharison, a Seneca chief, represented the Onon-
daga Council of the Six Nations among the Seneca. Considered one of the
most reliable of England's Indian allies, he was one of the most prominent of
the Indian chiefs at the Treaty of Logstown in 1752 and accompanied GW
on his 1754 expedition.

[30] Davison was an experienced Indian interpreter, operating a trading business out of Logstown and generally acting as interpreter for the Half-King in
his negotiations with the English and French. On occasion he was employed
by the governor of Pennsylvania in negotiating with the Indians (PA. ARCH.
COL. REC., 6:194). It is uncertain whether he joined the party at Logstown or
whether GW acquired his services at Winchester, Cresap's, or Wills Creek
(see FREEMAN, 1:290 n.82). Pennsylvania trader George Croghan, not un-
prejudiced in his views of other traders, observed that he "talks a Little of
ye Indian Languidge, and makes a great Deal of Disturbance" (PA. ARCH.,
1st ser., 2:119).

new Settlement (which we pass'd by) bears about W: N: W: 70 Miles from Wills Creek, Shanapins,[31] or the Forks N: B[y]: W: or N: N: W: about 50 Miles from that; & from thence to the Logstown, the Course is nearly West, about 18 or 20 Miles; so that the whole Distance, as we went & computed it, is at least 135 or 40 Miles from our back Settlements.[32]

25th: Came to Town four of ten French Men that Deserted from a Company at the Cuscusas, which lies at the Mouth of this

[31] Gist's "new Settlement" was above the headwaters of Red Stone Creek in the vicinity of present-day Mount Braddock, Pa.

Shanopin's Town was a Delaware village near the Forks of the Ohio. When Gist was there on his journey for the Ohio Company in 1750, he found about 20 families living in the village (GIST, 34).

[32] Gist also kept a diary account of the expedition's movements from the time he joined the party on 14 Nov. His entries for the period 14–24 Nov. read as follows:

"Wednesday 14 November, 1753.—Then Major George Washington came to my house at Will's Creek, and delivered me a letter from the council in Virginia, requesting me to attend him up to the commandant of the French fort on the Ohio River.

"Thursday 15.—We set out, and at night encamped at George's Creek about eight miles, where a messenger came with letters from my son, who was just returned from his people at the Cherokees, and lay sick at the mouth of Conegocheague. But as I found myself entered again on public business, and Major Washington and all the company unwilling I should return I wrote and sent medicines to my son, and so continued my journey, and encamped at a big hill in the forks of Youghiogany, about eighteen miles.

"Friday 16—The next day set out and got to the big fork of said river, about ten miles there.

"Saturday 17.—We encamped and rested our horses, and then we set out early in the morning.

"Sunday 18.—And at night got to my house in the new settlement, about twenty-one miles; snow about ancle deep.

"Monday 19.—Set out, cross Big Youghiogany, to Jacob's cabins, about twenty miles. Here some of our horses straggled away, and we did not get away until eleven o'clock.

"Tuesday 20.—Set out, had rain in the afternoon; I killed a deer; travelled about seven miles.

"Wednesday 21.—It continued to rain. Stayed all day.

"Thursday 22.—We set out and came to the mouth of Turtle Creek, about twelve miles, to John Frazier's; and he was very kind to us, and lent us a canoe to carry our baggage to the forks, about ten miles.

"Friday 23.—Set out, rid to Shannopin's town, and down Allegheny to the mouth of Monongahela, where we met our baggage, and swimmed our horses over Allegheny, and there encamped that night.

"Saturday 24.—Set out; we went to king Shingiss, and he and Lawmolach [Lowmolach] went with us to the Logstown, and we spoke to the chiefs this evening, and repaired to our camp" (GIST, 80–81).

River; I got the following Account from them. They were sent from New Orlians with 100 Men, & 8 Canoe load of Provisions, to this Place; where they expected to have met the same Number of Men, from the Forts this Side Lake Erie to convoy them, & the Horses up, but were not arriv'd when they ran off.[33] I enquir'd into the Situation of the French on the Mississippi, their Number, & what Forts they had Built: They inform'd me that there were four small Forts between New Orlians, & the Black Islands,[34] Garrison'd with about 30 or 40 Men, & a few small Pieces of Cannon in each. That at New Orlians, which is near the Mouth of the Mississippi, there is 35 Companies of 40 Men each, with a pretty strong Fort, mounting 8 large Carriage Guns; & at the Black Islands there is several Companies, & a Fort with 6 Guns. The Black Islands is about 130 Leagues above the Mouth of the Ohio, which is 150 above New Orlians: They also acquainted me, that there was a small Palisadoed Fort on the Ohio, at the Mouth of the Obaish,[35] about 60 Leagues from the Mississippi: the Obaish heads near the West End of Lake Erie, & affords the Communication between the French on Mississippi, & those on the Lakes. These Deserters came up from the lower Shawnesse Town, with one Brown an Indian Trader, & were going to Philadelphia.[36]

About 3 o'Clock this Evening the Half King came to Town; I went up & invited him & Davison privately to my Tent, & desir'd him to relate some of the Particulars of his Journey to the French

[33] Although it has been suggested (DIARIES, 1:46) that GW is referring to the Indian village of Kuskuskies on Beaver Creek (New Castle, Pa.), it is probable that the deserters were from the French post of Kaskaskia on the Mississippi, above the mouth of the Ohio River. As Hugh Cleland has pointed out, GW notes that the deserters were "picked up by an English trader at Lower Shawnee Town (now Portsmouth, Ohio) and were heading for Philadelphia. If these men had deserted from Kuskuskies for Philadelphia and been picked up at Lower Shawnee Town, they had traveled two hundred miles in the wrong direction and *towards* the French settlements from which they were fleeing" (CLELAND, 47–48).

[34] Van Braam, in translating the deserter's information, understood *Isles Noires* for Illinois, which was at that time an administrative district of the province of Louisiana.

[35] Either the deserters were misinformed, or Van Braam misinterpreted their information; the French had no fort at this place. The reference may have been to Vincennes.

[36] Lower Shawnee Town was located near present-day Portsmouth, Ohio. The Indian trader was possibly James Brown, who signed a treaty with the Indians at Logstown in May 1751 (PA. ARCH. COL. REC., 5:532).

Paul Revere made this engraving showing a typical council with the Indians for the *Royal American Magazine*, 1774. (Spencer Collection, New York Public Library, Astor, Lenox and Tilden Foundations)

Commandant, & reception there, & to give me an Account of the Way & Distance.[37] He told me that the nearest & levelest Way was now impassable, by reason of the many large miry Savannas; that we must be oblig'd to go by Venango,[38] & shou'd not get to the near Fort under 5 or 6 Nights Sleep, good Traveling. When he went to the Fort he said he was receiv'd in a very stern Manner by the late Commander, who ask'd him very abruptly, what he had come about, & to declare his Business; which he says he did in the following Speech.

FATHERS I am come to tell you your own Speeches, what your own Mouths have declar'd. FATHERS You in former Days set a Silver Bason before us wherein there was the Leg of a Beaver, and desir'd of all Nations to come & eat of it; to eat in Peace & Plenty, & not to be Churlish to one another; & that if any such Person shou'd be found to be a Disturber; I here lay down by the Edge

[37] In Sept. 1753 the Half-King and a representative group of Indians from the Ohio tribes had traveled to Presque Isle to warn the sieur de Marin against French expansion into the Ohio country. For an account of the meeting, see "Counseil tenu par des Tsonnontouans venus de la Belle-Rivière," PAPIERS CONTRECOEUR, 53–58. The versions of the Half-King's speeches and Marin's replies reported in this source differ considerably from the account given to GW by the chief.

[38] Venango was an important French trading and supply post at the juncture of French Creek and the Allegheny River. It is now Franklin, Pa.

of the Dish a rod, which you must Scourge them with; & if Me your Father shou'd get Foolish in my old Days, I desire you may use it upon me as well as others.

NOW FATHERS it is you that is the Disturber in this Land, by coming & building your Towns, and taking it away unknown to us & by Force. FATHERS We kindled a Fire a long Time ago at a Place call'd Morail,[39] where we desir'd you to stay, & not to come & intrude upon our Land. I now desire you may dispatch to that Place; for be it known to you Fathers, this is our Land, & not yours. FATHERS I desire you may hear me in Civilness; if not, We must handle that rod which was laid down for the Use of the obstropulous. If you had come in a peaceable Manner like our Brothers the English, We shou'd not have been against your trading with us as they do, but to come Fathers, & build great Houses upon our Land, & to take it by Force, is what we cannot submit to.

FATHERS Both you & the English are White. We live in a Country between, therefore the Land does not belong either to one or the other; but the GREAT BEING above allow'd it to be a Place of residence for us; so Fathers, I desire you to withdraw, as I have done our Brothers the English, for I will keep you at Arm's length. I lay this down as a Tryal for both, to see which will have the greatest regard to it, & that Side we will stand by, & make equal Sharers with us: Our Brothers the English have heard this, & I come now to tell it to you, for I am not affraid to discharge you off this Land. This, he said, was the Substance of what he said to the General, who made this Reply.

NOW MY CHILD I have heard your Speech. You spoke first, but it is my Time to speak now. Where is my Wampum that you took away, with the Marks of Towns in it? This Wampum I do not know, which you have discharg'd me off the Land with; but you need not put yourself to the Trouble of Speaking for I will not hear you: I am not affraid of Flies or Musquito's; for Indians are such as those; I tell you down that River I will go, & will build upon it according to my Command: If the River was ever so block'd up, I have Forces sufficient to burst it open, & tread under my Feet all that stand in Opposition together with their Alliances; for my Force is as the Sand upon the Sea Shoar: therefore here is your Wampum, I fling it at you. Child, you talk foolish; you say this Land belongs to you, but there is not the

[39] Presumably the Half-King is referring to the council held at Montreal in 1732 between the French administration and the Shawnee and the Seneca.

Black of my Nail yours, I saw that Land sooner than you did, before the Shawnesse & you were at War: Lead [40] was the Man that went down, & took Possession of that River; it is my Land, & I will have it let who will stand up for, or say against it. I'll buy & sell with the English (mockingly). If People will be rul'd by me they may expect Kindness but not else.

The Half King told me, he enquir'd of the General after two English Men that were made Prisoners,[41] & receiv'd this Answer.

CHILD You think it is a very great Hardship that I made Prisoners of those two People at Venango, don't you concern yourself with it we took & carried them to Canada to get Intelligence of what the English were doing in Virginia.

He inform'd me that they had built two Forts, one on Lake Erie, & another on French Creek,[42] near a small Lake about 15 Miles asunder, & a large Waggon Road between; they are both built after the same Model, but different in the Size; that on the Lake the largest; he gave me a Plan of them of his own drawing. The Indians enquir'd very particularly after their Brothers in

[40] In the version of this speech in PAPIERS CONTRECOEUR, 57, the reference is to Robert Cavelier, sieur de La Salle, who explored the Ohio country in the 1680s. Marin was apparently more concerned by the Half-King's attitude than his words indicated. He wrote to his superiors complaining about the chief's insolence and requesting the dispatch of other representatives of the tribes to repudiate his words (Marin to Joncaire, n.d., PAPIERS CONTRECOEUR, 58–59). In fact, the Half-King's anti-French sentiments do not appear to have had wide support from other Indians in the area (see "Parole des Chaouanons," 3 Sept. 1753, PAPIERS CONTRECOEUR, 61–62).

[41] The "two Englishmen" were John Trotter and his servant James McLaughlin. According to Trotter's deposition, written 22 Mar. 1754 after his return to Philadelphia, the two were taken prisoner at Venango on 15 Aug. 1753 by a party of 110 Frenchmen, who confiscated their goods and took them in irons to Montreal. After a period of imprisonment, first in Montreal and then Quebec, they were "put on board a Man of War of thirty-six Guns, and arriv'd at Rochel, and there put into Jayl for thirty Days, having only Bread and Water for their Sustenance; and then the Commanding Officer . . . set them at Liberty and gave them a Pass, with which they Begged their way to Bourdeaux, and . . . embarqued on Board the Betty and Sally . . . bound for this City, where they Arrived on Saturday, the sixteenth Instant." McLaughlin was left at Bordeaux "for want of Conveniencies in the Vessel" (PA. ARCH., 1st ser., 2:131–32).

[42] These forts were Presque Isle on Lake Erie (now Erie, Pa.) and Fort Le Boeuf (now Waterford, Pa.), on a branch of French Creek.

Carolina Goal.[43] They also ask'd what sort of a Boy it was that was taken from the South Branch; for they had, by some Indians heard, that a Party of French Indians had carried a White Boy by the Cuscusa Town, towards the Lakes.[44]

26th: We met in council at the Long House, about 9 o'Clock, where I spoke to them as follows,

BROTHERS I have call'd you together in Council, by Order of your Brother the Governor of Virginia, to acquaint you that I am sent with all possible Dispatch to visit & deliver a Letter to the French Commandant of very great Importance to your Brothers the English: & I dare say to you their Friends & Allies. I was desir'd Brothers, by your Brother the Governor, to call upon you, the Sachems of the Six Nations, to inform you of it, & to ask your Advice & Assistance to proceed the nearest & best Road to the French. You see Brothers I have got thus far on my Journey. His Honour likewise desir'd me to apply to you for some of your young Men to conduct and provide Provisions for us on our Way: & to be a Safeguard against those French Indians, that have taken up the Hatchet against us. I have spoke this particularly to you Brothers, because His Hon. our Governor, treats you as good

[43] This is a reference to six Shawnee who had been apprehended on the South Carolina frontier during the summer of 1753 by the South Carolina militia. The area had suffered a series of raids by Shawnee, who frequently carried local Indians north as slaves. As a result, Gov. James Glen had offered a reward for the capture of the invaders. On 3 Oct. 1753 Glen wrote to Pennsylvania Gov. James Hamilton that he was sending two of the captured Shawnee north "to be sent, or detained by you as you may judge it most likely to obtain the good End of having our friendly Indians or Mustee Slaves sent back to us, and . . . the other four . . . will be returned to their Friends upon restoring all the Prisoners they have taken from us, and upon their engaging to you in the most solemn Manner not to permit any of their People to come into this Province for the Future" (S.C. IND. AFF. DOCS., 21 May 1750–7 Aug. 1754, 462–64). By Jan. 1754 all six of the Indians had been released ("George Croghan's Journal, 1754," PA. ARCH. COL. REC., 5:732). See also WAINWRIGHT, 57–58.

[44] This may have been the child referred to by Claude Pierre Pécaudy, sieur de Contrecoeur, who informed the commander of the British forces on the Ohio that, learning that Indians of the Six Nations "had fallen upon, and destroyed an English Family towards *Carolina;* he stopped their Passage, and obliged them to deliver him up a little Boy belonging to that Family, and who was the only one left alive; he was brought back to Boston" (MEMOIR, 66–67).

"Cuscusa" is a reference to Kuskuskies, a Delaware village in the vicinity of present-day New Castle, Pa.

Friends & Allies, & holds you in great Esteem. To confirm what I have said I give you this String of Wampum.

After they had considered some Time on the above, the Half King got up & spoke.

NOW MY BROTHERS. In Regard to what my Brother the Governor has desir'd of me, I return you this Answer. I rely upon you as a Brother ought to do, as you say we are Brothers, & one People. We shall put Heart in Hand, & speak to our Fathers the French, concerning the Speech they made to me, & you may depend that we will endeavour to be your Guard.

BROTHER, as you have ask'd my Advice, I hope you will be ruled by it, & stay 'til I can provide a Company to go with you. The French Speech Belt is not here, I have it to go for to my hunting Cabbin likewise the People I have order'd are not yet come, nor can 'til the third Night from this, 'till which Time Brother I must beg you to stay. I intend to send a Guard of Mingoes, Shawnesse, & Delawar's, that our Brothers may see the Love and Loyalty We bear them.

As I had Orders to make all possible Dispatch, & waiting here very contrary to my Inclinations; I thank'd him in the most suitable Manner I cou'd, & told that my Business requir'd the greatest Expedition, & wou'd not admit of that Delay: He was not well pleas'd that I shou'd offer to go before the Time he had appointed, & told me that he cou'd not consent to our going without a Guard, for fear some Accident shou'd befall us, & draw a reflection upon him—besides says he, this is a Matter of no small Moment, & must not be enter'd into without due Consideration, for I now intend to deliver up the French Speech Belt, & make the Shawnesse & Delawars do the same, & accordingly gave Orders to King Singess, who was present, to attend on Wednesday Night with the Wampum, & two Men of their Nation to be in readiness to set off with us next Morning. As I found it impossible to get off without affronting them in the most egregious Manner, I consented to stay.

I gave them back a String of Wampum that I met with at Mr. Frazer's, which they had sent with a Speech to his Honour the Governor, to inform him, that three Nations of French Indians, (vizt.) Chippaway's, Ottaway's, & Arundacks, had taken up the Hatchet against the English, & desired them to repeat it over again; which they postpon'd doing 'til they met in full Council with the Shawnesse, & Delawar Chiefs.

27th: Runners were dispatch'd very early for the Shawness Chiefs, the Half King set out himself to fetch the French Speech Belt from his hunting Cabbin.[45]

28th: He return'd this Evening, & came with Monacatoocha & two other Sachems to my Tent, & beg'd (as they had comply'd with his Honour the Governor's Request in providing Men, &ca.) to know what Business we were going to the French about? This was a Question I all along expected, & had provided as satisfactory Answers as I cou'd, which allay'd their Curiosity a little. Monacatoocha Informed me, that an Indian from Venango brought News a few Days ago; that the French had call'd all the Mingo's, Delawar's &ca. together at that Place, & told them that they intended to have been down the River this Fall, but the Waters were geting Cold, & the Winter advancing, which obliged them to go into Quarters; but they might assuredly expect them in the Spring, with a far greater Number; & desired that they might be quite Passive, & not intermeddle, unless they had a mind to draw all their Force upon them; for that they expected to fight the English three Years, (as they suppos'd there would be some Attempts made to stop them) in which Time they shou'd Conquer, but if they shou'd prove equally strong, that they & the English wou'd join to cut them off, & divide the Land between them: that though they had lost their General, & some few of their Soldiers, yet there was Men enough to reinforce, & make them Masters of the Ohio. This Speech, he said, was deliver'd to them by an Captn. Joncaire, their Interpreter in Chief, living at Venango, & a Man of Note in the Army.[46]

29th: The Half King and Monacatoocha came very early &

[45] The entry in Gist's diary for 27 Nov. 1753 reads:
"Tuesday 27.—Stayed in our camp. Monacatoocha and Pollatha Wappia gave us some provisions. We stayed until the 29th when the Indians said, they were not ready. They desired us to stay until the next day and as the warriors were not come, the Half-King said he would go with us himself, and take care of us" (GIST, 81).

[46] Philippe Thomas de Joncaire, sieur de Chabert (1707–c.1766), captain of marines in the French army, was a member of a family known in Canada for its influence among the Indians. He is frequently confused with his father, Louis Thomas de Joncaire, sieur de Chabert, and his younger brother Daniel de Joncaire, sieur de Chabert et de Clausonne, both of whom were active in Indian diplomacy. The older brother was among the most adroit of French negotiators among the Indians, particularly the Seneca. In 1739 he succeeded his father as agent to the Iroquois and in 1749 accompanied Céloron in his exploration of the Ohio country. As one of the leaders in the French advance during the summer of 1753, he had arrived to take up quarters at Venango about 1 Dec. 1753.

beg'd me to stay one Day more, for notwithstanding they had used all the Diligence in their Power, the Shawnesse Chiefs had not brought the Wampum they order'd, but wou'd certainly be in to Night, if not they wou'd delay me no longer, but send it after us as soon as they arriv'd: When I found them so pressing in their request; & knew that returning of Wampum, was the abolishing of Agreements; & giving this up was shaking of all Dependence upon the French, I consented to stay, as I believ'd an Offence offer'd at this Crisis, might have been attended with greater ill Consequence than another Day's Delay.

They also inform'd me that Singess cou'd not get in his Men, & was prevented from coming himself by His Wife's Sickness, (I believe by fear of the French) but that the Wampum of that Nation was lodg'd with Custaloga, one of their Chiefs at Venango.[47] In the Evening they came again, & acquainted me that the Shawnesse were not yet come, but it shou'd not retard the Prosecution of our Journey. He deliver'd in my Hearing the Speeches that were to be made to the French by Jeskakake, one of their old Chiefs,[48] which was giving up the Belt the late Commandant had ask'd for, & repeating near the same Speech he himself had done before. He also deliver'd a String of Wampum to this Chief, which was sent by King Singess to be given to Custaloga, with Orders to repair to, & deliver up the French Wampum. He likewise gave a very large String of black & white Wampum, which was to be sent immediately up to the Six Nations, if the French refus'd to quit the Land at this Warning, which was the third & last Time, & was the right of this Jeskakake to deliver.

30th: Last Night the great Men assembled to their Council House to consult further about this Journey, & who were to go; the result of which was, that only three of their Chiefs, with one of their best Hunters shou'd be our Convoy: the reason they gave for not sending more, after what had been propos'd in Council the 26th. was, that a greater Number might give the French Suspicion of some bad Design, & cause them to be treated rudely; but I rather think they cou'd not get their Hunters in.

---

[47] Custaloga was a Delaware chief. Custaloga's Town (Meadville, Pa.) was on the west side of French Creek. In July 1753 Pennsylvania trader William Trent noted that Custaloga's people were helping the French move their supplies across the Presque Isle portage (DARLINGTON, 18–19). By 1754 the chief was openly supporting the French.

[48] Jeskakake is presumably the Cayuga referred to in PAPIERS CONTRECOEUR, 189, as Déjiquéqué. He became a supporter of the French and was given for his services a *commission de chef* in June 1754.

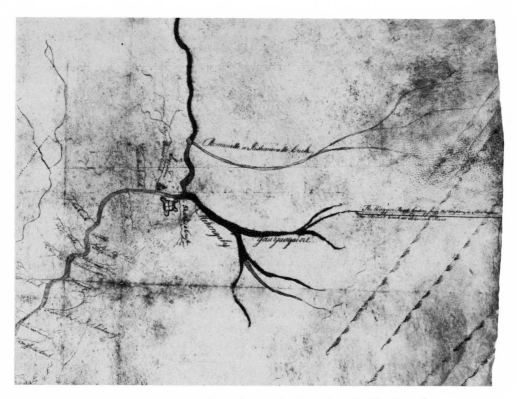

Christopher Gist's 1750 map of the Ohio River and tributaries. (Public Record Office, London. Crown Copyright)

We set out about 9 o'Clock, with the Half King, Jeskakake, White Thunder, & the Hunter; [49] & travel'd on the road to Venango, where we arriv'd the 4th: of December, without any Thing remarkably happening, but a continued Series of bad

[49] White Thunder, or Belt of Wampum, was an Iroquois chief (SARGENT [1], 378). The Hunter, also known as Guyasuta or Kiasutha, was a Seneca who later became a principal chief of the Six Nations and participated in many of the councils between the Iroquois and the English before the Revolution. After Braddock's Defeat in 1755, Guyasuta went over to the French and led the Indians in the defeat of Maj. James Grant in 1758 (SIPE, 372). GW encountered him again during his journey to the Ohio in 1770.

Weather.[50] This is an old Indian Town, situated on the Mouth of French Creek on Ohio, & lies near No. about 60 Miles from the Logstown, but more than 70 the Way we were oblig'd to come. We found the French Colours hoisted at a House where they drove Mr. John Frazer an English Subject from: I immediately repair'd to it, to know where the Commander resided: There was three Officers, one of which, Capt. Joncaire, inform'd me, that he had the Command of the Ohio, but that there was a General Officer at the next Fort, which he advis'd me to for an Answer.

He invited us to Sup with them, & treated with the greatest Complaisance. The Wine, as they dos'd themselves pretty plentifully with it, soon banish'd the restraint which at first appear'd in their Conversation, & gave license to their Tongues to reveal their Sentiments more freely. They told me it was their absolute Design to take Possession of the Ohio, & by G—— they wou'd do it, for tho' they were sensible, that the English cou'd raise two Men for their one; yet they knew their Motions were too slow & dilatory to prevent any Undertaking of theirs. They pretended to have an undoubted right to the river from a Discovery made by one La Sol 60 Years ago, & the use of this Expedition is to prevent our Settling on the River or Waters of it, as they have heard of some Families moving out in order thereto.

From the best Intelligence I cou'd get, there has been 1,500 Men this Side Oswago Lake, but upon the Death of the General, all were recall'd to about 6 or 7 Hundred, which were left to Garrison four Forts, 150 or thereabouts in each, the first of which is on French Creek, near a small Lake, about 60 Miles from Venango near N: N: W: the next lies on Lake Erie, where the greatest Part of their Stores are kept about 15 Miles from the other; from that it is 120 Miles from the Carrying Place, at the

---

[50] Gist's description of the journey from Logstown to Venango reads:

"Friday 30.—We set out, and the Half-King and two old men and one young warrior, with us. At night we encamped at the Murthering town, about fifteen miles, on a branch of Great Beaver Creek. Got some corn and dried meat.

"Saturday 1 December.—Set out, and at night encamped at the crossing of Beaver creek from the Kaskuskies to Venango about thirty miles. The next day rain; our Indians went out a hunting; they killed two bucks. Had rain all day.

"Monday 3.—We set out and travelled all day. Encamped at night on one of the head branches of Great Beaver creek about twenty-two miles.

"Tuesday [4].—Set out about fifteen miles, to the town of Venango, where we were kindly and complaisantly received by Monsieur Joncaire, the French interpreter for the Six Nations" (GIST, 81).

Fall of Lake Erie, where there is a small Fort, which they lodge their Goods at, in bringing them from Morail, the Place that all their Stores come from; the next Fort lies about 20 Miles from this, on Oswago Lake; between this Fort & Morail there are three others; the first of which is near the English Fort Oswago. From the Fort on Lake Erie to Morail is about 600 Miles, which they say if good Weather, requires no more than 4 Weeks Voyage, if they go in Barks or large Vessells that they can cross the Lake; but if they come in Canoes, it will require five or six Weeks for they are oblig'd to keep under the Shoar.

5th: Rain'd successively all Day, which prevented our traveling. Capt. Joncaire sent for the half King, as he had but just heard

Washington and Gist crossing the Allegheny River. From *Columbian Magazine,* Nov. 1844. (George Washington Masonic National Memorial Association)

that he came with me: He affected to be much Concern'd that I did not make free to bring him in before; I excused it in the best Manner I was capable, & told him I did not think their Company agreeable, as I had heard him say a good deal in dispraise of Indians in General. But another Motive prevented my bringing them into his Company: I knew that he was Interpreter, & a Person of very great Influence among the Indians, & had lately used all possible means to draw them over to their Interest; therefore I was desirous of giving no more Opportunity than cou'd be avoided. When they came in there was great Pleasure express'd at seeing them, he wonder'd how they cou'd be so near without coming to visit him, made several trifling Presents, & applied Liquors so fast, that they were soon render'd incapable of the Business they came about notwithstanding the Caution that was given.[51]

6th: The Half King came to my Tent quite Sober, & insisted very much that I shou'd stay & hear what he had to say to the French. I fain wou'd have prevented his speaking any Thing 'til he came to the Commandant, but cou'd not prevail. He told me that at this Place Council Fire was kindled, where all their Business with these People were to be transacted, & that the Management of the Indian Affairs was left solely to Monsieur Joncaire. As I was desirous of knowing the Issue of this, I agreed to stay, but sent our Horses a little Way up French Creek, to raft over & Camp, which I knew wou'd make it near Night.

About 10 oClock they met in Council, the King spoke much the same as he had done to the General, & offer'd the French Speech Belt which had before been demanded, with the Marks of four Towns in it, which Monsieur Joncaire refused to receive; but desired him to carry it to the Fort to the Commander.

7th: Monsieur La Force, Commissary of the French Stores,[52] &

---

[51] Gist's diary entry for this day reads:

"Wednesday 5.—Rain all day. Our Indians were in council with the Delawares, who lived under the French colors, and ordered them to deliver up to the French the belt, with the marks of the four towns, according to the desire of King Shingiss. But the chief of these Delawares said, 'It was true King Shingiss was a great man, but he had sent no speech, and,' said he, 'I cannot pretend to make a speech for a King.' So our Indians could not prevail with them to deliver their belt; but the Half-King did deliver his belt, as he had determined. Joncaire did every thing he could to prevail on our Indians to stay behind us, and I took all care to have them along with us" (GIST, 82).

[52] Michel Pépin, called La Force, was captured by the British near Great Meadows in the spring of 1754 and sent to Williamsburg as a hostage after the surrender of Fort Necessity. His abilities were as respected by the British

three other Soldiers came over to accompany us up. We found it extreamly difficult getting the Indians off to Day; as every Stratagem had been used to prevent their going up with me. I had last Night left John Davison (the Indian Interpreter that I brought from Logstown with me) strictly charg'd not to be out of their Company, as I cou'd not get them over to my Tent (they having some Business with Custaloga, to know the reason why he did not deliver up the French Belt, which he had in keeping,) but was oblig'd to send Mr. Gist over to Day to fetch them, which he did with great Perswasion.

At 11 o'Clock we set out for the Fort, & was prevented from arriving there 'till the 11th: by excessive rains, Snows, & bad traveling, through many Mires & Swamps, which we were oblig'd to pass to avoid crossing the Creek, which was impassible either by Fording or Rafting, the Water was so high & rapid. We pass'd over much good Land since we left Venango, & through several extensive & very rich Meadows, one of which was near 4 Miles in length, & considerably wide in some Places.[53]

12th: I prepar'd early to wait upon the Commander, & was receiv'd & conducted to him by the 2d. Officer in Command; I

---

as by the French: "looseing La Force, I really think, w'd tend more to our disservice, than 50 other Men, as he is a Person whose active Spirit, leads him into all parlys, and brought him acquainted with all parts, add to this a perfect use of the Indian Tongue, and g't influence with the Indians" (GW to Dinwiddie, 29 May 1754, DLC:GW).

[53] According to Gist's diary, the party left Venango on 6 April. His entries for the journey to Fort Le Boeuf read as follows:

"Thursday 6.—We set out late in the day accompanied by the French General and four servants or soldiers, and

"Friday 7.—All encamped at Sugar creek, five miles from Venango. The creek being very high we were obliged to carry all our baggage over on trees, and swim our horses. The Major and I went first over, with our boots on.

"Saturday [8].—We set out and travelled twenty-five miles to Cussewago, an old Indian town.

"Sunday 9.—We set out, left one of our horses here that could travel no further. This day we travelled to the big crossing, about fifteen miles, and encamped, our Indians went out to look out logs to make a raft; but as the water was high, and there were other creeks to cross, we concluded to keep up this side the creek.

"Monday 10.—Set out, travelled about eight miles, and encamped. Our Indians killed a bear. Here we had a creek to cross, very deep; we got over on a tree, and got our goods over.

"Tuesday 11.—We set out, travelled about fifteen miles to the French fort, the sun being set. Our interpreter gave the commandant notice of our being over the creek; upon which he sent several officers to conduct us to the fort, and they received us with a great deal of complaisance" (GIST, 82–83).

acquainted him with my Business, & offer'd my Commission & Letter, both of which he desir'd me to keep 'til the Arrival of Monsieur Riparti, Capt. at the next Fort, who was sent for & expected every Hour.[54]

This Commander is a Knight of the Military Order of St: Lewis, & named Legadieur St. Piere, he is an elderly Gentleman, & has much the Air of a Soldier; he was sent over to take the Command immediately upon the Death of the late General, & arriv'd here about 7 Days before me. At 2 o'Clock the Gentleman that was sent for arriv'd, when I offer'd the Letters &ca. again, which they receiv'd, & adjourn'd into a private Appartment for the Captain to translate, who understood a little English, after he had done it, the Captain desir'd I wou'd walk in & bring my Interpreter to peruse & correct it, which I did.[55]

13th: The chief Officer retired to hold a Council of War, which gave me an Opportunity of taking the Dimensions of the Fort, & making what Observations I cou'd. It is situated on the South or West Fork of French Creek, near the Water, & is almost surrounded by the Creek, & a small Branch of it which forms a Kind of an Island, as may be seen by a Plan I have here annexed,[56] it is

[54] The commander was Jacques Le Gardeur, sieur de Saint-Pierre (1701–1755), who had succeeded the sieur de Marin as commandant of the French forces in the Ohio country upon the latter's death (see note 26). He had been commissioned an ensign in 1732 and served as a lieutenant in the Chickasaw campaign in 1739. Commissioned captain in 1749, he engaged in extensive western exploration. He was killed at Lake George 8 Sept. 1755 (PAPIERS CONTRECOEUR, 74 n.1). "Monsieur Riparti" was Louis Le Gardeur de Repentigny, commandant at Fort Presque Isle and probably a kinsman of Le Gardeur de Saint-Pierre. Repentigny had become commandant of Fort Le Boeuf upon the death of Marin and remained there until he was relieved by Le Gardeur de Saint-Pierre.

[55] Gist's diary entry for this day reads:

"Wednesday 12.—The Major gave the passport, showed his commission, and offered the Governor's letter to the commandant; but he desired not to receive them, until the other commander from Lake Erie came, whom he had sent for, and expected next day by twelve o'clock" (GIST, 83).

[56] A search of British repositories has failed to uncover this plan of Fort Le Boeuf. A map drawn by GW of the area covered by his journey to the French commandant is in P.R.O., M.P.G. 118. However, the above reference is clearly to a detailed plan of the French fort rather than to the map. Dinwiddie included the plan with GW's journal and other enclosures in a letter of 29 Jan. 1754 to the Board of Trade (P.R.O., C.O.5/1328, ff. 97–100). However, in the journal of the Board of Trade for 2 April 1754, when Dinwiddie's letter and accompanying documents were read, "A Map describing the situation of the French forts on the River Ohio" is noted as an enclosure, but no mention is made of the plan of the fort (BD. OF TRADE JL., 10:25). For an

THE

JOURNAL

OF

Major *George Washington,*

SENT BY THE

Hon. *ROBERT DINWIDDIE,* Esq;
His Majesty's Lieutenant-Governor, and
Commander in Chief of *VIRGINIA,*

TO THE

COMMANDANT

OF THE

FRENCH FORCES

ON

O H I O.

To WHICH ARE ADDED, THE

GOVERNOR's LETTER,

AND A TRANSLATION OF THE

FRENCH OFFICER's ANSWER.

―――――――――――――

WILLIAMSBURG:

Printed by WILLIAM HUNTER. 1754

Rushed into print at Williamsburg, Washington's report was widely discussed. (Rare Book Division, New York Public Library, Astor, Lenox and Tilden Foundations)

built exactly in that Manner & of that Dimensions. 4 Houses compose the Sides; the Bastions are made of Piles drove into the Ground, & about 12 Feet above sharpe at Top, with Port Holes cut for Cannon & Small Arms to fire through; there are Eight 6 lb. Pieces Mounted, two in each Bastion, & one of 4 lb. before the Gate: In the Bastions are a Guard House, Chapel, Doctor's Lodgings, & the Commander's private Store, round which is laid Platforms for the Cannon & Men to stand on: there is several Barracks without the Fort for the Soldiers dwelling, cover'd some with Bark, & some with Boards, & made chiefly of Logs, there is also several other Houses such as Stables, Smiths Shop &ca: all of which I have laid down exactly as they stand, & shall refer to the Plan for Explanation.

I cou'd get no certain Account of the Number of Men here; but according to the best Judgement I cou'd form, there is an Hundred exclusive of Officers, which are pretty many. I also gave Orders to the People that were with me, to take an exact Account of the Canoes that were haled up, to convey their Forces down in the Spring, which they did, and told 50 of Birch Bark, & 170 of Pine; besides many others that were block'd out, in Readiness to make.[57]

―――――――――――――

account of GW's map of the Ohio country, see FORD [1]. The map is reproduced on p. 153.

[57] The entry for this day in Gist's diary states:

"Thursday 13.—The other General came. The Major delivered the letter,

14th: As the Snow increased very fast, & our Horses daily got weaker, I sent them off unloaded, under the Care of Barnaby Currin & two others, to make all convenient Dispatch to Venango, & there wait our Arrival, if there was a Prospect of the Rivers Freezing, if not, then to continue down to Shanapin's Town at the Forks of Ohio, & there wait 'till we came to cross Allegany; intending my Self to go down by Water, as I had the Offer of a Canoe or two.

As I found many Plots concerted to retard the Indians Business, & prevent their returning with me, I endeavour'd all in my Power to frustrate their Schemes, & hurry them on to execute their intended Design. They accordingly pressed for admittance this Evening, which at length was granted them privately with the Commander, & one or two other Officers. The Half King told me that he offer'd the Wampum to the Commander, who evaded taking it, & made many fair Promises of Love & Friendship; said he wanted to live in Peace & trade amicably with them; as a Proof of which, he wou'd send some Goods immediately down to the Logstown for them, but I rather think the Design of that is to bring away all of our stragling traders that they may meet with; as I privately understood they intended to carry an Officer, &ca. with them; & what rather confirms this Opinion, I was enquiring of the Commander by what Authority he had taken & made Prisoners of several of our English Subjects. He told me the Country belong'd to them, that no English Man had a right to trade upon them Waters; & that he had Orders to make every Person Prisoner that attempted it on the Ohio or the Waters of it.

I enquir'd of Capt. Riparti about the Boy that was carried by, as it was done while the Command devolved upon him, between the Death of the late General & the Arrival of the Present. He acknowledg'd that a Boy had been carried past, & that the Indians had two or three white Scalps, (I was told by some of the Indians at Venango 8) but pretended to have forgot the Name of the Place that the Boy came from, & all the Particulars, tho' he Question'd him for some Hours as they were carrying him past. I likewise enquired where & what they had done with John Trotter, & James McClocklan, two Pensylvania Traders, which they had

---

and desired a speedy answer; the time of year and business required it. They took our Indians into private council, and gave them several presents" (GIST, 83).

taken with all their Goods: they told me that they had been sent to Canada, but were now return'd Home.[58]

This Evening I receiv'd an Answer to His Honour the Governor's Letter from the Commandant.[59]

15th: The Commander order'd a plentiful Store of Liquor, Provisions & ca. to be put on board our Canoe, & appear'd to be extreamly complaisant, though he was ploting every Scheme that the Devil & Man cou'd invent, to set our Indians at Variance with us, to prevent their going 'till after our Departure. Presents, rewards, & every Thing that cou'd be suggested by him or his

[58] See note 41.

[59] This letter was written in reply to Gov. Robert Dinwiddie's letter of 31 Oct. 1753, warning against a French invasion of the Ohio country (see note 17). The letter from Le Gardeur de Saint-Pierre, dated 15 Dec. 1753, is in the Virginia State Library at Richmond. A translation reads:

"As I have the honor of commanding here in chief, Mr. Washington delivered me the letter which you wrote to the commander of the French troops.

"I should have been glad if you had given him orders, or he had been inclined, to proceed to Canada to see our General, to whom it belongs, rather than to me, to set forth the evidence and the reality of the rights of the King, my master, to the lands situated along the Belle Rivière, and to contest the pretensions of the King of Great Britain thereto.

"I am going to send your letter to the Marquis Duquesne. His reply will be a law to me, and, if he should order me to communicate it to you, Sir, I can assure you that I shall neglect nothing to have it reach you very promptly.

"As to the summons you send me to retire, I do not think myself obliged to obey it. Whatever may be your instructions, I am here by virtue of the orders of my General, and I entreat you, Sir, not to doubt for a moment that I have a firm resolution to follow them with all the exactness and determination which can be expected of the best officer.

"I do not know that anything has happened in the course of this campaign which can be construed as an act of hostility, or as contrary to the treaties between the two Crowns; the continuation of which interests and pleases us as much as it does the English. If you had been pleased, Sir, to go into detail regarding the deeds which caused your complaints, I should have had the honor of answering you in the most positive manner, and I am sure that you would have had reason to be satisfied.

"I have made it a particular duty to receive Mr. Washington with the distinction owing to your dignity, his position, and his own great merit. I trust that he will do me justice in that regard with you, and that he will make known to you the profound respect with which I am, Sir, Your most humble and most obedient servant,

Legardeur de St. Pierre

"From the Fort of the Rivière au Beuf, December 15, 1753" (KENT, 75–76).

Le Gardeur de Saint-Pierre forwarded Dinwiddie's letter to Governor Duquesne on 22 Dec. The governor found the claims of the Virginians to be without foundation; the area incontestably belonged to the French (Du-

Officers was not neglected to do. I can't say that ever in my Life I suffer'd so much Anxiety as I did in this affair: I saw that every Stratagem that the most fruitful Brain cou'd invent: was practis'd to get the Half King won to their Interest, & that leaving of him here, was giving them the Opportunity they aimed at: I went to the Half King and press'd him in the strongest Terms to go. He told me the Commander wou'd not discharge him 'till the Morning; I then went to the Commander & desired him to do their Business, & complain'd of ill Treatment; for keeping them, as they were Part of my Company was detaining me, which he promis'd not to do, but to forward my Journey as much as he cou'd: He protested he did not keep them but was innocent of the Cause of their Stay; though I soon found it out. He had promis'd them a Present of Guns, &ca. if they wou'd wait 'till the Morning. As I was very much press'd by the Indians to wait this Day for them; I consented on a Promise that Nothing shou'd hinder them in the Morning.

16th: The French were not slack in their Inventions to keep the Indians this Day also; but as they were obligated, according to promise, to give the Present: they then endeavour'd to try the Power of Liquor; which I doubt not wou'd have prevail'd at any other Time than this, but I tax'd the King so close upon his Word that he refrain'd, & set off with us as he had engag'd. We had a tedious & very fatiguing Passage down the Creek, several Times we had like to have stove against Rocks, & many Times were oblig'd all Hands to get out, & remain in the Water Half an Hour or more, getting her over the Shoals: on one Place the Ice had lodg'd & made it impassable by Water; therefore we were oblig'd to carry our Canoe across a neck Land a quarter of a Mile over. We did not reach Venango 'till the 22d: where we met with our Horses. This Creek is extreamly crooked, I dare say the Distance between the Fort & Venango can't be less than 130 Miles to follow the Meanders.[60]

---

quesne to Le Gardeur de Saint-Pierre, 30 Jan. 1754, PAPIERS CONTRECOEUR, 98–99).

The entry in Gist's diary for this date reads:

"Friday 14.—When we had done our business, they delayed and kept our Indians, until Sunday; and then we set out with two canoes, one for our Indians, and the other for ourselves. Our horses we had sent away some days before, to wait at Venango, if ice appeared on the rivers and creeks" (GIST, 83).

[60] Here Gist describes the return trip from Fort Le Boeuf to Venango:

"Sunday 16.—We set out by water about sixteen miles, and encamped. Our

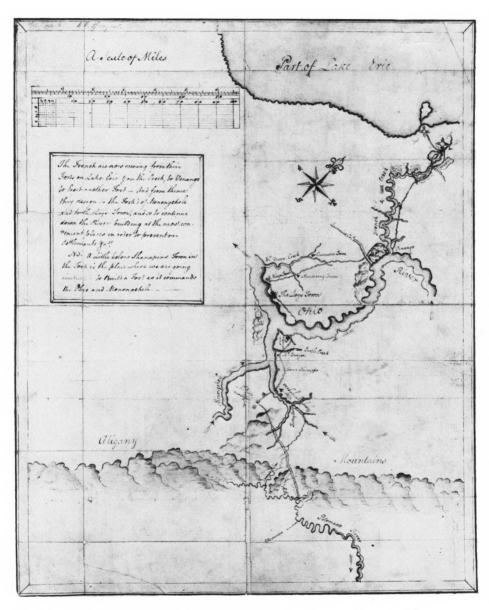

Washington's map of the Ohio country accompanied his report to Governor Dinwiddie. (Public Record Office, London. Crown Copyright)

23d: When I got Things ready to set off I sent for the Half King, to know whether they intended to go with us, or by Water. He told me that the White Thunder had hurt himself much, & was Sick & unable to walk, therefore he was oblig'd to carry him down in a Canoe: As I found he intended to stay a Day or two here, & knew that Monsieur Joncaire wou'd employ every Scheme to set him against the English, as he had before done; I told him I hoped he wou'd guard against his Flattery, & let no fine Speeches Influence Him in their Favour: He desired I might not be concern'd, for he knew the French too well, for any Thing to engage him in their Behalf, & though he cou'd not go down with us, he wou'd endeavour to meet at the Forks with Joseph Campbell,[61] to deliver a Speech for me to carry to his Honour the Governor. He told me he wou'd order the young Hunter to attend us, & get Provision &ca. if wanted. Our Horses were now so weak & feeble, & the Baggage heavy; as we were oblig'd to provide all the Necessaries the Journey wou'd require, that we doubted much their performing it; therefore my Self & others (except the Drivers which were oblig'd to ride) gave up our Horses for Packs, to assist along with the Baggage; & put my Self into an Indian walking Dress, & continue'd with them three Day's, 'till I found there

Indians went before us, passed the little lake, and we did not come up with them that night.

"Monday 17.—We set out, came to our Indians' camp. They were out hunting; they killed three bears. We stayed this day, and

"Tuesday 18.—One of our Indians did not come to camp. So we finding the waters lower very fast, were obliged to go and leave our Indians.

"Wednesday 19.—We set out about seven or eight miles, and encamped, and the next day

"Thursday 20.—About twenty miles, where we were stopped by ice, and worked until night.

"Friday 21.—The ice was so hard we could not break our way through, but were obliged to haul our vessels across a point of land and put them in the creek again. The Indians and three French canoes overtook us here, and the people of one French canoe that was lost, with her cargo of powder and lead. This night we encamped about twenty miles above Venango.

"Saturday 22.—Set out. The creek began to be very low and we were forced to get out, to keep our canoe from oversetting, several times; the water freezing to our clothes; and we had the pleasure of seeing the French overset, and the brandy and wine floating in the creek, and run by them, and left them to shift for themselves. Came to Venango, and met with our people and horses" (GIST, 83–84).

[61] Campbell was an unlicensed Pennsylvania trader in 1747 and 1748, employed by Alexander Moorhead. He was represented by George Croghan to be "a bad man, and corrupted by the French" (PA. ARCH. COL. REC., 5:693). He was killed by an Indian of the Six Nations at Parnell's Knob in Sept. 1754 (PA. ARCH., 1st ser., 2:173).

was no Probability of their getting in, in any reasonable Time; the Horses grew less able to travel every Day. The Cold increas'd very fast, & the Roads were geting much worse by a deep Snow continually Freezing; And as I was uneasy to get back to make a report of my Proceedings to his Honour the Governor; I determin'd to prosecute my Journey the nearest way through the Woods on Foot. Accordingly I left Mr. Vanbraam in Charge of our Baggage, with Money and Directions to provide Necessaries from Place to Place for themselves & Horses & to make the most convenient Dispatch in. I took my necessary Papers, pull'd off my Cloths; tied My Self up in a Match Coat; & with my Pack at my back, with my Papers & Provisions in it, & a Gun, set out with Mr. Gist, fitted in the same Manner, on Wednesday the 26th.

The Day following, just after we had pass'd a Place call'd the Murdering Town [62] where we intended to quit the Path & steer across the Country for Shanapins Town, we fell in with a Party of French Indians, which had laid in wait for us, one of them fired at Mr. Gist or me, not 15 Steps, but fortunately missed. We took this Fellow into Custody, & kept him 'till about 9 o'Clock at Night, & then let him go, & then walked all the remaining Part of the Night without making any Stop; that we might get the start, so far as to be out of the reach of their Pursuit next Day, as were well assur'd they wou'd follow upon our Tract as soon as it was Light: The next Day we continued traveling 'till it was quite Dark, & got to the River about two Miles above Shanapins; we expected to have found the River Froze, but it was not, only about 50 Yards from each Shoar; the Ice I suppose had broke up above, for it was driving in vast Quantities.

There was no way for us to get over but upon a Raft, which we set about with but one poor Hatchet, & got finish'd just after Sunsetting, after a whole days Work: We got it launch'd, & on board of it, & sett off; but before we got half over, we were jamed in the Ice in such a Manner, that we expected every Moment our Raft wou'd sink, & we Perish; I put out my seting Pole, to try to stop the Raft, that the Ice might pass by, when the Rapidity of the Stream through it with so much Violence against the Pole, that it Jirk'd me into 10 Feet Water, but I fortunately saved my Self by catching hold of one of the Raft Logs. Notwithstanding all our Efforts we cou'd not get the Raft to either Shoar, but were oblig'd, as we were pretty near an Island, to quit our Raft &

---

[62] Murdering Town, or Murthering Town, was a Delaware village on Conoquenessing Creek, a subsidiary of Beaver Creek. According to Gist's diary it was about 15 miles from Logstown (GIST, 81).

wade to it. The Cold was so extream severe, that Mr. Gist got all his Fingers, & some of his Toes Froze, & the Water was shut up so hard, that We found no Difficulty in getting off the Island on the Ice in the Morning, & went to Mr. Frazers. We met here with 20 Warriors that had been going to the Southward to War, but coming to a Place upon the Head of the Great Cunnaway, where they found People kill'd & Scalpt, all but one Woman with very Light Hair, they turn'd about; & ran back, for fear of the Inhabitants rising & takeing them as the Authors of the Murder: They report that the People were lying about the House, & some of them much torn & eat by Hogs; by the Marks that were left, they say they were French Indians of the Ottaway Nation, &ca. that did it.[63]

As we intended to take Horse here, & it requir'd some Time to hunt them; I went up about 3 Miles to the Mouth of Yaughyaughgane to visit Queen Aliquippa,[64] who had express'd great Concern that we pass'd her in going to the Fort. I made her a Present of a Match Coat; & a Bottle of rum, which was thought much the best Present of the two.[65]

[63] This is probably a reference to the massacre of the family of Robert Foyles, "his wife & 5 children," who were killed on the Monongahela rather than the Great Kanawha (INDIAN WARS, 399). In Mar. 1754 Dinwiddie in writing to Gov. James Hamilton noted that "the Incursions of these People with their Ind's on our present Settlem'ts, will be constantly, and attended with Robberies and Murders, w'ch was the Case last Year w'n some of their Ind's Came to our Frontiers, Murder'd a Man, his Wife and five Children, Robbed them of all they had, and left their Bodies to be tore in Pieces by the wild Beasts" (DINWIDDIE, 1:119). See also *Md. Gaz.*, 7 Mar. 1754.

[64] Queen Alliquippa (Allaquippa), who died about 1754, was frequently described as a Delaware (HODGE, 1:45; DIARIES, 1:66 n.1). Conrad Weiser, Pennsylvania's leading Indian negotiator, who met her at Logstown in 1748, described her as the old Seneca queen (WALLACE, 269). In 1749 she was living at McKee's Rocks when Céloron visited her. "The Iroquois inhabit this place, and it is an old woman of this nation who governs it. She regards herself as sovereign; she is entirely devoted to the English" (CÉLORON, 27). George Croghan stated in Dec. 1754 that "Alequeapy ye old quine is Dead and Left Several Children" (PA. ARCH., 1st ser., 2:218). See also SIPE, 255–58.

[65] Gist described the journey from Venango to John Fraser's trading post at Turtle Creek as follows:

"Sunday 23.—We set out from Venango, travelled about five miles to Lacomick creek.

"Monday 24.—Here Major Washington set out on foot in Indian dress. Our horses grew weak, that we were mostly obliged to travel on foot, and had snow all day. Encamped near the barrens.

"Tuesday 25.—Set out and travelled on foot to branches of Great Beaver creek.

"Wednesday 26.—The Major desired me to set out on foot, and leave

Tuesday 1st: Day of Jany: We left Mr. Frazers House, & arriv'd at Mr. Gists at Monangahela the 2d. where I bought Horse Saddle &ca. The 6th: We met 17 Horses loaded with Materials & Stores for a Fort at the Forks; & the Day after, a Family or two going out

---

our company, as the creeks were frozen, and our horses could make but little way. Indeed, I was unwilling he should undertake such a travel, who had never been used to walking before this time. But as he insisted on it, I set out with our packs, like Indians, and travelled eighteen miles. That night we lodged at an Indian cabin, and the Major was much fatigued. It was very cold; all the small runs were frozen, that we could hardly get water to drink.

"Thursday 27.—We rose early in the morning, and set out about two o'clock. Got to the Murthering town, on the southeast fork of Beaver creek. Here we met with an Indian, whom I thought I had seen at Joncaire's, at Venango, when on our journey up to the French fort. This fellow called me by my Indian name, and pretended to be glad to see me. He asked us several questions, as how we came to travel on foot, when we left Venango, where we parted with our horses, and when they would be there, etc. Major Washington insisted on travelling on the nearest way to forks of Alleghany. We asked the Indian if he could go with us, and show us the nearest way. The Indian seemed very glad and ready to go with us. Upon which we set out, and the Indian took the Major's pack. We travelled very brisk for eight or ten miles, when the Major's feet grew very sore, and he very weary, and the Indian steered too much north-eastwardly. The Major desired to encamp, to which the Indian asked to carry his gun. But he refused that, and then the Indian grew churlish, and pressed us to keep on, telling us that there were Ottawa Indians in these woods, and they would scalp us if we lay out; but to go to his cabin, and we should be safe. I thought very ill of the fellow, but did not care to let the Major know I mistrusted him. But he soon mistrusted him as much as I. He said he could hear a gun to his cabin, and steered us more northwardly. We grew uneasy, and then he said two whoops might be heard to his cabin. We went two miles further; then the Major said he would stay at the next water, and we desired the Indian to stop at the next water. But before we came to water, we came to a clear meadow; it was very light, and snow on the ground. The Indian made a stop, turned about; the Major saw him point his gun toward us and fire. Said the Major, 'Are you shot?' 'No,' said I. Upon which the Indian ran forward to a big standing white oak, and to loading his gun; but we were soon with him. I would have killed him; but the Major would not suffer me to kill him. We let him charge his gun; we found he put in a ball; then we took care of him. The Major or I always stood by the guns; we made him make a fire for us by a little run, as if we intended to sleep there. I said to the Major, 'As you will not have him killed, we must get him away, and then we must travel all night.' Upon which I said to the Indian, 'I suppose you were lost, and fired your gun.' He said, he knew the way to his cabin, and 'twas but a little way. 'Well,' said I, 'do you go home; and as we are much tired, we will follow your track in the morning; and here is a cake of bread for you, and you must give us meat in the morning.' He was glad to get away. I followed him, and listened until he was fairly out of the

to settle; this Day we arriv'd at Wills Creek, after as fatiguing a Journey as it is possible to conceive, rendered so by excessive bad Weather: From the first Day of December 'till the 15th. there was but one Day, but what it rain'd or snow'd incessantly & throughout the whole Journey we met with nothing but one continued Series of cold wet Weather; which occasioned very uncumfortable Lodgings, especially after we had left our Tent; which was some Screen from the Inclemency of it.[66]

On the 11th. I got to Belvoir,[67] where I stop'd one Day to take necessary rest; & then set out for, & arrived at Williamsburg, the 16th. & waited upon His Honour the Governor with the Letter I had brought from the French Commandant, & to give an Account of the Proceedures of my Journey. Which I beg leave to do by offering the Foregoing, as it contains the most remarkable Occurrences that happen'd to me.

I hope it will be sufficient to satisfy your Honour with my Proceedings; for that was my Aim in undertaking the Journey: & chief Study throughout the Prosecution of it.

---

way, and then we set out about half a mile, when we made a fire, set our compass, and fixed our course, and travelled all night, and in the morning we were on the head of Piney creek.

"Friday 28.—We travelled all the next day down the said creek, and just at night found some tracks where Indians had been hunting. We parted, and appointed a place a distance off, where to meet, it being then dark. We encamped, and thought ourselves safe enough to sleep.

"Saturday 29.—We set out early, got to Alleghany, made a raft, and with much difficulty got over to an island, a little above Shannopin's town. The Major having fallen in from off the raft, and my fingers frost-bitten, and the sun down, and very cold, we contented ourselves to encamp upon that island. It was deep water between us and the shore; but the cold did us some service, for in the morning it was frozen hard enough for us to pass over on the ice.

"Sunday 30.—We set out about ten miles to John Frazier's, at Turtle creek, and rested that evening.

"Monday 31.—Next day we waited on queen Aliquippa, who lives now at the mouth of Youghiogany. She said she would never go down to the river Alleghany to live, except the English built a fort, and then she would go and live there."

[66] The remainder of the journey is described by Gist as follows:

"Tuesday January 1, 1754.—We set out from John Frazier's and at night encamped at Jacob's cabins.

"Wednesday 2.—Set out and crossed Youghiogany on the ice. Got to my house in the new settlement.

"Thursday 3.—Rain.

"Friday 4.—Set out for Will's creek, where we arrived on Sunday January 6" (GIST, 84–87).

[67] Belvoir was the estate of Col. William Fairfax on the southern shore of the Potomac.

On Wednesday the 31st of October 1753, I was Comissiond & appointed by the Honble. Robert Dinwiddie Esqr. Governor &c. of Virginia

57

To visit & deliver a Letter to the Comandant of the French Forces on the Ohio, & set out on the intended Journey the same Day. The next I arrivd at Fredericksburg & engagd Mr. Jacob Vanbraam Interpreter, & proceeded with him to Alexandria where we provided Necessaries: From thence we went to Winchester & got Baggage Horses &c—: & from there we pursued the new Road to Wills Creek, where we arrived the 14th of November.

Here I engagd Mr. Gist to Pilot us out; & also hired four others as Servitors (vizt) Barnaby Currin, & John McGuier, Indian Traders) Henry Steward, & William Jenkins; & in Company with those Persons I left the Inhabitants the Day following. The excessive Rains, & vast Quantity of Snow that had fallen prevented our reaching Mr. Frazer's, an Indian Trader at the Mouth of Turtle Creek, on Monongehela, til Thursday.

22: We were informd here, that Expresses were sent a few Days ago to the Traders down the River to acquaint them with the General's Death & return of Major Part of the French Army into Winter Quarters. The Waters were quite impassable, without Swiming our Horses, which obligd us to get the Loan of a Canoe from Mr. Frazer, & to send Barnaby Currin & Henry Steward down Monongehela, with our Baggage, to meet us at the Forks of Ohio, about 10 Miles to cross Allegany.

As I got down before the Canoe, I spent some Time in viewing the Rivers, & the Land in the Fork, which I think extreamly well situated for a Fort; as it has the absolute Comand of both Rivers. The Land at the Point is 20 or 25 Feet above the Common Surface of the Water; & a considerable Bottom of flat well timber'd Land all around it, very convenient for Building. The Rivers are each a quarter of a Mile, or more, across, & run here very nigh at Right Angles; Allegany bearing N.E. & Monongehela S.E. The former of these two is a very rapid swift running Water, the other deep & still, with scarce any perceptable Fall. About two Miles from this, on the S.E. Side of the River, at the Place where the Ohio Company intended to erect a Fort, lives Singess King of the Delawares; We call'd upon him to invite him to Council at the Logstown—

As I had taken a good deal of Notice Yesterday of the Situation at the Forks; my Curiosity led me to examine this more particularly, & my Judgement to think it greatly inferior, either for Defence or Advantages, especially the latter; For a Fort at the Forks would be equally well situated on Ohio, & have the entire Command of Monongehela, which runs up to our Settlements

A clerk's copy of the report to Dinwiddie. (Public Record Office, London. Crown Copyright)

With the Assurance, & Hope of doing it, I with infinite Pleasure subscribe my Self Yr. Honour's most Obedt. & very Hble. Servant.

Go: Washington [68]

[68] Upon GW's arrival in Williamsburg, he presented the French commandant's letter and this journal of the expedition to the governor. His verbal account of French activities was accorded equal attention by Dinwiddie. The governor informed the council and the House of Burgesses that "Major Washington further reports that he ask'd why they [the French] had seized the Goods of our Traders, and sent their Persons Prisoners to Canada, to w'ch the Com'd't answer'd; 'That his Orders from their Gen'l, the Governor of Canada, were, Not to permit any English Subjects to trade on the Waters of the Ohio, but to seize their Goods and send them Prisoners to Quebeck.' He also ask'd the reason of taking Mr. Frazier's House from him, w'ch he had built and lived in upwards of twelve years. . . . He s'd that Man was lucky that he made his Escape, or he w'd have sent him Prisoner to Canada" (DINWIDDIE, 1:73–74). A further account of GW's comments was forwarded by the governor to the Board of Trade, together with his journal, his map of the frontier, and his plan of Fort Le Boeuf, on 29 Jan. 1754: "Mr. Washington had my Orders to make what Observations he cou'd on his Journey, & to take a Plan of their Fort, which I now enclose You, & from these Directions his Journal becomes so large. He assures me that they had begun another Fort at the Mouth of the Creek, which he thinks will be finish'd by the Month of March. There were in the Fort where the Commander resided, about 300 regular Forces; & nine hundred more were gone to Winter Quarters (in order to save their Provisions) to some Forts on Lake Erie &ca. but that they were to return by the Month of March; then they fully determin'd with all the Forces they cou'd collect, which he understood wou'd be fifteen hundred regulars, besides Indians, to go down the River Ohio, & propose building many other Forts, & that their chief residence wou'd be at the Logstown; & that they had near three hundred Canoes to transport their Soldiers, Provisions & Ammunition &ca." (P.R.O., C.O.5/1328, ff. 43–44).

Almost immediately upon GW's return to Williamsburg, Dinwiddie ordered publication of his journal. It appeared as *The Journal of Major George Washington, Sent by the Hon. Robert Dinwiddie, Esq; His Majesty's Lieutenant-Governor, and Commander in Chief of Virginia, to the Commandant of the French Forces on Ohio. To Which Are Added, the Governor's Letter, and a Translation of the French Officer's Answer* (Williamsburg: William Hunter, 1754). GW prefaced the publication with the following "Advertisement":

"As it was thought adviseable by his Honour the Governor to have the following Account of my Proceedings to and from the French on Ohio, committed to Print; I think I can do no less than apologize, in some Measure, for the numberless Imperfections of it.

"There intervened but one Day between my Arrival in Williamsburg, and the Time for the Council's Meeting, for me to prepare and transcribe, from the rough Minutes I had taken in my Travels, this Journal; the writing of which only was sufficient to employ me closely the whole Time, consequently admitted of no Leisure to consult of a new and proper Form to offer it in, or to correct or amend the Diction of the old; neither was I apprised, or did in the least conceive, when I wrote this for his Honour's Perusal, that it ever would be published, or even have more than a cursory Reading; till I was informed, at the Meeting of the present General Assembly, that it was already in the Press.

"There is nothing can recommend it to the Public, but this. Those Things which came under the Notice of my own Observation, I have been explicit and just in a Recital of:—Those which I have gathered from Report, I have been particularly cautious not to augment, but collected the Opinions of the several Intelligencers, and selected from the whole, the most probable and consistent Account.

G. Washington.

The journal was printed in various colonial newspapers (see, for example, *Md. Gaz.*, 21 & 28 Mar. 1754; *Boston Gaz.*, 16 April–21 May 1754). On 15 Feb. 1754 the journal was delivered to the House of Burgesses, and on 21 Feb. the burgesses voted the sum of £50 to GW "to testify our Approbation of his Proceedings on his Journey to the *Ohio*" (H.B.J., 1752–58, 182, 185).

Expedition to the Ohio

31 March–27 June 1754

EDITORIAL NOTE. In the weeks after GW's return from his journey to the French commandant, reports of further French infiltration into the Ohio Valley continued to reach Williamsburg and Gov. Robert Dinwiddie made preparations to resist. He appealed to other colonial governors for aid in repelling the French.[1] Capt. William Trent[2] was ordered to raise a force of 100 men and march them to the Ohio to construct a fort at the Forks. Dinwiddie had already sent ten cannon and a supply of ammunition to Alexandria for transportation to the Ohio.[3] GW, now adjutant of the Northern Neck, was instructed to raise 50 men from Frederick County and 50 men from Augusta County, then "Having all Things in readiness You are to use all Expedition in proceeding to the Fork of Ohio with the Men under Com'd and there you are to finish and compleat in the best Manner and as soon as You possibly can, the Fort w'ch I expect is there already begun by the Ohio Comp'a. You are to act on the Defensive, but in Case any Attempts are made to obstruct the Works or interrupt our Settlem'ts by any Persons whatsoever You are to

[1] DINWIDDIE, 1:61–71.

[2] Dinwiddie to Trent, [Jan. 1754], DINWIDDIE, 1:55–57. William Trent (1715–1787) was a native of Lancaster, Pa. His military experience dated from the 1746 campaign against Canada, when he was appointed captain of one of the four companies raised in Pennsylvania. After the campaign he returned to Pennsylvania and served as justice of the court of common pleas for Cumberland County. Trent was an experienced frontiersman who had acted for the Pennsylvania Assembly in carrying messages and gifts to the Indians. In the 1740s he had built up a considerable Indian trade and formed a partnership with George Croghan. He was an agent for the Ohio Company in the construction of storehouses and a fort. During the French and Indian War he served with both the Pennsylvania and Virginia forces, attended the Indian council at Easton in 1757, and took part in the Forbes campaign against Fort Duquesne in 1758. He lost much of his holdings during Pontiac's rebellion in 1763 and became a leader of the "Suffering Traders," who perennially requested restitution of their losses from the crown.

[3] DINWIDDIE, 1:73–79.

This engraving of Washington at twenty-five is after a miniature by Charles Willson Peale. (New-York Historical Society)

restrain all such Offenders, and in Case of resistance to make Prisoners of or kill and destroy them." However, neither Augusta nor Frederick complied with the request for men, and in mid-February GW returned to Williamsburg.[4] To encourage enlistments Dinwiddie issued a proclamation on 19 Feb. promising that a grant of 200,000 acres on the east side of the Ohio would be distributed among those who volunteered for service in the army.[5]

When the House of Burgesses met in February, Dinwiddie immediately informed it of the French threat. The burgesses proved less cooperative than Dinwiddie had hoped. An inadequate grant of £10,000 for protecting the frontier was hedged with restrictions as to the terms under which the money could be spent.[6] By

[4] DINWIDDIE, 1:59, 82; VA. EXEC. JLS., 5:460.

[5] The proclamation is in VA. EXEC. JLS., 5:499–500.

[6] Dinwiddie's relations with the House of Burgesses had been exacerbated by the recent conflict over the pistole fee (see GREENE [1]). However, some of the reluctance on the part of Virginia and the other colonies to support Dinwiddie's plans stemmed from the widespread suspicion that these military activities were to be used to further the schemes of the Ohio Company and to protect its interests on the frontier. GW noted that even after he had returned from his journey to the French commandant with evidence that the French were infiltrating the Ohio Valley, "it was yet thought a Fiction; and Scheme to promote the Interest of a private Company (by many Gentlemen that had a share in Government. . . . These unfavourable Surmises caus'd great delays in Raiseing the first Men and Money" (GW to the earl of Loudoun, 10 Jan. 1757, CSmH). "An Act for the encouragement and protec-

this time Dinwiddie realized the futility of relying on the counties to raise enough militia for the campaign and decided to use the funds voted by the Assembly to raise a force of six companies composed of 50 men each. "I am in hopes they will soon meet at Alexandria . . . and that they will be on their March to the Ohio the latter End of this Mo. or early in April." [7] Both New York and South Carolina were to send independent companies of regular troops, and it was hoped that contributions would be forthcoming from the other colonies.

GW was definitely interested in a command for the campaign against the French. In a letter to Richard Corbin, a member of the Council, he stated: "In a conversation with you at Green Spring, you gave me some room to hope for a commission above that of major, and to be ranked among the chief officers of this expedition. The command of the whole forces is what I neither look for, expect, nor desire; for I must be impartial enough to confess, it is a charge too great for my youth and inexperience to be entrusted with. . . . But if I could entertain hopes, that you thought me worthy of the post of lieutenant-colonel, and would favor me so far as to mention it at the appointment of officers, I could not but entertain a true sense of the kindness." Corbin, and probably others, apparently spoke for GW, since he did indeed receive the appointment he sought—forwarded to him by Corbin. General command of the Virginia forces was given to Joshua Fry, who was ordered to march first to Alexandria and then on to Wills Creek to aid in construction of a fort at the Forks of the Ohio. [8]

---

tion of the settlers upon the waters of the Mississippi" voted the sum of £10,000 for defense but appointed a committee of prominent Virginians who should "with the consent and approbation of the governor or commander in chief . . . direct and appoint how the said money shall be applied, towards the protecting and defending his majesty's subjects" (HENING, 6:418). Although a similar committee had existed in the administration of Gov. William Gooch, the council maintained "many Things in the said Bill to be unconstitutional." However, the need for money to meet the French emergency compelled the governor to give his assent (VA. EXEC. JLS., 5:462–63).

[7] Dinwiddie to James De Lancey, 1 Mar. 1754 (DINWIDDIE, 1:83–85).

[8] GW's letter to Corbin is in WRITINGS, 1:34–35. Joshua Fry (c.1700–1754) was born in Crewkerne, Somerset, Eng., and educated at Oxford. He emigrated to Virginia some time before 1720. In 1729 he became master of the grammar school at the College of William and Mary and in 1731 profes-

One of the most important maps of Virginia was drawn by Joshua Fry and Peter Jefferson in 1751. The above cartouche is taken from the revised map of 1755. (Rare Book Department, University of Virginia Library)

Even before the receipt of his commission as lieutenant colonel, GW had established headquarters at Alexandria and was actively engaged in recruiting and preparations for the campaign. Dinwiddie wrote GW on 15 Mar. that the French were moving down

sor of mathematics and natural philosophy. After the formation of Albemarle County in 1744, he filled a variety of posts, including county surveyor and justice of the peace. He represented Albermarle County in the House of Burgesses from 1745 until his death. He collaborated with Peter Jefferson in 1751 to produce the "Map of the Inhabited Parts of Virginia," one of the most famous of colonial maps. In 1745 he was appointed county lieutenant for Albemarle County. He received a commission as colonel of the Virginia Regiment in 1754 and was put in command of the campaign to drive the French from the Ohio. On his way to Wills Creek, Fry fell from his horse and died of his injuries 31 May, leaving the command of the regiment to devolve on GW. Fry's instructions are in DINWIDDIE, 1:88–90.

the Ohio more rapidly than expected, "w'ch, I think, makes it necessary for You to march what Soldiers You have enlisted, imediately to the Ohio, and escort some Waggons with the necessary Provisions. Colo. Fry to march w'th the others as soon as possible."[9] GW's diary of the campaign begins 31 Mar. 1754 and includes the march from Alexandria to the frontier, the defeat of a party of French troops under the command of Joseph Coulon de Villiers, sieur de Jumonville, and the construction of Fort Necessity in the Great Meadows. The last entry is for 27 June 1754, with GW's force planning to move to erect a fort on Red Stone Creek. On 28 June word was received from Chief Monacatoocha that the French at the Forks were preparing to send out "800 of their own men & 400 Indians" under the command of Louis Coulon de Villiers.[10] It was clear that the Indians with GW's troops would leave unless he returned to Great Meadows. Accordingly, the retreat was ordered, and after a backbreaking march over a mountainous terrain, the Virginia troops and Capt. James Mackay's Independent Company of regulars arrived at little Fort Necessity on Great Meadows 1 July. There they found almost no provisions—but the exhausted men were in no condition to retreat farther. GW ordered them to dig in. Their Indian allies quietly disappeared. On 1 July scouts informed GW that the French had advanced as far as Red Stone, and about 11:00 A.M. on 3 July the French command approached the fort. After a day of fighting, faced by a greatly superior force, GW was compelled to surrender. On 3 July he and Captain Mackay signed the articles of capitulation including the controversial admission that they had "assassinated" Jumonville.

The diary was among the papers lost by GW at the surrender of Fort Necessity. Retrieved by the French, it became part of a pamphlet published in Paris in 1756 under the title *Mémoire contenant le précis des faits, avec leurs pièces justificatives pour servir de réponse aux observations envoyées par les ministres d'Angleterre, dans les cours de l'Europe.*

In addition to GW's journal which appeared as document No. VIII in the first part of the pamphlet, numerous other letters and journals were included with editorial notes justifying French activities in the Ohio Valley. In 1757 a copy of the pamphlet was

[9] ViHi.   [10] HAMILTON [1], 1:17.

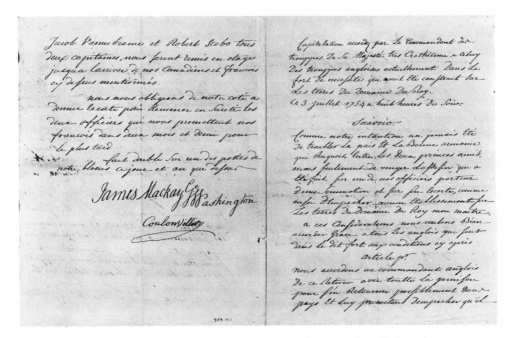

The capitulation at Fort Necessity was signed on 3 July 1754. (Royal Ontario Museum, Toronto)

captured on board a French ship taken as a prize, and was translated and published by Hugh Gaine in New York under the title *A Memorial Containing a Summary View of Facts with Their Authorities, in Answer to the Observations Sent by the English Ministry to the Courts of Europe.* This translation is hereafter referred to as MEMOIR and has been used in this volume as the source for the text of the 1754 diary. Two additional printings, one by J. Parker in New York and one by James Chattin in Philadelphia, appeared also in 1757. Two English editions were published.[11]

[11] *The Conduct of the Late Ministry; or Memorial Containing a Summary of Facts, with Their Vouchers, in Answer to the Observations Sent by the English Ministry to the Courts of Europe* (London, 1757). Upon the pamphlet's publication the *Monthly Review* commented: "We are probably

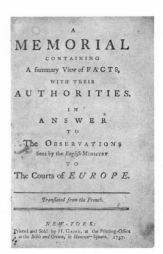

The first American publication of Washington's campaign against the French in 1753-54. (Tracy W. McGregor Library, University of Virginia)

As the original of GW's journal has not been found, the accuracy of the version published in the MEMOIR must remain questionable. The authenticity of at least one of the documents in the MEMOIR was disputed in England in 1756 before an English translation appeared in print. Document No. XII of the first part of the MEMOIR is a letter, purportedly from Col. Robert Napier to Gen. Edward Braddock, 25 Nov. 1754, containing the duke of Cumberland's orders for the 1755 campaign against the French in the Ohio country. In 1756 a pamphlet, *Reasons Humbly Offered, to Prove, That the Letter Printed at the End of the French Memorial of Justification, Is a French Forgery, and Falsely Ascribed to His R——l H——s*, was published in London, challenging the authenticity of the letter on the basis of its content.[12] GW expressed reservations concerning the accuracy of the

obliged to certain restless spirits among us, for this unnatural importation. We cannot, indeed, blame our *open enemies* for publishing whatever *they* may have to allege against us, and in support of their own cause; but what business have *we* to strengthen their efforts, and extend the circulation of their sophistry, by the additional aid of our own language?" (16 [1757], 468). In 1759 a second English edition appeared: *The Mystery Reveal'd; or, Truth Brought to Light. Being a Discovery of Some Facts, in Relation to the Conduct of the Late M——Y, Which However Extraordinary They May Appear, Are Yet Supported by Such Testimonies of Authentik Papers and Memoirs As Neither Confidence, Can, Outbrave; nor Cunning Invalidate. By a Patriot. Monstrum Horrendum!* (London: W. Carter, 1759).

[12] See also *Monthly Review*, 15 (1756), 302-4.

MEMOIR in a letter used by Jared Sparks in his edition of GW's writings:

I am really sorry, that I have it not in my power to answer your request in a more satisfactory manner. If you had favored me with the journal a few days sooner, I would have examined it carefully, and endeavoured to point out such errors as might conduce to your use, my advantage, and the public satisfaction; but now it is out of my power.

I had no time to make any remarks upon that piece, which is called my journal. The enclosed are observations on the French notes. They are of no use to me separated, nor will they, I believe, be of any to you; yet I send them unconnected and incoherent as they were taken, for I have no opportunity to correct them.

In regard to the journal, I can only observe in general, that I kept no regular one during that expedition; rough minutes of occurrences I certainly took, and find them as certainly and strangely metamorphosed; some parts left out, which I remember were entered, and many things added that never were thought of; the names of men and things egregiously miscalled; and the whole of what I saw Englished is very incorrect and nonsensical; yet, I will not pretend to say that the little body, who brought it to me, has not made a literal translation, and a good one.

Short as my time is, I cannot help remarking on Villiers' account of the battle of, and transactions at, the Meadows, as it is very extraordinary, and not less erroneous than inconsistent.[13] He says the French

---

[13] Document No. IX of the MEMOIR was "Journal of M. de Villiers." Louis Coulon de Villiers (1710–1757), Jumonville's brother, had been given command of the forces sent out against the English force on the Ohio. The portions of Villiers's journal to which GW objected in this letter concern the French attack on Fort Necessity and the capitulation of the fort: "As we had no Knowledge of the Place, we presented our Flank to the Fort, when they began to fire upon us, and almost at the same Time, I perceived the *English* on the Right, in order of Battle, and coming towards us. . . . Towards Six at Night, the Fire of the Enemy increased with more Vigour than ever, and lasted until Eight. We briskly returned their Fire. We took particular Care to secure our Posts, to keep the *English* fast up in their Fort all Night; and after having fixed ourselves in the best Position we could, we let the *English* know, that if they would speak to us, we would stop firing. They accepted the Proposal. There came a Captain to the Place where I was: I sent M. *le Mercier* to receive him, and I went to the Meadow, where I told him, that as we were not at war, we were very willing to save them from the Cruelties to which they exposed themselves, on Account of the *Indians*. . . . We considered, that nothing could be more advantageous than this Capitulation, as it was not proper to make Prisoners in a Time of Peace. We made the *English* consent to sign, that they had assassinated my

received the first fire. It is well known, that we received it at six hundred paces' distance. He also says, our fears obliged us to retreat in a most disorderly manner after the capitulation. How is this consistent with his other account? He acknowledges, that we sustained the attack warmly from ten in the morning until dark, and that he called first to parley, which strongly indicates that we were not totally absorbed in fear. If the gentleman in his account had adhered to the truth, he must have confessed, that we looked upon his offer to parley as an artifice to get into and examine our trenches, and refused on this account, until they desired an officer might be sent to them, and gave their parole for his safe return. He might also, if he had been as great a lover of the truth as he was of vainglory, have said, that we absolutely refused their first and second proposals, and would consent to capitulate on no other terms than such as we obtained. That we were wilfully, or ignorantly, deceived by our interpreter in regard to the word *assassination,* I do aver, and will to my dying moment; so will every officer that was present. The interpreter was a Dutchman,[14] little acquainted with the English tongue, therefore might not advert to the tone and meaning of the word in English; but, whatever his motives were for so doing, certain it is, he called it the *death,* or the *loss,* of the Sieur Jumonville. So we received and so we understood it, until, to our great surprise and mortification, we found it otherwise in a literal translation.

That we left our baggage and horses at the Meadows is certain; that there was not even a possibility to bring them away is equally certain, as we had every horse belonging to the camp killed or taken away during the action; so that it was impracticable to bring any thing off, that our shoulders were not able to bear; and to wait there was impossible,

---

Brother in his own Camp. We had Hostages for the Security of the *French* who were in their Power; we made them abandon the King's Country; we obliged them to leave us their Cannon, consisting of nine Pieces; we destroyed all their Horses and Cattle, and made them to sign that the Favour we granted them was only to prove, how desirous we were to use them as Friends. . . . The 4th, at Break of Day, I sent a Detachment, to take Possession of the Fort; the Garrison filed off, and the Number of their Dead and Wounded, moved me to Pity, notwithstanding my Resentment for their having in such a Manner, taken away my Brother's Life. The *Indians,* who had obeyed my Orders in every Thing, claimed a right to the Plunder; but I opposed it: However, the *English* being frightened, fled and left their Tents, and one of their Colours" (MEMOIR, 101). A more complete version than that printed in the MEMOIR is in PAPIERS CONTRECOEUR, 196–202.

[14] The translation of the articles of capitulation was made by Jacob Van Braam. The surrender of Fort Necessity and the articles of capitulation will be fully treated in vol. 1 of the *Papers.* See also FREEMAN, 1:402–11, 546–49.

for we had scarce three days' provisions, and were seventy miles from a supply; yet, to say we came off precipitately is absolutely false; notwithstanding they did, contrary to articles, suffer their Indians to pillage our baggage, and commit all kinds of irregularity, we were with them until ten o'clock the next day; we destroyed our powder and other stores, nay, even our private baggage, to prevent its falling into their hands, as we could not bring it off. When we had got about a mile from the place of action, we missed two or three of the wounded, and sent a party back to bring them up; this is the party he speaks of. We brought them all safe off, and encamped within three miles of the Meadows. These are circumstances, I think, that make it evidently clear, that we were not very apprehensive of danger. The colors he speaks of as left were a large flag of immense size and weight; our regimental colors were brought off and are now in my possession. Their gasconades, and boasted clemency, must appear in the most ludicrous light to every considerate person, who reads Villiers' journal; such preparations for an attack, such vigor and intrepidity as he pretends to have conducted his march with, such revenge as by his own account appeared in his attack, considered, it will hardly be thought that compassion was his motive for calling a parley. But to sum up the whole, Mr. Villiers pays himself no great compliment in saying, we were struck with a panic when matters were adjusted. We surely could not be afraid without cause, and if we had cause after capitulation, it was a reflection upon himself.

I do not doubt, but your good nature will excuse the badness of my paper, and the incoherence of my writing; think you see me in a public house in a crowd, surrounded with noise, and you hit my case. You do me particular honor in offering your friendship; I wish I may be so happy as always to merit it, and deserve your correspondence, which I should be glad to cultivate.[15]

Discovery of a contemporary copy of GW's diary in the Contre-coeur Papers, Archives du Seminaire de Québec, Université Laval, indicates that the amount of deliberate French "editing" of the journal was probably less than historians have believed

[15] SPARKS, 2:463–65. The original of this letter has not been located and the version published by Sparks is undated and unaddressed. It is possible, however, that the letter was sent to the historian William Smith (1727–1803), of Philadelphia. On 10 Nov. 1757 Smith wrote GW: "I have not been unmindful of the Papers you sent relating to the French Memorial, & you would have seen proper use made ⟨of⟩ them before now, if they had not been designed to be inter⟨   ⟩ in the general History of the present War" (DLC:GW).

and was probably confined to critical annotation and comments. Duquesne sent this copy of the journal to his subordinate, the sieur de Contrecoeur, on 8 Sept. 1754:

I attach hereto the extract of the journal of Colonel Washington who commanded the 500 Englishmen whom we fought. You will see that he is the most impertinent of all men, but that he has wit only in the degree that he is cunning with credulous savages. For the rest, he lies very much to justify the assassination of sieur de Jumonville, which has turned on him, and which he had the stupidity to confess in his capitulation![16]

This piece which the baron de Longueuil has transmitted to me is extraordinary. The hypocrisy of the Englishman is unmasked. That of the Five Nations is no less uncovered, but after all, the Englishman is their dupe, because after so many pretty promises they abandoned him at the moment when he had the most need of them. On the other hand, you will see that the Englishman, wishing to make them believe that he would march only at the solicitation of the Five Nations, marched. The blunderer, thinking that with this strong assistance he could not fail to defeat us, and then become the peaceful possessor of La Belle Rivière [the Ohio River]! What has struck me in this journal, is that they came in wagons as far as the place where Sr. de Villiers found them, but that captain doubts all the same that they were able to cross the high mountains which they would have had to climb in order to go to the English camp. . . .

What desertion! What difficulties in the provinces where Washington has passed! What discord in these troops from different provinces who pretend to independence! It is that which makes me believe that we shall always be fighting a troop as poorly composed as they are poor warriors.

I beg you to comment on this journal in order to improve, if it can be done, upon my ideas and the precautions on which your safety depends, for they certainly are sensible that only treason can destroy our establishments.

There is nothing more unworthy and lower, and even blacker, than the sentiments and the way of thinking of this Washington. It would have been a pleasure to read his outrageous journal under his very nose.[17]

[16] PAPIERS CONTRECOEUR, 133–81, contains a side-by-side comparison of the Contrecoeur copy of the diary with the version printed in the MEMOIR. For a complete discussion of the Contrecoeur copy, see CONTRECOEUR DIARY.

[17] PAPIERS CONTRECOEUR, 249–53 (translation).

It is evident that Duquesne did not regard the journal as a fabrication; a comparison of the version in the Contrecoeur Papers with the version in the MEMOIR reveals only minor differences in wording, although there are several entries in the Contrecoeur copy which do not appear in the MEMOIR. Aside from variations in spelling of places and proper names, the French translator probably closely followed GW's original diary.

On the 31st of *March,* I received from his Honour a Lieutenant Colonel's Commission,[18] of the *Virginia* Regiment, whereof *Joshua Fry,* Esq; was Colonel, dated the 15th; with Orders to take the Troops, which were at that Time quartered at *Alexandria,* under my Command, and to march with them towards the *Ohio,* there to help Captain *Trent* to build Forts, and to defend the Possessions of his Majesty against the Attempts and Hostilities of the *French.*[19]

April the 2d, Every Thing being ready, we began our march according to our Orders, the 2d of *April,* with two Companies of Foot, commanded by Captain *Peter Hog,*[20] and Lieutenant *Jacob Vambraam,*[21] five Subalterns, two Serjeants, six Corporals, one

[18] The date of the commission's receipt as given here is in error. Dinwiddie wrote to GW 15 Mar. enclosing the commission as lieutenant colonel of the Virginia Regiment, "pay, 12s. 6d. per day" (ViHi), and GW acknowledged its receipt 20 Mar. (WRITINGS, 1:35–36).

[19] In Alexandria, GW was facing the perennial problems of recruiting and supply. On 9 Mar. he wrote to Dinwiddie: "I have increased my number of Men to abt. 25, and dare venture to say, I should have had several more if the excessive bad weather did not prevent their meeting agreeable to their Officer's Commands. We daily Experience the great necessity for Cloathing the Men, as we find the generality of those, who are to be Enlisted, are of those loose, Idle Persons, that are quite destitute of House, and Home, and, I may truly say, many of them of Cloaths; which last, renders them very incapable of the necessary Service, as they must unavoidably be expos'd to inclement weather in their Marches, &c., and can expect no other than to encounter almost every difficulty, that's incident to a Soldiers Life. There is many of them without Shoes, others want Stockings, some are without Shirts, and not a few that have Scarce a Coat, or Waistcoat to their Backs; in short, they are as illy provided as can well be conceiv'd" (ViHi).

[20] Peter Hog (1703–1782), a native of Edinburgh, settled in Augusta County about 1745. He was commissioned a captain in the Virginia Regiment 9 Mar. 1754. In July 1756 he was chosen to erect a line of frontier forts commissioned by the Virginia Assembly. Hog was licensed to practice law on 10 May 1759, and in 1772 Lord Dunmore appointed him prosecuting attorney for Dunmore County. He eventually became a landowner of considerable importance with extensive holdings in Kentucky and western Virginia.

[21] Jacob Van Braam had accompanied GW on his journey to the French commandant in 1753. According to a memorial Van Braam presented to Lord George Germain 31 July 1777, he was "formerly a Lieutenant in the Dutch Service—that having some connections in America, he went to that Country in the Year 1752. In 1753 he was sent with Mr. Washington to the French who were at that time erecting Forts on the Ohio—that the Year after (the French still pursuing their incroachments) the Virginians raised a Regiment of which your Memorialist had the sole disciplining—that Mr. Washington who was Colonel of the said Regiment being compelled by a superior force of Canadians and Indians to surrender Fort Necessity, your Memorialist was sent as an Hostage to Canada, where he was kept in a Gaol

Drummer, and one Hundred and twenty Soldiers, one Surgeon,[22] one *Swedish* Gentleman,[23] who was a Volunteer, two Waggons, guarded by one Lieutenant, Serjeant, Corporal, and Twenty-five Soldiers.

We left *Alexandria* on Tuesday Noon, and pitched our Tents about four miles from *Cameron,* having travelled six Miles.[24]

---

for several years 'till the reduction of that Country" (P.R.O., C.O.5/116, ff. 2–24). Van Braam's role in translating the articles of capitulation of Fort Necessity aroused so much criticism in Virginia that his name was omitted from the list of officers thanked by the Assembly for their participation in the campaign. By 1761, however, tempers had cooled and Van Braam was specifically recommended by Gov. Francis Fauquier for a commission in the British army (Fauquier to William Pitt, 3 April 1761, P.R.O., C.O.30./8/32, ff. 17–18). He was also granted 9,000 acres of land as an officer in the Virginia Regiment (VA. EXEC. JLS., 6:440, 549). He subsequently received a commission in the Royal American Regiment. At the end of the war he went on half pay and settled on "a considerable farm" in Wales. In 1775 he was again appointed to a company in one of the battalions of the Royal American Regiment and sent to Saint Augustine in East Florida (P.R.O., C.O.5/116, ff. 21–24). He served as captain in the British army in the Georgia campaign and sold his commission in 1779. After the war he apparently settled in France (see Van Braam to GW, 20 Dec. 1783, DLC:GW).

[22] The surgeon who accompanied the expedition was Dr. James Craik (1730–1814), a native of Arbigland, Scot. Educated at the University of Edinburgh, he emigrated in 1750, first to the West Indies and then to Virginia, opening a practice in Norfolk, where he was living when commissioned in the Virginia Regiment 7 Mar. 1754. During the French and Indian War he was stationed at Winchester and served in the Braddock campaign. At the close of the war he settled on a plantation at Port Tobacco, Charles County, Md. During the Revolution, Craik held, among other posts, that of chief physician and surgeon of the Continental Army. He was a frequent visitor to Mount Vernon, especially when there was illness in the family and among the slaves, accompanied GW on his journey to the Ohio and Kanawha rivers in 1770 and 1784, and attended him in his last illness.

[23] Carolus Gustavus de Spiltdorf was commissioned an ensign in the Virginia Regiment 21 July 1754 and promoted to lieutenant 29 Oct. 1754. He was killed during Braddock's Defeat 9 July 1755.

[24] Cameron was located at the head of Hunting Creek, Fairfax County. Although only the site of an inn or ordinary, it gained some importance from its site at the junction of several roads and as a mustering place for militia meetings (see HARRISON [1], 414–15).

Although the printed diary does not indicate the route taken by the expedition from Cameron, it can be partially reconstructed from the account of GW's expenses submitted to the colony of Virginia in Oct. 1754 (DLC:GW). It appears likely that after leaving Cameron he proceeded through Loudoun County to the establishment of the Quaker Edward Thompson at the later site of Hillsboro ("To Expences of the Regimt. at Edward Thompsons in Marching up 2.16.6"). The regiment crossed the Blue Ridge at Vestal's Gap 8 April and proceeded across the Shenandoah by ferry ("To Bacon for

Washington's lifelong friend and physician, Dr. James Craik. (Richmond Academy of Medicine)

(From the 3d of *April,* to the 19th of said Month, this Journal only contains the March of the Troops, and how they were joined by a Detachment which was brought by Captain *Stevens.*) [25]

[the regiment] of John Vestal at Shanandoah & Ferriages over 1.9.0") and on to Winchester. The next stage was to Joseph Edwards's fort on Cacapon Creek ("To an Express at Edwards's 2.6"), then to Job Pearsal's on the right bank of the South Branch of the Potomac, then to Thomas Cresap's establishment near the mouth of the South Branch, and on to Wills Creek.

In the Contrecoeur version the following entry appears for 17 April: "About noon I met Mr. Gist who had been sent from Oyo on express by the Half King in order to find out when the English could be expected there. He informed me that the Indians are very angry at our delay, and that they threaten to abandon the country; that the French are expected every day at the lower part of the river; that the fort is begun, but hardly advanced; and several other particulars" (CONTRECOEUR DIARY, 12).

[25] Adam Stephen (c.1718–1791) was born in Scotland and studied medicine at the University of Edinburgh. After briefly pursuing a career in the British navy, Stephen settled down to the practice of medicine in Virginia. He joined the Virginia Regiment in 1754 as a captain and was later promoted to lieutenant colonel. He took part in the Braddock campaign in 1755 and in 1756 was among the forces sent against the Creeks in South Carolina, serving with the Virginia troops until 1758. During Pontiac's rebellion he again joined the army and faced charges in 1764 that he used militia to guard wagons carrying his own property. The charges were dismissed, but he was censured for sending Virginia troops out of the colony (H.B.J., 1761–65, 296–98). In Feb. 1776 he was appointed colonel of the 4th Virginia Regiment and in Sept. 1776 a brigadier general in the Continental Army. In Oct. 1777 he was charged with "Acting unlike an officer" at Germantown. He was dis-

The 19th, Met an Express who had Letters from Captain *Trent,* at the *Ohio,* demanding a Reinforcement with all Speed, as he hourly expected a Body of Eight Hundred *French.* I tarried at *Job Pearsall's* [26] for the Arrival of the Troops, where they came the next Day. When I received the above Express, I dispatched a Courier to Colonel *Fry,* to give him Notice of it.

The 20th, Came down to Colonel *Cresap,* to order the Detachment, and on my Rout, had Notice that the Fort was taken by the *French.* That News was confirmed by Mr. *Wart,* [27] the Ensign of Captain *Trent,* who had been obliged to surrender to a Body of One Thousand *French* and upwards, under the Command of Captain *Contrecoeur,* [28] who was come from *Venango* (in *French,* the Peninsula) with Sixty Battoes, and Three Hundred Canoes, and who having planted eighteen Pieces of Cannon against the Fort, afterwards had sent him a Summons to depart. [29]

Mr. *Wart* also informed me, that the *Indians* kept stedfastly

---

missed from the service in Nov. 1777. After the war he lived on his farm in Berkeley County (now West Virginia) and in 1788 served as a member of the Virginia Convention to ratify the Constitution.

[26] Job Pearsal was "one of the first settlers on the south branch of the Potomac, at or near the site of the present town of Romney. His cabin, on the right bank of the stream, was surrounded by a stockade. . . . This was on the line of the main road between Winchester, the forts on Patterson creek, Oldtown and Fort Cumberland" (TONER [3], 30). See also KOONTZ, 138.

[27] Trent had left Ens. Edward Ward in charge of the construction of the proposed fort at the mouth of the Monongahela while he returned to Wills Creek for provisions. Shortly after Trent's departure, Ward received word that a body of French were marching on the fort. Upon the advice of the Half-King, Ward hastily threw up a stockade at the Forks. On 17 April the French forces appeared with a summons to surrender. Since the French had some 1,000 men to Ward's 41 he was forced to comply. For Ward's deposition on his surrender, see GIST, 275–78.

[28] Claude Pierre Pécaudy, sieur de Contrecoeur (1706–1775), had begun his military career in the French army as an ensign in 1729. He advanced to the rank of lieutenant in 1742 and to captain in 1748, and in 1754 was ordered to construct a fort at the Forks of the Ohio and put in command of French forces in the Ohio country. He retired from the army in 1759 and established residence in Canada, where, in 1774, he was appointed to the legislative council of the Province of Quebec.

Contrecoeur's "Summons" to Ward to surrender the stockade is in PAPIERS CONTRECOEUR, 117–19. In it he warned the English that the French government would not tolerate expansion into the Ohio country.

[29] Venango (now Franklin, Pa.) was at the junction of the Allegheny River and French Creek. "Peninsula" is a translation, not of Venango, but of Presque Isle (Erie, Pa.), on Lake Erie.

attached to our Interest.[30] He brought two young *Indian* Men
with him, who were *Mingoes,* that they might have the Satisfaction to see that we were marching with our Troops to their Succour.

He also delivered me the following Speech, which the *Half-King*
sent to me.

Fort-Ohio, April 18th, 1754.

A SPEECH *from the* Half-King, *for the Governors of* Virginia *and*
Pennsylvania. MY Brethren the *English.* The Bearer will let you
understand in what Manner the *French* have treated us. We
waited a long Time, thinking they would come and attack us; we
now see how they have a Mind to use us.

We are now ready to fall upon them, waiting only for your
Succour. Have good Courage, and come as soon as possible; you
will find us as *ready to encounter with them as you are yourselves.*

We have sent those two young Men to see if you are ready to
come, and if so, they are to return to us, to let us know where you
are, that we may come and join you. We should be glad, if the
Troops belonging to the two Provinces could meet together at
the Fort which is in the Way. If you do not come to our Assistance now, we are intirely undone, and imagine we shall never
meet together again. I speak it with a Heart full of Grief.

A Belt of Wampum.

The *Half-King* directed to me the following Speech. I am ready,
if you think it proper, to go to both the Governors, with these
two young Men, for I have now no more Dependance on those
who have been gone so long, without returning or sending any
Message.

A Belt of Wampum.

April 23d. A COUNCIL of WAR held at *Wills-Creek,* in order to
consult upon what must be done on Account of the News brought
by Mr. *Wart,*

The News brought by Ensign *Wart,* having been examined into,
as also the Summons sent by Captain *Contrecoeur,* Commander
of the *French* Troops, and the Speeches of the *Half-King,* and of

[30] Ward noted in his deposition the strong support given to his detachment
by the Half-King, who had helped him to erect the fort. The chief
"stormed greatly at the French at the Time they were oblieged to march
out of the Fort and told them it was he Order'd that Fort and laid the first
Log of it himself, but the French paid no Regard to what he said" (GIST, 278).

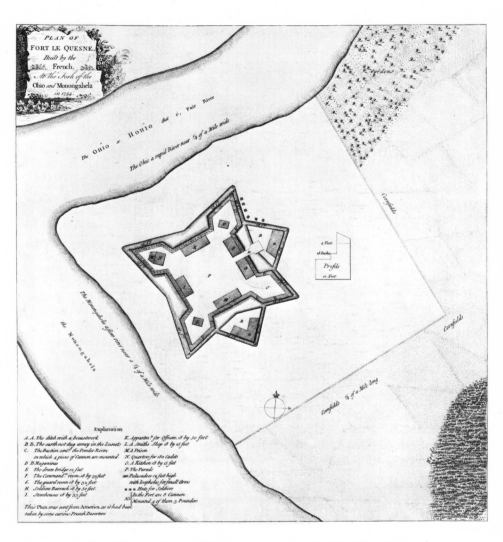

A plan of Fort Duquesne as it appeared in 1754. From a broadside, London: J. Payne, 1756. (Public Record Office, London, Crown Copyright)

the other Chiefs of the *Six-Nations;* it appears, that Mr. *Wart,* was forced to surrender the said Fort, the 17th of this Instant, to the *French,* who were above One Thousand strong, and had eighteen Artillery Pieces, some of which were nine Pounders, and also that the Detachment of the *Virginia* Regiment, amounting to One Hundred and Fifty Men, commanded by Colonel *Washington* had Orders to reinforce the Company of Captain *Trent,* and that the aforesaid Garrison consisted only of Thirty-three effective Men.

It was thought a Thing impracticable to march towards the Fort without sufficient Strength; however, being strongly invited by the *Indians,* and particularly by the Speeches of the *Half-King,* the President gave his Opinion, that it would be proper to advance as far as *Red-Stone-Creek,* on *Monaungahela,* about Thirty-seven Miles on this Side of the Fort, and there to raise a Fortification, clearing a Road broad enough to pass with all our Artillery and our Baggage, and there to wait for fresh Orders.

The Opinion aforesaid was resolved upon, for the following Reasons;

1st, That the Mouth of *Red-Stone* is the first convenient Place on the River *Monaungahela.*

2d, That Stores are already built at that Place for the Provisions of the Company, wherein our Ammunition may be laid up; [31] our great Guns may be also sent by Water whenever we should think it convenient to attack the Fort.

3d, We may easily (having all these Conveniences) preserve our People from the ill Consequences of Inaction, and encourage the *Indians* our Allies, to remain in our Interest. Whereupon, I sent Mr. *Wart* to the Governor, with one of the young *Indians* and an Interpreter: I thought it proper also to acquaint the Governors of *Maryland* and *Pennsylvania* of the News; [32] and I

[31] The Ohio Company had erected a store on the right bank of Red Stone Creek (Brownsville, Pa.) in Jan. 1754.

[32] Ward was in Williamsburg by 4 May. On that day Dinwiddie informed the council of Ward's surrender and presented it a copy of "the Resolve of a Council of War held thereupon." The council requested "that his Honour would Signifie by a Letter to Col. Washington that his Conduct in General has been approved of, more particularly the Caution he has taken in halting at Red Stone Creek, til they have Assembled a Sufficient Body to secure themselves & Cannon and then to proceed to Monongahela" (VA. EXEC. JLS., 5:468–69).

GW's letter to Gov. Horatio Sharpe of Maryland is printed, under 27 April, in WRITINGS, 1:43–44. The letter to Gov. James Hamilton of Pennsylvania, dated 24 April, is in the University of Pittsburgh libraries.

sent away the other *Indian* to the *Half-King,* with the Speeches inclosed in the following Letter.

To the Honourable Robert Dinwiddie, *Esq; Governor, &c.*[33]

SIR,

Mr. *Wart,* an Ensign of Captain *Trent's* Company, is this Day come from *Monaungahela,* and has brought the sorrowful News of the Reduction of the Fort, on the 17th of this Instant; having been summoned by Captain *Contrecoeur* to surrender to a Body of *French* Troops who were a Thousand strong, who came from *Venango,* with eighteen Pieces of Cannon, sixty Battoes, and Three Hundred Canoes; they permitted all our Men to retire, and take with them their Working-Tools out of the Fort, which was done the same Day.

Upon receiving this News, I called a Council of War, in order to consult what was best to be done in such Circumstances; and have sent you a particular Account of every Thing agreed upon at the said Council by the same Express, that you may know Things yet more particularly.

Mr. *Wart* is the Bearer of the Summons, as also of the Speech from the *Half-King,* wherein I inclosed the Wampum; he is in Company with one of those *Indians* mentioned in the Speech, who had been sent to see our Forces, and to know what Time they might expect us; the other *Indian,* I have sent back with a Message. I hope you will find it necessary, to send us our Forces as soon as they are raised, as also a sufficient Number of Canoes, and other Boats with Decks; send us also some Mortar-Pieces, that we may be in a Condition to attack the *French* with equal Forces. And as we are informed that the *Indians* of the *Six Nations,* and the *Outawas,* are coming down *Sciodo-Creek,* in order to join the *French* who are to meet at the *Ohio;* so I think it would not be amiss to invite the *Cherokees, Catawbas,* and the *Chickasaws* to come to our Assistance; and as I have received Intelligence, that there is no good Understanding between them and the *Indians* of the *Six Nations* aforesaid, it would be well to perswade them to make a Peace with them; otherwise if they should meet at the *Ohio,* it might cause great Disorder, and turn out to our Disadvantage.[34]

[33] For GW's letter to Dinwiddie, dated 25 April 1754, see P.R.O., C.O.5/14, f. 191. It is entirely possible that a copy of the letter was not included in the original diary but was found among GW's papers by the French after the capture of Fort Necessity.

[34] Dinwiddie relayed GW's plan regarding the southern Indians to South

We find the great Advantage there is in Water-Carriage, wherefore, I would remind you to provide a Number of Boats for that Purpose.

This Day, arrived the Men belonging to Captain *Trent*, who by your Orders had been inlisted as Militia-Troops; the Officers having imprudently promised them *Two Shillings* per Day, they now refuse to serve for less Pay; *Wart* shall receive your Orders on that Head.[35]

To his Excellency Horatio Sharpe, *Governor of* Maryland.

SIR,

I AM here arrived with a Detachment of One Hundred and Fifty Men: We daily expect Colonel *Fry* with the remaining Part of the Regiment and the Artillery; however, we shall march gently a-cross the Mountains, clearing the Roads as we go, that our Cannon may with the greater Ease be sent after us; we propose to go as far as *Red-Stone River,* which falls into *Monaungahela,* about Thirty-seven Miles this Side of the Fort which the *French* have taken, from thence all our heavy Luggage may be carried as far as the *Ohio*. A Store is built there by the *Ohio* Company, wherein may be placed our Ammunition and Provisions.

Besides the *French* Forces above mentioned, we have Reason to

---

Carolina Gov. James Glen. Glen, unenthusiastic about the proposal, replied, 1 June 1754, that "the Catawbas, the Cherokees, Creeks, and Chickasaws . . . are not only in perfect Peace and Friendship with one another, but were never more strongly attached to the British Interest. If this were to be disputed, let Facts speak; they come when we send for them, they go when they are bid and they do whatever is desired of them. . . . What Benefit then do you propose by sending so many pressing Messages to prevail with these Four Nations or with the Five Nations in New York to come to Virginia. . . . I will answer for their good Behavior with my Life, if your Province does not interfere" (S.C. IND. AFF. DOCS., 21 May 1750–7 Aug. 1754, 524–28).

[35] In recruiting men to construct the fort at the Forks, Trent had apparently promised them pay of 2s. per day, the amount commonly allowed volunteers; however, he had enlisted the men in the militia, where the rate allowed private soldiers was 8d. per day (DINWIDDIE, 1:117). Although Dinwiddie's instructions to Trent are not specific on this point, he may have intended Trent's men to be enlisted for a brief period as volunteers (see DINWIDDIE, 1:55–56). GW had additional reason to fear unrest among his men since four of them had been detected in a plan to desert when the company had arrived in Winchester. An entry in GW's account book notes: "April 10. To Cash to B: Hamilton for discovering the Plot of 4 Soldrs. to Desert. 1.4" (DLC:GW). GW continued to have trouble with Trent's soldiers until, against his orders, they finally dispersed (GW to Dinwiddie, 18 May 1754, ViHi).

believe, according to the Accounts we have heard, that another Party is coming to the *Ohio;* we have also learnt that Six Hundred of the *Chippowais* and *Ollowais Indians,* are coming down the River *Sciodo,* in order to join them.

The following is my Answer to the Speech of the *Half-King;*

"To the *Half-King,* and to the Chiefs and Warriors of the *Shawanese* and *Loups* our Friends and Brethren. I received your Speech by Brother *Bucks,*[36] who came to us with the two young Men six Days after their Departure from you. We return you our greatest Thanks, and our Hearts are fired with Love and Affection towards you, in Gratitude for your constant Attachment to us, as also your gracious Speech, and your wise Counsels.

This young Man will inform you, where he found a small Part of our Army, making towards you, clearing the Roads for a great Number of our Warriors, who are ready to follow us, with our great Guns, our Ammunition and Provisions. As I delight in letting you know with speed the Thoughts of our Heart, I send you back this young Man, with this Speech, to acquaint you therewith, and the other young Man I have sent to the Governor of *Virginia,* to deliver him your Speech and your Wampum, and to be an Eye-witness of those Preparations we are making, to come in all Haste to the Assistance of those whose Interest is as dear to us as our Lives. We know the Character of the treacherous *French,* and our Conduct shall plainly shew you, how much we have it at Heart. I shall not be satisfied if I do not see you before all our Forces are met together at the Fort which is in the Way; wherefore, I desire, with the greatest Earnestness, that you, or at least one of you, would come as soon as possible to meet us on the Road, and to assist us in Council. I present you with these Bunches of Wampum, to assure you of the Sincerity of my Speech, and that you may remember how much I am your Friend and Brother."

Signed, WASHINGTON
or CONOTOCARIOUS [37]

[36] "Brother Bucks" was the Indian name of the trader George Croghan, Ens. Edward Ward's half brother; however, it was Ward who brought the Half-King's speech to GW in company with two young men of the Mingoes.

[37] GW inherited the Indian name given to his great-grandfather, John Washington. The name signified "town taker" or "devourer of villages." In his "Biographical Memoranda," comments written in 1786 on a projected biography of him by David Humphreys, GW stated that during the 1753 journey to the French commandant he "was named by the half-King (as he

April 28.   Came to us some Pieces of Cannon, which were taken up to the Mouth of *Patterson's* River.

(From the 29th of *April,* to the 11th of *May,* the Journal only contains Marches, and Things of little Consequence.) [38]

---

was called) and the tribes of Nations with whom he treated, Caunotaucarius (in English) the Town taker; which name being registered in their Manner and communicated to other Nations of Indians, has been remembered by them ever since in all their transactions with him during the late War" (anonymous donor).

[38] The version of GW's diary found among Contrecoeur's papers contains the following entries for some of the missing days:

"May 4. We met Captain Trente's factor who informed us that 400 more French had certainly arrived at the fort and that the same number were expected in a short time. He also informed us that they were busy building two strong houses, one upon the Oyo, and the other upon the River Mal engueulée [Monongahela], both of them about three hundred rods from their junction; and that they are setting up a battery on an islet between them.

"May 5. We were joined by another trader coming from Aliganie who confirmed the same news, and who added that the French were building in the place where the Oyo Company had at first intended to build a fort, at the mouth of the small River Shuttiés [Chartier's Creek].

"May 7. We met a trader who informed us that the French had come to the mouth of the River Rouge [Red Stone Creek], and that they had taken possession of it with about four hundred men.

"May 8. This report was contradicted by some other traders who came directly from there.

"May 10. A trader arrived from the Wyendot country, having passed by the Mal engueulé forks where he had seen the Half King and the other chiefs of the Six Nations who had just received the speech I had sent them. The Half King showed the pleasure it had given him and, before the trader left, a detachment of 50 men was sent to meet us. He informs me that the French are working with all their might to build a fort on the point which I had indicated to the government. On the way this same merchant met M. La Force at Mr. Gist's new plantation with three other Frenchmen and two Indians who had come to reconnoiter the country of the River Rouge and the vicinity under the specious pretense of hunting deserters" (CONTRECOEUR DIARY, 18–20).

Some of GW's activities for the missing period can be reconstructed from his letter written from the Little Meadows to Robert Dinwiddie 9 May (ViHi). During these days his command began the slow push from Wills Creek. The initial problem was transportation. William Trent had been ordered to have packhorses waiting at Wills Creek to convey troops and supplies, but when GW arrived "there was none in readiness, nor any in expectation, that I could perceive." The troops were therefore compelled to wait until wagons could be procured from the South Branch of the Potomac some 40 miles away. The wagons probably did not arrive until 29 April. For the party to reach the Ohio Company's new store at Red Stone Creek, it was necessary to improve and widen the existing road; GW detached a body of 60 men for the work, "which party since the 25th. of Apl., and the main

May the 11th, Detached a Party of Twenty-five Men, commanded by Captain *Stevens* and Ensign *Peronie*,[39] with Orders to go to Mr. *Gist's,* to enquire where *La Force,* and his Party were; [40] and in case they were in the Neighbourhood, to cease pursuing and to take care of themselves. I also ordered them to examine closely all the Woods round about, and if they should find any *Frenchman* apart from the rest, to seize him and bring him to us, that we might learn what we could from him: We were exceedingly desirous to know, if there was any Possibility of sending

---

body since the 1st. Instt. have been laboriously employ'd, and have got no further than these Meadows abt. 20 Miles from the new Store, where we have been two Days making a Bridge across and are not done yet." The pace slowed to as little as four miles a day, and reports poured into camp that the French were on the march.

[39] William La Péronie (Peyroney), a native of France who settled in Virginia about 1750, had apparently had previous military experience and was appointed an ensign in the Virginia Regiment. He was wounded in the engagement at Fort Necessity. In a letter of 12 June 1754 to Dinwiddie, GW warmly recommended him for promotion to adjutant, noting that he had been "sensibly chagrined, when I acquainted him with your pleasure, of giving him an ensigncy. This he had twelve years ago, and long since commanded a company" (WRITINGS, 1:76–84). He received the appointment of adjutant and was killed at Braddock's Defeat.

[40] Christopher Gist's new settlement was in central Fayette County, Pa., near present-day Mount Braddock.

Adam Stephen described this incident in his "Autobiography": "On the 11th of May 1754 he [Stephen] was detached by Col. Washington from the Little Meadows, an Encampment about 20 miles above Fort Cumberland, with Monsieur Perony an Ensign, & 25 men; to apprehend Monsieur Jumonville, La Force & other Frenchmen, detached from Fort du Quesne to Reconnoitre the Country.

"Stephens Carried only four days provision with him; & there fell such a heavy rain, that it raisd all the Rivers in the Mountains; he sent out Hunters to kill provisions; employd the Rest in making Rafts, & with labour & difficulty crossd all the Rivers.

"He at last arrivd with his detachmt. on the Monongahela near Redstone, & was informed by Some Indian Traders, whom the French had permitted to Retire; that Joumonville & his party finding the Weather unsuitable for Reconnoitering had returnd down the River to Fort du Quesne the day before. Stephens unwilling to Return to Washington without Some thing to Say, bethought himself of sending a Spy to Fort du Quesne for Intelligence. It was distant about 37 miles.

"He pitched upon a person that in five days brought him the most Satisfactory & Accurate Acct of every thing at Fort du Quesne. . . .

"Stephens was amazed at so great an Accuracy, & it immediately enterd into his head; that the fellow had got five pounds of him for the Scout, & that probably he had Recevd. as much of the French for informing them of his Strength & Situation. This occasiond as Quick a Return to Meet Washington as possible" (PPL: Benjamin Rush Papers).

Hon.ble Sir   Little Meadows 9th of May 1754

I acquainted your Honour by Mr. Ward with the determination's, which we prosecuted in 2 Days after his Departure, as soon as Waggons arrived to convey our Provisions — The want of proper Conveyances has much retarded this Expedition, and at this time, unfortunately delay'd the Detachment I have the Honour to command — Even When we came to Wills Ck. my disappointments, were not less than before, for there I expected to have found a sufficient number of pack Horses provided by Capt. Trent conformable to his Promise, Maj. Carlyle's Letter's and my own (that I might prosecute my first intention with light expeditious Marches) but inst.d of Wt., there was none in readiness, nor any in expectation, that I could perceive, which added me to the necessity of waitg. till Waggon's ed be procured from the Branch (20 Miles distant) However in the mean time I detach'd a party of 60 Men

Here Washington reports to Dinwiddie his problems of transport in pursuing the French. (Virginia Historical Society)

[186]

down any Thing by Water, as also to find out some convenient
Place about the Mouth of *Red-Stone-Creek,* where we could build
a Fort, it being my Design to salute the *Half-King,* and to send
him back under a small Guard; we were also desirous to enquire
what were the Views of the *French,* what they had done, and what
they intended to do, and to collect every Thing, which could give
us the least Intelligence.

The 12th, Marched away, and went on a rising Ground, where
we halted to dry ourselves, for we had been obliged to ford a deep
River, where our shortest Men had Water up to their Arm-pits.

There came an Express to us with Letters, acquainting us, that
Col. *Fry,* with a Detachment of One Hundred Men and upwards,
was at *Winchester,* and was to set out in a few Days to join us; as
also, that Col. *Innis* [41] was marching with Three Hundred and
Fifty Men, raised in *Carolina;* that it was expected *Maryland*
would raise Two Hundred Men, and that *Pennsylvania* had
raised *Ten T[h]ousand Pounds* (equal to about *Fifty-two Thousand Five Hundred Livres*) to pay the Soldiers raised in other
Colonies, as that Province furnisheth no Recruits, as also that
Governor *Shirley* had sent 600 Men to harrass the *French* in
Canada; I hope that will give them some Work to do, and will
slacken their sending so many Men to the *Ohio* as they have
done.[42]

The 16th, Met two Traders, who told us they fled for Fear of

[41] James Innes (d. 1759) was born in Scotland and emigrated to North
Carolina some time after 1733. He settled in Wilmington and in 1740–41
commanded the Cape Fear Company in the campaign against Cartagena.
After his return to North Carolina, he became a planter and served as
colonel of the New Hanover County militia. In 1750 he was appointed to
the North Carolina Council. At the outbreak of the French and Indian
War, he was named commander of the North Carolina forces and, after
Joshua Fry's death, was appointed by his friend Governor Dinwiddie to
overall command of the combined colonial forces for the expedition against
the French in the Ohio Valley (DINWIDDIE, 1:194–95). He held various posts
during the war—among them campmaster general and governor of Fort
Cumberland.

[42] Although these estimates were optimistic, similar information was sent
by Dinwiddie to Capel Hanbury of London 10 May 1754 (DINWIDDIE, 1:153–
55).

The Contrecoeur version of the diary has the following entry: "May 15.
I learned by letter, among other things, that Governor Charlay [William
Shirley of Massachusetts] had sent six hundred men to harass the French in
Canada. I hope that that will give them something to do, and will hinder
them from sending so many forces to the River Oyo" (CONTRECOEUR DIARY,
20). As the information is similar to that contained in the entry for 12
May, the date may be in error.

the *French,* as Parties of them were often seen towards Mr. *Gist's.* These Traders are of Opinion, as well as many others, that it is not possible to clear a Road for any Carriage to go from hence to *Red-Stone-Creek.*

The 17th, This Night Mr. *Wart* arrived with the young *Indian* from *Williamsburg,* and delivered me a Letter, wherein the Governor is so good as to approve of my Proceedings, but is much displeased with Captain *Trent,* and has ordered him to be tried, for leaving his Men at the *Ohio:* The Governor also informs me, that Capt. *Mackay,* with an Independant Company of 100 Men, excluding the Officers, were arrived, and that we might expect them daily; and that the Men from *New-York* would join us within ten Days.[43]

This Night also came two *Indians* from the *Ohio,* who left the *French* Fort five Days ago: They relate that the *French* Forces are all employed in building their Fort, that it is already Breast-high, and the Thickness of twelve Feet, and filled up with Earth and Stone, &c. They have cut down and burnt up all the Trees which were about it, and sown Grain instead thereof. The *Indians* believe there were only 600 in Number; though they say themselves they are 800: They expect a greater Number in a few Days, which may amount to 1600, then they say they can defy the *English.*

---

[43] Dinwiddie's letter to GW is dated 4 May 1754 (DINWIDDIE, 1:148–49). Capt. James Mackay and his company from South Carolina did not catch up with the Virginians until 14 June. The South Carolina force and its captain were part of the regular British army establishment, a fact which raised the delicate question of rank between Mackay, who held the king's commission, and GW, whose commission was provincial. Officers holding royal commissions had proved reluctant on other occasions to take orders from officers of higher rank in the provincial forces. Dinwiddie himself may have had misgivings about possible friction; in his letter of 4 May to GW he noted that Mackay "appears to be an Officer of some Experience and Importance, You will . . . so well agree as not to let some Punctillios ab't Com'd render the Service You are all engag'd in, perplexed or obstructed" (ViHi).

James Mackay (d. 1785) had been appointed an ensign in a Georgia independent company of foot in 1737 and had served at Fort Diego, Fla., where he was promoted to lieutenant in May 1740. In Feb. 1741/42 he was promoted to captain lieutenant and in July 1745 to captain in Oglethorpe's Regiment. After the disbandment of this regiment in 1749, he was made captain of one of the newly organized independent companies in South Carolina. He apparently resigned his commission in 1755 and returned to Georgia, where he was an active politician, an extensive landowner, and proprietor of Strathy Hall. In 1785 he went to Rhode Island for his health and died at Alexandria, Va., on his return journey to Georgia (GW to Robert Sinclair, 6 May 1792, DLC:GW). For the friction of command between GW and Mackay, see also HARDEN.

The 18th, The Waters being yet very high, hindred me from advancing on Account of my Baggage, wherefore I determined to set myself in a Posture of Defence against any immediate Attack from the Enemy, and went down to observe the River.[44]

The 19th, I dispatched the young *Indian* which was returned with Mr. *Wart*, to the *Half King*, with the following Speech.

To the Half King, *&c.*

My Brethren,

It gives me great Pleasure, to learn that you are marching to assist me with your Counsels; be of good Courage, my Brethren, and march vigorously towards your Brethren the *English;* for fresh Forces will soon join them, who will protect you against your treacherous Enemy the *French.* My Friends whom I send to you,

[44] The question of the discrepancy between the pay of British officers and that of provincial officers had rankled with GW's troops throughout the campaign. By 18 May the irritation of GW and the officers of his command reached the boiling point. At the beginning of the campaign the question was not definitely decided, but the estimate was 15s. per day for a lieutenant colonel and 12s. 6d. for a major. GW had objected to the sums at the time as being lower than the pay of corresponding ranks in the British regular army (GW to Dinwiddie, 29 May 1754, ViHi). Dinwiddie, however, had assured him that subsistence for the officers would be provided. When GW's commission was sent to him, the pay had been reduced to 12s. 6d. for a lieutenant colonel and 10s. for a major, with a corresponding reduction for lesser ranks (DINWIDDIE, 1:106–7, 112–15). Ward had presumably brought word to GW's camp that the committee of the General Assembly overseeing expenditure had refused an increase. GW wrote to Dinwiddie 18 May, transmitting a written memorial from his officers protesting pay and rations: "I am heartily concerned, that the officers have such real cause to complain of the Committee's resolves; and still more to find my inclinations prone to second their just grievances." Although GW was reluctant to surrender his commission, "I would rather prefer the great toil of a daily laborer, and dig for a maintenance . . . than serve upon such ignoble terms; for I really do not see why the lives of his Majesty's subjects in Virginia should be of less value, than of those in other parts of his American dominions. . . . Upon the whole, I find so many clogs upon the expedition, that I quite despair of success" (ViHi). Dinwiddie responded angrily 25 May, expressing surprise at "Such ill timed Complaints. . . . The Gent. very well knew the Terms on w'ch they were to serve. . . . Thus much, in answer to the paper signed by Capt. Stephen and others. Now, Colo. W., I shall more particularly answer w't relates to Y'rself, and I must begin with expressing both Concern and Surprize to find a Gent. . . . from whom I had so great Expectat's and Hopes . . . concuring with Complaints in general so ill-founded" (ViHi). The importance of this pay issue to GW and his officers during the campaign is indicated by the fact that before giving Dinwiddie a detailed account of his defeat of Jumonville's forces he prefaced his report with a lengthy refutation of the governor's letter of 25 May (GW to Dinwiddie, 29 May 1754, ViHi).

will acquaint you of an agreeable Speech which the Governor of *Virginia* adresses to you: He is very sorry for the bad Usage you have received. The great Waters do not permit us to make such Haste towards you as we would do; for that Reason I have sent the young Men to invite you to come and meet us: They can tell you many Things which they have seen in *Virginia,* and also how well they were received by the most Part of our Grandees; they did not use them as the *French* do your People who go to their Fort: they refuse them Provisions; this Man has had given him, all that his Heart could wish: For the Confirmation of all this, I here give you a Belt of *Wampum.*

The 20th, Embarked in a Canoe with Lieut. *West,* three Soldiers, and one *Indian;* [45] and having followed the River along about Half a Mile, were obliged to come ashore, where I met *Peter Suver,* a Trader,[46] who seemed to discourage me from seeking a Passage by Water; that made me alter my Mind of causing Canoes to be made; I ordered my People to wade, as the Waters were shallow enough; and continued myself going down the River in the Canoe: Now finding that our Canoe was too small for six Men, we stopped to make some Sort of a Bark;[47] with which, together with our Canoe, we gained *Turkey-Foot,*[48] by the Beginning of the Night. We underwent several Difficulties about

[45] John West, Jr. (d. 1777), of Fairfax County was commissioned a lieutenant in the Virginia Regiment 27 Feb. 1754 and served until August, when he resigned (VA. TROOPS, 284; GW to Robert Dinwiddie, 20 Aug. 1754, ViHi). His resignation may have been prompted by the death about this time of his father, Hugh West (Hugh West's will, 9 Feb. 1754, Fairfax County Wills, Book B-1, 74–75, Vi Microfilm). John West, Jr., like GW, was a trained surveyor, and during the previous year had been appointed surveyor for Fairfax County (John West, Jr.'s bond, Fairfax County Deeds, Book C-1, 546, Vi Microfilm). He was Fairfax County sheriff 1759–61, justice of the Fairfax County court 1757–76, and clerk of Truro Parish 1758–63.

The Indian who accompanied the party refused to proceed beyond the Forks until GW "promised him a ruffled shirt, which I must take from my own, and a match-coat" (GW to Joshua Fry, 23 May 1754, WRITINGS, 1:52–53).

[46] John C. Fitzpatrick suggests that the name Peter Suver was a French interpretation of Philip Sute, "among . . . the earliest settlers in the Red Stone Creek region" (DIARIES, 1:83 n.2). A more likely suggestion is Peter Shaver (Shafer), a licensed trader in Pennsylvania in 1744 who lived "four miles from the Susquehanna River" in 1750 (HANNA, 2:340). Shaver was killed by Indians in the fall of 1755.

[47] "Washington's journal shows that the time spent at the task would have sufficed only for the building of a raft" (FREEMAN, 1:364n).

[48] Turkey Foot, present-day Confluence, Pa., is at the confluence of Laurel Creek, Casselman's River, and the Youghiogheny.

eight or ten Miles from thence, though of no great Consequence, finding the Waters sometimes deep enough for Canoes to pass, and at other times more shallow.

The 21st, Tarried there some Time to examine the Place, which we found very convenient to build a Fort, not only because it was gravelly, but also for its being at the Mouth of three Branches of small Rivers: The Plan thereof, which may be seen here, is as exact as could be done, without Mathematical Instruments.[49]

We went about two Miles to observe the Course of the River, which is very strait, has many Currents, is full of Rocks, and rapid; we waded it, though the Water was pretty high, which made me think it would not be difficult to pass it with Canoes.

We also found other Places where the Water was rapid, but not so deep, and the Current smoother; we easily passed over them; but afterwards we found little or scarce any Bottom: There are Mountains on both Sides of the River. We went down the River about ten Miles, when at last it became so rapid as to oblige us to come ashore.

(*From the 22d to the 24th, the Journal contains only a Description of the Country.*)[50]

The 24th, This Morning arrived an *Indian,* in Company with him I had sent to the *Half King,* and brought me the following Letter from him.

To any of his Majesty's Officers whom these may concern.
AS 'tis reported that the *French* Army is set out to meet M. *George Washington,* I exhort you, my Brethren, to guard against them; for they intend to fall on the first *English* they meet; they have been on their March these two Days; the *Half King,* and the other Chiefs, will join you within five Days, to hold a Council,

[49] The plan of Turkey Foot has not been located.
[50] On 23 May GW wrote to Joshua Fry that he has "returned from my discoveries down the Youghiogany, which I am sorry to say, can never be made navigable." The group had traveled some 30 miles in a fruitless search for a water route. GW had been pessimistic about the possibility of finding the Youghiogheny navigable and had ordered the soldiers on by land in the direction of Red Stone Creek. "By concurring intelligence, which we received from the Indians, the French are not above seven or eight hundred strong, and by a late account we are informed, that one half of them were detached in the night, without even the Indians knowledge, on some secret expedition; but the truth of this, though it is affirmed by an Indian lately from their fort, I cannot yet vouch for, not tell where they are bound" (WRITINGS, 1:52–53). Upon his return to the Great Crossing of the Youghiogheny, GW met Adam Stephen and his party (see note 40).

though we know not the Number we shall be. I shall say no more; but remember me to my Brethren the *English.*

Signed, The HALF-KING.[51]

I Examined those two young *Indians* in the best Manner I could, concerning every Circumstance, but was not much the better satisfied.

They say there are Parties of them often out, but they do not know of any considerable Number coming this Way. The *French* continue raising their Fort, that Part next to the Land is very well inclosed, but that next to the Water is much neglected, at least without any Defence: They have only nine Pieces of Cannon, and some of them very small, and not one mounted. There are two on the Point, and the others some Distance from the Fort next to the Land.

They relate that there are many sick among them, that they cannot find any *Indians* to guide their small Parties towards our Camp, these *Indians* having refused them.

The same Day at Two o'Clock, we arrived at the Meadows,[52] where we saw a Trader, who told us that he came this Morning from Mr. *Gist's,* where he had seen two *Frenchmen* the Night before; and that he knew there was a strong Detachment out, which confirmed the Account we had received from the *Half King:* Wherefore I placed Troops behind two natural Intrenchments, where our Waggons also entered.

The 25th, Detached a Party to go along the Roads, and other

[51] This letter was written for the Half-King by his interpreter, John Davison. GW copied the letter verbatim in his letter to Dinwiddie, 27 May 1754, retaining Davison's highly original spelling and punctuation. In GW's version the letter reads: "To the forist his Majesties Commander Offeverses to hom this meay concern: On acct of a french armey to meat Miger Georg Wassiontton therfor my Brotheres I deesir you to be awar of them for deisin'd to strik the forist Englsh they see tow deays since they marchd I cannot tell what nomber the half King and the rest of the Chiefes will be with you in five dayes to consel, no more at present but give my serves to my Brother's the English" (ViHi).

[52] GW is referring to Great Meadows, near Laurel Hill (approximately 11 miles southeast of present-day Uniontown, Pa.). It was here that he erected Fort Necessity. In 1767 GW acquired ownership of more than 200 acres in the area of Great Meadows, including the site of Fort Necessity. On the evening of 24 May, GW received another report that the French were at the crossing of the Youghiogheny some 18 miles away; he decided upon Great Meadows as a convenient place to make a stand. "We have, with Natures assistance made a good Intrenchment and by clearing the Bushes out of these Meadows prepar'd a charming field for an Encounter" (GW to Dinwiddie, 27 May 1754, ViHi).

small Parties to the Woods, to see if they could make any Discovery. I gave the Horse-men Orders to examine the Country well, and endeavour to get some News of the *French,* of their Forces, and of their Motions, *&c.*

At Night all these Parties returned, without having discovered any thing, though they had been a great way towards the Place from whence it was said the Party was coming.

The 26th, Arrived *William Jenkins;* Col. *Fry* had sent him with a Letter from Col. *Fairfax,*[53] which informed me, that the Governor himself, as also Colonels *Corbin* and *Ludwell,* were arrived at *Winchester,*[54] and were desirous to to see the *Half King* there, whereupon I sent him an Account thereof.[55]

The 27th, Arrived Mr. *Gist,* early in the Morning, who told us, that Mr. *la Force,* with fifty Men, whose Tracks he had seen five Miles off, had been at his Plantation the Day before, towards Noon; and would have killed a Cow, and broken every Thing in the House, if two *Indians,* whom he had left in the House, had not persuaded them from their Design: I immediately detached 65 Men,[56] under the Command of Captain *Hog,* Lieut. *Mercer,*[57]

[53] William Fairfax was at this time lieutenant colonel of the Fairfax County militia. The letter has not been found.

[54] Dinwiddie was preparing for a conference at Winchester with chiefs of both northern and southern tribes. He hoped to settle the differences between these traditional enemies and to hold them to the British interest. The governor left for Winchester 13 May 1754, and as he reported to Sir Thomas Robinson 18 June, "I waited in that Town 16 days, in expectation of the Ind's, agreeable to their Promise. I rec'd a Message from the Chiefs of some of their Tribes, acquaint'g me that they could not come to W. at that Time, because the French had invaded and taken Possession of their Lands, and that they c'd not properly leave their People, but that they had joined our Forces under the Com'd of Colo. Geo. Washington, but desir'd me to send them some of the Present sent them from their Father, the King of G. B., w'ch I accordingly did to Colo. W——" (DINWIDDIE, 1:201–5).

Richard Corbin and Philip Ludwell, both members of the governor's council, accompanied Dinwiddie to the Winchester council.

[55] Upon GW's arrival at Great Meadows he had sent out "small light partys of Horse (Wagn. Horses) to reconnoitre the Enemy, and discover their strength & motion, who return'd Yesterday with't seeing any thing of them nevertheless, we were alarm'd at Night and remaind under Arms from two oClock till near Sun rise. We conceive it was our own Men, as 6 of them Deserted, but can't be certain whether it was them or other Enemy's. Be it as it will, they were fired at by the Centrys, but I believe without damage" (GW to Dinwiddie, 27 May 1754, ViHi).

[56] According to GW's letter of 27 May to Dinwiddie (ViHi) and Adam Stephen's "Autobiography" (PPL:Benjamin Rush Papers), he dispatched 75 men.

[57] George Mercer (1733–1784) was educated at William and Mary and

Portrait of George Mercer. (From a
photograph at the Virginia Historical
Society)

Ensign *Peronie,* three Sergeants, and three Corporals, with Instructions.

The *French* enquired at Mr. *Gist's,* what was become of the
Half King? I did not fail to let the young *Indians* who were in
our Camp know, that the *French* wanted to kill the *Half King;*
and that had its desired Effect. They thereupon offered to accompany our People to go after the *French,* and if they found it
true that he had been killed, or even insulted by them, one of
them would presently carry the News thereof to the *Mingoes,* in
order to incite their Warriors to fall upon them. One of these
young Men was detached towards Mr. *Gist's;* that if he should
not find the *Half King* there, he was to send a Message by a
Delaware.

About eight at Night, received an Express from the *Half
King,* which informed me, that, as he was coming to join us, he
had seen along the Road, the Tracts of two Men, which he had

served in the 1st and 2nd Virginia regiments from 1754 to 1760. For a period
he was GW's aide. When the Ohio Company renewed its activities after the
French and Indian War, Mercer was an active promoter of its interests,
serving as its London agent 1763–70. He was a burgess from Frederick
County from 1761 to 1765, although he missed some sessions when he was on
Ohio Company business in London. He returned to Virginia in the autumn
of 1765 for a brief but stormy career as stamp officer for the colony under the
Stamp Act and went back to London at the end of the year. By 1776 his
personal finances were in serious disorder, and he moved from London to
Paris, although he apparently retained some nebulous connection with the
British government (see JAMES, 78–80).

followed, till he was brought thereby to a low obscure Place; that he was of Opinion the whole Party of the *French* was hidden there. That very Moment I sent out Forty Men, and ordered my Ammunition to be put in a Place of Safety, under a strong Guard to defend it, fearing it to be a Stratagem of the *French* to attack our Camp; and with the rest of my Men, set out in a heavy Rain, and in a Night as dark as Pitch, along a Path scarce broad enough for one Man; we were sometimes fifteen or twenty Minutes out of the Path, before we could come to it again, and so dark, that we would often strike one against another: All Night long we continued our Rout, and the 28th, about Sun-rise, we arrived at the *Indian* Camp, where, after having held a Council with the *Half King,* it was concluded we should fall on them together; so we sent out two Men to discover where they were, as also their Posture, and what Sort of Ground was thereabout; after which, we formed ourselves for an Engagement, marching one after the other, in the *Indian* Manner: We were advanced pretty near to them, as we thought, when they discovered us; whereupon I ordered my Company to fire; mine was supported by that of Mr. *Wager's,*[58] and my Company and his received the whole Fire of the *French,* during the greatest Part of the Action, which only lasted a Quarter of an Hour, before the Enemy was routed.

We killed Mr. *de Jumonville,* the Commander of that Party, as also nine others; we wounded one, and made Twenty-one Prisoners, among whom were M. *la Force,* M. *Drouillon,* and two Cadets.[59] The *Indians* scalped the Dead, and took away the most

[58] Thomas Waggoner held the rank of lieutenant in Jacob Van Braam's company and was slightly wounded during the skirmish with Jumonville.

[59] The site of the French camp is present-day Jumonville's Rocks, three miles north of Summit, Pa. (CLELAND, 80 n.30). The officers were Michel Pépin, called La Force, and Pierre Jacques Drouillon de Macé (b. 1725). Drouillon had been commissioned in 1750 and had served with Marin in constructing forts in the Ohio country. The cadets were Boucherville and Dusablé (PAPIERS CONTRECOEUR, 204 n.3). See also DINWIDDIE, 2:227–28.

The historical controversy over this engagement has continued to recent times. The French claimed that Jumonville's mission was that of an ambassador, similar to GW's own journey to the French forts a few months earlier, and that the English opened fire on the French without warning. Joseph Coulon de Villiers, sieur de Jumonville (1718–1754), had joined the French army in 1738 and served in the French campaign against the Chickasaw in 1739. After further service in Canada he was appointed in 1754 by Contrecoeur to carry an ultimatum to the English forces to leave the Ohio country. According to the French, he was on this peaceful mission when he was attacked by the English early on the morning of 28 May 1754. What was to become the French version of the engagement is contained in a letter from Contrecoeur to Duquesne, 2 June 1754: "I expected Mr. *de Jumonville,*

Part of their Arms, after which we marched on with the Prisoners and the Guard, to the *Indian* Camp, where again I held a Council with the *Half-King;* and there informed him, that the Governor was desirous to see him, and was waiting for him at *Winchester;*

within four Days; the *Indians* have just now informed me, that that Party is taken and defeated; they were Eight in Number, one whereof was Mr. *de Jumonville.* One of that Party, *Monceau* by Name, a *Canadian,* made his Escape, and tells us that they had built themselves Cabbins, in a low Bottom, where they sheltered themselves, as it rained hard. About seven o'Clock the next Morning, they saw themselves surrounded by the *English* on one Side and the *Indians* on the Other. The *English* gave them two Volleys, but the *Indians* did not fire. Mr. *de Jumonville,* by his Interpreter, told them to desist, that he had something to tell them. Upon which they ceased firing. Then Mr. *de Jumonville* ordered the Summons which I had sent them to retire, to be read. . . . The aforesaid *Monceau,* saw all our *Frenchmen* coming up close Mr. *de Jumonville,* whilst they were reading the Summons, so that they were all in Platoons, between the *English* and the *Indians,* during which Time, said *Monceau* made the best of his Way to us, partly by Land through the Woods, and partly along the River *Monaungahela,* in a small Canoe.

"This is all, Sir, I could learn from said *Monceau.* The Misfortune is, that our People were surprized; the *English* had incircled them, and came upon them unseen. . . .

"The *Indians* who were present when the Thing was done, say, that Mr. *de Jumonville* was killed by a Musket-Shot in the Head, whilst they were reading the Summons; and that the *English* would afterwards have killed all our Men, had not the *Indians* who were present, by rushing in between them and the *English,* prevented their Design" (MEMOIR, 69; see also ROBITAILLE; FAY, 73–75).

The British version of the engagement follows closely GW's own account sent to Dinwiddie on 29 May: "I set out with 40 Men before 10, and was from that time till near Sun rise before we reach'd the Indian's Camp, hav'g March'd in [a] small path, a heavy Rain, and a Night as Dark as it is possible to concieve. We were frequently tumbling one over another, and often so lost, that 15 or 20 Minutes' search would not find the path again.

"When we came to the Half King, I council'd with him, and got his assent to go hand in hand and strike the French. Accordingly, himself, Monacatoocha, and a few other Indians set out with us, and when we came to the place where the Tracts were, the Half King sent Two Indians to follow their Tract, and discover their lodgment, which they did abt. half a mile from the Road in a very obscure place surrounded with Rocks. I thereupon in conjunction with the Half King and Monacatoocha, form'd a disposition to attack them on all sides, which we accordingly did and after an Engagement of abt. 15 Minutes we killed 10, wounded one, and took 21 Prisoner's. . . . [The] Officers pretend they were coming on an Embassy, but the absurdity of this pretext is too glaring as your Honour will see by the Instructions and Summons inclos'd. . . . These Enterprising Men were purposely choose out to get intelligence. . . . This with several other Reasons, induc'd all the Officers to believe firmly that they were sent as spys, rather

he answered that, he could not go just then, as his People were in too eminent a Danger from the *French,* whom they had fallen upon; that he must send Messengers to all the allied Nations, in order to invite them to take up the Hatchet. He sent a young *Delaware Indian* to the *Delaware* Nation, and gave him also a *French* Scalp to carry to them. This young Man desired to have a Part of the Presents which were allotted for them, but that the remaining Part might be kept for another Opportunity: He said he would go to his own Family, and to several others, and would wait on them at Mr. *Gist's,* where he desired Men and Horses should be sent ready to bring them up to our Camp. After this I marched on with the Prisoners; *They informed me that they had been sent with a Summons to order me to depart.*[60] A plausible Pretence to discover our Camp, and to obtain the Knowledge of our Forces and our Situation! It was so clear that they were come to reconnoitre what we were, that I admired at their Assurance, when they told me they were come as an Embassy; for their Instructions mentioned that they should get what Knowledge they could of the Roads, Rivers, and of all the Country as far as *Potowmack:* And instead of coming as an Embassador, publickly, and in an open Manner, they came secretly, and sought after the most hidden Retreats, more like Deserters than Embassadors in

than any thing else, and has occasiond my sending them as prisoners, tho' they expected (or at least had some faint hope, of being continued as ambassadors) " (ViHi) .

See also LEDUC. Accounts of the engagement by Adam Stephen appeared in the *Md. Gaz.,* 29 Aug. 1754, the *Pa. Gaz.,* 19 Sept. 1754, and in his "Autobiography" (PPL: Benjamin Rush Papers) . Photostats of a deposition by Pvt. John Shaw are in PPiU.

In a letter to his brother, John Augustine, 31 May 1754, GW wrote a brief description of the engagement and its aftermath, which was printed in the *London Magazine,* Aug. 1754. According to this letter there were 12 Frenchmen killed. "We had but one man killed, and two or three wounded. . . . We expect every hour to be attacked by superior force, but, if they forbear one day longer, we shall be prepared for them. We have already got entrenchments, are about a pallisado which I hope will be finished to-day. . . . I fortunately escaped without any wound, for the right wing, where I stood, was exposed to and received all the enemy's fire. . . . I heard the bullets whistle, and, believe me, there is something charming in the sound" (WRITINGS, 1:70) . It was the latter observation which prompted George II's wry remark: "He would not say so, if he had been used to hear many" (WALPOLE, 1:400) . Another account by GW of the engagement is in his "Biographical Memoranda" (anonymous donor) .

[60] A translation of the summons is in MEMOIR, 68. A copy of the French version found among the Contrecoeur Papers is in PAPIERS CONTRECOEUR, 130–31. Contrecoeur's orders to Jumonville are in MEMOIR, 67.

such Retreat they incamped, and remained hid for whole Days together, and that, no more than five Miles from us: From thence they sent Spies to reconnoitre our Camp; after this was done, they went back two Miles, from whence they sent the two Messengers spoken of in the Instruction, to acquaint M. *de Contrecour* of the Place we were at, and of our Disposition, that he might send his Detachments to inforce the Summons as soon as it should be given.

Besides, an Embassador has princely Attendants; whereas this was only a simple petty *French* Officer; an Embassador has no Need of Spies, his Character being always sacred: And seeing their Intention was so good, why did they tarry two Days, at five Miles distance from us, without acquainting me with the Summons, or, at least, with something that related to the Embassy? That alone would be sufficient to raise the greatest Suspicions, and we ought to do them the Justice to say, that, as they wanted to hide themselves, they could not pick out better Places than they had done.

The Summons was so insolent, and savoured the Gasconnade so much, that if it had been brought openly by two Men, it would have been an immediate Indulgence, to have suffered them to return.

It was the Opinion of the *Half-King* in this Case, that their Intentions were evil, and that it was a pure Pretence; that they never intended to come to us but as Enemies; and if we had been such Fools as to let them go, they would never help us any more to take other *Frenchmen*.

They say they called to us as soon as they had discovered us; which is an absolute Falshood, for I was then marching at the Head of the Company going towards them, and can positively affirm, that, when they first saw us, they ran to their Arms, without calling; as I must have heard them, had they so done.

The 29th, Dispached Ensign *Latour*[61] to the *Half-King*, with about Twenty-five Men, and almost as many Horses; and as I expected some *French* Parties would continually follow that which we had defeated, I sent an Express to Colonel *Fry* for a Reinforcement.

After this the *French* Prisoners desired to speak with me, and asked me in what Manner I looked upon them, whether as the Attendants of an Embassador, or as Prisoners of War: I answered

[61] Ens. James Towers, of Capt. Peter Hog's company, resigned from the Virginia Regiment at the end of 1754.

them that it was in Quality of the Latter, and gave them my Reasons for it, as above.

The 30th, Detached Lieutenant *West,* and Mr. *Spindorph,* to take the Prisoners to *Winchester,* with a Guard of Twenty Men.

Began to raise a Fort with small Pallisadoes, fearing that when the *French* should hear the News of that Defeat, we might be attacked by considerable Forces.

June the 1st, Arrived here an *Indian* Trader with the *Half-King:* They said that when Mr. *de Jumonville* was sent here, another Party had been detached towards the lower Part of the River, in order to take and kill all the *English* they should meet.

We are finishing our Fort.

Towards Night arrived Ensign *Towers,* with the *Half-King,* Queen *Alguipa,* and about Twenty-five or Thirty Families, making in all about Eighty or One Hundred Persons, including Women and Children. The old King being invited to come into our Tents, told me that he had sent *Monakatoocha* to *Log's Town,* with Wampum, and four *French* Scalps, which were to be sent to the *Six Nations,* to the *Wiendots, &c.* to inform them, that they had fallen upon the *French,* and to demand their Assistance.

He also told me he had something to say at the Council, but would stay till the Arrival of the *Shawanese,* whom we expected next Morning.

The 2d, Arrived two or three Families of the *Shawanese:* We had Prayers in the Fort.

The 3d, The *Half-King* assembled the Council, and informed me that he had received a Speech from *Grand-Chaudiere,*[62] in Answer to the one he had sent him.

The 5th, Arrived an *Indian* from the *Ohio,* who had lately been at the *French* Fort: This *Indian* confirms the News of two Traders being taken by the *French,* and sent to *Canada;* he saith they have set up their Pallisadoes, and enclosed their Fort with exceeding large Trees.

There are eight *Indian* Families on this side the River, coming to join us: He met a *Frenchman* who had made his Escape in the Time of M. *de Jumonville's* Action,[63] he was without either Shoes or Stockings, and scarce able to walk; however he let him pass, not knowing we had fallen upon them.

---

[62] Big Kettle (Canajachrera) was a Seneca chief living in the Ohio country. The Pennsylvanians referred to him as Broken Kettle (HANNA, 1:344–46).

[63] Contrecoeur identified the fugitive as a Canadian called Monceau (see note 59).

The 6th, Mr. *Gist* is returned, and acquaints me of the safe Arrival of the *French* Prisoners at *Winchester,* and of the Death of poor Colonel *Fry.*[64]

It gave the Governor great Satisfaction to see the *French* Prisoners safely arrived at *Winchester.*

I am also informed that, Mr. *Montour,*[65] is coming with a Commission to command Two Hundred *Indians.*

Mr. *Gist* met a *French* Deserter, who assured him, that they were only Five Hundred Men, when they took Mr. *Wart's* Fort, that they were now less, having sent Fifteen Men to *Canada,* to acquaint the Governor of their Success: That there were yet Two Hundred Soldiers who only waited for a favourable Opportunity to come and join us.

The 9th, Arrived the last Body of the *Virginia* Regiment, under the Command of Colonel *Must,*[66] and we learnt that the Independent Company of *Carolina* was arrived at *Wills-Creek.*

The 10th, I received the Regiment, and at Night had Notice, that some *French* were advancing towards us; whereupon I sent a Party of *Indians* upon the Scout towards *Gist's,* in order to dis-

[64] Fry had died on 31 May (see note 8). On 4 June Dinwiddie wrote to GW, appointing him to the command of the Virginia Regiment (DINWIDDIE, 1:193–94).

[65] Andrew Montour, a French and Indian fur trader, was the son of Madam Montour, a prominent frontier figure who frequently acted as interpreter, and of Roland Montour, a Seneca. He attended the councils at Logstown in 1750 and 1752 and was at various times Indian agent and interpreter for both Virginia and Pennsylvania. For his service he received a grant of land on Sherman's Creek in Perry County, Pa. Montour served in Braddock's campaign in 1755 and was present at the battle on the Monongahela. He continued his service throughout the French and Indian War and during Pontiac's rebellion in 1763. In 1769 he was given a grant of 300 acres below the mouth of the Monongahela and was probably living there when his death occurred some time before 1775. In 1754 Montour held a commission from Dinwiddie to organize scouts for the English forces. GW had requested 3 June that Montour join him since "he would be of singular use to me here at this present, in conversing with the Indians" (GW to Dinwiddie, 3 June 1754, PHi: Dreer Collection).

[66] George Muse (1720–1790), was born in England, had served in the campaign against Cartegena, and in 1752 had been appointed adjutant of the Middle Neck. He served in the Virginia Regiment as captain, major, and lieutenant colonel. Muse apparently behaved badly at the Fort Necessity engagement during the 1754 campaign. According to Landon Carter, "instead of bringing up the 2d division to make the Attack with the first, he marched them or rather frightened them back into the trenches" (CARTER [3], 1:110). His name was specifically omitted from the list of officers thanked by the House of Burgesses after the campaign (H.B.J., 1752–58, 198).

cover them, and to know their Number: Just before Night we had an Alarm, but it proved false.

The 12th, Returned two of the Men, whom we had sent out Yesterday upon the Scout; they discovered a small Party of *French;* the others went on as far as *Stuart's.*[67] Upon this Advice, I thought it necessary to march with the major Part of the Regiment, to find out those Ninety Men, of whom we had Intelligence. Accordingly I gave Orders to Colonel *Must,* to put away all our Baggage and Ammunition, and to place them in the Fort, and set a good Guard there till my Return; after which I marched at the Head of One Hundred and Thirty Men, and about Thirty *Indians;* but at the Distance of half a Mile, I met the other *Indians,* who told me, there were only nine Deserters; whereupon I sent Mr. *Montour,* with some few *Indians,* in order to bring them safe to me; I caused them to be drest, and they confirmed us in our Opinion, of the Intention of M. *de Jumonville's* Party; that more than One Hundred Soldiers were only waiting for a favourable Opportunity to come and join us; that M. *de Contrecour* expected a Reinforcement of Four Hundred Men; that the Fort was compleated; and its Artillery a shelter to its Front and Gates; that there was a double Pallisadoe next to the Water; that they have only eight small Pieces of Cannon; and know what Number of Men we are.

They also informed us, that the *Delaware* and *Shawanese* had taken up the Hatchet against us; whereupon, resolved to invite those two Nations to come to a Council at Mr. *Gist's.* Sent for that Purpose Messengers and Wampum.

The 13th, Perswaded the Deserters to write the following Letter, to those of their Companions who had an Inclination to Desert.[68]

(It is not in the Journal.)

The 15th, Set about clearing the Roads.

[67] Stewart's Crossing was on the Youghiogheny River below present-day Connellsville in Fayette County, Pa.

[68] This letter was omitted from the published diary, and no copy has been found. However, GW apparently dispatched a Delaware carrying the letter into Contrecoeur's headquarters at the Forks. On 8 Sept. Duquesne wrote to Contrecoeur concerning GW's action: "You see how treacherous he is, having expected he could, in trusting our nine vile deserters, make your garrison revolt, by which means they flattered themselves they could take the fort. Inform yourself, without seeming to do so, if this Delaware, who is said to have transmitted the letter to the Soldiers of your garrison, again frequents the fort" (PAPIERS CONTRECOEUR, 249–53).

16th, Set out for *Red-Stone-Creek,* and were extremely per-plexed, our Waggons breaking very often.

17th, Dispatched an Express to the *Half-King,* in order to perswade him to send a Message to the *Loups* [Delawares]; which he did.

18th, Arrived eight *Mingoes* from *Loiston* [Logstown], who at their Arrival told me of a Commission they had, and that a Coun-cil must be held. When we assembled, they told us very shortly, that they had often desired to see their Brethren out in the Field with Forces, and begged us not to take it amiss, that they were amongst the *French,* and that they complied with some of their Customs; notwithstanding which they were naturally inclined to fall upon them, and other Words to that Purport: After which they said, they had brought a Speech with them; and desired to deliver it with Speed. These, and other Discourses to the same Purpose, made us suspect that their Intentions towards us were evil; wherefore I delayed giving them Audience until the Ar-rival of the *Half-King,* and desired also the *Delawares* to have Patience till then, as I only waited their Arrival to hold a Coun-cil, which I expected would be that same Day. After the eight *Mingoes* had conferred a while together, they sent me some Strings of Wampum, desiring me to excuse their insisting on the Delivery of their Speech so speedily, that they now perceived it necessary to wait the Arrival of the *Half King.*

When the *Half-King* arrived, I consented to give them Au-dience.

A Council was held in the Camp for that Purpose, where the *Half-King,* and several of the *Six Nations, Loups* and *Shawanese,* to the Number of Forty, were present.

The Speaker of the Six-Nations *directed the following Speech to the Governor of* Virginia.

Brethren,

WE *your Brothers of the* Six Nations, *are now come to acquaint you, that we have been informed you threaten to destroy entirely all your Brethren the* Indians, *who will not join you on the Road; wherefore we who keep in our own Towns, expect every Day to be cut in Pieces by you. We would desire to know from your Mouth, if there be any Truth in that Information, and that you would not look upon it as preposterous, that we are come to enquire into it, since you very well know, that bad News com-monly makes a deeper Impression upon us than good; that we may be fully satisfied by your Answers of the Truth thereof, we give you this Belt of* Wampum.

We know the French *will ask us at our Return, of what Number our Brethren are whom we went to see? Therefore we desire you, by this Belt, to let us know it, as also the Number of those whom you expect, and at what Time you expect them, and when you reckon to attack the* French, *that we may give Notice thereof to our Town, and know also, what we shall have to tell the* French.

ANSWER.

Brethren,

WE are very glad to see you, and sorry that such Reports disquiet you: The *English* do not intend to hurt you, or any of your Allies; this News, we know, must have been forged by the French, who are constantly treacherous, asserting the greatest Falshoods whenever they think they will turn out to their Advantage; they speak well, promise fine Things, but all from the Lips outward; whilst their Heart is corrupted and full of venomous Poison. You have been their Children, and they would have done every Thing for you, but they no sooner thought themselves strong enough, than they returned to their natural Pride, and drove you off from your Lands, declaring you had no Right on the *Ohio.* The *English,* your real Friends, are too generous, to think of using the *Six Nations,* their faithful Allies, in like Manner; when you made your Address to the Governors of *Virginia* and *Pennsylvania,* they (at your repeated Request) sent *an Army to maintain your Rights;* to put you in the Possession of your Lands, and to take Care of your Wives and Children, to dispossess the *French,* to support your Prerogatives, and to make that whole Country sure to you; for those very Ends are the *English* Arms actually employed; it is for the Safety of your Wives and your Children that we fight; and as this is the only Motive of our Conduct, we cannot reasonably doubt of being joined by the remaining Part of your Forces, to oppose the common Enemy.

Those that will not join us, shall be answerable, for whatever may be the Consequence; we only desire you, Brethren, to chuse that Side which shall seem most agreeable to them.

The *Indians* of the *Six Nations* are those, who have the most Interest in this War; for them it is that we fight; and it would greatly trouble me to do them the least Hurt: We have engaged in this War, in order to assist and protect you; our Arms are open to receive you, and our Hands ready to nourish your Families during the Course of this War. The Governor of *Virginia* has often desired they might be sent to him, that he might see them in Person, nourish and cloath them according to their own Desire; but as you could not be determined to send them to him, we are ready to share in a friendly Manner, all our Provisions with you, and shall take such Measures, and give such Orders, that enough shall be brought to maintain your Wives and Children. Such a Conduct will evidently prove how much more the *English* love and esteem their Allies the *Six Nations,* than the *French* do; as we have drawn the Sword in your Cause, and in your Defence, delay not one Moment, be no more in Suspence, but put your Wives and Children under our Protection; and they shall find Plenty of Provisions; in the mean while, set your young Men and your Warriors to sharpen their Hatchets, in order to join and unite with us vigorously in our Battles.

The Present, my Brethren, which I offer you, is not so considerable as I could wish, but I expect in a short Time a Quantity of Goods, which are to be at my Disposal, in order to reward those who shall have shewn themselves brave and active on this Occasion; however, I shall recompense them most generously.

Be of good Courage, my Brethren, deliver your Country, and make it sure to your Children; let me know the Thoughts of your Hearts on this Affair, that I may give an Account of your Sentiments to your great Friend and Brother the Governor of *Virginia*. In order to assure you of my Sincerity and Esteem, I present you this Belt.

The 20th, The Council still continued.

When the *Delawares* knew that they were suspected of being in the *French* Interest, they demanded the Reason why they had been sent for, and what they should tell the *French* at their Return.

I answered them, it was to let them know, that we were come at their reiterated requests to assist them with Sword in Hand; that we intended to put them in the Possession of those Lands which the *French* had taken from them.

And as they had often demanded our Assistance, in Quality of our ancient and faithful Allies, I invited them to come and place themselves under our Protection, together with the Women and Children.

Whereupon the *Indian* Speaker stretched out his Blanket on the Floor, and laid several Belts and Strings of Wampum thereon, in the same order he had received them from the *French*. This done, he repeated the Speeches of M. *de Contrecour;* after which, the *Delaware* Speaker directed to me the following Speech.

Brethren,
THE *Governors of* Virginia *and* Pennsylvania; *We your Brethren, the* Delawares *remember perfectly well the Treaty of* Loiston, *where you and your Uncles the* Six-Nations, *considering the bad Situation we were in, for want of a Man to be our Leader, you then gave us a King,*[69] *and told us, he should transact all our publick Affairs between you and us; you gave us a Charge, not to listen to every vain Report that might be spread, but to consult ourselves, and to do, what would seem to us, to be right: We assure you, that we have given no Credit to any of those Reports, nor ever shall; but will be guided by you, our Brethren; and by our Uncles the* Six-Nations: *And will do, on all Occasions, what is just and right, taking Advice from you alone. To assure you of the Desire we have to fulfill our Engagements with you, we present you this Belt.*

After which they made the following Discourse, to the *Six-Nations.*

Uncles, Thirteen Days are now past since we have received this Belt from the Onondago *Council; I do not doubt your knowing it: They exhorted us to remember old Times, when they cloathed us with a Robe reaching down to our Heels; afterwards told us, to raise it up to our Knees, and there to make it very fast, and come to them at the Head of* Susquehanna, *where they had provided a Place for us to live; that they had also sent a Speech to those of our Nation, who live near the* Minisinks, *inviting them to go to the Place by them appointed, that they might live with us: They also sent us a Speech, to give us Notice that the* English *and* French *were upon the Point of coming to an Engagement on the River* Ohio, *and exhorted us to do nothing in that Juncture, but what was reasonable, and what they would tell us themselves.* Lastly, *They recommended to us, to keep fast Hold of the Chain of Friendship, which has so long subsisted between us and them; and our Brethren the* English. A Belt.

Then the *Delawares* spoke to the *Shawanese* as follows:

[69] At the Logstown council in 1752, Shingas had been made head chief of the Delaware Nation by the Half-King (see SIPE, 287–88). For Shingas, see 25 Nov. 1753, n.27.

"Grand Sons, by this Belt, we take you between our Arms, and fetch you away from the Ohio, *where you now are, to carry you amongst us, that you may live where we live, and there live in Peace and Quiet.*["]

The Council after this was adjourned to the next Morning.

The 21st, Met very early, and I spoke first to the *Delawares* in the following Manner.

"Brethren,

BY your open and generous Conduct on this Occasion, You have made yourselves dearer to us than ever; we return you our Thanks, that you did not go to *Venango,* when the *French* first invited you there; their treating you in such childish Manner, as we perceive they do, raises in us a just and strong Resentment: They call you their Children, and speak to you, as if you in reality were Children, and had no more Understanding than such.

Consider well my Brethren, and compare all their Discourse, and you will find that all it tends to do, is to tell you, I am going to open your Eyes, to unstop your Ears, and such like Words to no Purpose, only proper to amuse Children. You also observe Brethren, that if they deliver a Speech, or make a Promise, and confirm it by a Belt, they imagine it binds them no longer than they think it consistent with their Interest to stand to it. They have given one Example of it; and I will make you observe it, in the Jump which they say they have made over the Boundaries, which you have set them; which ought to stir you up my Brethren, to a just Anger, and cause you to embrace the favourable Opportunity that we offer You, as we are come, at your Request, to assist you, and by Means of which, you may make them Jump back again, with more Speed than they advanced.

A String of Wampum.

The *French* are continually telling you, not to give Heed to the ill Reports that are told you concerning them who are your Fathers. If they did not know in their very Souls, how richly they deserve it on your Account, why should they suspect being accused? Why should they forewarn you of it, in order to hinder you from believing what is told you concerning them? With Regard to what they tell you of us, our Conduct alone will answer in our Behalf: Examine the Truth yourselves; you know the Roads leading to our Habitations, you have lived amongst us, you can speak our Language; but in order to justify ourselves from whatever might be said against us, and assure you of our brotherly Love; we once more invite your old Men, your Wives and your Children, to take Sanctuary under our Protection, and between our Arms, in order to be plentifully fed, whilst your Warriors and young Men join with ours, and espouse together the common Cause.

A String of Wampum.

Brethren, we thank you with all our Hearts, for having declared unto us, your Resolution of accomplishing the Engagements which you have entered into, at the Treaty of *Loiston* [Logstown], and we can do no otherwise than praise your generous Conduct with Regard to your Grand Sons the *Shawanese;* it gives us infinite Pleasure.

We are greatly obliged to the Council given you by *Onondago,* charging you to hold fast the Chain of Friendship by which we are bound; I dare say, that had he known, how nearly you are interested in this War, or that it is for the Love of you, and at your Request, we have taken up Arms, he would have ordered you to DECLARE and to act immediately against the COMMON ENEMY of the *Six Nations.* In order to assure you of my Affection, and to confirm the Truth of what I have said, I present you these

Two great Strings."

After this, the Council broke up, and those treacherous Devils, who had been sent by the *French* as Spies, returned, though not without some Tale ready prepared to amuse the *French,* which may be of Service to make our own Designs succeed.

As they had told me there were Sixteen Hundred *French,* and Seven Hundred *Indians* on their March, to reinforce those at the Garrison, I perswaded the *Half King* to send three of his Men to inquire into the Truth of it; though I imagined this News to be only Soldiers Discourse; these *Indians* were accordingly sent in a secret Manner, before the Council broke up, and had Orders to go to the Fort, and get what Information they could from all the *Indians* they should meet, and if there was any News worth while, one of them should return, and the other two continue their Rout as far as *Venango,* and about the *Lake,* in order to obtain a perfect Knowledge of every Thing.

I also perswaded King *Shingas,* to send out Rangers towards the River, to bring us News, in Case any *French* should come; I gave him also a Letter, which he was to send back again by an Express, to prevent my being imposed upon by a false Alarm.

Though King *Shingas,* and others of the *Delawares,* could not be persuaded to retire to our Camp with their Families, through the Fear they were in of *Onondago's* Council, they nevertheless gave us strong Assurances of their Assistance, and directed us in what Manner to act, in order to obtain our Desire: the Method was this; we were to prepare a great War-Belt, to invite all those Warriors who would receive it, to act independantly from their King and Council; and King *Shingas* promised to take privately the most subtil Methods to make the Affair succeed, though he did not dare to do it openly.

The very Day the Council broke up, I perswaded *Kaque-huston*,[70] a trusty *Delaware,* to carry that Letter to the Fort which the *French* Deserters had written to their Comrades, and gave him Instructions how he should behave in his Observations, upon several Articles of which I had spoken to him; for I am certain the Fort may be surprized, as the *French* are encamped outside, and cannot keep a strict Guard, by Reason of the Works they are about.

I also perswaded *George,*[71] another trusty *Delaware,* to go and take a View of the Fort, a little after *Kaquehuston,* and gave him proper Instructions recommending him particularly to return with Speed, that we might have fresh News.

Presently after the Council was over, notwithstanding all that Mr. *Montour* could do to disswade them, the *Delawares,* as also the *Half-King,* and all the other *Indians,* returned to the Great Meadows; but though we had lost them, I still had Spies of our own People, to prevent being surprised.

As it had been told me, that if I sent a Belt of *Wampum* and a Speech, that might bring us back both the *Half-King* and his young Men; accordingly I sent the following Speech by Mr. *Croghan.*[72]

[70] This is probably a reference to Kekeuscung, "the healer," who later became a Delaware chief. Like most of his tribe, he eventually supported the French. See n. 68.

[71] Delaware George later became a chief and went over to the French.

[72] George Croghan (d. 1782) was probably the best-known Indian trader on the Pennsylvania frontier. He was born in Ireland and emigrated to Pennsylvania around 1741, settling near Carlisle. In the years before the French and Indian War he established a network of trading posts on the frontier and became Pennsylvania's chief agent to the Indians. During the war he served with Washington and Braddock in their campaigns and in 1756 was appointed deputy superintendent of Indian affairs by Sir William Johnson. Like most of the traders, his business had been destroyed by the war, and after 1763 he turned his attention to western lands. From Croghan Hall, his estate near Pittsburgh, where he had moved in 1758, he engaged in extensive speculation in Ohio and Illinois lands, participating in the Illinois Company and the Grand Ohio Company. The Revolution wrecked most of these western land schemes, and Croghan died near Philadelphia in comparative poverty.

'Tis but lately since we were assembled together; we were sent here by your Brother the Governor of Virginia, *at your own Request, in Order to succour you, and fight for your Cause; wherefore my Brethren, I must require that you and your young Men come to join and encamp with us, that we may be ready to receive our Brother* Monacotocha, *whom I daily expect: That this Request may have its desired Effect, and make a suitable Impression upon your Minds, I present you with this String of* Wampum.

As those *Indians,* who were Spies sent by the *French,* were very inquisitive, and asked us many Questions in order to know by what Way we proposed to go to the Fort, and what Time we expected to arrive there; I left off working any further at the Road, and told them we intended to keep on across the Woods as far as the Fort, falling the Trees, *&c.* That we were waiting here for the Reinforcement which was coming to us, our Artillery, and our Waggons to accompany us there; but, as soon as they were gone, I set about marking out and clearing a Road towards *Red-Stone.*

The 25th, Towards Night came three Men from the Great Meadows, amongst whom was the Son of Queen *Aliguipa.*[73]

He brought me a Letter from Mr. *Croghan,*[74] informing me what Pains he was at to perswade any *Indians* to come to us; that the *Half-King* was inclined, and was preparing to join us, but had received a Blow which was a Hindrance to it. I thought it proper to send Captain *Montour* to *Fort-Necessity,* in order to try if he could, possibly, gain the *Indians* to come to us.

The 26th, Arrived an *Indian,* bringing News that *Monacotoocha,* had burnt his Village (*Loiston*) and was gone by Water with his People to *Red-Stone,* and may be expected there in two Days. This *Indian* passed close by the Fort, and assures us, that the *French* had received no Reinforcement, except a small Number of *Indians,* who had killed, as he said, two or three of the *Delawares.* I did not fail to relate that Piece of News to the *Indians* in its proper Colours, and particularly to two of the *Delawares* who are here.

The 27th, Detached Captain *Lewis,*[75] Lieutenant *Wagghener,*

[73] This was probably Canachquasy, also known as Captain New Castle (d. 1756), an important agent of the Pennsylvania government in its relations with the Indians (see SIPE, 258–66).

[74] Letter from George Croghan not found.

[75] Andrew Lewis (1720–1781) was a native of Ulster, Ireland, came to Virginia in 1732, and settled in what is now Augusta County. He served in

and Ensign *Mercer*,[76] two Serjeants, two Corporals, one Drummer, and Sixty Men, in order to endeavour to clear a Road, to the Mouth of *Red-Stone-Creek* on *Monaungahela*.

---

the Augusta militia, received a commission as captain in the Virginia Regiment in 1754, and was present at the capitulation of Fort Necessity. During the French and Indian War he served in Braddock's campaign and as commissioner to the Cherokee and to the Six Nations. Lewis was captured by the French during James Grant's ill-fated attack on Fort Duquesne in Sept. 1758 and was taken to Montreal. He had settled near present-day Salem, Va., and after the war served as justice of the peace for the newly formed Botetourt County. He represented the county in the House of Burgesses and participated in the Virginia conventions of Mar. and Dec. 1775. In 1774 he led the Virginia forces that defeated the Indians under Cornstalk at the Battle of Point Pleasant. During the Revolution he held the rank of brigadier general and took part in the campaign against Dunmore. He resigned his commission in 1777 but continued to maintain an active interest in military affairs.

[76] John Fenton Mercer (1735–1756), a son of John Mercer (1704–1768), served successively as ensign, lieutenant, and captain in the Virginia Regiment. He was killed by Indians while on scouting duty for GW in Apr. 1756.

Washington the Planter and Farmer

1760

[January]

January 1 Tuesday.   Visited my Plantations and receivd an Instance of Mr. French's great Love of Money in disappointing me of some Pork because the price had risen to 22/6 after he had engagd to let me have it at 20/.

Calld at Mr. Possey's in my way home and desird him to engage me 100 Barl. of Corn upon the best terms he coud in Maryland.

And found Mrs. Washington upon my arrival broke out with the Meazles.

Daniel French (1733–1771), a wealthy Fairfax County planter, lived at Rose Hill, about five miles west of Alexandria. Although his main plantation lay in the vicinity of his house, he also owned a plantation on Dogue Creek a short distance west of Mount Vernon. At this time it contained about 416 acres, but with the purchase of another tract of land later this year, he would own a total of about 552 acres in the Mount Vernon area (see entry for 6 Mar. 1760; will of French, 20 May 1771, Fairfax County Wills, Book C-1, 134–36, Vi Microfilm). French was a Fairfax County justice 1743–71 and a vestryman of Truro Parish 1744–65 and of Fairfax Parish 1765–71.

John Posey, whose home, Rover's Delight, stood near the Potomac River about a mile southwest of Mount Vernon, was a regular in GW's social circle in the 1760s, often joining him in fox hunts. Posey farmed a plantation of about 400 acres and operated a public ferry from a landing near his house across the Potomac to Maryland, where he had many personal contacts.

Mrs. Washington, born Martha Dandridge (1731–1802), first married (1749) Daniel Parke Custis (1711–1757), of the White House, New Kent County. They had two children who survived infancy, John Parke Custis (1754–1781) and Martha Parke Custis (1756–1773). Following Martha's wedding to GW 6 Jan. 1759 in her home county of New Kent, GW took Martha and the two Custis children to their new home at Mount Vernon (see FREEMAN, 3:1–2, 13).

Jany. 2d. Wednesy.   Mrs. Barnes who came to visit Mrs. Washington yesterday returnd home in my Chariot the Weather being too bad to Travel in an open Carriage—which together with Mrs. Washington's Indisposition confind me to the House and gave me an oppertunity of Posting my Books and putting them in good Order.

Fearing a disappointment elsewhere in Pork I was fein to take Mr. French upon his own terms & engagd them to be delivd. at my House on Monday next.

The Custis children, Jacky and Patsy, in a painting by John Wollaston. (Washington and Lee University, Washington-Custis-Lee Collection)

Sarah Barnes was the daughter of Col. William Ball of Northampton County and thus a distant relation to GW. After the death in 1743 of her first husband, Dennis McCarty, of Prince William County, she married Abraham (Abram) Barnes, of Truro Parish, Fairfax County.

PORK: After GW resigned Dec. 1758 from the command of the Virginia troops in the French and Indian War, he retired to Mount Vernon and

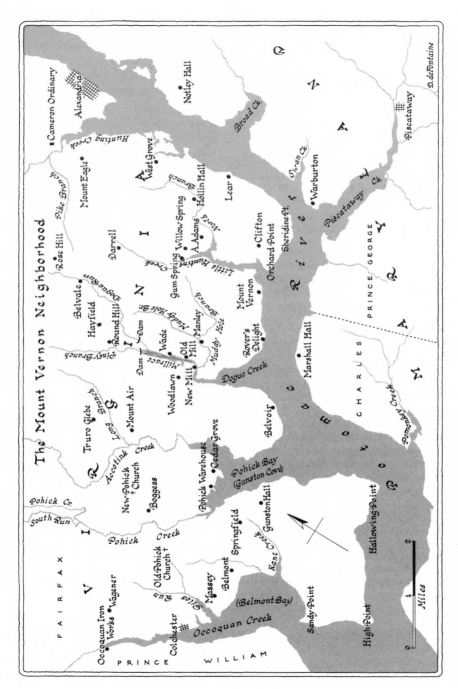

The Mount Vernon Neighborhood

Sarah Ball McCarty Barnes, one of many visitors to Mount Vernon in 1760. (Smithsonian Institution photo no. 75–1942)

began working to make it a paying plantation. On 27 April 1763 he wrote to Robert Stewart, one of his old officers: "when I retired from the Publick Service of this Colony . . . I had Provision's of all kinds to buy for the first two or three years; and my Plantation to stock, in short, with every thing" (DLC:GW) .

Thursday Jany. 3d.   The Weather continuing Bad & the same causes subsisting I confind myself to the House.

Morris who went to work Yesterday caught cold, and was laid up bad again—and several of the Family were taken with the Measles, but no bad Symptoms seemd to attend any of them.

Hauled the Sein and got some fish, but was near being disappointd of my Boat by means of an Oyste⟨r⟩ Man who had lain at my Landing and plagud me a good deal by his disorderly behaviour.

MORRIS: Because Mrs. Washington's first husband died without a will, his property was divided according to English common law, which allowed the widow one-third of the property for her life only (called her right of dower), after which it would revert to their children or their descendants (BLACK [2], 580–81) . Upon her marriage to GW, all of Martha's property came under his control during her lifetime, including her share of the slaves from the Custis estate. One of her "dower slaves" that was transferred to Mount Vernon by GW was Morris (born c.1730), who worked as a carpenter 1760–63, a tradesman 1764–65, and overseer of GW's Dogue Run plantation 1766–94. Morris's wife was Hannah, who, with a child, had been purchased by GW from William Cloptan 16 June 1759 for £80 (LEDGER A, 56). Morris and

Hannah were married c.1765 when both were transferred to the Dogue Run plantation. Like most large planters, GW referred to his plantation workers collectively either as his "people" or his "family."

Friday Jany. 4th. The Weather continud Drisling and Warm, and I kept the House all day. Mrs. Washington seemg. to be very ill ⟨I⟩ wrote to Mr. Green this afternoon desiring his Company to visit her in the Morng.

Rev. Charles Green (c.1710–1765) was the first permanent rector of Truro Parish, recommended to that post in 1736 by GW's father. He also practiced medicine. "Ministers were frequently the only ones who could 'read medicine,' since before 1700 the greater part of the literature was in Latin. Clerical practice survived incidentally in rural areas well into the eighteenth century" (SHRYOCK [1], 280).

Saturday Jany. 5th. Mrs. Washington appeard to be something better. Mr. Green however came to see her abt. 11 Oclock and in an hour Mrs. Fairfax arrivd. Mr. Green prescribd the needful and just as we were going to Dinnr Captn. Walter Stuart appeard with Doctr. Laurie.

The Evening being very cold, and the wind high Mrs. Fairfax went home in the Chariot & soon afterwards Mulatto Jack arrivd from Fredk. with 4 Beeves.

Mrs. Fairfax is Sarah (Sally) Cary Fairfax (c. 1730–1811), wife of George William Fairfax. Walter Stuart (Stewart) served with GW in the Virginia Regiment and in 1754 was wounded in Braddock's Defeat. At Grant's Defeat in 1758, where he was again wounded, Stuart "distinguished himself greatly. . . . He was left in the Field, but made his escape afterwards" (GW to Francis Fauquier, 25 Sept. 1758, DLC:GW). Dr. James Laurie (Lowrie), a physician of Alexandria, may have come that day to tend those in GW's "family" who were down with measles.

Mulatto Jack, a dower Negro from the Custis estate, was regularly used by GW as a courier, often to and from his Bullskin plantation in the Shenandoah Valley, which at this time was part of Frederick County (later Berkeley County and now Jefferson County, W. Va.; see entry for 19 Jan. 1760).

Sunday Jany. 6th. The Chariot not returng. time enought from Colo. Fairfax's we were prevented from Church.

Mrs. Washington was a good deal better today, but the Oyster Man still continuing his Disorderly behaviour at my Landing I was obligd in the most preemptory manner to order him and his Compy. away which he did not Incline to obey till next morning.

In colonial Virginia the established church—paid for by an annual levy on all tithables—was the Anglican Church of England. By 1760 there were a number of Methodists, Baptists, Presbyterians, Quakers, and German Pietists in Virginia; but GW, like the majority of Virginians, still adhered to the

Mount Vernon was named for Adm. Edward Vernon, under whom Lawrence Washington had served. (Mount Vernon Ladies' Association of the Union)

established church. Each Anglican parish was administered by a 12-man vestry elected by the voters upon the creation of the new parish by the Virginia Assembly. Subsequent vacancies were filled by the vestry itself, which had broad civil and religious duties within the parish boundaries and enjoyed great power in the choice of rector. The parish boundaries did not always follow county lines; while populous counties were served by two or even three parishes, more thinly settled counties often had but one. Mount Vernon was in Truro Parish, which in 1760 served all but the upper edge of Fairfax County. In the 1760s "Church" for GW was the old wooden Pohick Church, built sometime before 1724 in Mason's Neck, two miles up the road from Colchester toward Alexandria and about a seven-mile ride from Mount Vernon. Originally called Occoquan Church, it became the main church for Truro Parish when that parish was formed in 1732 and was renamed Pohick Church the following year (see HARRISON [1], 285–86; SLAUGHTER [1], 5; FREEMAN, 1:136–37).

Monday Jany. 7th.   Accompanied Mrs. Bassett to Alexandria and engagd a Keg of Butter of Mr. Kirkpatrick being quite out of that Article.

Wrote from thence to Doctr. Craik to endeavour if possible to engage me a Gardener from the Regiment and returnd in the dusk of the Evening.

Mrs. Bassett, the former Anna Maria Dandridge (1739–1777), younger sister of Mrs. Washington, in 1757 married Burwell Bassett, of Eltham, New Kent County, by whom she had seven children. Mr. Kirkpatrick was one of two brothers, John or Thomas, merchants and partners in Alexandria. John was GW's personal secretary, 1755–57. The keg of butter weighed 71 pounds and cost GW £2 13s. 3d., which he paid on 25 Jan. (LEDGER A, 63).

A GARDENER FROM THE REGIMENT: Dr. Craik did not find a gardener, so GW asked Capt. Robert Stewart of the Virginia Regiment, then stationed at Winchester, to locate one and then find a replacement for him in the regiment. Stewart quickly found a replacement, but the chosen gardener—whose surname was Allen or Allan—balked at the terms. An appeal went

A portrait of Sally Cary Fairfax, done
by Duncan Smith from a copy of the
lost original by an unknown artist.
(Mrs. Charles Baird, Jr.)

out to the commandant at Pittsburgh—to no avail. Finally, in Dec. 1762,
Allen went to Mount Vernon to be interviewed for the gardener's position.
Apparently he did not take it.

Tuesday Jany. 8.   Directed an Indictment to be formd by Mr.
Johnston against Jno. Ballendine for a fraud in some Iron he sold
me.

Got a little Butter from Mr. Dalton and wrote to Colo. West
for Pork.

In the Evening 8 of Mr. French's Hogs from his Ravensworth
Quarter came down one being lost on the way as the others might
as well have been for their goodness.

Nothing but the disappointments in this Article of Pork which
he himself had causd and my necessities coud possibly have
obligd me to take them.

Carpenter Sam was taken with the Meazles.

John Ballendine (d. 1782) of Prince William County, an enthusiastic
promoter, builder, and operator of a series of mills, ironworks, and canals,
had moved in 1755 to a site on Occoquan Creek about two miles above Colchester and now operated "an iron furnace, a forge, two saw mills, and a
bolting mill" there (BURNABY, 66). The "fraud" was a shortage in weight of
an iron shipment from the Occoquan works to Mount Vernon. On 19 Dec.
1759 GW had paid Ballendine £44 12s. 3d. for 2 tons of bar iron, but he
received only 3,556 pounds, leaving a balance of £8 5s. 7d. charged against
Ballendine (LEDGER A, 69). GW wished to recover that sum in iron or cash

and at the same time to teach Ballendine a lesson, but George Johnston (d. 1766) of Alexandria and Belvale, a distinguished lawyer and Fairfax County burgess, today told him that a suit in the county court would be expensive and that a conviction would have little, if any, effect on Ballendine, because he had been previously found guilty and punished severely in a similar case without producing any change in his behavior (Johnston to GW, 8 Jan. 1760, DLC:GW). Although Ballendine wrote GW 18 Nov. 1760, expressing a desire to send iron to make up the deficiency and thus to clear his name of all suspicion of dishonesty, the dispute was never settled (DLC: GW). GW continued to charge £8 5s. 7d. against Ballendine in his ledgers until about 1773, when he wrote the sum off as "lost" (LEDGER B, 7).

John Dalton (d. 1777), a merchant in Alexandria and one of the founders of that town, had supplied GW during the French and Indian War. Col. John West (d. 1777), uncle of John West, Jr., lived on the south side of Hunting Creek near the Potomac River, his house being about two miles by water and four by road from Alexandria (*Va. Gaz.*, P&D, 24 Nov. 1774). He had succeeded his brother Hugh West as Fairfax County burgess soon after Hugh's death in 1754 and served in the house until 1774 (H.B.J., 1752–55, 197). He was a Fairfax County justice 1745–77 and a vestryman 1744–65 for Truro Parish, and after 1765, for Fairfax Parish. He married twice, having children both by his first wife, Mary, and his second wife, Margaret Pearson (John West's will, 27 Mar. 1776, Fairfax County Wills, Book D-1, 25–33, Vi Microfilm; BROCKETT, 104). Because John West, Jr., lived in the same general neighborhood and died only a few months before his uncle did, the two men are often confused with one another. In the diaries, GW distinguishes between them by referring to the elder John West as colonel—apparently a militia title—and to his nephew as Mr. or Capt. John West. The title of captain may also have been a militia designation or may have derived from an earlier involvement in merchant shipping (*Va. Gaz.* 5 Mar. 1752; LEDGER A, 135).

Ravensworth was originally a patent for 21,996 acres of land granted to William Fitzhugh 1 Oct. 1694 (Northern Neck Deeds and Grants, Book 2, 14, Vi Microfilm). Lying west of Alexandria and north of Mount Vernon, this large area was now divided into several plantations and quarters belonging to various planters (see map of GW's lands in MVAR, 1965, 25).

Sam, who was one of GW's slave carpenters, recovered.

Wednesday. Jany. 9. Killd and dressd Mr. French's Hogs which weighd 751 lbs. neat.

Colo. West leaving me in doubt about his Pork yesterday obligd me to send to him again to day, and now no definitive answr was receivd—he purposing to send his Overseer down tomorrow to agree abt. it.

Colo. Bassetts Abram arrivd with Letters from his Master appointing Port Royal, & Monday next as a time and place to meet him. He brought some things from me that Lay in Mr. Norton's Ware house in York Town.

Burwell Bassett (1734–1793), husband of Mrs. Washington's sister Anna Maria, lived at Eltham on the Pamunkey River, where the Washingtons usually stayed when visiting Williamsburg. The two families were close, particularly before the death of Mrs. Bassett in 1777. Port Royal, a small port town on the Rappahannock River, was a convenient rendezvous almost equidistant between Eltham and Mount Vernon. The warehouse at Yorktown, at the mouth of the York River, was being run in 1760 by John Norton, of the London tobacco firm of Flowerdewe & Norton. As recently as 30 Nov. 1759 GW had complained in a letter (DLC:GW) to his London agent Robert Cary that "it is almost as much trouble and expence getting Goods from any of the Rivers round to Potomack as the Original Charges of Shipping them amounts to."

Thursday Jany. 10th.   Accompanied Mrs. Bassett in a Visit to Belvoir.

She this day determind on setting of for Port Royal on Saturday.

Colo. West wrote me word that he had engag'd his Pork.

Killd the Beeves that Jack brought down two of which were tolerable good.

Belvoir, located on a bluff overlooking the Potomac on the next "neck" downriver from Mount Vernon, was the first seat of the Fairfax family of Virginia, built around 1741 by William Fairfax (1691–1757), cousin and agent of Thomas, Lord Fairfax. GW first visited there while in his early teens, during stays with his brother Lawrence at Mount Vernon. It was then that the long friendship began between GW and William Fairfax's son George William. From 1757 to 1773, when Belvoir was the permanent home of George William and Sarah Cary Fairfax, the Washingtons often visited it. Years later, in reflecting to George William on his days at Belvoir, GW observed that "the happiest days of my life had been spent there" (27 Feb. 1785, DLC:GW). For the house itself, see WATERMAN, 329–34.

Friday Jany. 11th.   Deliverd Rd. Stephens two Hogs in part of his Years Provisions weight

$$
\begin{array}{r}
69 \\
90 \\
\hline
159.
\end{array}
$$

He had one before of 100 lbs. weight. Two Hogs were also reservd for Foster of the following weights

$$
\begin{array}{r}
90 \\
83 \\
\hline
173
\end{array}
$$

which with

$$
\begin{array}{r}
100 \\
100 \\
97 \\
90 \\
\hline
387
\end{array}
$$

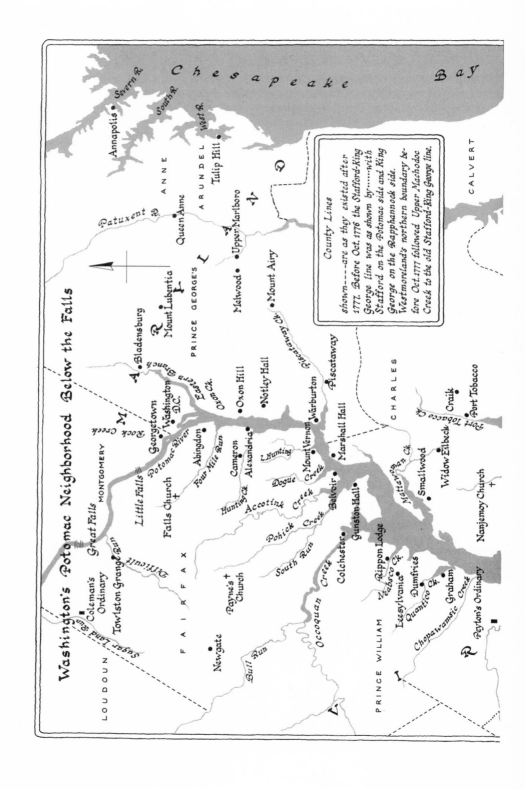

Washington's Potomac Neighborhood Below the Falls

Chesapeake Bay

Annapolis
Severn R.
South R.
West R.
Tulip Hill

ANNE ARUNDEL

CALVERT

Patuxent R.

Queen Anne

Upper Marlboro
Mount Airy
Melwood

PRINCE GEORGE'S

Mount Lubentia
Bladensburg

Eastern Branch

Washington D.C.
Georgetown

Oxon Ck.
Oxon Hill
Notley Hall
Warburton
Piscataway Ck.
Piscataway

Rock Creek
MONTGOMERY

Abingdon
Four Mile Run
Camgron
Alexandria
L. Hunting
Mount Vernon
Marshall Hall

Potomac River

Falls Church
Little Falls
Great Falls

Coleman's Ordinary
Towlston Grange
Sugar Land Run
Difficult

LOUDOUN

FAIRFAX

Newgate
Payne's Church
Bull Run

Huntin Ck.
Dogue
Accotink Creek
Pohick Creek
South Run
Occoquan Creek
Colchester
Gunston Hall
Belvoir
Rippon Lodge

CHARLES

Mattawoman Ck.
Smallwood
Widow Elbeck
Craik
Port Tobacco

Port Tobacco Ck.

Nanjemoy Church

PRINCE WILLIAM

Neabsco Ck.
Leesylvania Ck.
Quantico Ck.
Dumfries
Graham
Chopawamsic Creek
Peyton's Ordinary

County Lines

shown----are as they existed after 1777. Before Oct. 1776 the Stafford-King George line was as shown by.....with Stafford on the Potomac side and King George on the Rappahannock side. Westmoreland's northern boundary before Oct. 1777 followed Upper Machodoc Creek to the old Stafford-King George line.

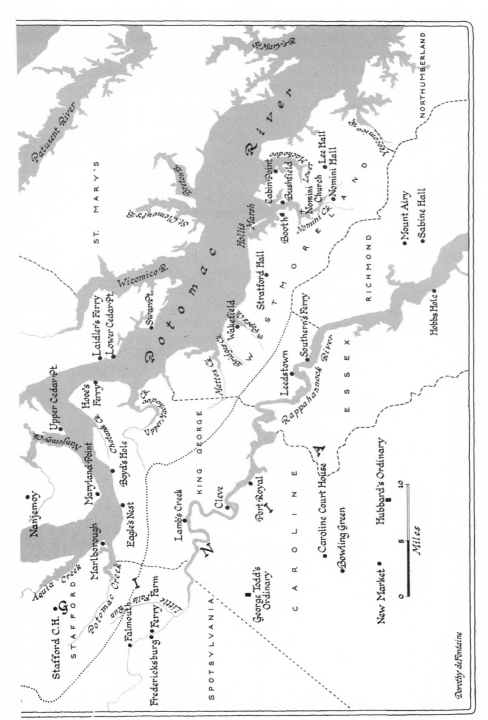

Washington's Potomac Neighborhood below the Falls

Dorothy deFontaine

that were cut out and Salted makes up 719 lbs. and accts. for Mr. French's 8 Hogs; shewing the loss of weiging Meat so soon as kills which cannot be less than 5 pr. Ct.

Richard Stephens (Stevens) was overseer of the Muddy Hole farm and John Foster was overseer of the Dogue Run farm, both on the Mount Vernon plantation.

Saturday Jany. 12th.   Sett out with Mrs. Bassett on her journey to Port Royal. The morning was clear and fine but soon clouded and promisd much Rain or other falling weather wch. is generally the case after remarkable white Frosts—as it was to day. We past Occoquan witht. any great difficulty notwithstanding the Wind was something high and Lodgd at Mr. McCraes in Dumfries—sending the Horses to the Tavern.

Here I was informd that Colo. Cocke was disgusted at my House, and left it because he see an old Negroe there resembling his own Image.

The ferry at Occoquan Creek, about ten miles south of Mount Vernon, was owned by George Mason of Gunston Hall and run by one of his slaves. At the ferry crossing, the creek was quite shallow and about 100 yards wide, thus being treacherous in high winds. By 1760 Dumfries, on Quantico Creek in lower Prince William County, was losing in its commercial competition with Alexandria. Allan Macrae (d. 1766) was one of the Scottish merchants who built the town on the tobacco trade. He had come to Virginia about 1750 and in 1756 married Elizabeth Pearson (VIRKUS, 5:162).
    Catesby Cocke (b. 1702), son of William Cocke (1672–1720), served successively as clerk of Stafford, Prince William, and Fairfax counties. In 1746 he retired and lived in Dumfries near his daughter Elizabeth, who had married John Graham (1711–1787), founder of Dumfries.

Sunday Jany. 13th.   The Wind last Night Chopd about from Southerly to the No. West blew extreame hard and made it excessive cold.

We reachd Mr. Seldons abt. 3 Oclock and met with a certain Captn. Dives there a Man who, as I have been informd is pretty well known for some of his Exploits and suspected to be an Instrument in carrying Dickenson whose Character and Memory are too well established to need any Commentaries.

Samuel Selden, who married a daughter of John Mercer of Marlborough, lived at Selvington on the south side of the mouth of Potomac Creek in Stafford (now King George) County (*Va. Mag.*, 18:455, note g; HAYDEN, 63). Dickenson is probably William Dickenson, who came to Virginia with two partners about 1754. They opened a store in Williamsburg and began buying up tobacco at advanced prices. In the spring of 1759, when they were unable to pay their creditors, they fled the colony, leaving debts of over £20,000 and taking their profits with them.

Monday Jany. 14th.   The Wind at No. West, and the Morning being clear and cold but otherwise fine we set out—Mr. Seldon obligingly accompanying us a few Miles to prevent any misapprehensions of the Road. We arrivd about 2 Oclock to the Plantation late Colo. Turners but now Inhabited by an Overseer directly opposite to Port Royal (at this place also Mr. Giberne lodges) and here we were disagreably disappointed of meeting him for a few hours but at length he arrivd almost at the same Instant that Colo. Bassett did. From hence we moved over to Port Royal and spent the Evening at Fox's with Mr. & Mrs. Bassett.

Mr. Bassett brought me a letter from Captn. Langbourn Inclosing a Bill of Lading for 20 Hhds. pr. the Deliverance Captn. Wm. Whyte. One other was sent by the Ship neither of which signifying to whom the Tobo. was Consignd which is not less strange than that only two Bills shd. be given when 4 and never less than three is customary in War time.

The Wind freshned up as the Evening came on and causd a most intense frost. Indeed no thaw had been the whole day.

Thomas Turner, whose plantation was Walsingham in King George County, was an old family friend from the days of GW's youth. At the age of 16 GW had won 1s. 3d. from Turner in a game of billiards. Rev. Isaac William Giberne was licensed in 1758 and came to Virginia the next year to find a parish. In 1760 he left his bachelor's quarters at Walsingham to marry a wealthy widow, Mary Fauntleroy Beale, and moved to her home, Belle Ville, in Richmond County, Lunenburg Parish, which he served 1762-95. A hard drinker, an avid cardplayer, and an active Whig, Giberne was generally considered to be the most popular preacher in the colony (FITHIAN, 25n). The original Roy's tavern at Port Royal was bought in 1755 by Capt. William Fox (d. 1772) and was run by his wife Ann during the captain's sailing trips between England and Virginia (CAMPBELL [1], 398).

Capt. William Langbourne (Langborn) (1723-1766) was a ship captain who sailed between Virginia and Bristol, Eng. Langbourne's home, in King William County, was about three miles up the Pamunkey River from Williams' Ferry. The bill of lading, for tobacco from a Custis estate in York County, was directed to the Hanbury firm of London. In 1754 Capt. William Whyte was commanding the *Deliverance* between Virginia and Barbados (*Va. Gaz.*, 19 July and 7 Nov. 1754).

In 1760 the Seven Years' (French and Indian) War was raging on three continents and in most of the world's oceans, putting every British merchant ship in danger of being captured or sunk by the French. Thus, commercial communications between America and Britain were usually sent in triplicate or quadruplicate in different ships, so that at least one copy would get through. GW was not overcautious; the *Deliverance* was, in fact, taken by the French. The tobacco had been insured, and GW reflected that "accidents of this Nature are common & ought not to be repin'd at" (GW to Capel & Osgood Hanbury, 10 Aug. 1760, DLC:GW).

Tuesday Jany. 15th.   Mr. Gibourne and I, leaving Mr. Bassett Just ready to set out recrossd the River and proceeded to Colo. Carters where we dind and in the Evening reachd Colo. Champes.

Several Gentlemen dind with us at Colo. Carters (neighbours of his) but we spent a very lonesome Evening at Colo. Champes not any Body favouring us with their Company but himself.

The Morning of this day was exceeding cold the Wind still continuing at No. West but in the Evening it died away grew something more moderate and promisd falling weather but no appearance of a thaw.

Charles Carter (1707–1764), of Cleve, King George County, was the third son of Robert "King" Carter. In 1760 Charles was one of the most powerful members of the House of Burgesses.

Col. John Champe (d. 1765), of Lamb's Creek, King George County, served variously as sheriff, coroner, and justice of the peace. Champe's daughter Jane became the first wife of GW's younger brother Samuel.

During the previous summer GW, Colonel Carter, Colonel Champe, and 15 other gentlemen had been commissioned justices for King George County by the governor and council (King George County Order Book for 1751–65, 874, Vi Microfilm). GW was entitled to be a King George justice by virtue of owning Ferry Farm and other property in the county, but he declined to serve, apparently finding the distance from Mount Vernon to the King George courthouse too great to attend the frequent court sessions. Like several others named in the commission, he did not take the required oaths of office, and his name was explicitly deleted from the county's next commission of the peace, which was issued in 1770 (VA. EXEC. JLS., 6:345).

Wednesday Jany. 16.   I parted with Mr. Gibourne, leaving Colo. Champes before the Family was Stirring and abt. 10 reachd my Mothers where I breakfasted and then went to Fredericksburg with my Brothr. Saml. who I found there.

Abt. Noon it began Snowing, the Wind at So. West but not Cold; was disappointed of seeing my Sister Lewis & getting a few things which I wanted out of the Stores returnd in the Evening to Mother's—all alone with her.

MY MOTHER'S: the Ferry Farm of GW's youth. When GW was about three years old the Washingtons moved from his birthplace at Pope's Creek, Westmoreland County, about 60 miles up the Potomac River to a new home near Little Hunting Creek. There the family lived three years on the plantation that later became Mount Vernon in Prince William (after 1741, Fairfax) County. In Nov. 1738 GW's father bought 260 acres on the north bank of the Rappahannock River just below the new town of Fredericksburg, and

A tobacco plantation as it might have appeared in Washington's day. (Arents Collections, New York Public Library, Astor, Lenox and Tilden Foundations)

the next month he moved his family to this new home. Although GW, by his father's will, inherited the farm upon reaching his majority in 1753, his mother remained there until the early 1770s.

Samuel Washington (1734–1781), the eldest of GW's three younger brothers, left Ferry Farm in the mid-1750s and settled on a 600-acre plantation in the Chotank district of Stafford County that he had inherited from his father. He also had a house in the town of Fredericksburg, which in 1760, with a population of about 2,500, was a flourishing commercial and cultural center, serving most of the Rappahannock valley and a large part of the backcountry.

GW's sister was Betty Washington (1733–1797), born at Pope's Creek and raised at the Ferry Farm. In 1750 she married the widower Fielding Lewis (1725–1782), son of John and Frances Fielding Lewis, of Warner Hall in Gloucester County. Fielding Lewis was a second cousin to both GW and Betty. The Lewises, who had seven children that survived to adulthood, lived in Fredericksburg at a home built for Lewis in 1752 called Kenmore.

In the Fredericksburg stores GW today bought 27½ pounds of German steel, a Dutch oven, and an iron pot (LEDGER A, 63).

Thursday Jany. 17th.   The Snow had turnd to Rain & occasiond a Sleet, the Wind at No. Et. and the Ground coverd abt. an Inch and half with Snow, the Rain continued with but little Intermission till Noon and then came on a Mist which lasted till Night.

Abt. Noon I set out from my Mother's & Just at Dusk arrivd at Dumfries.

Friday Jany. 18th. Continued my Journey home, the Misling continuing till Noon when the Wind got Southerly and being very warm occasiond a great thaw. I however found Potomk. River quite coverd with Ice & Doctr. Craik at my House.

Saturday Jany. 19. The Wind got abt. to the No[rth] ward last Night and froze the Ground hard. The Morning Lowerd, and threatned Rain; but about Noon the clouds dispersd and grew Warm, the Wind coming about Southerly again.

Recd. a Letter from my Overseer Hardwick, informing me that the Small Pox was surrounding the Plantation's he overlookd—& requiring sundry Working Tools.

Bought 4 Hogs weighing—1—103
2—102
3—130
4—108
443 lbs. a 22/.

and deliverd them to Richd. Stephens wch. fully compleats his own & Sons allowance of Provision's.

During the surveying trips of his early years GW discovered the rich lands in the lower Shenandoah Valley. The first real property GW owned was several tracts of land along Bullskin Run in Frederick County, which he bought in 1750. These lands he named the Bullskin plantation and on them were raised crops of corn, wheat, and tobacco. In 1756 GW hired Christopher Hardwick to be resident overseer. The smallpox epidemic in Frederick County was, by Jan. 1760, in its seventh month. It had already become so general by Oct. 1759 that the county court had closed down for the duration, thus bringing all legal and much other business to a standstill.

The pork that GW bought today did not come from Daniel French, but from some unidentified person. In his ledger GW recorded the total price as £4 17s. 6d. (LEDGER A, 63).

Sunday Jany. 20th. My Waggon after leaving 2 Hogsheads of Tobo. at Alexandria arrivd here with 3 Sides of Sole Leather and 4 of upper Leather 2 Kegs of Butter one of which for Colo. Fairfax and 15 Bushels of Salt which She took in at Alexandria.

Visited at Belvoir to day carrying Doctr. Craik with us who spent the Evening there.

The wind Continued Southerly the whole day the Ground very soft, & ⟨rain⟩—till 10 Oclo⟨ck A.⟩M. It Raind witht. intermission, but then the Clouds dispers'd and promisd fair Weather till Noon when it again set in to Raining and continued by Intervals the whole Afternoon being Warm.

The wagon apparently came from Bullskin plantation.

Monday Jany. 21st.   Warm with Rain, the Wind at South till Noon when it veerd abt. to the No. Ward & cleard.

The Ice in the River almost gone. The Rains that fell last Night, & to day in some measure hardned the Ground from the Rotton condition it appeard in Yesterday.

Tuesday Jany. 22d.   The Wind continued No[rth]wardly—the weather clear & cold—the ground hard froze & the River blockd up again.

Killd 17 more Hogs which were bought of Mr. French who was here ready to see them weighd & to receive his Money. Doctr. Craik Dind here. Hogs wd. 1722 lbs. nett.

These hogs made the total amount of pork received from French 2,473 pounds. Paying the agreed rate of 22s. 6d. a pound, GW today gave him £27 12s. 6d. Virginia currency (LEDGER A, 63).

Wednesday Jany. 23d.   Clear and more moderate than Yesterday—but the g[roun]d & r[iver] still hard frozen. Abt. Noon the wind (what little blew) came Westerly and Inclining South.

My Waggon set of for Frederick with Sundry's that were wrote for by the Overseer there.

Doctr. Craik left this for Alexandria and I visited my Quarter's & the Mill. According to Custom found young Stephen's absent.

GW's gristmill at this time was on the east side of Dogue Run, about 2 miles northwest of Mount Vernon. Lawrence Washington, acting on behalf of his father, Augustine, had apparently obtained this mill for the family in 1738, when he bought a 56-acre tract of land on the run from William Spencer (deed of Spencer to Lawrence Washington, 1–2 Mar. 1738, Prince William County Deeds, Book D, 110–16, Vi Microfilm). This property was transferred to Augustine and remained his until his death in 1743, when Lawrence was bequeathed the Mount Vernon tract "with the water mill Adjoining thereto or Lying Near the same" (will of Augustine Washington, 11 April 1743, DLC:GW). Lawrence may have improved the mill and the milldam near it, because in 1750 he bought 94 acres of land on the west side of Dogue Run onto which his millpond had overflowed and in the following year bought 22 acres adjoining the "Mill Tract" on the north, probably for the same reason (deed of Henry Trenn to Lawrence Washington, 4–5 Feb. 1750, Fairfax County Deeds, Book C-1, 152–55, Vi Microfilm; deed of Thomas Marshall to Lawrence Washington, 28 Mar. 1751, Fairfax County Deeds, Book C-1, 159–60, Vi Microfilm). Thus, there were now 172 acres around GW's mill, land which he later called his mill plantation.

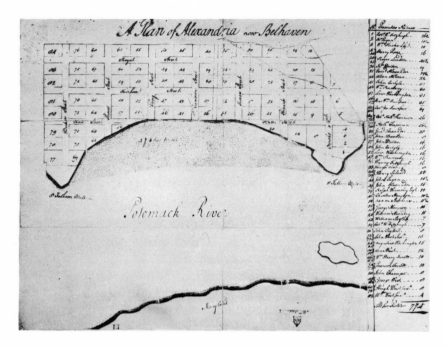

Washington drew this plan of Alexandria (Belhaven) about 1749. From *George Washington Atlas,* Washington, D.C., 1932. (Rare Book Department, University of Virginia Library)

Robert Stephens, son of Richard, worked on GW's Williamson farm in 1760. He apparently left before the harvest, for GW directed the 1760 Williamson farm harvest himself (see entry for 26 Jan. 1760).

Thursday Jany. 24th.   Moderate and fine, the Wind at So. and a gradual thaugh.

Friday Jany. 25th.   Fine warm morning with the wind at So. till abt. 10 Oclock when it came westerly and then No. Wt. blewing exceeding hard till 3 in the afternoon.

Went to Alexandria and saw my Tobo. wch. came from the Mountns. lying in an open shed with the ends of the Hhds out and in very bad order. Engagd the Inspection of it on Monday.

Wrote to Doctr. Ross to purchase me a Joiner, Bricklayer, and Gardner if any Ship of Servants was in.

Also wrote to my old Servt. Bishop to return to me again if he was not otherwise engagd. Directed for him at Phila. but no certainty of his being there.

SAW MY TOB[ACC]O: *Nicotiana tabacum*, tobacco, was GW's main cash crop during this period but less important to him later (see the Introduction, p. xxx). Tobacco was inspected in tobacco warehouses, established in compliance with the acts of 1730 and 1732 of the General Assembly to prevent the exportation of "bad, unsound, and unmerchantable tobacco" (HENING, 4:247, 331). FROM THE MOUNTNS.: from Bullskin plantation in Frederick County.

Dr. David Ross (d. 1778) was a merchant in Bladensburg, Md. GW had dealt with him during the French and Indian War, when Ross was a commissary for the Maryland troops. The servants would be white indentured servants emigrating from the British Isles. Thomas Bishop (c.1705–c.1795) came to America with General Braddock in the spring of 1755. Soon after GW was appointed colonel of the new Virginia Regiment he hired Bishop as his personal servant, paying him £10 per year. Seven months after GW retired from military life, Bishop resigned from GW's service, apparently with the intention of rejoining a unit of the British army. Philadelphia had been since 1757 the eastern headquarters for the frontier expeditions in which GW and Bishop had served.

Saturday Jany. 26th.   A Very white frost the ground and River hard froze. The wind at Sun Rise at No. Et. In an hour afterwards it got to south and continued there the whole day. Rode to Williamsons Quarter—the Overseer not there—a very remarkable Circle round the Moon—another Indication of falling Weather.

In 1756 Benjamin Williamson rented a farm from GW near Mount Vernon on Little Hunting Creek. During the next four years he slowly slipped behind in his rent. The rental was not renewed for 1760, and in that year GW turned Williamson's farm (possibly combined with the farm of Thomas Petit) into a Mount Vernon quarter called Williamson's. He assigned six hands to it and hired Robert Stephens as overseer. By 1761 Stephens was replaced by Josias Cook and the quarter was renamed the Creek plantation.

Sunday Jany. 27th.   A high South Wind continued to blow till about 4 in the afternoon and then it got to No. Wt. blew fresh, and grew Cold.

Abt. 10 oclock it began to Rain, and continued witht. Intermission till the wind changd and then grew clear and began to freeze.

The Southerly Wind had almost opend the River of Ice.

Monday Jany. 28th.   The River close again & the ground very Knobby & hard. The wind got So. about [   ] and blew fresh which allmost cleard the River of Ice.

Visited my Plantation. Severely reprimanded young Stephens for his Indolence, & his father for suffering of it.

Found the new Negroe Cupid ill of a pleurisy at Dogue Run Quarter & had him brot. home in a Cart for better care of him.

Cupid was a dower Negro, and hence new. In 1760 he was one of four slaves assigned to the Dogue Run quarter, which was divided into tracts and was still being planted in tobacco. Through various land acquisitions this farm came by 1793 to comprise close to 649 working acres.

Tuesday Jany. 29th.   White Frost, and Wind at So. till 3 oclock then No. Wt. but not very cold—clear all day.

Darcus—daughter to Phillis died, which makes 4 Negroes lost this Winter viz. 3 Dower Negroes namely—

Beck—appraisd to £50—

Dolls Child born since—

Darcus appd. at

and Belinda a Wench of mine in Frederick.

Wednesday Jany. 30th.   Very Cloudy. Wind at So. till 9 Oclock at Night when it instentaniously shifted to No. West & blew a mere hurricane.

Cupid was extreame Ill all this day and at Night when I went to Bed I thought him within a few hours of breathing his last.

Thursday Jany. 31st.   He was somewhat better; The wind continued at No. West all day—very cold & clear.

[February]

Friday Feby. 1st. 1760.   Wind at [   ] and Snow till 9 Oclock then cleard & became tolerable warm. Visited my Plantation's. Found Foster had been absent from his charge since the 28th. Ulto. Left Order's for him to come immediately to me upon his return & reprehended him severely.

Mr. Johnston & Mr. Walter Stewart came here this Afternoon.

Saturday Feby. 2d. 17[60].   The Gentlemen went of after Breakfast and I rid out to my Plantns. and to my Carpenter's. Found Richd. Stephens hard at Work with an ax—very extraordinary this! Desird him to see after Wm. Nations' Rent, who died t'other day.

The wind for the most part was Northerly yet the Day was mild

—the Evening fine & promisd settle Weathr. Mrs. Possey and 2 of her Children came, and Stayd the Night here.

In 1755 William Nations began renting a quarter from GW for 1,000 pounds of tobacco per year.

MRS. POSSEY: Martha Posey (née Price) first married George Harrison (d. 1748) and then Capt. John Posey of Rover's Delight. She bore Posey at least four children: John Price, Hanson, St. Lawrence, and Amelia. Of the two children who came with her this day one was probably Amelia, who appears in the diaries as "Milly."

Sunday Feby. 3d.   Very white Frost—and wind shifting from So. to East.

Breechy was laid up this Morning with pains in his breast & head attended with a fever.

Mrs. Possey went home and we to Church at Alexandria. Dind at Colo. Carlyles and returnd in the Evening.

One Newell offerd himself to me to be Overseer. Put him of to another day.

Episcopal services in Alexandria at this time were held in a small building furnished jointly by local subscription and by Truro Parish. The Rev. Mr. Green preached there every third Sunday from 1753 until 1765, when Fairfax Parish was formed. John Carlyle (1720–1780), of Dumfrieshire, Scot., was a merchant and a founder of Alexandria. In 1745 he married Sarah Fairfax (1728–1761), of Belvoir, a sister-in-law of GW's brother Lawrence. During the French and Indian War, Carlyle was a supplier of GW's troops.

Monday Feby. 4th.   White Frost & So[uther]ly Wind. Sometimes cloudy & sometimes clear. The Frost seemed to be getting out of the Ground.

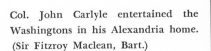

Col. John Carlyle entertained the Washingtons in his Alexandria home. (Sir Fitzroy Maclean, Bart.)

Dispatchd Foster to Occoquan, to proceed from thence in Bailey's Vessell to Portobacco for 100 Barrls. of Corn wch. Captn. Possey purchased of Mr. Hunter the Priest for my use. Sent money to pay for the Corn viz.—37 pistoles and a Shilling, each pistole weighing 4 d[ram]s 8 gr.

Breechy's pains Increasd and he appeard extreamely ill all the day. In Suspence whither to send for Doctr. Laurie or not.

Visited my Plantations and found two Negroes Sick at Williamson's Quarter viz. Greg and Lucy—orderd them to be Blooded. Stepns. at Wk.

Colo. Fairfax giving me Notice that he shoud send up to Frederick in the Morning, sat down & wrote to my Overseer there.

Father George Hunter (1713–1779) was one of the handful of Roman Catholic priests—all Jesuits—who served the small Catholic populace living in colonial Maryland. As there was no official support (in the form of taxes or glebe land) to provide a living for the Jesuits, the Roman Catholic community of Maryland made use of Maryland's manor system of land tenure by establishing several manors that were held in trust by the community's leaders in the name of one or more of the Jesuits residing in the colony. Each manor, like St. Thomas Manor, in Charles County, had a chapel and usually slaves to work the manor's fields. Port Tobacco, founded in 1728 as the county seat (1728–1895) of Charles County, Md., was literally a small tobacco port on Port Tobacco Creek, which joined the Potomac opposite the Chotank district of King George County in Virginia. The town's official name, Charlestown, which was seldom used, was legally dropped in 1820 (KLAPTHOR, 46, 105; W.P.A. [2], 490). Roman Catholic priests in this period were commonly addressed as "Mister." In 1760 Mr. Hunter was the superior for the Maryland Mission.

The 37 pistoles and 1 shilling were, according to GW's ledger, equal to £40 2s. 8d. Virginia currency (LEDGER A, 63; see entries for 21 Feb. 1760).

Tuesday Feby. 5th. Breechy's pains Increasg. & he appearing worse in other Respects inducd me to send for Dr. Laurie. Wrote to Mr. Ramsay Begging the favour of him to enquire in to the price of Mr. Barnes Sugar Land Tract & he informd me that the value set on it by Mr. Barnes was £400.

Visited my Plantation and found to my great surprise Stephens constt. at Work. Greg and Lucy nothing better.

Passing by my Carpenters that were hughing I found that four of [them] viz. George, Tom, Mike & young Billy had only hughd 120 Foot Yesterday from 10 Oclock. Sat down therefore and observd.

Tom and Mike in a less space than 30 Minutes cleard the Bushes from abt. a Poplar Stock-lind it 10 Foot long and hughd each their side 12 Inches deep.

Then, letting them proceed their own way—they spent 25 Min-

Martha Washington ordered this English songbook from a London merchant, and her husband wrote her name and the date on the title page. (Mount Vernon Ladies' Association of the Union)

utes more in getting the cross cut saw standing to consider what to do—sawing the Stock of in two places—putting it on the Blocks for hughing it square lining it &ca. and from this time till they had finishd the Stock entirely; requird 20 Minutes more, so that in the Spaces of one hour and a quarter they each of them from the Stump finishd 20 Feet of hughing: from hence it appears very clear that allowing they work only from Sun to Sun and require two hour's at Breakfast they ought to yield each his 125 feet while the days are at their present length and more in proportion as they Increase.

While this was doing George and Billy sawd 30 Foot of Plank so that it appears as clear making the same allowance as before (but not for the time requird in pilling the Stock) that they ought to Saw 180 Feet of Plank.

It is to be observd here, that this hughing, & Sawing likewise was of Poplr. What may be the difference therefore between the working of this Wood and other some future observations must make known.

The Weather to day was variable, often Rainy but the Wind hung chiefly between the So. & West. No Frost last Night & the Ground Vastly Rotton.

Colo. Fairfax, his Lady, & Doctr. Laurie dind here. The Dr. went away afterwards but the others stayd the Evening.

William Ramsay (1716–1785) migrated to Virginia from the Galloway district of Scotland and became a founder and merchant of Alexandria. During the French and Indian War, Ramsay, then in financial straits, was appointed a commissary of British troops on the recommendation of GW. The land of Abraham Barnes was part of an area full of sugar-bearing maple trees and hence called the Sugar Lands which lay along Sugar Land Run. After 1798 the confluence of Sugar Land Run with the Potomac River described the northern point of the boundary between Fairfax and Loudoun counties.

STOCK-LIND IT: cut it into sections before hewing it into square timbers.

Wednesday Feby. 6th.   Fine warm day and the ground much dried. The wind which was extreamely little appeard to be shifting.

Colo. Fairfax & Mrs. Fairfax Dind here.

The Dr. sent his Servant down with things to Breechy. Grig came here this afternoon, worse and I had 15 Hogs arrivd from Bullskin.

Thursday Feby. 7th.   The Hogs which arrivd Yesterday were killd—weighg. as follows viz.

142	140	140	139
130	130	110	90
90	90	90	90
83	80	70	
445	440	410	319
			410
			440
			445
		Total	1614

Out of which Jno. Foster recd. the remainder of his Years Provisions viz.

177 lbs.

had before <u>173</u>

350 — the years Allowe.

Doctr. Lauries Man attended the Sick this day also.

I went to Mr. Craigs Funeral Sermon at Alexandria — and there met my Waggons with 4 Hhds. Tobo. more. Unloaded & sent them down to Mt. Vernon.

One of the Boys that came down with them & the Hogs (Nat) was taken with the Meazles last Night.

The Wind was Southerly, and very warm & drying, but the Earth extreamely Rotton.

The funeral was probably for Charles Craig (Craik), who had rented a Mount Vernon quarter from GW since 1756.

Friday Feby. 8th. 1760. The Wind had got to No. West, but as it did not blew fresh, so neither was it cold.

Rode to my Plantatns. and orderd Lucy down to H[ome] House to be Physickd.

Saturday Feby. 9th. The Ground was a little crusted but not hard — a remarkable white Frost.

Visited my Plantation's before Sunrise & forbid Stephen's keeping any horses upon my Expence.

Set my Waggon's to draw in Stocks and Scantling, and wrote to Mr. Stuart of Norfolk for 20 or 30 or more thousd. shingles 6 Barrls. Tar 6 of Turpentine & 100 wt. of Tallow or Myrtle wax or half as much Candles.

Remarkable fine day but the Wind at No. Et.

MR. STUART: possibly Charles Steuart, a merchant in Norfolk active in the 1750s (*Va. Gaz.*, 12 Mar. 1752).

Sunday Feby. 10th. The Wind got to North and often, clouded up and threatend Rain but in the Evening at sunsetting it cleard and seemd to promise fair Weather.

Captn. Possey, and Mrs. Possey dind here. He obliquely hinted a design of selling his 145 Acres of Wood Land on Muddy hole.

Orderd all the Fellows from the different Quarter's to Assembly at Williamson's Quarter in the Morning to move Petits House.

On 20–21 Sept. 1759 GW's youngest brother, Charles Washington, had sold John Posey two separate tracts lying between Mount Vernon and Dogue

Creek: one of about 200 acres on the Potomac River and the one mentioned here, which supposedly contained 145 acres of uncleared land and lay on Muddy Hole Branch, a tributary of Dogue Creek (Fairfax County Deeds, Book D-1, 669–73, Vi Microfilm). Not part of the original Mount Vernon tract, these lands had been bought for GW's father, Augustine, in 1738 and 1739 by Lawrence Washington and had subsequently been inherited by Charles (deed of William Spencer to Lawrence Washington, 1–2 Mar. 1738, Prince William County Deeds, Book D, 110–16, Vi Microfilm; deed of George Harrison to Lawrence Washington, 20–21 Nov. 1739, Prince William County Deeds, Book D, 425–29, Vi Microfilm; will of Augustine Washington, 11 April 1743, DLC:GW). Posey combined the tract on the Potomac with adjacent land that his wife held by right of dower from her first husband to form the plantation that he was farming, but he either did not want or could not afford to keep the tract on Muddy Hole Branch (see entry for 6 Mar. 1760).

Thomas Petit rented a Mount Vernon quarter from GW in 1759 and 1760, after which he disappears from GW's records.

Monday Feby. 11th.   Went out early myself and continued with my People till 1 Oclock in which time we got the house abt. 250 yards. Was informd then that Mr. Digges was at my House upon which I retd. finding him & Doctr. Laurie there.

The Ground being soft and Deep we found it no easy matter with 20 hands and 8 Horses & 6 Oxen to get this House along.

Exceeding clear & fine, wind Northwardly.

The Digges family of Virginia and Maryland descended from Edward Digges, who settled in Virginia in the mid-seventeenth century and served as governor of Virginia 1655–57. His eldest son, William, later moved north of the Potomac River and founded the Maryland branch of the Digges family. The Mr. Digges who appears here is William Digges (1713–1783), a grandson of the elder William. This William, a prominent layman in the Roman Catholic church in Maryland, married Ann Atwood and lived at his plantation, Warburton Manor, across the Potomac River within sight of Mount Vernon. For many years the families of Warburton Manor and Mount Vernon exchanged visits across the Potomac.

Tuesday Feby. 12th.   A Small Frost happening last Night to Crust the Ground causd the House to move much lighter and by 9 Oclock it was got to the spot on wch. it was intended to stand.

Visited at the Glebe the day being very fine clear & still. No wind blowing from any Quarter perceivably.

Sett Kate & Doll to heaping the Dung abt. the Stable.

Recd. a Letter & Acct. Currt. from Messrs. Hanbury the former dated Octr. 1 – 1759 the other Septr. 1st. same yr.

The Truro Parish glebe, which grew from 176 acres in 1752 to 385 in 1767, included a house and outbuildings for the Rev. and Mrs. Green (Truro

Ann Atwood Digges, of Warburton, Prince George's County, Md. (Mr. and Mrs. Walter Slowinski)

Vestry Book, 70, 121, DLC). The house, begun in 1752 by Green and Thomas Waite, had been newly completed in 1760 by William Buckland (1734–1774), a talented joiner previously imported from England for the construction of George Mason's Gunston Hall.

The Hanbury firm, a powerful London merchant house, had served the Custis plantations for a number of years. On 12 June 1759 GW had written to the firm, then known as Capel & Osgood Hanbury, informing them of his marriage to Martha Custis and stating: "I must now desire that you will please to address all your Letters which relate to the Affairs of the Deceas'd Colo. Custis to me" (DLC:GW), which directions the Hanburys acknowledged in a letter to GW, 1 Oct. 1759 (DLC:GW).

Wednesday Feby. 13th.   A fresh gale So. continued the whole day with clear and Warm Sun.

Visited all my Quarters.

Thursday Feby. 14th.   Mr. Clifton came here and we conditiond for his Land viz., if he is not bound by some prior engagemt. I am to have all his Land in the Neck (500 Acres about his house excepted) and the Land commonly calld Brents for 1600 £ Curry. He getting Messrs. Digges &ca. to join in making me a good & Sufft. Title. But Note I am not bound to Ratifie this bargain unless Colo. Carlyle will let me have his Land adjoining Brents at half a Pistole an Acre.

Visited my Quarters and saw a plant patch burnt at the Mill.

Brought home 4003 lbs. of Hay from Mr. Digges's.

The Southerly wind still continued to blow fresh till abt. 9 Oclock at Night and then it suddenly changd to No. Et. Clouded up, and threatned Rain every moment.

William Clifton (died c.1770) was descended from an English Roman Catholic family, several branches of which began leaving England for Maryland and Virginia in the mid-seventeenth century. William left England in the early eighteenth century and settled in Truro Parish, where he was living in 1739 when he bought 500 acres of the Neck land from his brother-in-law George Brent (d. 1778) of Stafford County. By 1760 Clifton's land was a plantation of about 1,806 acres in Clifton's Neck, which lay on the east side of Little Hunting Creek, facing the Potomac River, across which Clifton ran a ferry often used by GW.

BRENTS: George Brent's remaining land in the Neck, 238 acres lying between Little Hunting Creek and Clifton's plantation.

GW paid William Digges £14 for hay on 5 June 1760 (LEDGER A, 95).

Friday Feby. 15th.   A Small fine Rain from No. Et. wet the Top of my Hay that had been landed last Night. It was all carted up however to the Barn & the Wet and dry seperated.

Went to a Ball at Alexandria—where Musick and Dancing was the chief Entertainment. However in a convenient Room detachd for the purpose abounded great plenty of Bread and Butter, some Biscuets with Tea, & Coffee which the Drinkers of coud not Distinguish from Hot water sweetned. Be it remembered that pocket handkerchiefs servd the purposes of Table Cloths & Napkins and that no Apologies were made for either. I shall therefore distinguish this Ball by the Stile & title of the Bread & Butter Ball.

The Proprietors of this Ball were Messrs. Carlyle Laurie & Robt. Wilson, but the Doctr. not getting it conducted agreeable to his own taste woud claim no share of the merit of it.

We lodgd at Colo. Carlyles.

A man named Robert Wilson voted for GW in the 1758 Frederick County election for the House of Burgesses.

GW apparently played cards at the ball, because on the following day he recorded the loss of 7s. "By Cards" (LEDGER A, 63).

Saturday Feby. 16.   Returnd home—receiving an Invitation to Mrs. Chews Ball on Monday night next, first.

The Morning lowerd, and dript as yesterday, but abt. 10 Oclock the Wind So[uther]ly, blew fresh, and cleard.

Mercy Chew (d. 1775), with her husband Joseph Chew, kept a tavern in Alexandria which GW patronized in the early 1760s (Fairfax County Deeds, Book C-1, 63, Vi Microfilm; Fairfax County Wills, Book C-1, 244, Vi Microfilm; LEDGER A, 141, 160).

Sunday Feby. 17th.   The Wind blew cold & fresh from the No. West.

Went to Church & Dind at Belvoir.

Sent 4 Yews & Lambs to the Mill to be fatted.

Monday Feby. 18th.   Dispatchd my Waggon with Tools &ca. for Frederick.

Sent over for two more Tons of Hay—to Mr. Digges.

The Morning was cold the Wind being at No. West. It afterwards changd to So. and grew more moderate but towards Night it agn. Shifted to the No. East, but made no perceptable change in the Air, as to heat or cold.

Tuesday Feby. 19th.   Went to Court, and Administerd upon Nations Effects. Got Mr. Smiths Lease to me recorded and Mr. Johnston not having Darrels Deeds ready I was obligd to get the acknowledging of them postpond.

Recd. a Letter from my Brothr. Austin by Mr. Lane & answerd it.

Fine moderate day with a brisk Southerly Wind which brought up the Vessell with my Corn.

Mike and Tom began sawing in the Pit some considerable time after Sun rise and Cut 122 feet of Oak Scantling.

GW's first expansion of the Mount Vernon property occurred in Dec. 1757, when he bought two pieces of land on the plantation's northern boundary from Sampson Darrell (d. 1777) of Fairfax County: a tract of 200 acres on Dogue Run and an adjoining tract of 300 acres on Little Hunting Creek. The total price of these two tracts was £350, which GW paid with £260 in cash and a bond for £90 due in two years, and in return he received Darrell's bond guaranteeing him title to the land (LEDGER A, 49; bond of Darrell to GW, 20 Dec. 1757, ViMtV). But the official deeds were not immediately signed and recorded in court because the property was held under right of dower by Darrell's mother, Ann, for her lifetime; only after her death would it revert to Darrell as a surviving son. Thus, although GW owned Darrell's rights to the land, he could not obtain the deeds until Ann died or rented the land to him. GW did not have to await her death, because on 20 Sept. 1759 he signed a lease with her and her present husband, Thomas Smith (d. 1764) of Fairfax County, agreeing thereby to pay them 1,030 pounds of tobacco a year until Ann died (lease of Thomas and Ann Smith to GW, PHi: Gratz Collection; LEDGER A, 111). Having recorded the lease on this day, GW was eager to get and record Darrell's deeds, but he was obliged to wait for the May court session (deeds of Darrell to GW, 19–20 May 1760, Fairfax County Deeds, Book D-1, 681–92, Vi Microfilm).

Augustine Washington (1720–1762), half brother of GW by his father's first wife, Jane Butler, married Anne Aylett (d. 1773) and lived at Pope's Creek in Westmoreland County. GW usually called him "Austin." Mr. Lane

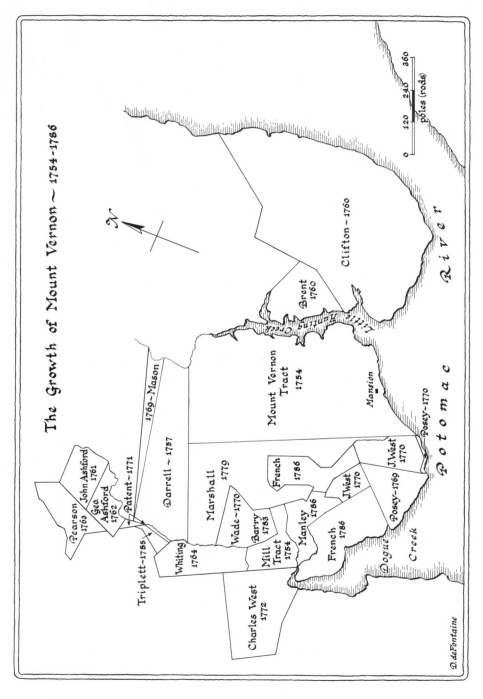

The Growth of Mount Vernon, 1754–86

Map Key: The Growth of Mount Vernon, 1754–86

Date GW acquired tract	Name of tract	Estimated acreage of tract	Estimated total acreage of plantation
1754 Dec. 17	Mount Vernon Tract	2,126	2,126
1754 Dec. 17	Mill Tract	172	2,298
1757 Dec. 20	Sampson Darrell	500	2,798
1760 May 20	William Clifton	1,806	4,604
1760 Sept. 23–24	George Brent	238	4,842
1761 Jan. 29–30	John Ashford	135	4,977
1762 Jan. 13–14	George Ashford	135	5,112
1763 Feb. 14	Simon Pearson	178	5,290
1764 c. June	William and Diana Whiting	200	5,490
1769 Oct. 23–25	John Posey	200	5,690
1769 Oct. 24	George Mason	100	5,790
1770 April 23	John Posey	6	5,796
1770 Sept. 18	John West, Jr.	200	5,996
1770 Dec. 17–18	Valinda Wade	75	6,071
1771 Mar. 4	Patent from Lord Fairfax	20½	6,091½
1772 Oct. 27–28	Charles West	412	6,503½
1779 c. Mar. 16	Thomas Hanson Marshall	480½	6,984
1783 June 16	William Barry	118	7,102
1785 Feb. 25	Land deeded to Lund Washington from the John and George Ashford, Simon Pearson, and 1771 Patent tracts	−434	6,668
1785 May 18	Land deeded to William Triplett from the George Ashford, Simon Pearson, and 1771 Patent tracts	−26	6,642
1785 May 18	William Triplett	29	6,671
1786 Sept. 22	Harrison Manley's executors	142	6,813
1786 Oct. 18	Penelope French	552	7,365

NOTE. The dates listed here are the ones on which GW first gained effective title to each tract. In several instances he rented land or purchased rights to it with the understanding that he would obtain full legal ownership at a later date. The Mount Vernon and mill tracts were leased in 1754 from

The Growth of Mount Vernon, 1754–86 (*cont.*)

Lawrence Washington's widow, Ann, for her lifetime and reverted to GW upon her death in 1761 by virtue of Lawrence's will. Darrell's rights to his 500 acres were bought in 1757, but because his mother had been given the land for her lifetime, arrangements had to be made with her, and the deeds were not signed until 19–20 May 1760. A dispute between John Posey and John West, Jr., over Posey's 6-acre strip on the Potomac delayed the signing of deeds for that land and West's property north of it. Thus, while GW began leasing both tracts during 1770, Posey did not deed the 6-acre strip to him until 8 June 1772 and West did not deed his land until 22 Sept. 1772. In the case of the Wade-Barry tract, GW had to wait for a division with Barry on 19 Sept. 1772 before taking possession of the land that he bought from Valinda Wade in 1770. Because a copy of that division has not been found, no line is shown on the map between the Wade and Barry portions. GW's purchase of Mrs. French's land in 1786 was conditioned on the payment of an annual rent to her by GW or his heirs until her death, which, as it happened, did not occur until after GW died.

The acreages given are based on GW's deeds and leases wherever possible and on contemporary ledger entries, quitrent lists, or letters in all other cases. However, these figures should not be considered exact because of the vagueness or inaccuracy of most eighteenth-century surveys. Thus, although GW was an experienced surveyor, he apparently did not know the precise total acreage of the Mount Vernon plantation as it existed at the time of his death. In an advertisement dated 1 Feb. 1796 offering the plantation for lease, he stated that it contained "altogether about eight thousand acres" (WRITINGS, 34:433–41), and in his will of 9 July 1799, he was equally vague, bequeathing the plantation in three sections: one to Bushrod Washington "containing upwards of four thousand acres, be the same more or less"; one to George Fayette Washington and Lawrence Augustine Washington "containing in the whole, by Deeds, Two thousand and seventy seven acres, be it more or less"; and one to Lawrence and Eleanor Parke Lewis containing "about two thousand Acres, be it more or less" (Fairfax County Courthouse). In the case of Bushrod Washington's land, the acreage was shown by an 1831 survey to be much less: 3,593 acres instead of 4,000 (ViMtV). The most accurate estimate of Mount Vernon's final size may be the one made by Warrington Gillingham, who surveyed the area in the 1850s and declared that the plantation had contained "about 7600 acres" (MUIR, between pp. 90 and 91).

was probably one of the three sons of William Lane (1690–1760) of Nomini Forest, Westmoreland County: James Lane (d. 1777), William Carr Lane (d. 1770), and Joseph Lane (d. 1796).

Wednesday Feby. 20.   Landed 65 Barrels of Corn. Fine moderate day. Very little wind. George & Billy sawd 155 feet of Oak Scantling.

Thursday Feby. 21.   Finished landing the Corn, which held out only 1½ Bushells above measure. Paid the Skipper for the Freight.

Visited at Mr. Clifton's and rode over his Lands—but in an especial manner view'd that tract calld Brents, which wd. have pleas'd me exceedingly at the price he offerd it at viz. half a pistole an Acre provided Colo. Carlyle's 300 Acres just below it coud be annexd at the same price and this but a few Months ago he offerd it at but now seeming to set a higher value upon it, and at the same time putting on an air of indifference inducd me to make Clifton another for his Land—namely £1700 Cury. for all his Lands in the Neck Including his own Plantn. &ca. which offer he readily accepted upon Condition of getting his wife to acknowledge her Right of Dower to it and of his success in this he was to inform me in a few days.

A fresh So[uther]ly Wind blew the whole day and often Clouds towards Night. It threatned ⟨Rain very much.⟩

Clifton's wife was his cousin Elizabeth Brent (d. 1773), a daughter of Robert Brent of Woodstock, Stafford County, whose seventeenth-century ancestor Giles Brent had originally patented most of the land in what was now called Clifton's Neck. Mrs. Clifton's "Right of Dower" referred to that portion of the Neck which, although controlled by her husband under the law of marital right, could only be alienated (given or sold) by Mrs. Clifton, the legal owner. This situation was common in eighteenth-century Virginia; sometimes the wife allowed her husband to sell her land and sometimes not.

GW received a total of 100 barrels of corn. The shipping cost was £5 (LEDGER A, 63).

Friday Feby. 22.   The Wind in the Night encreasd to a mere Storm and raind exceedg. hard; towards day it moderated and ceasd Raining but the whole day afterwards was Squally.

Laid in part the Worm of a fence round my Peach Orchard, & had it made. Waited on Lord Fairfax at Belvoir & engd. him to dine at Mt. Vernon on Monday next.

Upon my return found one of my best Waggon Horses (namely Jolly) with his right foreleg Mashd to pieces which I suppose

Washington owned a copy of the work in which this drawing appears, William Gibson's *A New Treatise on the Diseases of Horses*, London, 1754. (Beinecke Rare Book and Manuscript Library, Yale University)

happend in the Storm last Night by Means of a Limb of a tree or something of that sort falling upon him.

Did it up as well as I coud this Night.

This was GW's birthday according to the Gregorian calendar (see entry for 11 Mar. 1748), but there is no indication that he took note of it either on this day or 11 Feb., the Old Style date on which he actually was born. In 1798 and 1799 the citizens of Alexandria celebrated his birthday on or near the old date.

WORM OF A FENCE: the bottom course of rails in a rail fence.

Saturday Feby. 23.   Had the Horse slung upon Canvas and his leg fresh set—following Markhams directions as near as I coud.

Laid the Worm round my Apple Orchard & made the Fence.

The Wind for the first part was So[uther]ly but afterwards it shifted to No. West. blew fresh and grew a little Cool.

Captn. Bullet came here from Alexandria, and engagd to secure me some Lands on the Ohio being lately appointed Surveyor of a District there.

MARKHAM'S DIRECTIONS: Gervase Markham (1568–1637) wrote many treatises on diseases of cattle and horses. In 1759 GW purchased a much more current work, William Gibson's *Treatise on the Diseases of Horses* (London, 1751).

Thomas Bullitt, son of Benjamin Bullitt (d. 1766) of Fauquier County, served with GW in the Virginia Regiment, rising to captain. He was with GW at Fort Necessity and at Braddock's Defeat, and held his Virginians in a bloody skirmish at Grant's Defeat. For Bullitt's appointment as a surveyor, see George Mercer to GW, 17 Feb. 1760, DLC:GW.

Sunday Feby. 24th.   Captn. Bullet dind here to day also. So did Mr. Clifton but the latter was able to give me no determinate answer in regard to his Land.

Was unprovided for a demand of £90 made by Mr. Alligood in favour of Messrs. Atchinson & Parker of Norfolk. My note of Hand to Sampson Darrel but promisd the payment, & Interest, at the April Court next.

Fresh Southerly Wind and Cloudy Weather.

MY NOTE: the two-year bond for £90 that GW had given Sampson Darrell as final payment for land bought from Darrell in Dec. 1757. Darrell had apparently used the bond to settle an account, and the firm of Aitcheson & Parker had now sent their collector to Mount Vernon for payment. GW paid them the £90 as promised while in Williamsburg in April (LEDGER A, 49, 89).

Monday Feby. 25th. Lord Fairfax, Colo. F[airfa]x & his Lady, Colo. Martin, Mr. B. F[airfa]x, Colo. Carlyle, & Mr. Green & Mrs. Green dind here.

So[uther]ly Wind and remarkable fine clear day. Set my People to Carting and carrying Rails round the Peach Orchard.

The Broken Legd. horse fell out of his Sling and by that means and strugling together hurt himself so much that I orderd him to be killd.

Thomas Bryan Martin (1731–1798), a nephew of Lord Fairfax, came to Virginia in 1751 and the next year was appointed land agent for the Fairfax Grant, taking up residence with Lord Fairfax at Greenway Court in the Shenandoah Valley. In 1758 Martin and GW were elected burgesses for

Frederick County. Bryan Fairfax (1737–1802) was a half brother of George William Fairfax. After an erratic youth Bryan married Elizabeth Cary, a sister of Sarah Cary Fairfax, and settled in Fairfax County, making his home at Towlston Grange on Difficult Run. He was one of GW's frequent fox-hunting companions before the Revolution.

Tuesday Feby. 26th.   Began Plowing the Field by the Stable and Quarter for Oats and Clover. Set two plows to Work under the care of Mulatto, & Cook Jacks.

Layd the Worm round my Peach Orchard & had the Fence put up.

Made an absolute agreement with Mr. Clifton for his Land (so far as depended upon him) on the following terms—to wit, I am to give him £1150 Sterling for his Neck Lands, containg. 1806 Acres, and to allow him the use of this Plantn. he lives on till fall twelve months.

He on his part is to procure the Gentlemen of Maryland to whom his Lands are under Mortgage to join in a Conveyance and is to put me into possession of the Land so soon as this can be done. He is not to cut down any Timber, nor clear any Ground nor to use more Wood than what shall be absolutely necessary for Fences and firing. Neither is he to assent to any alterations of Tenants transferring of Leases &ca. but on the contrary is to discourage every practice that has a tendancy to lessen the value of the Land.

N.B. He is also to bring Mr. Mercers opinion concerning the validity of a private sale made by himself.

Went down to Occoquan, by appointment to look at Colo. Cockes Cattle, but Mr. Peakes being from home I made no agreemt. for them not caring to give the price he askd for them.

Calld & dind at Captn. McCarty's in my way home & left the order of Court appointing him and others to appraisers of Nation's Estate (which I had sent my Boy down for) and at the same time got a promise of him to Prize & Inspect his Tobo. at the Warehouse.

Bottled 35 dozn. of Cyder, the weather very warm, & Cloudy with some Rain last Night.

The "Gentlemen of Maryland" who held mortgages were Charles Carroll (1702–1782) of Annapolis, Benjamin Tasker (1690–1768) of Anne Arundel County, and William Digges, Ignatius Digges, and John Addison, all of Prince George's County. The Carroll and Digges families of Maryland had married into the Brent family of Maryland and Virginia, and all of these parties were now in the fifteenth year of a struggle over Clifton's Neck, producing a maze of lawsuits involving leases, inheritances, mortgages, injunctions, and ejectments. Clifton's suit for a final settlement in Virginia's General Court (sitting in chancery) was now awaiting the report of court-appointed commissioners, one of whom was GW.

Since the court case was still pending, the validity of such a "private sale" was a moot point, and GW wisely advised Clifton to seek a legal opinion. Mr. Mercer is probably John Mercer (1704–1768), who emigrated from Ireland to Virginia in 1720 and made his home near the Potomac River at Marlborough, Stafford County. As a lawyer Mercer became so aggressive in the courtroom that in 1734 he was barred from practice. He then turned to legal scholarship, spending the next few years preparing *An Exact Abridgement of All the Public Acts of Assembly, of Virginia, in Force and Use,* issued by the *Virginia Gazette* printer William Parks (Williamsburg, 1737; 2d ed., Glasgow, Scot., 1759). This work was the first such edition of Virginia's laws, and all county justices of the peace, including those who had complained about Mercer, were advised to possess a copy. Mercer himself was later appointed a justice of Stafford County. In the process of his scholarly pursuits, Mercer collected one of the finest libraries in the colony, about a third of which related to law.

GW had known John Mercer for years. Mercer's home of Marlborough, on the neck between Aquia and Potomac creeks, was only a few miles up the Potomac from the Chotank neighborhood, so well known to GW from youth and later so thickly populated with his cousins. As early as 1754 GW had asked for Mercer's legal advice regarding the disposition of Mount Vernon after Lawrence Washington's death. Mercer had also served the Custis family for 16 years during a major legal battle in which GW took an interest following his marriage to Martha Custis in 1759.

Speculating in large tracts of land in Fauquier and Loudoun counties, Mercer was also interested in western lands in the Ohio River valley. To pursue this interest the Mercers and the Lees were instrumental in forming the Ohio Company, although the two families later had a falling-out in the debate over the 1764 Stamp Act. While Mercer was the company's secretary, GW's brother Lawrence was its second president.

Three of John Mercer's sons served with GW in the Virginia Regiment, one of whom, John Fenton Mercer (1735–1756), was killed in battle. The other two sons, George Mercer (1733–1784) and James Mercer (1735/6–1793), appear in the diaries along with other members of the family (see: HARRISON [1], 369; FREEMAN, 2:2, 290; COUNCIL, 232–35).

The Peake family of the Northern Neck descended in two branches through the two grandsons of John Peake the immigrant. The elder of the two grandsons was John Peake (d. 1758), of Prince William County, whose wife Lucy bore him eight sons. The younger grandson, William Peake (d. 1761), of Fairfax County, lived at Willow Spring in the fork of Little Hunting Creek and was hence GW's closest neighbor. William was a Truro Parish vestryman for many years, and upon his death GW was chosen by the vestry to take his place. William had two daughters, Sarah and Mary, and three sons, Humphrey, John, and William Jr., the last of whom served in the French and Indian War and died in 1756. Although it is the Willow Spring Peakes who usually appear in the diaries, the Mr. Peake mentioned here may have been a Peake of Prince William County (MCDONALD, 437–53).

From Daniel McCarty (d. 1724), planter of Pope's Creek, Westmoreland County, and Speaker of the House of Burgesses, 1715–18, were descended three branches of the Pope's Creek McCartys, many of whom appear in the diaries. Speaker Daniel's oldest son, Dennis McCarty (d. 1742), founder of the Cedar Grove McCartys, married Sarah Ball in 1724 and settled at Cedar Grove, which was in Truro Parish when that parish was created in 1732. His oldest son, Daniel McCarty (d. 1791), whom GW refers to before the Revolution as "Captain" and afterwards as "Colonel," was in his lifetime one of the wealthiest men in Virginia (MAIN, 378–79). Captain McCarty, his wife Sinah Ball McCarty (d. 1798), and their five children, all of whom appear in the diaries, lived at Mount Air about three miles up Accotink Creek from Cedar Grove. Both McCarty homesteads were located a few miles down the Potomac River from Mount Vernon. Captain McCarty served in the Truro vestry 1748–84, and the Washingtons and McCartys often appear to have dined together after services at Pohick Church. Through his mother GW was related to both Captain McCarty and his wife.

Wednesday Feby. 27.   Very little Wind & that Southerly but raind of and on the whole day.

Continued plowing while the Weather woud permit, and the People, viz. George, Kate, Doll, & little George were employd in Grubing the Field by the Garden.

Nations's horse that was destraind on for my Rent was sold at Publick Auction to Mr. Tom Triplet for £5.

Peter had got his Coal drawn & brought in one load.

Thomas Triplett (died c.1780), one of several sons of Francis Triplett (d. 1757) of Truro Parish, may have been living at this time on land he had inherited from his father on Goose Creek in Loudoun or Fauquier County (will of Francis Triplett, 4 Oct. 1757, Fairfax County Wills, Book B-1, 195–98, Vi Microfilm). However, by 1763 he was living on the North Branch of Little Hunting Creek where he had rented a small plantation from George Mason of Gunston Hall (lease of Mason to Triplett, 26 April 1763, Fairfax County Deeds, Book E-1, 262–69, Vi Microfilm). In 1771 he leased additional land in that area from Mason and continued living there until his death (lease of Mason to Triplett, 19 Dec. 1771, Fairfax County Deeds, Book K-1, 14–23, Vi Microfilm). This land later passed to Mason's son Thomson Mason (1759–1820) and became part of Hollin Hall plantation (deed of George Mason to Thomson Mason, 16 June 1786, Fairfax County Deeds, Book Q-1, 249–54, Vi Microfilm). Thomas Triplett and his brother William regularly joined GW in fox hunting.

Thursday Feby. 28th.   Measurd the Fields by the Quarter & Garden as the Fences was intended to be run and found Six Acres in the former & Nine in the Latter.

Also run the Round the Fields in the Lower pasture according as the dividing Fence is to go but the Compass being bad or some mistake happening I coud not close the plot with any exactness.

Finished Grubbing the Field by the Garden.

Between Sul [sun] setting & Dark, came Mr. Ramsay, Mr. Piper, Captn. Stanly & Captn. Littledale.

Warm, & little or no wind the first part of the Day. Towards Night it clouded and the Wind getting No. Easterly it begn. raining & grew colder.

Bought 3000 Shingles a 22/6 of [   ] Newbold also wood ware, & Bees Wax.

Harry Piper (d. 1780), a merchant of Alexandria, was a factor for John Dixon & Isaac Littledale, of Whitehaven, Eng. Captain Stanley may have been Capt. Edward Stanley, who sailed in the tobacco trade for Peter How & Co., also of Whitehaven (P.R.O., C.O.5/1447, f. 66).

GW paid Purnell Newbold a total of £5 4s. 7½d. Maryland currency for his goods (LEDGER A, 89).

CLOSE THE PLOT: In running the lines of this survey, GW did not return to his exact beginning point as he should have, and thus a gap was left in the boundaries of the plot.

Friday Feby. 29th.   The Rain continued by Intervals through the Night, and till afternoon when the Wind came to No. West and ceasd, growing clear. Stopd my Plows.

The Gentlemen Dind here to day and two, viz. Mr. Ramsay & Captn. Stanley, returnd to Alexandria. The others went to Belvoir.

A very great Circle rd. the Moon.

[March]

Saturday Mar. 1–1760.   Finishd Bottling 91 dozn. Cyder.

The wind for the first part was at No. West & very cold, but shifting Easterly & then to So. it grew something warmer but continued Cloudy.

The Ground being hard froze stopd my Plows this day also—and employd all hands in running the dividing fence of my Pastures.

Traversd the Fields in the Lower Pasture again & set a Course from the head of the drain that Runs into my Meadow [   ] which leaves in the Tobo. House Field [   ] and in the other [   ].

Also found the contents of my Meadow to be [   ] and that the Pocoson at Cotton patch measurd [   ].

Note. The Ground cleard this year measures [   ] and the fallow Ground is only [   ]. The Marsh and Pocoson at the Creek point contains [   ].

POCOSON (pocosin): from an Algonquin Indian word meaning a tidal swamp in its last stages before turning into dry land. In the miry pocosin soil, alternately covered and uncovered by water, would grow grass, shrubs, and pine trees.

Sunday Mar. 2. The Morning calm & Serene. About 10 Oclock the Wind freshned from the No. West, and died away by two. At 5 it came Southerly & blew again seeming unsettled.

Mr. Clifton came here to day, & under pretence of his Wife not consenting to acknowledge her Right of Dower wanted to disengage himself of the Bargain he had made with me for his Land on the 26th. past and by his Shuffling behaviour on the occasion convincd me of his being the trifling body represented.

Monday Mar. 3d. Bought 100 Bushels of Oats at 1/6. of Reuben Joyne.

Finishd plowing the Clover field but not the dividing Fence in the Pastures.

Wind for the most part was Southerly—sometimes blewing fresh & at other times quite calm but the day was cloudy & felt cold till towards Night.

Tuesday Mar. 4th. Rain without Intermission till Noon—thence at Intervals till Night, with strong So[uther]ly wind the whole time.

Plows Stopd—but the dividing fence finishd. Gave up the Horse Cart, & the Dun horse and Jack to R. Stephens.

Wednesday Mar. 5. High Wind from the West—the day clear & somewhat cold. Began plowing the field by the Garden for Lucern.

Put in the great bay mare ⟨& horse⟩ King. The latter coud not be prevaild upon to plow. The other did very well: but the Plows run very badly.

Finishd Plow Harness for my Chariot Horses.

LUCERN: alfalfa or lucerne, *Medicago sativa*. Although this perennial legume is widely grown in Virginia today as a hay crop, GW tried unsuccessfully for at least 35 years to raise it. On 12 Sept. 1795 he wrote to Jefferson that he was giving it up because, even with manuring, he had experienced less success with it than with chicory. He probably would have fared better by using more limestone, and much better had he had available the inoculating bacteria in use today for such nitrogen-fixing crops.

Thursday Mar. 6. Fitted a two Eyed Plow instead of a Duck Bill Plow and with much difficulty made my Chariot Wheel horses plow.

Surveyd Captn. Posseys 145 Acres of Woodland Ground which he bought of my Bror. Chs. & find some of the Courses and distances to vary from those in the Deeds and that 136 Acres only, are Included.

Also run the upper Courses of Frens Land and find some great Errors as may be seen by my Plot of it.

Wind Southerly & day fine.

Charles Washington (1738–1799) was married in 1757 to Mildred Thornton, daughter of Col. Francis Thornton of Spotsylvania County, and was probably living in the Fredericksburg area at this time. Although GW was very interested in buying lands near Mount Vernon, he did not purchase the woodland tract from Posey, and it was sold 16–17 June 1760 to Daniel French for £217 10s. (Fairfax County Deeds, Book D-1, 730–36, Vi Microfilm).

Henry Trenn (variously spelled Tren, Frenn, and Fren), who died in 1751, had owned a tract of about 300 acres on the west bank of Dogue Run, above the road from Gum Spring to Colchester. In 1750 he had sold 94 acres at the lower end of the tract to GW's half brother Lawrence, and the remainder was inherited at his death by two of his orphaned children, Absolom and Diana (deed of Trenn to Lawrence Washington, 4 Feb. 1750, Fairfax County Deeds, Book C-1, 152–53, Vi Microfilm; will of Trenn, 3 Oct. 1751, Fairfax County Wills, Book A-1, 490–91, Vi Microfilm). Absolom had apparently died since his father's death, and the tract was now solely owned by Diana, who was living in Maryland.

Friday Mar. 7th. Fine Morning, but Cloudy Afternoon, wind Southerly.

Put the Poll end Horses into the Plow in the Morng. and the Postilion & hand Horse in the Afternoon but the Ground being well sworded over & very heavy plowing I repented putting them in at all for fear it should give them a Habit of Stopping in the Chariot.

Saturday Mar. 8. No. Et. Wind & Rain—Plows stopd.

Gave Captn. Cawseys Skipper namely William Vicars—1 Tobo. Note and an Order on Hunting Creek Warehouses for 7 Hhds. of my Mountain Tobo.

John Cawsey was captain of the *Tyger,* a 120-ton British-built ship which took a crew of nine and sailed in the Virginia tobacco trade for John Farrel & Co. of Bristol, Eng. William Vicars was probably Cawsey's first mate. HUNTING CREEK WAREHOUSES: These tobacco warehouses at Alexandria had been established by the inspection acts of 1730 and 1732 (see entry for 25 Jan. 1760).

Sunday Mar. 9. No. Et. wind, and Snow by Intervals the whole day.

Monday Mar. 10th.   No. W. wind and clear, but the Ground too Wet for Plowing.

Rode to my Plantation and the Mill, & there partly agreed with Jerry Mitchell to rebuild my Mill when She runs dry in the Summer.

Dispatchd Mulatto Jack to Frederick for some Mares from thence to Plow.

The Snow (which was not more than an Inch & half deep) was entirely dissolvd today.

Jeremiah Mitchell, an independent artisan, contracted to do this repair work for 4s. 6d. a day. He put in 97 days in all, finishing the job by 1 Dec. 1760 (LEDGER A, 102).

Tuesday Mar. 11th.   Visited at Colo. Fairfax and was informd that Clifton had sold his Land to Mr. Thompsons Mason for 1200 £ Sterlg. which fully unravelled his Conduct on the 2d. and convincd me that he was nothing less than a thorough pacd Rascall—disregardful of any Engagements of Words or Oaths not bound by Penalties.

The day clear but something cold, Wind at No. West.

George William Fairfax was one of GW's fellow commissioners in the Clifton case. Thomson Mason (1733–1785), of Raspberry Plain in Loudoun County, was a younger brother of George Mason of Gunston Hall. He

This pastel of Thomson Mason, brother of George Mason of Gunston Hall, is apparently from a miniature done from life. (Board of Regents of Gunston Hall)

studied law in England at the Middle Temple and in 1760 was a burgess for Stafford County.

Wednesday Mar. 12.   Returnd home, Mrs. Carlyle accompanying us, the day being exceeding fine. Wind at South.

Found William Lodwick here with one Beef from Frederick. He set of with two but lamd the other and left him at Ricd. Colemans at the Sugar Lands.

Lodwick was apparently hired for this job only. In 1756 Richard Coleman (d. 1764) and his son James received a license to run an ordinary on the Leesburg Pike at Sugar Land Run.

Thursday Mar. 13th.   Incessant Rain and No. Et. Wind.

Mr. Carlyle (who came here from Port Tobo. Court last Night) and Mrs. Carlyle were confind here all day.

Mulatto Jack returnd home with the Mares he was sent for, but so poor were they, and so much abusd had they been by my Rascally Overseer Hardwick that they were scarce able to go highlone, much less to assist in the business of the Plantations.

Merchants or their agents regularly made rounds of county courts, which met monthly to transact business and legal cases. Port Tobacco was the seat of Charles County, Md.

HIGHLONE: alone, without support.

Friday Mar. 14th.   No. Et. Wind & rain witht. Intermission till after Noon. The Rain then abated, but clouds continued.

Mr. Carlyle & his Wife still remaind here. We talkd a good deal of a Scheme of setting up an Iron Work on Colo. Fairfax's Land on Shannondoah. Mr. Chapman who was proposd as a partner being a perfect Judge of these matters was to go up and view the Conveniences and determine the Scheme.

Colonel Fairfax's land on the Shenandoah River included the east bank of the crossing for Vestal's ferry. Carlyle and his brother-in-law George William Fairfax went ahead with the ironworks project. Nathaniel Chapman, who died later this year, had iron experience both with the Principio Company of Maryland and the Accokeek works in Stafford County. Chapman had also served as an executor for the estates of Augustine and Lawrence Washington, both of whom had had interests in ironworks.

Saturday Mar. 15. Snowd in the Morng. but afterwards clearing. Mr. Carlyle and his Wife returnd home.

Wm. Lodwick & the boy (Nat) who came down with him went up for the lame Beef they left upon the Road coming down.

The Vast quantity of Rain which had fallen in the last two

days had Swelld the Waters so high that dogue Run carried of the Tumbling Dam of my Mill and was near carrying of the House also.

Wind at No. Et. & fair from a settled Sky. Sent word to Mr. Clifton by my Negro Will that I shoud be glad to see him here in the Morning having something to propose to him.

The bad Weather this Week put a Total stop to plowing except a little on Wednesday with one Plow.

GW's dam was an earthwork with a tumbling bay, or spillway, in one portion. Excess water flowed over this outfall, normally preventing the water level behind the dam from rising too high. But on this occasion water came downstream faster than it could flow out the spillway, and the dam collapsed.

Sunday Mar. 16th.   In the Morning early began Snowing with a Strong No. Et. Wind and continued without the least Intermission, or Remission till dark, & how long after I know not.

Monday Mar. 17th.   The Snow this Morng. was much drifted, & many places of considerable depth. It kept Snowing by Intervals till Noon & appeard unsettled the whole day.

Went to my Mill and took a view of the Ruins the Fresh had causd. Determind however to repr. it with all expedition & accordingly set my Carpenters to making Wheel & Handbarrows.

Beef from Coleman's was brought down.

Mr. Possey being here and talking of the Orphan Fren's Land adjoining mine on Dogue Run, he undertook to purchase it for me of the said Orphan Diana, who lives at Nangemy in Maryland with one————Wright who I think he said Married her Aunt.

Mr. Possey thinks it may be bought for £50 or 60 pound & there shoud be 207 Acres of it.

Posey finally purchased this land for GW in 1764, by which time Diana had married William Whiting. The Whitings received £75 in several installments for the property, which was then estimated to contain 200 acres (LEDGER A, 168; GW's list of quitrent lands for 1764, DLC:GW).

Nanjemoy, according to an English traveler who saw it in 1774, was "a small Village of about five houses" lying west of Nanjemoy Creek in Charles County, Md. All the inhabitants were planters except two men who ran a store there (CRESSWELL, 17).

Tuesday Mar. 18th.   Cool in the morning, Wind at No. West, but afterwards Shifting to South grew more moderate and Melted the Snow much.

Went to Court partly on my own private Business and partly on Cliftons Affair but the Commissioners not meeting nothing was done in regard to the Latter. Much discourse happend between him and I con⟨cer⟩ning his ungenerous treatment of me. The whole turning to little Acct. tis not worth reciting here the result of which was that for £50 more than Mr. Mason offerd him he undertook if possible to disengage himself from that Gentleman & to let me have his Land. I did not think Myself restraind by any Rules of Honour, Conscience or &ca. from makeg. him this offer as his Lands were first engagd to me by the most Solemn assurances that any Man coud give.

Mr. Johnston not being in Town I coud not get Mr. Darrel's Deeds to me acknowledgd.

Killd the Beeves that came from Frederick.

The following month this move by GW in the Clifton affair was criticized by the General Court sitting in chancery. GW was putting himself into a potentially awkward situation, for as a commissioner he was responsible for giving a disinterested report to the chancery court on how the Clifton case should be settled.

GW dined today at Mrs. Chew's tavern (LEDGER A, 89).

Wednesday Mar. 19. Cold Southerly Wind & Lowring Weather till towds. Evening when the Clouds dispersing it became more moderate.

Peter (my Smith) and I after several efforts to make a plow after a new model—partly of my own contriving—was fiegn to give it out, at least for the present.

Snow but little dissolvd. Colo. Fairfax & Mrs. Fx. came here in the Evening.

Thursday Mar. 20th. Cold Northerly Wind. Colo. F[airfa]x and I set out to Alexa. by appointmt. to Settle & adjust (with the other Comrs.) Cliftons & Carrols accts. conformable to a decree of our Genl. Court but not being able to accomplish it then the 28th. was a further day appointed to meet and my house the place resolvd upon.

The other commissioners were Rev. Charles Green and John West, Jr., now sheriff of Fairfax County. It was the common practice in such cases for the court to appoint four commissioners, any three of whom could act as a quorum.

Friday Mar. 21st. Colo. Fairfax & Mrs. Fx. returnd home. The Wind being No. Easterly the Morng. and indeed the best half of the day was very Cold and Cloudy. The Wind towards Evening seemd to be getting So[uther]ly.

Brought 47 Bushels of Wheat from my Mill.

Saturday March 22d.   Cold southerly Wind and Cloudy, with Rain from 10 O'clock till Night.

Doctr. Laurie came here. Agreed with George Taylor for 3 Sows and Pigs—at 45/.

Taylor is a local small planter who apparently moved to Loudoun County later in 1760.

Sunday Mar. 23d.   Southerly Wind and Warm. Miss Fairfax & Miss Dent came here.

Hannah Fairfax was a younger sister of George William Fairfax. Miss Dent was possibly Elizabeth Dent (1727–1796) or one of her younger sisters, all daughters of Peter Dent (c.1694–1757), of Whitehaven, on Mattawoman Creek in the Piscataway region of Prince George's County, Md. (NEWMAN, 36–39).

Monday Mar. 24th.   Began repairing my Mill Dam—with hands from all my Quarters Carpenters Included.

In digging Earth for this purpose great Quantities of Marle or Fullers Earth appeard.

In the Evening, in a Bed that had been prepard with a mixture of Dung on Saturday last, I sowed Clo⟨ver,⟩ Lucerne, & Rye Grass Seeds in the Garden, to try their Goodness—doing it in the following Order. At the end next the Corner are two Rows of Clover Seed—in the 3d., 4, 5 & 6th. Rye Grass the last Row thinest Sowd 7th. & 8th. Barley (to see if it woud come up) the last also thinnest Sown—9, 10, 11, 12th. Lucerne—first a few seeds at every 4 Inches distance the next thicker & so on to the last wch. was very thick.

Carried the Sows I bot. of George Taylor to my Mill by Water.

The carpenters were needed to work on the spillway, which was made of timber. In addition, the dam probably had a timber foundation and may have been further strengthened by vertical planking on its upstream or downstream sides or in its center (CRAIK [1], 167–70).

CLOVER SEED: *Trifolium pratense,* red clover. Unless he specifies another clover by name, GW is referring to this species.

Tuesday Mar. 25th.   Set one Plow to Work on the Field below the Garden.

All hands being employd on the Dam again the Water was Stopd. and the Work in a fair way of receiving a finish by tomorrow Night.

The Wind was Southerly—the Day Changeable.

Mrs. Possey, & some young woman whose name was unknown to any Body in this family, dind here.

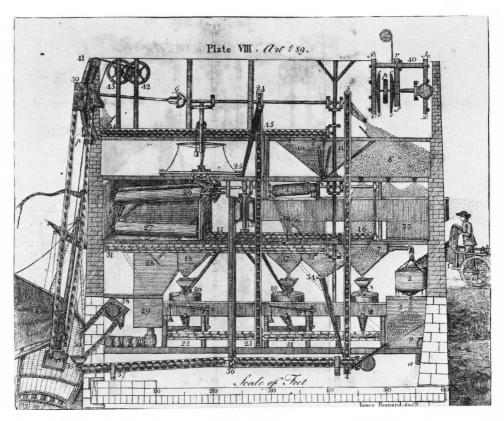

Milling machinery as depicted by Oliver Evans in *The Young Mill-Wright and Miller's Guide*, Philadelphia, 1795. (Beinecke Rare Book and Manuscript Library, Yale University)

Wednesday Mar. 26.   One Plow at Work today also.

Miss Dent & Miss Fairfax returnd home.

My Dam was entirely compleated by Evening.

Spent the greatest part of the day in making a new plow of my own Invention.

Wind at No. West & very boisterous.

Thursday Mar. 27.   Southerly Wind, day warm and very fine.

Sat my Plow to work and found She Answerd very well in the

Field in the lower Pasture wch. I this day began Plowing with the large Bay Mare & Rankin. Mulatto Jack conting. to Plow the Field below the Garden.

Agreed to give Mr. William Triplet £18 to build the two houses in the Front of my House (plastering them also) and running Walls for Pallisades to them from the Great house & from the Great House to the Wash House and Kitchen also.

William Triplett (d. 1803) of Truro Parish lived with his wife Sarah Massey Triplett at Round Hill about four miles northwest of Mount Vernon. He had participated in a recent remodeling of GW's mansion house, doing brickwork on the foundation and chimneys and plastering the interior of the house. His bill for those jobs, which totaled £52 8s. 4d., had been discharged by GW on 26 Feb. 1760 (LEDGER A, 72). GW had planned to have the two outbuildings mentioned here built earlier, but Triplett's many engagements to work for other planters in the area had prevented him from undertaking the task until now (John Patterson to GW, 2 Sept. 1758, DLC:GW).

Friday Mar. 28. According to appointment, Colo. F⟨airfa⟩x & Mr. Green met here upon Clifton's Affair, he being present as was Mr. Thompson Mason (as Council for him). Mr. Digges and Mr. Addison were also here and after examining all the Papers and Accts. on both sides, and stating them in the manner wch. seemd most equitable to Us, the debt due from Mr. Clifton according to that Settlement amounted to £[   ] that is to say— to Mr. Carroll £[243 135.1d.] to Mr. Tasker pr. Mr. Digges [£304 155.3d.] to Do. pr. Mr. Addison [£364 19s.].

We also agreed to report several things which appeard necessary, as well, in behalf of Mr. Clifton as the other party.

The Gentlemen from Maryland, Mr. Mason & Clifton left this; but Colo. Fairfax and Mr. Green stayd the Night.

Abt. Noon Mulatto Jack finishd plowing the Field below the Garden and went into the lower Pasture to work.

Sun shone Warm but the Wind blew strong from South.

The Addison family of Maryland descended from John Addison, who emigrated from England in 1677. His son Thomas Addison (1679–1727) built the family home of Oxon Hill in Prince George's County, Md., across the Potomac from Alexandria. By his second wife, Eleanor Smith Addison, Thomas had one daughter and four sons, one of whom was John Addison (1713–1764) of Oxon Hill, who appears here.

The gross amounts filled in here are taken from the Virginia General Court decree of 12 April 1760 (NjWoG). They are probably the amounts decided upon at this meeting but left blank by GW because interest and court costs were still to be figured into the final totals.

Saturday Mar. 29th. About noon sat one Plow into the Fallow Ground below the Hill, & about an hour before Sunset the other.

Fresh and variable Wind chiefly from South. Carried out about [   ] Tumbril Load of Dung from the Stable upon the Clover Field.

Sunday Mar. 30th.   Little Wind, but moist Weather. A misty Rain continuing at Short Intervals through the day.

Monday Mar. 31st.   Strong So[uther]ly Wind in the first part of the day with light Showers but Abt. Noon the Wind got No[rther]ly.

Went to Belvoir (according to Appointment on the 28th. past) and drew up and Signd a Report of our Proceedings in Clifton's affair to be sent with the Accts. to the Genl. Court.

Finishd plowing the Fallowd Ground abt. Sun Setting.

Mr. Walter Stuart who I met with at Belvoir gave me a Letter from Dr. Macleane and another from Bishop.

The Latter very desirous of returning but enlisted in the 44th. Regimt. the Former wrote to Colo. Byrd to ask his discharge of the Genl.

Wrote to Lieutt. Smith to try if possible to get me a Careful Man to Overlook my Carpenters. Wrote also to Harwick ordering down two Mares from thence & desiring him to engage me a Ditcher. Inclosd a Letter from my Brother Jno. to his Overseer Farrell Littleton and directed him what to do if the Small pox shd. come amongst them.

REPORT: The report included a recommendation that all sales by Clifton be set aside in favor of an auction. See entry for 28 Mar.

Dr. Lauchlin MacLeane (d. 1778), of England, served with units of the British army and practiced medicine in Philadelphia 1755–61. MacLeane, Stewart, Bishop, Byrd, and GW had all served together in the Forbes expedition against Fort Duquesne in 1758. GW knew that MacLeane was now in Philadelphia and may have written to Bishop in care of the doctor (see entry for 25 Jan. 1760). The 44th Regiment was brought from Ireland for Braddock's campaign and may have been Bishop's old unit. Col. William Byrd III (1729–1777), of Westover, had succeeded GW as commander of the Virginia Regiment, now stationed at Winchester. Bishop did not appear at Mount Vernon until Sept. 1761, when he resumed his service which continued to his death 33 years later.

Lt. Charles Smith, who was given command of Fort Loudoun at Winchester in 1758, had been recommended to that post by GW as an officer both "diligent" and "exceedingly industrious" (GW to John Blair, 28 May 1758, DLC:GW). Having lost an arm in the service, Smith received a life pension from the House of Burgesses on the recommendation of a committee which included GW (H.B.J., 1761–65, 179, 185).

DITCHER: an employee to supervise the construction of drainage ditches, along field boundaries and elsewhere. The customary boundaries delineating

GW's fields consisted of two parallel ditches with a row of dense hedge along the center ridge. They served the dual purpose of draining wet lands and making it more difficult for livestock to pass through the hedge.

GW's brother John Augustine Washington (1736–1787), who lived at Bushfield in Westmoreland County, had inherited land in Frederick County which lay near GW's Bullskin plantation.

[April]

Tuesday April 1 – 1760.   Crossd plowd the Fallow Field to day wch. contains 3.2.38 wch. shews that 2 Acres a day in Level ground already broke up may easily be accomplishd.

Doctor Laurie came here.

The Wind at No. West. Weather clear, somewhat Cool and drying.

Moon at its first rising remarkably red.

Recd. a Letter from Mr. Digges, Inclosing a Packet for Messrs. Nichos. & Withe wch. he desird I woud send under Cover to some Friend of mine in Williamsburg as it was to go by Clifton suspecting that Gentleman woud not deal fairly by it.

Began to prepare a Small piece of Ground of abt. [   ] Yards Square at the lower Corner of my Garden to put Trefoil in—a little Seed given me by Colo. F[airfa]x Yesterday.

The next day GW wrote a covering letter to accompany the packet. In the letter, addressed to Benjamin Waller, of the General Court, GW recited his differences with Clifton and Thomas Mason and argued strongly for his own position, which was that the court should "confirm the Opinion of the Commissioners" (2 April 1760, ViMtV). Of the two interested parties named Digges, this reference is probably to William, since Ignatius, as an agent for Charles Carroll of Carrollton, consistently refused to cooperate in the Clifton proceedings (GW to Carroll, 31 July 1791, DLC:GW). In 1760 Robert Carter Nicholas (1728–1780), a burgess for York County, and George Wythe (1726–1806), the burgess for the College of William and Mary, were already recognized as having two of Virginia's most talented legal minds.

CONTAINS 3.2.38: He means 3 acres, 2 roods, 38 perches. A rood is 40 square rods or ¼ acre; a perch is 1 square rod or $\frac{1}{160}$ acre.

TREFOIL: *Trifolium procumbens,* hop clover, or hop trefoil. GW is probably referring to this plant when he mentions yellow clover and yellow trefoil.

Wednesday Apl. 2d.   Got the above Ground ready for Sowing tomorrow. Begn. to Cross plow the first plowd Ground in the lower Pasture endeavouring to get it in Order for Sowg. Lucerne Seed In.

A Drying Southerly Wind & Warm.

Thursday April 3d.   Sowd 17½ Drills of Trefoil Seed in the ground adjoining the Garden, numbering from the side next the

Stable (or Work Shop) the residue of them viz. 4 was sowd with Lucerne Seed—both done with design to see how these Seeds answer in that Ground.

Sowd my Fallow Field in Oats to day, and harrowed them in viz. 101½ Bushels. Got done about three Oclock.

Cook Jack after laying of the Lands in this Field went to plowing in the 12 Acre Field where they were Yesterday as did the other plow abt. 5 oclock after Pointing.

Got several Composts and laid them to dry in order to mix with the Earth brot. from the Field below to try their several Virtues.

Wind blew very fresh from South. Clouds often appeard, and sometimes threatned the near approach of Rain but a clear setting Sun seemd denoted the Contrary.

SOWD . . . OATS TO DAY: *Avena sativa,* the "common oat" in GW's papers. GW did far less experimenting with varieties of oats than with wheat or field peas, perhaps because there was less selection in process among English and American growers. While president, he wrote to manager James Anderson, 29 Jan. 1797, that he was obtaining several bushels of an oat from beyond the Alleghenies "of a quality, it is said, inferior to none in the world" (DLC:GW). See entry for 8 Mar. 1787 for a note on the Poland oat.

Friday Apl. 4th.   Sowd abt. one Bushl. of Barley in a piece of Ground near the Tobo. House in the 12 Acre Field.

Harrowd, & crossd Harrowd the Ground in the sd. Field intended for Lucerne.

Apprehending the Herrings were come Hauled the Sein but catchd only a few of them tho a good many of other sorts. Majr. Stewart and Doctr. Johnston came here in the Afternoon and at Night Mr. Richie attended by Mr. Ross solliciting Freight—promisd none.

BUSHL. OF BARLEY: *Hordeum vulgare,* barley. Here GW is sowing spring barley, but his common practice is to use the winter variety (see entry for 2 Sept. 1763). "I tried it [spring barley] two or three years unsuccessfully" (GW to William Pearce, 23 Mar. 1794, NBLiHi). Elsewhere he mentions summer barley, Minorca barley, and English barley. For naked barley, see entry for 3 May 1788, and for bere barley, see entry for 10 April 1787.

Herring came up the rivers of tidewater Virginia and Maryland every spring to spawn near the falls (VOYAGE, 335). On 15 Mar. 1760 Cary & Co. of London sent GW an invoice listing two new fish seines which were described as being "35 fathoms long each, each 20 feet deep all through, made of the best 3 thd. laid twine, small Inch Meshes, hung loose on the lines & well fixd with Leads & Corks" (DLC:GW). Those seines, however, probably did not arrive in time to be of much use to GW during this fishing season.

Robert Stewart entered the Virginia Regiment in 1754. He was soon made captain and was with GW at Fort Necessity and Braddock's Defeat, becoming

Lucerne Flower.

Lucerne Leaves.

Burnet.

Sheeps Fescue.

Washington eventually gave up trying to raise lucerne, now called alfalfa. From *Farmer's Magazine*, Sept. 1776. (Beinecke Rare Book and Manuscript Library, Yale University)

one of GW's favorite officers. In the fall of 1758 he became brigade major of the Virginia troops on GW's recommendation, and in 1760 he was still in the service, stationed at Winchester. Dr. Johnston is probably Robert Johnston (Johnson), originally of James City County, who served as the surgeon in Col. William Byrd's Virginia Regiment; he may have been attending the Virginia troops in Winchester at this time. Johnston, who voted for GW in the lively 1758 burgesses' election in Frederick County, died in Frederick County in 1763 (CROZIER [1], 40; election poll for Frederick County, 24 July 1758, DLC:GW).

Archibald Ritchie (d. 1784) was a Scottish merchant in Hobbs Hole (Tappahannock, on the Rappahannock River, Essex County). Hector Ross, a merchant at Colchester, Fairfax County, bought tobacco and Indian corn from GW, and his establishment, in turn, served as a local store of convenience for clothing and minor necessities for GW's white servants, his tenants, and his slaves.

Saturday Apl. 5th.　Planted out 20 young Pine trees at the head of my Cherry Walk.

Recd. my Goods from York.

Hauld the Sein again catchd 2 or 3 White Fish more Herring than Yesterday & a great Number of Cats.

Richie and Ross went away.

Made another Plow the same as my former excepting that it has two Eyes and the other one.

So[uther]ly Wind, but not so fresh as that wch. blew Yesterday. However, it blew up a little Rain abt. Dark with a good deal of Lightning & some Thunder.

WHITE FISH: shad. These fish usually ran in large numbers during April and May. CATS: catfish (VOYAGE, 335).

Sunday April 6th.　Wind at No. Et. and Cool. About 3 Oclock it began Raining and continued to do so (moderately) for about an hour when it cleard, the Wind shifting So[uther]ly.

I just perceivd the Rye grass Seed wch. I sowd in the Garden to try its goodness was beginning to come up pretty thick; the Clovr., Lucerne, & Barley I discoverd above Ground, on the first Instant.

Majr. Stewart & Doctr. Johnston set out for Winchesr.

Monday April 7th.　Raind till 6 Oclock pretty hard and then cleard—Wind So[uther]ly and Cloudy all day.

In the Evening Colo. Frog came here, and made me an offer of 2400 Acres of Land wch. he has in Culpeper for £400. This Ld. Lyes (according to his acct.) 46 Miles above The Falls of Rappahannock—is well Water'd Timberd & of a Fertile Soil—no Impr[ove]ments on it. I told him that I woud get Captn. Thomas

Fitzhugh to give me his Opinion of the Land when he went next to his Quarter not far from it—or I woud take it in my way from Fredk. when I next went up there as it lies he says only 8 Miles from the place where Josh. Nevil livd at the Pignut Ridge.

One Captn. Kennelly lives within a Mile of the Land and is well acquainted with it.

People kept Holliday.

Col. John Frogg was living in Fauquier County but held land across Hedgman's River in Culpeper County. The falls were just above Fredericksburg. Capt. Thomas Fitzhugh (1725–1768) lived at Boscobel in King George (now Stafford) County. Many of the military ranks held by men appearing in the diaries are in the colonial militia, in which the highest rank was that of colonel; Fitzhugh was a captain in the militia. Joseph Neville (many spellings) lived in the vicinity of the Neville's ordinary shown on the 1755 edition of the Fry-Jefferson Map. KENNELLY: probably James Kennerley, of Culpeper County, whose land was close to John Frogg's (PRICHARD, 31).

HOLLIDAY: Easter Monday.

Tuesday April 8th.   What time it began Raining in the Night I cant say, but at day break it was pouring very hard, and continued so, till 7 oclock when a Messenger came to inform me that my Mill was in great danger of blowing. I immediately hurried off all hands with Shovels &ca. to her assistance and got there myself just time enough to give her a reprieve for this time by Wheeling dirt into the place which the Water had Washd.

While I was here a very heavy Thunder Shower came on which lasted upwards of an hour.

Here also, I tried what time the Mill requird to grind a Bushel of Corn and to my Surprize found She was within 5 Minutes of an hour about. This old Anthony attributed to the low head of Water (but Whether it was so or not I cant say—her Works all decayd and out of Order wch. I rather take to be the cause).

This Bushel of Corn when Ground measurd near a Peck more Meal.

No. Et. Wind and Cloudy all day. Towards Night it dripd of Rain.

The mill was probably a small, one- or two-story wooden structure with an overshot or breast wheel and a single set of grinding stones. GW's assessment of the mill's machinery must have been correct, but Anthony recognized an equally important problem. The head of water was not high enough to generate much force when the water fell on the wheel, and without more power, better machinery could not be used to its full capacity. Some work was done on the millrace by Hosea Bazell during the late summer, but any improvement made in the head of water was probably minimal (LEDGER A,

102). Jerry Mitchell apparently confined his efforts this year to rebuilding the mill's internal works.

The slave carpenter Anthony was in his middle fifties when he was brought to Mount Vernon in 1759 as part of Martha Custis's dower. GW made him his miller but the next year reassigned him to the crew of carpenters, where by 1762 he had become head slave carpenter. After 1763 Anthony disappears from GW's tithable lists.

Wednesday Apl. 9th.   Wind at No. Et. Very Cloudy and sometimes Misty.

The Heavy Rains that had fallen in this few days past had made the Ground too wet for Plowing; I therefore set about the Fence which Incloses my Clover Field.

Doctr. Laurie came here. I may add Drunk.

Observd the Trefoil wch. I sowd on the 3d. Inst. to be coming up, but in a Scattg. manner. The Lucerne wch. was sewd at the same time and in the same manner appeard much better; & forwarder.

Thursday Apl. 10th.   Mrs. Washington was blooded by Doctr. Laurie who stayd all Night.

This Morning my Plows began to Work in the Clover Field, but a hard Shower of Rain from No. Et. (where the Wind hung all day) abt. 11 Oclock, stopd them for the Remainder of the day. I therefore Employd the hands in making two or three hauls of the Sein, & found that the Herrings were come.

Val Crawford brought 4 Hhds. of my Mountain Tobo. to the Warehouses in Alexa. two in my own Waggon and with a Plow such as they use mostly in Frederick came here in the Night.

He informd me of my worthy Overseer Hardwicks lying since the 17th. Ulto. in Winchester of a Broken Leg.

Valentine Crawford (d. 1777) lived near GW's Bullskin plantation in Frederick County and was regularly hired to bring down GW's mountain tobacco from those quarters. Valentine was the brother of Col. William Crawford (1732–1782) and half brother to John, Hugh, Richard, and Marcus Stephenson, sons of Richard and Onora (née Grimes) Crawford Stephenson, all of whom appear in the diaries.

Friday Apl. 11th.   Set one Plow to Work again in the Morning the other about 10 Oclock in the Clover Field.

Tryd the new Plow brot. Yesterday, found she did good Work and run very true but heavy—rather too much so for two Horses, especially while the Gd. was moist.

Abt. 11 Oclock set the People to Hauling the Sein and by Night and in the Night Catchd and dressd [   ] Barrels of Herring and 60 White Fish.

Observd that the Flood tide was infinitely the best for these Fish.

The Wind came fresh from So. Et. the day Cool. Cloudy till Noon, but very clear promising settled Weather afterwards.

After cleaning, the catch was packed with salt into barrels and stored for use on the plantation, fish being a staple of the slaves' diet (MIDDLETON [2], 202–5).

Saturday April 12th.   Hard No. West the whole day, very clear and Cool.

Hauld the Sein but without Success. Some said it was owing to the wind setting of the Shore, which seems in some Measure confirmd by the quantity we catchd Yesterday when the Wind blew on upon it.

About 11 Oclock finishd plowing the Clover Field. Abt. 1 Mullatto Jack began harrowing it with the wide Toothd Harrow and got half over the Field by Night. Cook Jack went to Plowing in the 12 Acre Field.

Perceivd my Barley and Oats to be coming up very thick and well.

Engag'd 150 Bushels of Oats of an Eastern shore Man & got 40 of them Landd. before I found they were damagd.

GW paid £2 16s. for 39½ bushels of the oats (LEDGER A, 89).

Sunday April 13th.   Fine clear still Morng. Abt. 10 Oclock the Wind (what little there was before being So.) came Easterly, blew fresh and Clouded. Towards Evening the Atmostphere was quite Overcast and threatned Instant Rain.

My Negroes askd the lent of the Sein to day but caught little or no Fish. Note the Wind blew upon the shore to day.

Monday Apl. 14.   Fine warm day, Wind So[uther]ly and clear till the Eveng. when it clouded.

No Fish were to be catchd to day neither.

Mixd my Composts in a box with ten Apartments in the following manner viz.–in No. 1 is three pecks of the Earth brought from below the Hill out of the 46 Acre Field without any mixture–in No.

  2. is two pecks of the said Earth and one of Marle taken out of the said Field which Marle seemd a little Inclinable to Sand.

3. Has 2 Pecks of sd. Earth and 1 of Riverside Sand.
4. Has a Peck of Horse Dung.
5. Has Mud taken out of the Creek.
6. Has Cow Dung.
7. Marle from the Gullys on the Hill side wch. seemd to be purer than the other.
8. Sheep Dung.
9. Black Mould taken out of the Pocoson on the Creek side.
10. Clay got just below the Garden.

All mixd with the same quantity & sort of Earth in the most effectual manner by reducing the whole to a tolerable degree of fineness & jubling them well together in a Cloth.

In each of these divisions were planted three Grains of Wheat 3 of Oats & as many of Barley, all at equal distances in Rows & of equal depth (done by a Machine made for the purpose).

The Wheat Rows are next the Numbered side, the Oats in the Middle, & the Barley on that side next the upper part of the Garden.

Two or three hours after sowing in this manner, and about an hour before Sun set I waterd them all equally alike with Water that had been standing in a Tub abt. two hours exposd to the Sun.

Began drawing Bricks burning Lime & Preparing for Mr. Triplet who is to be here on Wednesday to Work.

Finishd Harrowing the Clover Field, and began reharrowing of it. Got a new harrow made of smaller, and closer Tinings for Harrowing in Grain—the other being more proper for preparing the Ground for sowing.

Cook Jack's plow was stopd he being employd in setting the Lime Kiln.

GRAINS OF WHEAT: *Triticum aestivum,* wheat, was second to tobacco as a cash crop during GW's early farming years and his prime cash crop after he reduced his tobacco plantings in later years. When he speaks of "wheat" he means the common English red winter wheat, but during his lifetime he tried at least a dozen different kinds and experimented (as above) with various modes of culture. A common method of cropping was to sow wheat between corn rows after the corn had been topped in late summer. GW's diaries and papers show him trying early wheat, summer wheat, red-straw wheat, lamas wheat, double-headed wheat, yellow-bearded wheat, and Russian wheat sent him by British agriculturist Arthur Young. White wheat became his favorite variety but during the Revolution, when his farms were neglected, his seed became so mixed that it lost its original characteristics. Much of his experimentation with wheat after that time involved finding an ideal white variety. He sent a sack of early white wheat to Sir John Sinclair 10 July 1798, saying it had been developed in America about seven years earlier and was a white, full, and heavy grain. Possibly this is the strain which Thomas Jefferson sent home from Georgetown, Md., in 1790, reporting that Washington had assured him it was the best he had ever seen. It was a white wheat widely used in Maryland with a small, plump grain, weighing 62 to 64 pounds per bushel (BETTS [2], 153–54).

Tuesday April 15th.   Sent Tom and Mike to Alexandria in my Boat for 20 or 25 Bushels of Oats.

Went up myself there to Court after calling at Mr. Green's & leaving Mrs. Washington there.

Mr. Darrell not being there the Execution of his Deeds were again put of.

Being informd that French, Triplet and others were about buying (in conjunction) a piece of Land of Simon Piarson lying not far from my Dogue Run Quarter I engagd him to give me the first offer of it so soon as he shoud determine upon selling it.

About 3 Oclock fell a very heavy Shower of Rain attended with much Wind at So. wch. Instantaneously abt. an hour by Sun changd to No. West & blew for a few Minutes most violently but soon after fell calm.

Good part of my New Fencing that was not Riderd was leveld.

Simon Pearson (c.1738–1797) owned 558 acres of land which lay on the main road from Alexandria to Colchester, northwest of the land on Dogue Run that GW had bought from Sampson Darrell in 1757. To sell his tract Pearson had to dock the entail on it, which he achieved in 1762, and on 14 Feb. 1763 GW bought 178 acres of Pearson's land for £191 7s. (deed of Pearson to GW, DLC:GW). The remainder went to William Triplett and George Johnston.

FENCING . . . NOT RIDERD: In a rail fence, a rider is the top rail placed in a crotch of crossed stakes at the end of each panel, to lock all the rails in place and keep the fence firm.

Wednesday Apl. 16.   My Boat which the Wind and Rain prevented from returning Yesterday came home this Morning the Wind being at North West and Fresh.

Mr. Triplet & his Brother came this day to Work. Abt. 10 Oclock they began, and got the Wall between the House and Dairy finishd.

Thinking the Ground Rather too wet for Sowing I set my Horses to Carting Rails, and both my Plows were stopd Cook Jack being employd abt. the Lime.

Finishd a Roller this day for Rolling my Grain.

Thursday April 17th.   By 3 Oclock in the afternoon Mr. Triplet finishd the Wall between the Dairy and Kitchen. The Rain from that time prevented his Working.

Sowed my Clover Field with Oats, 24 Bushels. The upper part next the Peach Orchard was Harrowed in during the Rain but before it began to Clog much.

Also sowd 18 Rows of Lucerne in the 12 Acre Field below the Hill. The first 4 Rows were Sowd in Drils the others by a line stretchd and the Seed Raked In.

Richd. Stephens brot. down 9 Hogsheads of Tobo. to go to the Inspection at Hunting [Creek Warehouse] in a flat which I borrowd (or I rather suppose hird) from Messrs. Carlyle and Dalton —wch. Flat brot. down 4 Barrels of Corn—being part of Eight that I was to have had of William Garner at the rate of 9/. pr. Barl. to be paid in Pistoles or Dollars. It seems the other 4 Barrels I am to get from Garner's House.

A Fresh Southerly Wind blew all day. Towards Noon it shifted more East and by 3 Oclock it began Raining and continued so to do witht. Intermission till we went to Bed & how long afterwards I know not.

The Alexandria retail partnership of John Carlyle & John Dalton lasted from 1744 to Dalton's death in 1777, an unusually long time in an age when most partnerships were entered into for one year at a time and few lasted more than a decade. GW carried this firm on his books from 1760 to 1769. William Gardner was a Truro vestryman from 1765 to 1776, when he apparently moved out of the parish. In 1766 and 1767 he served as a churchwarden with GW. FLAT: flatboat.

Friday April 18th.   Righted up all my Fencing.

Planted other Pine Trees in the Fencd place at the Cornr. of the Garden the first being broke, and much hurt by Creatures.

Began Sowing my Clovr. and got 4 Acres sowd 14 lb. to the Acre. Harrowd it in with the fine toothd Harrow as light as I coud.

Tryd my Roller wch. find much too light.

Sowd 69 Rows more of Lucerne which makes 87 in all.

Got my Cloaths &ca. packd up for my Journey to Williamsburg tomorrow.

Mr. Barnes's Davy brot. home my Negroe fellow Boson who Ran away on Monday last.

Davy was one of Abraham Barnes's slaves. In 1760 Boson was assigned to the Mount Vernon quarter called Williamson's. GW today paid Davy 10s. for taking up Boson (LEDGER A, 89). For colonial Virginia slaves who "ran away" from their masters, see MULLIN.

Saturday Apl. 19th.   Crossd at Mr. Possey's Ferry and began my journey to Williamsburg about 9 Oclock. Abt. 11 I broke my

Chair and had to Walk to Port Tobo. where I was detaind the whole day getting my Chair mended—no Smith being with 6 Miles. Lodgd at Doctr. Halkerston's.

John Posey's ferry crossed the Potomac River from the lower point of the Mount Vernon neck to Marshall Hall in Charles County, Md., home of Capt. Thomas Hanson Marshall (1731–1801) and his wife Rebecca Dent Marshall (c.1737–1770). By using Posey's ferry, GW could cut across Charles County, past Port Tobacco, and recross the Potomac, entering Virginia in the Chotank area of King George County. In this way he saved himself from traveling the lower "Potomac Path" on the Virginia side of the Potomac, which crossed a number of swamps and small streams now swollen by a week of hard rains. Robert Halkerston had lived in Fredericksburg during GW's youth, where he was a founding member of the Masonic Lodge in 1752 and was probably present at the 1753 lodge meetings in which the young GW was initiated, passed, and raised into Masonry.

Sunday Apl. 20th.   Set out early, and crossd at Cedar point by 10; the day being very calm & fine, Dind and lodgd at my Brother's. The Evening Cloudy with Rain. Wind tho little at So. West.

The lower of the two Cedar Points in Maryland was about a 13-mile ride south from Port Tobacco. GW most likely used Hooe's ferry, although several ferries crossed the Potomac from Cedar Point in 1760. His brother Samuel's plantation in the Chotank area of Stafford County (now King George County) was originally one of their father's quarters, inherited by Samuel when he came of age in 1755 (HENING, 6:513–16). There Samuel settled and built a "dwelling house with six rooms below and three above . . . situated on a hill, that opens a most agreeable prospect for some miles up and down the [Potomac] river" (*Va. Gaz.,* R, 18 Aug. 1768, supp.). In the 1760s Samuel served as a justice of the peace for Stafford County and as a vestryman for St. Paul's Parish.

Monday Apl. 21st.   Crossd at Southern's and Tods Bridge and lodgd at Major Gaines's.

After leaving his brother's home GW rode about three miles below Leedstown to Southern's (earlier Southings) ferry on the Rappahannock River, whose owner lived on the far side of the river in Essex County. In 1755 the ferryboat was manned by two Negroes (HENING, 3:22; FISHER, 170). GW then rode southwest through Essex and King and Queen counties to arrive at Todd's Bridge, where he crossed the Mattaponi River into King William County a short way upriver from Aylett's Warehouse (later the village of Aylett, Va.). In 1760 William Todd, who lived on the King and Queen side of the bridge, also had a warehouse and an ordinary at this crossing (GRAY [1], 303). Maj. Harry Gaines (d. 1766), a local planter, was elected a burgess for King William County in 1758.

Tuesday April 22d.   Crossd Pamunky at Williams's Ferry, and visited all the Plantations in New Kent. Found the Overseers

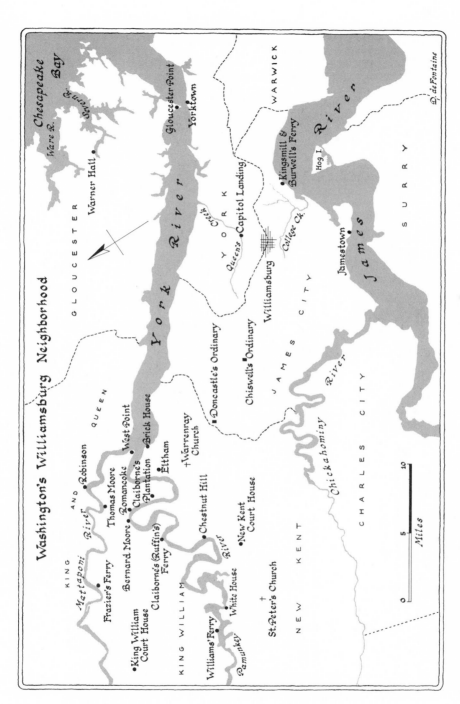

Washington's Williamsburg Neighborhood

much behind hand in their Business. Went to Mrs. Dandridges and lodgd.

From Major Gaines's, GW rode south through King William County to cross the Pamunkey River into New Kent County at Williams's ferry. The crossing brought him very near the Custis plantations in the vicinity of the White House, which had been the home of Martha Dandridge Custis when GW met her. Mrs. Frances Jones Dandridge (1710–1785), widow of John Dandridge (1700–1756), was GW's mother-in-law. She lived at Chestnut Grove in New Kent County, about midway along the Pamunkey River between the White House and the Bassett's home, Eltham (GRAY [1], 304, 315).

Wednesday Apl. 23d. Went to Colo. Bassetts and remaind there the whole day.

Burwell Bassett's home, Eltham in New Kent County, was less than a mile up the Pamunkey River from West Point, where the Pamunkey joins the Mattaponi to form the York River.

Thursday April 24th. Visited my Quarters at Claibornes and found their business in tolerable forwardness. Also went to my other Quarter at [   ] where their was an insufficiently quantity of Ground prepard—but all that coud be had—it was sd.

Dind at Mr. Bassetts and went in the Evening to Williamsburg.

CLAIBORNES: This Custis plantation lay in King William County on the neck of land the Pamunkey River forms just above Eltham. Containing an estimated 3,080 acres, nearly half of which were marsh, Claiborne's was so named because Martha Washington's first husband, Daniel Parke Custis, had purchased it 14–15 Dec. 1750 from the executors of William Claiborne (d. 1746) of Romancoke (survey by William Groveham 14–18 April 1789 and 25–29 Mar. 1791, Vi). When the Custis estate was apportioned among Martha and the two children, Claiborne's was one of the plantations assigned to her by right of dower. As her second husband, GW was entitled to use the dower plantations as if they were his own, except that he could not sell them or encumber them "to the prejudice of her ultimate rights or those of her heirs," for on her death the dower plantations were to go to John Parke Custis (FREEMAN, 3:20). At this time 19 dower slaves worked at Claiborne's, growing tobacco, wheat, and corn under the direction of the plantation's overseer, John Roan ("Part of John Roan's Crop—1759," and "A List of Working Dower Negroes, where settld & under whose care, 1760," DLC:GW; both lists are at the beginning of the 1760 *Virginia Almanack* in which GW kept his diary for this year).

Friday Apl. 25th. Waited upon the Govr.

The governor of Virginia was an appointee of the king. Since, in the British imperial practice, the governorship was considered to be a source of revenue as well as an administrative responsibility, the governor often obtained the royal appointment of a lieutenant governor, who would live in Virginia as the colony's chief executive officer, and with whom the governor would come to some agreement over the income and perquisites of the office. In 1760 the governor of Virginia was Sir Jeffery Amherst, and the resident lieutenant governor was Francis Fauquier (1703–1768). Fauquier was commissioned lieutenant governor of Virginia 10 Feb. 1758, took the oaths of office in Williamsburg 5 June 1758, and died in office. He had thus been GW's superior during part of the 1758 campaigns against the French. It was Lieutenant Governor Fauquier whom he visited on this date; he was following the common practice of Virginians in referring to him as simply the governor.

Saturday Apl. 26th. Visited all the Estates and my own Quarters about Williamsburg. Found these also in pretty good forwardness.

Receivd Letters from Winchester informing me that the Small Pox had got among my Quarter's in Frederick; determind therefore to leave Town as soon as possible and proceed up to them.

ESTATES: John Parke Custis's plantations in York County. He had also inherited the Custis lands in New Kent, Hanover, and Northampton counties as well as lots in Williamsburg and Jamestown (Custis to GW, 11 May 1778, ViHi; *Va. Gaz.*, P, 16 Oct. 1778). MY OWN QUARTERS: Martha Washington's dower plantations in York County—Bridge Quarter and the Ship Landing, both of which lay near the Capitol Landing on Queen's Creek about two miles north of Williamsburg. Together they contained about 1,000 acres, of which "100 or more" were "firm hard marsh, supporting a numerous flock of cattle winter and summer," and 10 to 12 were swamp (*Va. Gaz.*, P&D, 2 April 1767). Tobacco and corn were grown on the higher ground by 19 dower slaves who worked there at this time. The dower property also included a gristmill, which adjoined the two York plantations, plus lots in Williamsburg

Francis Fauquier, governor of Virginia, arrived in the colony 5 June 1758. (Thomas Coram Foundation for Children, London)

and Jamestown ("A List of Working Dower Negroes, where settled, & under whose care, 1760," DLC:GW, at the beginning of GW's 1760 *Virginia Almanack;* GW to Custis, 12 Oct. 1778, DLC:GW).

Sunday Apl. 27th. Went to Church. In the Afternoon some Rain, & a great deal of severe Lightning but not much Thunder.

CHURCH: probably Bruton Parish Church on Duke of Gloucester Street in Williamsburg.

Monday Apl. 28th. Let my House in Town to Colo. Moore, for Colo. Dandridge, who is to come into it in the Fall, and pay me 45 £ pr. Ann. In the meanwhile I am to paint it.

In the Afternoon after collecting what Money I coud I left Town and reachd Colo. Bassetts.

This day agreed with Mr. Jno. Driver of Nansemond for 25,000 shingles to be deliverd in October. They are to be 18 inch shingles and of the best sort. Desird him if he coud not cause them to be deliverd for 18/ a Thousd. not to send them but let me know of it as soon as possible.

By "my House in Town," GW refers to a Williamsburg house in Martha's dower estate which was now under GW's management.

Colonel Moore is either Thomas Moore or his brother and near neighbor, Bernard Moore (d. 1775), of Chelsea, who was a burgess for King William County 1744–65 and again, 1769–71. Both were colonels and lived in the Custis-Dandridge-Bassett neighborhood along the Pamunkey River; both were heavily in debt to the Custis estate. Colonel Dandridge is Bartholomew Dandridge (1737–1785), a brother of Mrs. Washington.

The money GW collected today was for burgesses' wages and an old account from the colony of Virginia £60 4d. in all (LEDGER A, 89).

John Driver was a merchant in the port town of Suffolk, Va., on the Nansemond River. One of the major sources of roofing shingles for Virginians was the Dismal Swamp area just south of Suffolk in Nansemond County.

Tuesday Apl. 29th. Reachd Port Royal by Sunset.

GW crossed the Pamunkey River at Thomas Dansie's ferry and dined at Todd's ordinary on his way to Port Royal (LEDGER A, 89).

Wednesday 30th. Came to Hoes Ferry by 10 Oclock but the wind blew too fresh to cross: detained there all Night.

Hooe's ferry, running from Mathias Point in Virginia to lower Cedar Point in Maryland, was established in 1715 by Col. Rice Hooe (Hoe, Howe), grandson of Rice (Rhuys) Hooe, a seventeenth-century immigrant from Wales. At Colonel Hooe's death (1726), the ferry was inherited and run by his son John (1704–1766), and following John's death by John's widow, Ann Alexander Hooe, and their son Gerard Hooe (1733–1786), who married

Sarah Barnes (1742–1815) and lived at the family home of Barnsfield in Mathias Neck, Stafford County (HENING, 4:93; *Va. Gaz.*, R, 24 Mar. 1768; NICKLIN [1], 368).

From Hooe's ferry, GW probably retraced his steps home but entered no expense in his ledger for recrossing the Potomac to reach Mount Vernon.

[May]

Thursday May 1st. Got over early in the Morning and reachd home before Dinnertime and upon enquiry found that my Clover Field was finishd sowing & Rolling the Saturday I left home—as was the Sowing of my Lucerne: and that on the [   ] they began sowing the last field of Oats & finishd it the 25th.

That in box No. 6, two grains of Wheat appeard on the 20th.; one an Inch high—on the 22d. a grain of Wheat in No. 7 and 9 appeard—on the 23 after a good deal of Rain the Night before some Stalks appeard in Nos. 2, 3, 4, 5, & 8 but the Ground was so hard bakd by the drying Winds when I came home that it was difficult to say which Nos. lookd most thriving. However in

No.   1 there was nothing come up.

2.		2 Oats	1 barley
3.		1 Oat	2 barley
4.		1 Oat	4
5.	1 Wheat	2 Oats	
6.	1 Do.	3 Do.	1 Do.
7.	1 Do.	2 Do.	2 Do.
8.	1 Do.	1 Do.	
9.	2 Do.	3 Do.	2 Do.
10.			1 Do.

The two Grains in No. 8 were I think rather the strongest, but upon the whole No. 9 was the best.

Friday May 2d. Cold, & strong Westerly Winds.

My English Horse Coverd the great bay Mare.

GW had bought an English colt from Col. Bernard or Thomas Moore in Mar. 1759 for £17 10s. (LEDGER A, 55).

Saturday May 3d. Wind got Southerly, but blew fresh and Cool.

The Stallion coverd Ranken—and afterwards breaking out of his pasture Coverd the great bay Mare again.

Sunday May 4th.   Warm and fine. Set out for Frederick to see my Negroes that lay Ill of the Small Pox. Took Church in my way to Colemans where I arrivd about Sun setting.

Monday May 5th.   Reach'd Mr. Stephenson in Frederick abt. 4 Oclock just time enough to see Richd. Mounts Interrd. Here I was informd that Harry & Kit, the two first of my Negroes that took the Small Pox were Dead and Roger & Phillis the only two down with it were recovering from it.
    Lodgd at Mr. Stephenson.

Richard Stephenson (d. 1765) of Frederick County married the widow Onora Grimes Crawford, mother of William and Valentine Crawford. By Mrs. Crawford, Stephenson had five sons, four of whom appear in the GW diaries. As an early entrepreneur in the Shenandoah Valley, Stephenson joined John Vestal and others in 1742 to set up an iron bloomery project. He hired GW to survey land for him in 1750 and during the French and Indian War was a supplier to GW's troops. GW sometimes referred to Stephenson as "Stevens" or "Stephens."
    Richard Mount recorded a will in Frederick County in 1752.

Tuesday May 6.   Visited my Brother's Quarter, & just calld at my own in my way to Winchester where I spent the day & Evening with Colo. Byrd &ca.
    The Court was held to Day at Stephen's Town but adjournd to Winchester to Morrow.

Because of the smallpox epidemic in Frederick County, the county court was moved, by order of the governor 3 July 1759, to Stephensburg, "during the time the small pox rageth in the town of Winchester." Stephensburg (later Newton, later Stephens City), founded by Lewis Stephens in 1758, was competing with Winchester to become the seat for Frederick County. By Oct. 1759 the smallpox, according to a petition of the inhabitants of Winchester, "was raging at Stephensburg," and the court did not meet at all until Feb. 1760 (NORRIS [1], 121–22). GW is here noting the court's move back to its regular seat.

Wednesday May 7.   After taking the Doctrs. Direction's in regard to my People I set out for my Quarters and got there abt. 12 Oclock–time enough to go over them and find every thing in the utmost confusion, disorder & backwardness my Overseer lying upon his Back of a broken Leg, and not half a Crop especially of Corn Ground prepard.
    Engagd. Vale. Crawford to go in pursuit of a Nurse to be ready in case more of my People shd. be seizd with the same disorder.

Thursday May 8th.   Got Blankets and every other requisite from Winchester & settld things upon the best footing I coud to prevt.

the Small Pox from Spreading—and in case of its spreading for the care of the Negroes. Mr. Vale. Crawford agreeing in case any more of the People at the lower Quarter getting it to take them home to his House—& if any of those at the upper Quarter gets it to have them removd into my Room and the Nurse sent for.

GW today lent £15 to Crawford and gave £4 to his overseer Hardwick (LEDGER A, 89).

Friday May 9th.   Set out on my return Home. The Morning drizzling a little. Calld at the Bloomery and got Mr. Wm. Crawford to shew me the place that has been so often talkd of for erecting an Iron Work upon.

The Convenience of Water is great—first it may be taken out of the River into a Canal and a considerable Fall obtained—& ⟨then⟩ a Run comes from the Mountain on which the largest Fall may [be] got with Small Labour and expence. But of the constancy of this Stream I know nothing nor Coud Crawford tell me. I saw none of the Ore but all People agree that there is an inexhaustable fund of that that is rich—but Wood seems an obstacle not but that there is enough of it but the Gd. is so hilly & rugged as not to admit of making Coal or transporting it.

I did not examine the place so accurately myself as to be a com-

THE BLOOMERY: a primitive means of turning iron ore into iron, consisting of a hearth rather larger than that of a blacksmith. Iron ore and charcoal were fed into a fire fanned by a bellows that was powered by a waterwheel. When the heated iron formed a lump, or "bloom," it was lifted to an anvil and beaten into a bar by a hammer, also powered by the waterwheel. The product was an impure wrought iron used by local artisans and blacksmiths. A bloomery for making bar iron was begun in 1742 by a group which included William Vestal and Crawford's stepfather, Richard Stephenson. It was located on John Vestal's land about four miles above Key's (later Vestal's) ferry, on the right bank of the Shenandoah River and the mouth of Evitt's Run.

IRON WORK: a more sophisticated process producing a high grade of iron for commercial sale. Such a work, using limestone for flux, needed a much greater amount of capital to finance a 25- to 30-foot-high furnace, a large bellows (often 25 feet long) for the blast, a waterwheel over 20 feet in diameter, and a minimum of 10 to 12 full-time workers. But it could turn out 20 tons of relatively pure pig iron per week, which would either be worked in the colonies or shipped to England for sale (BINING, 76–84). Vast amounts of firewood were needed to produce charcoal for the iron furnace.

William Crawford, brother of Valentine Crawford, entered the Virginia Regiment in 1755 as an ensign and scout and later served with GW on the Forbes expedition of 1758. He lived in Frederick County until 1765, when he removed to the Youghiogheny country in western Pennsylvania.

Despite Crawford's approval of this site for an ironwork, GW did not join in the venture.

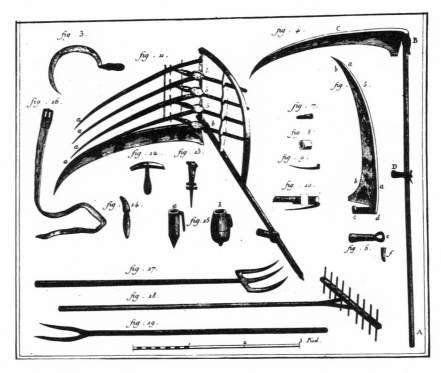

The familiar cradle for harvesting small grains, largest implement shown here, changed very little before mechanical devices replaced it. From *La Nouvelle Maison rustique*, Paris, 1798. (Mount Vernon Ladies' Association of the Union)

petent judge of this matter & Mr. Crawford says there will be no difficulty in the case.

Reachd Coleman's.

Saturday May 10.   Arrivd at home abt. 10 Oclock where I found my Brother Jno. And was told that my great Chesnut folded a Horse Colt on the 6 Instt. and that my Young Peach trees were Wed according to Order.

The Oats, & in short every thing else seemd quite at a stand, from the dryness of the Earth which was remarkably so partly for want of Rain and partly by the constant drying Winds which have blown for sometime past.

GW's younger brother, John Augustine Washington, had managed Mount Vernon for him during the former's absence in the French and Indian wars.

"Jack," as GW called him, brought his bride, Hannah Bushrod Washington, to Mount Vernon in 1756 and lived there until 1758. It was partly in acknowledgment of Jack's help and loyalty that GW in his will left part of the Mount Vernon estate to Jack's older son, Bushrod Washington (MVAR, 1964, 18–21; WRITINGS, 37:288–89).

Sunday May 11th.   Mrs. Washington we[nt] to Church.

My black pacing Mare was twice Coverd.

Proposd a purchase of some Lands which Col. F[airfa]x has at the Mouth of the Warm Spring Run joing. Barwicks bottom. He promisd me the preference if he shd. sell but is not inclind to do it at prest.

Monday May 12th.   Fine Rain began in the Morning and continued by Intervals all day.

Sent Cook Jack & my Horses to get in Stephens Corn.

Black Mare was coverd again to day. Mr. Alexander sent a Mare but She refusd the Horse.

CORN: *Zea mays,* Indian corn. GW's principal variety was probably Virginia Gourdseed, a coarse, white dent corn with a red cob and soft and starchy kernel (SINGLETON, 73). He wrote Charles Carter 14 Dec. 1787 that his normal yield at that time was 2 to 2½ barrels per acre, an estimated 8 to 10 bushels. When he obtained early seed corn from the North, it was most likely to be a flint variety with white cob and a round kernel, much harder than that of the dent variety.

There were two main branches of the Alexander family in eighteenth-century Virginia, descended respectively from Robert and Philip Alexander, the two sons of John Alexander the immigrant (d. 1677). It was this John Alexander who in 1669 purchased the 6,000-acre Howsing Patent out of which the city of Alexandria was carved in 1749. In 1760 the "Robert" branch of Alexanders was represented by the brothers John Alexander (1711–1764), of Caledon, in the Chotank area of Stafford County, and Col. Gerard Alexander (d. 1761), of Alexandria, whose oldest son, Robert Alexander (d. 1793), is probably the Mr. Alexander mentioned here.

Tuesday May 13th.   Cloudy with some slight Showers of Rain.

People all working at Muddy hole getting in Stephens's Corn.

My Brother Jno. returnd from Difficult.

DIFFICULT: Difficult Run, which empties into the Potomac River between the Great Falls and the Little Falls. From 1757 until 1798 it was the upper half of the boundary between Loudoun and Fairfax counties.

Wednesday May 14th.   Wind at No. Wt. fresh and drying. Visited at Belvoir.

People & Plows at Muddy Hole.

Thursday May 15th. Drying Winds—People at Muddy hole again.

Friday May 16th.   Still Cool and Windy—my People yet continuing at Muddy hole. My Brother Jno. left this and I got Nations Estate Appraisd by Messrs. McCarty Barry & Triplet—as follows viz.

One old Gun & lock	7.6
1 Small Bell	2.6
1 Suit of Cloaths viz.	
a Coat Waistt. Breechs.	10
Shirt, Hat, Shoes & Garters	
A Small parcel of Lea[the]r	1

Nations's estate still owed GW £1 11s. 1d., but GW wrote off that balance as "given to his Widow" (LEDGER A, 69). Barry is probably John Barry (died c.1776), the clerk of Pohick Church, an original trustee of the town of Colchester, and a neighbor of Daniel McCarty.

Saturday May 17th.   Mulatto Jack returnd from King William with 3 Yoke of Oxen & lost Punch the Horse he rid.
    Sent up 16 Hydes to Mr. Adams at Alexa. viz.
    12 large &
    4 Small ones to be Tan'd.
Brought a Pipe of Wine from there wch. Captn. McKie brought from Madeira also a Chest of Lemons and some other trifles.
    Began weeding my Trefoil below the Hill.
    The Great Bay was coverd. Got an Acct. that the Assembly was to meet on Monday. Resolvd to set of to Morrow.

Robert Adam (1731–1789) was born in Kilbride, Scot., migrated to America in the early 1750s, and settled in Alexandria, where he initiated a number of industries, including a tannery.
    McKie is possibly Capt. William Macky, who entered his ship into the York River Naval District records, 1 April 1760, as having come from South Carolina, a common port of call in the trade between Chesapeake Bay and the wine islands (P.R.O., C.O.5/1448, f. 25).
    GW was a burgess for Frederick County 1758–65. The House of Burgesses had met 4–11 Mar. 1760 to continue the existence of the Virginia Regiment for another six months, but GW had not attended that session (H.B.J., 1758–61, 157–68). The House met again 19–24 May 1760 to consider an urgent message from Governor Fauquier for men and money to relieve Fort Loudoun on the Little Tennessee River, which was in danger of falling to the Cherokees (H.B.J., 1758–61, 171–79).

Sunday May 18th.   Set out in Company with Mr. George Johnston. At Colchester was informd by Colo. Thornton and Chissel that the Assembly wd. be broke up before I could get down.

Turnd back therefore & found Colo. Fairfax and his Family and that Lightning wch. had attended a good deal of Rain had struck my Quarter & near 10 Negroes in it some very bad but with letting Blood they recoverd.

George Johnston, of Belvale, was a burgess for Fairfax County 1758–65. Colchester, a small settlement of Scottish merchants, lay on Occoquan Creek about eight miles below Mount Vernon. Colonels Thornton and Chissel may have been Col. Presley Thornton, burgess for Northumberland County, and John Chiswell, of Hanover County.

On 23 May the House of Burgesses passed a bill authorizing the raising of £32,000 and up to 700 soldiers plus officers for the relief of Fort Loudoun (H.B.J., 1758–61, 176).

Monday May 19th.   Went to Alexandria to see Captn. Littledales Ship Launchd wch. went of extreamely well. This day was attended with slight shower's. Colo. F[airfa]x had a Mare Cover'd. So had Captn. Dalton.

In 1760 Isaac Littledale was establishing his trade between his home in Whitehaven, Eng., and the Potomac River valley. For this trade the *Hero*, a 200-ton ship which required 14 hands, was built in the Alexandria shipyard in 1760. Littledale was her captain on the maiden voyage.

Tuesday May 20th.   Being Court day Mr. Clifton's Land in the Neck was exposd to Sale and I bought it for £1210 Sterlg. & under many threats and disadvantages paid the Money into the Comrs. hands and returnd home at Night with Colo. Fairfax & Famy. Captn. Dalton's Dun Mare again Covd.

The final decree of the General Court in chancery (decree, Clifton v. Carroll et al., 12 April 1760, NjWoG) ordered that the commissioners on 20 May at Alexandria sell at public auction to the highest bidder the lands in Clifton's Neck and that Clifton's creditors then be paid off. The "threats and disadvantages" to GW came from all sides. Thomson Mason threatened to appeal the sale decree; Ignatius Digges and Charles Carroll refused to show up at all to deliver their mortgages, thus barring GW from a clear title; and Carroll had already decided to appeal the case to the Privy Council in London (Charles Carroll of Annapolis to Charles Carroll of Carrollton, 26 April, 4 July 1762, CARROLL, 264–69). Finally, Clifton declared he would not vacate the land until 1762, which, among other problems, threatened GW with a two-year loss of rent from the Clifton's Neck tenant farmers (Robert Carter Nicholas and George Wythe to GW, 27 May 1760, anonymous donor).

Wednesday May 21.   Wrote to Messrs. Nicholas & With for Advice how to act in regard to Clifton's Land. Sent the Letter by the Post. A good deal of Rain in the Night.

Colo. Fairfax went home. Began shearing my Sheep. ⟨Dalton's sorrel⟩ Mare coverd.

In their reply of 27 May 1760 Robert Carter Nicholas and George Wythe stated they were "sorry to find you are likely to be involved in so much Trouble" and warned GW that they could advise nothing "with any Certainty" (Nicholas and Wythe to GW, 27 May 1760, anonymous donor). After giving their opinion that Mason had a strong case and that the Privy Council would probably find for Carroll, they referred GW to his local lawyer, George Johnston.

At this point in the diary GW inserts a lengthy paraphrase on the cultivation of lucerne from Jethro Tull, *Horse-Houghing Husbandry: An Essay on the Principles of Vegetation and Tillage* (London, 1731). This important British work on scientific agriculture ran through several editions—here GW is quoting the 1751 edition—and was still being published in 1829. GW relied heavily on it in his early years as a farmer; later he would turn to the books and personal communications of Arthur Young.

Material in angle brackets has been taken from DIARIES, 1:164.

Thursday May 22d.   Continued shearing my sheep. A good deal of Rain at Night—and Cool as it has been ever since the first Reign on the 12th.

Captn. Dalton had a sorrell Mare coverd.

My Black Mare that came Frederick was Coverd Yesterday & the day before.

Captn. McCarty had a Mare Coverd the 20th.

Memms.

To have 600 Tobo. Hills Marld at Williamsons quarter—to try the Virtues of it—to do it more effectually, tend 500 Hills of the same Ground witht. Marl giving both equal working and let them fare exactly alike in all Respects.

Illustration from Thomas Hale's *Husbandry*, London, 1758. (Mount Vernon Ladies' Association of the Union)

January 1760

For an Experimt.

Take 7 Pots (Earthen) or 7 Boxes of equal size and number them.

Then put in No. 1 pld. Earth taken out of the Field below, which is intend. for Wheat—in No. 2, 3, 4, 5, 6 and 7 equal proportion's of the same Earth—to No. 2 put Cow dung—to 3 Marle, 4 ⟨with⟩ Mud from the Marshes ⟨& bottoms⟩ adjoining the [   ] Field, to 5 Mud ⟨tak⟩en out of the River immediately, to 6 the same Mud lain to Mellow sum time, and to 7 the Mud taken from the Shoreside at low Water where it appears to be unmixd with Clay. Of each an equal quantity—and at the proper Season of Sowing Oats put in each of these Pots or boxes 6 Grains of the largest and heaviest Oats planted at proper distances—and watch their growth and different changes till Harvest.

N.B. To preserve them from Accidents put them in the Garden ⟨and⟩ let the Pots be buried ⟨up⟩ to their brims.

[The Weather]

[January]

1st.   Fine warm Sun Shine—wind Southerly.

2.   Warm, but Mist and Rain.

3.   Just the same kind of Weather as Yestery.

4.   Ditto.

5.   Wind at No. West. Blew hard & grew very Cold.

6.   Clear & tolerable warm.

7.   Ditto.

8.   The morng. fine, but Cloudy & cold afterwards.

9.   High wind, but clear & tolerably warm.

10.   Fine, clear & warm.

11.   Morng. Lowering, but fine & warm afterwards.

12.   White frost & clear in the Morng. but Cloudy afterwd.

13.   Wind at N. Wt. very clear, & extrame cold.

14.   Wind Do. but not hard—yet very cold & frosty.

15.   Do. pretty fresh & very cold & frosty.

16.   Wind at So. Wt. very cloudy in the Mg. At 12 begn. to Sn[ow].

17.   Wind at No. Et. and Rain till Noon then Mist.

18.   Great Sleet, & mist till Noon, then clear Wd. So.

19.   Wind So. tolerable clear—but cloudy afternn.

20.   Wind Contd. So[uther]ly with Rain, & Warm.

21.   So[uther]ly in the Morng. and Rain till Noon—then No[rther]ly & clear.

22.   Wind cond. No[rther]ly. Clear, cold, & hard frost.

23.   Clear and Moderate—wind Westerly.

24.   Fine day. Wind So[uther]ly. Gradual thaw.

25.   Warm & So[uther]ly wind in the Mg. Afterwds. at No. Wt.

26.   No. Et. in the Morng. So[uther]ly afterwards.

27.   Strong So. wind & Rain till 4 P.M. then No. Wt.

28.   Wind at So. again & fresh. Clear all day.

29.   Wind at Do. till 3 Oclock then No. W. clear all d[ay].

30.   So[uther]ly Wind & Cloudy till 9 at Night then No. W. & clear.

31.   ⟨N⟩o. Wt. clear and Cold.

[February]

1. Snow in the Morning, but clear afterwds.

2. Wind No[rther]ly but mild clear.

3. Wind shifting from East to So. Clear & ⟨warm⟩.

4. So[uther]ly cloudy & clear by turns—white Frost.

5. So[uther]ly with Rain—gd. very Rotton.

6. Very fine drying day. No wind.

7. W. So[uther]ly, very warm & drying.

8. W. No. Wt. but not hard, fine clear & Warm.

9. Sml. Frost. Wd. No. Et.

10. Do. wind at No. threatning Rain.

11. Clear & fine. Wind Northwardly.

12. Very clear, still and fine.

13. Strong, & warm southerly Wind—clear.

14. Ditto   Ditto   Do.   Do. but cloudy.

15. No. Et. wind and Rain.

16. Morng. cloudy—fair afterwds. & So[uther]ly Wind.

17. Wind at No. W. cloudy & very cold.

18. Cold in the Mg. Moderate afterwds. Wd. So[uther]ly.

19. Fine warm day. Fresh So[uther]ly Wind.

20. Fine Day & little wind.

21. Brisk So[uther]ly Wind & Cloudy with mch. Rain.

22. So[uther]ly Storm.

23. Fine day. Wind shifting from So. to No. Wt.

24. Fresh So[uther]ly Wind & Cloudy Weather.

25. Wind still So[uther]ly, warm & fine day.

26. So[uther]ly wind Cloudy & a little Rain.

27. So[uther]ly wind & dripping Weather.

28. Little or no Wind till Night then No. Et. & Wet.

29. Rain till 12 Oclock then Wind at No. West.

[March]

1. Cold & Cloudy—wind first at No. Wt. then East[er]ly.

2. Fair day, variable Wind.

3. Southerly Wind & Cloudy.

4. High Westerly Wind—clear & cool.

5. So[uther]ly wind & Rain.

6. Do. fine day.

7. Do. fine Morning but Cloudy Afterwds.

8. No. Et. Wind, and much Rain.

9. No. Et. Wind & Snow by Intervals all day.

10. No. W. Wind & Clear.

11. Ditto—Ditto—somewhat Cold.

12. Southerly Wind—clear & very fine.

13. No. Et. Wind & Incessant Rain.

14. Do. till Noon.

15. Wind at Do. Cloudy and little Snow.

16. No. Et. Wind and much Snow.

17. Snowd by Intervals all Day.

18. Wind in the Morng. at No. Wt. then So[uther]ly & War[m].

19. Lowg. & Cold, Wind So[uther]ly.

20. Cold No[rther]ly Wind–clear.

21. In the Morng. No. Et. Wind. So[uther]ly afterwards.

22. Cold south[er]ly Wind & Rain.

23. Southerly Wind and Warm.

24. South[er]ly in the Morng. Easterly After.

25. Do. but changeable Weather.

26. No. West & very boisterous.

27. So[uther]ly Wind, fine warm day.

28. Clear, & Warm strong So[uther]ly Wind.

29. Misty Rain at Intervals. Little wind.

30. Fresh & variable Wind, chiefly from So.

31. Do. & fresh, light Showers.

[April]

1. Clear, No. West Wind–a little Cool.

2. So[uther]ly drying Wind & Warm.

3. Do. and fresh, with Clouds.

4. Clear—So[uther]ly Wind—fresh.

5. So[uther]ly Wind. Rain at Dark.

6. No. Et. Wind. Cool & Cloudy with Rain.

7. So[uther]ly Wind—with Rain. Cloudy all day.

8. Much Rain, wind variable.

9. No. Et. very cloudy sometimes Misty.

10. Do.   Do.   Do.

11. So. Et. & fresh. Cleard abt. Noon.

A Diary Fragment

1761

[May]

May 24th.   Betty from Riverside Quarter came home Sick & did not again in a Condition to work till the 13th. July fol.

Riverside Quarter, or River Quarter, a newly developed part of the Mount Vernon crop land, was in the 1,806 acres of land GW had bought from William Clifton in 1760. Most of the remaining cleared land in the Neck owned by GW was, in 1760, being worked by tenants. Riverside Quarter became the basis for the larger River plantation (later River Farm) that GW developed in subsequent years.

GW had gone to Frederick County early in May to campaign for re-election to the House of Burgesses. He and George Mercer won the two seats in the assembly despite a determined campaign by GW's old lieutenant from the Virginia Regiment, Adam Stephen (see FREEMAN, 3:55–56, 61–62).

[July]

11th. July.   Edward Violette compleated his Planting at Muddy hole Quarter—that is, he planted 25,000 hills on the East side of the Plantn. & replanted all.

The same day Jno. Foster at Dogue Run Quarter finishd his, having 40,000 to plant besides replanting—18,000 of which lying at the south Extreame of the Plantn., 8,000 in the Orchard abt. the House, & the Rest around the New Tobo. House on the East.

N.B. The Reason of noting this late plantg. is to see how it succeeds.

Edward Violette (d. 1773) was overseer at Muddy Hole until he moved to the Bullskin plantation in 1762 (see entry for 27 Oct. 1762).

Friday July 31st.   Sowd Turnips—upon which fell a heavy Rain immediately—so that they were neither Rakd nor harrowd in—the seed I mean. In a few days they came up very thick and well.

[August]

Augt. 15th.   Sow'd abt. half an Acre of English Turnip Seed adjoining to the above and Raked them in the Ground being dry.

[289]

A tobacco plant from Rembert Dodoën's *Cruydeboeck,* Antwerp, 1554. (Arents Collections, New York Public Library, Astor, Lenox and Tilden Foundations)

Elsewhere GW calls his English turnips "Norfolk turnips," from the county in southeast England where the raising of turnips (*Brassica rapa*) as a field crop for livestock was highly developed. Tull's method of drilling the seed in rows to permit cultivation by horsedrawn equipment had become a technique of the agricultural revolution in England. Elsewhere GW mentions the Naper turnip, Swedish turnip, winter turnip, and summer turnip.

GW contracted a bad cold during the election campaign in Frederick County in May 1761, which turned into a long, serious illness during the summer and fall of 1761. In August he went to Berkeley Springs to try to recover his health. Although he felt an improvement after a few weeks at the warm springs, he had a slight relapse while attending the House of Burgesses in October and missed some of the meetings. (On GW's illness, see FREEMAN, 3:62–63, 67–68, 70.)

[September]

Septr. 8.   Sowed 12 Bushels of Ray Grass Seed and 2 Bushels of Hop Trafoil in the Inclosure adjoining the Quarter. The Weather was extremely dry when it was sowd, however their fell a slight Shower that day—as there did likewise the 10th. but not more than sufficient to lay the Dust thoroughly. The seed was Harrowed in with a Brush Harrow and it is apprehended buried too deep by that means as none of it appeard till towards the last of the Month after a great deal of Rainy Weather and then of none but the Ray grass. The other is not to be seen at this time Octr. 23d.

RAY GRASS: *Lolium perenne*, perennial, or English, ryegrass.

[21] Cattle bought at My Bro. John Washington's Sale 21st. Septr. 1761.

1 Cow and Calf		£ 2.10
1 Ditto	Ditto	2.3
1 Ditto	Ditto	2.16
1 Ditto	Ditto	2.17
1 Ditto	Ditto	3.3
1 Ditto	Yearling	2.9
1 Ditto	Ditto	3.1
1 Ditto	Ditto	2.10
1 Ditto		1.16
1 Steer		1.17
2 Ditto		2.
		£27.2

The list of cattle has been moved from the flyleaf of the almanac.

[October]

Octr. 15th.   Sowed a Bushel of Ray grass seed, a gallon of clean Timothy Seed, and abt. half a Bushel in Chaff of Ditto on my Meadow at Dogue Run quarter. Note this ground at the time of Sowing was very moist—but no Rain fell upon it afterwards Untill the 22d. of the Month, when it raind hard for two days. This Seed was also harrowd in with Bushes. Clean Timothy seed supposd not to be good.

English agriculturist Richard Parkinson wrote that American farmers usually sowed timothy grass, *Phleum pratense*, alone (PARKINSON, 2:343); here GW is mixing it with ryegrass. In his later years GW depended heavily on timothy, finding it suitable for a hot climate and able to survive in wet pasturelands.

Octr. 22d.   Began Captn. Posey's Barn with Turner Crump & Six Carpenters.

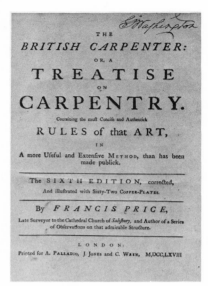

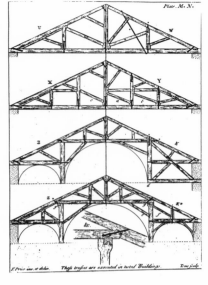

With books such as these, and the skill of his carpenters, Washington continually improved his expanding farms. (Boston Athenaeum)

Roof trusses illustrated in Francis Price's *British Carpenter*, London, 1768. (Sterling Memorial Library, Yale University)

Turner Crump was hired by GW in Dec. 1760 to oversee GW's slave carpenters at a wage of £30 per year. This construction project apparently marked the first time GW contracted Crump and his slave carpenters out to do work for others.

Concerns of a Tobacco Planter

1762

[January]

Note. Killed this 27th. of Jany.—18 hogs of abt. 15 Months old—and for an experiment weighed them alive, after they had fasted abt. 36 hours.

They turned out		2147
When killed nett Wt. was	1774	
Haslletts	63	1837
Difference allowg. nothg. for Gut Fat		310

by which it appears that the odds between gross and Nett Porke shoud be abt. 15 pr. Ct.

HASLLETTS: haslets, the edible viscera of a slaughtered animal.

[February]

9. Began Plowing for Oats.

20. Rented George Ashfords Plantn. to Nelson Kelly for 1000 lbs. Tobo. & Cash.

Sowed a good deal of Tobo. Seed at all my Quarters.

George Ashford of Fairfax County sold GW 135 acres of land on the west side of Dogue Run 13–14 Jan. 1762 for £165 (Fairfax County Deeds, Book E-1, 22–30, Vi Microfilm). Adjoining this land on the north was another 135-acre tract that GW had bought from Ashford's brother John 29–30 Jan. 1761 for £150 (Fairfax County Deeds, Book D-1, 822–27, Vi Microfilm). Both tracts lay on the east side of the land that GW purchased from Simon Pearson on 14 Feb. of this year, giving him a solid 448-acre section between Dogue Run and the main road from Alexandria to Colchester. Kelly later in the year became overseer of the Dogue Run plantation (see entry for 31 Aug. 1762).

27. Killed 27 Hogs after being Six days coming from Frederick and very well emptied—wch. hogs weighed gross as follows—viz.

320	202	254	206	220
130	128	160	134	132
178	178	150	126	206
128	172	131	154	181
181	120	240	214	144
120	134			
1057	934	935	834	883
	1057	1991	2926	3760
	1991	2926	3760	4643

4643 lbs. being the gross wt. I then tryed what they woud weigh nett, after being killd 12 & 18 hours.

124	142	100	106	100
174	252	180	162	212
106	146	186	94	104
140	122	174	146	150
126	164	114	114	108
94	96			
764	922	754	622	674
	764	1686	2440	3062
	1686	2440	3062	3736

deduct for a Rope, weighg. Nett Porke   81

3655

add for Hasllets   139
ditto for Gut fat   96

3890

The difference between Nett. & gross Porke is 753 by wch. it appears that there is a loss of 16 pr. Ct.

March

2. There having fallen a Snow of abt. 2 Inches depth the Night before—I sowed thereupon, at the Meadow at Fosters, where the grass was entirely destroyd by the Winter's Frosts, Six pecks of Ray grass Seed & three quarts of Timothy Seed mixed well in Ashes.

Also Sowed, from the North Side of the Inclosure by the Quarter, to the Quarter with Ray grass, hop Clover, & Lucerne Mixed —viz. for the whole Inclosure 8 Pecks of Ray seed, 3 ditto of the Clovr., & 1 ditto of the Lucerne—but the Snow dissolving & the Wind coming out very fresh at No. West I was obligd to desist and a prodigious severe frost happeng. that Night 'tis to be fear'd the Seed all perished.

In March GW's half brother Augustine Washington died; GW records an expenditure of £2 13s. 3d. for a trip to Westmoreland County to attend the funeral. He undoubtedly gave some advice and help to Augustine's family, but he refused to act as executor, probably because of the distance involved and the press of his own affairs (LEDGER A, 146; FREEMAN, 3:73n; GW to John West, 13 Jan. 1775, DLC:GW). After his trip to Augustine's home, GW traveled to Williamsburg to attend a meeting of the House of Burgesses which began on 30 Mar. At this meeting Governor Fauquier announced that, according to instruction from the assembly in Jan. 1762, the Virginia Regiment had been disbanded. Now, however, there was a possibility of trouble with the Spanish in Florida, and the assembly voted to raise 1,000 troops to form a new regiment (see FREEMAN, 3:74-75).

18th.   Agreed to give Turner Crump one Sixth part of what he can make by my Carpenters this Year, which is to commense the 22d. day of Octr. being the time when he began Captn. Poseys Work, and to give him the Seventh of what he can make by them the Year after.

20.   Finished Plowing for Oats—abt. 20 Acs.

22.   Began Plowg. and Ditchg. the Meadow at George Ashfords.
    Also began Sowing & Harrowing in of Oats.
    Also, grafted Six trees in the Garden. See Memorandum of this on 'tother side the Book.

24.   Burnt Tobo. Beds.
    Grafted 5 others of the same Cherry's on Scions standing in a Cluster in the Mint bed.
    Also, 3 Bullock hearts (from Colo. Mason) one under the Wall to the right of the gate—2 others under the Wall also, between the 5 Cornation Cherrys & opposite to the Plumb trees.
    Also—4 more of the fine early Cherrys from Colo. Masons, between the abo⟨ve⟩ and the Cherrys which were graf⟨ted⟩ last year from that tree by the Gra⟨pe⟩ Vine. These were all upon growg. Sc⟨ions⟩.
    Grafted likewise in the Peach Orch⟨ard⟩ 4 More Apricots & in the Apple Orchard 6 more. Note. These Apricots came from the Plantation where Mr. Clifton used to live.

Beginning with the word "Grafted," the remainder of the 24 Mar. entry has been transferred from a dated memorandum on the back cover of the diary.
    4 MORE APRICOTS: *Prunus armeniaca*, apricot. GW does not mention this fruit again in the diaries until 9 Feb. 1785, but other papers show that it was common in his orchards.

25.   Sowed them [tobacco beds] in the following Manner viz. in the first bed next towards the dividing fence Frederick Tobo. Seed – in 2d. Bed Thick joint in 3d. Sweetscented – 4th. Johnson's 5th. br[oa]d long Green.

27th.   Finished Sowing & harrowing in my Oats. Viz. 44 Bushels. Also, finished Sowing the grass Seed by Quar[te]r.

29.   Engagd my Ferriage at Fredksburg. by the Year of Mr. Jas. Hunter.

James Hunter, Jr. (1746–1788), inherited this Rappahannock River ferry from his father, William, who died in 1754. Since James Jr. was still a minor in 1762, GW must have dealt with his older cousin and guardian, James Hunter, Sr. (d. 1785), a major merchant, planter, and iron manufacturer then of King George County.

30.   Sowed in the Meadow at Ashfords, eight Quarts of Timothy Seed four Do. of Lucerne, and three pecks of Hop Trefoil.

April

5.   Sowed Timothy Seed in the old Apple Orchard below the Hill.

7.   Sowed – or rather sprinkled a little of Ditto on the Oats.

8. to the 10th.   Getting Swamp Mud, & laying it in heaps – also got a little of the Creek Mud – Both for tryal as Manures.

14.   Inspected 20 Hhds. Tobo.

15.   John Foster run away.

21.   Sent Jno. Alton to take charge of Plantation.

John Alton (d. 1785), a white servant, worked faithfully for GW for more than 30 years. He accompanied GW as his body servant in the Braddock campaign and later served in various capacities at Mount Vernon. When John Foster ran away from Mount Vernon, GW sent Alton to take over the overseer's duties at the Dogue Run farm. Later in the year Alton was transferred to Muddy Hole to succeed Edward Violette (see entry for 27 Oct. 1762), and at the time of his death was overseer at River Farm. For several years Alton also managed the Mill plantation.

22.   Attachts. in my hands for Fosters effects.

The royal arms of colonial Virginia. (Colonial Williamsburg Photograph)

24. Had the Plantn. viewed.
   Herrings run in gt. quantity's.
   Planted new gd. at Williamson's.

26. Began to plant Corn at all my Plantation's.

May

3. Mr. Daingerfields Negro Bricklayer Guy came here to work.

Three William Daingerfields were living in Virginia in 1762, all of whom GW knew. Col. William Daingerfield (d. 1769), of Greenfield, Essex County, whom GW had visited in 1752 as he was traveling home from Barbados, had a son and a nephew, both named William. The son William Daingerfield (d. 1781), of Coventry and Fredericksburg, Spotsylvania County, had served with GW as ensign and lieutenant in the Virginia Regiment and continued in service until the regiment was disbanded in 1762. The nephew William Daingerfield (d. 1783), of New Kent, was a first cousin to Burwell Bassett and lived in the Eltham neighborhood until about 1770, when he removed to Belvidera, just south of Fredericksburg (see RILEY [1], 172). GW hired Guy for £30 per year plus room and board and billed Daingerfield for Guy's clothing. Guy remained in GW's service until Oct. 1763.

4.   Finished Planting Corn at all Places.

10.   Counted the Tobo. Gd. at Doeg Run Qr. as follows—viz.—of

Cowpen Ground	7500
Dungd Gd. in Peach Orchard	3100
Ditto in Apple Orchard	3500
	14,100
New ground	12500
Old Ground J. Gists adjg.	10700
large Cut by Corn field fence	22000
Middle Cut adjoing.	9200
Small Cut next Woods Do.	4500
round New Tobo. House	8600
Branch between	
Jno. Gists old Gd. So. side Plann.	13,000

John Gist (d. 1778) was a planter who for many years had rented 106 acres on the east side of Dogue Run from Sampson Darrell—land that came under GW's ownership after his purchase of 500 acres from Darrell in 1757. Gist continued to rent his quarter from GW until 12 Aug. 1760, when GW bought out his lease for £30 (deed of Gist to GW, PHi: Gratz Collection; LEDGER A, 84). Gist apparently moved to Loudoun County.

11.   Told my Sheep as follows—viz. & Cut & Markd

Ewes in all	104	Ewe Lambs	38
Weather's Do.	29	left for Ram's	4
Ram's	6	Weather's	8
	139	left for killing	16
			66

Note. The above Includes falling Sheep Ewes & Lambs.
Put 31 hides in Soak for Tanning.
Guy began the Garden Wall, after having built an Oven in the Kitchen, laid the hearth, & repaird the back.
Brought 5 Cows & Calves from Muddy hole.

13.   Got a Cask of Leith Ale from Mr. Marshall Piscatwy.
   Agreed to do Mr. Bells Work for £59.

Marshall is probably James Marshall, who owned or managed a "Public House of Entertainment" in Piscataway in 1761 (*Md. Gaz.*, 23 April 1761). Piscataway is on Piscataway Creek in Prince George's County, Md., almost directly across the Potomac from Mount Vernon. At this time it was a thriving town made up largely of Scottish merchants engaged in the tobacco trade.

MR. BELLS WORK: On 15 Aug. 1763 GW received £41 15s. 8d. from "Mr. Josias Bell for Carpenters w[ork]" (LEDGER A, 166). Most of GW's carpenters were involved in this work during the summer of 1762 (see entries for 28 June, 19 July, 27 July, and 29 July 1762). Bell was probably Josias Beall (born c.1725) of Prince George's County, Md.

15.   6 Cows & Calves from S. Johnson. 3 Do. 2 Do. from C.

22.   Young Countiss & black Mare Covered by Alexanders Ho[rse].

Alexander is probably Robert Alexander, son of Col. Gerard Alexander and his wife Mary Dent Alexander. It is probable that GW sent some of his mares to Alexander's nearby plantation to be bred, possibly to an English stallion which he had previously sold to Alexander (LEDGER A, 96).

28.   Planted abt. 50, or 60,000—being the first—Tobo. put in. Roan's bay & sorrel covered by Mr. Rozers Traveller. English bay & black covered by Aeriel.

Roan may have been John Roan, overseer of Claiborne's, the Custis dower plantation in King William County.

Ariel was a thoroughbred black stallion from the famous Belair stables in Prince George's County, Md. In 1762 he was standing at William Digges's plantation (BELAIR STUD, 56).

Henry Rozer or Rozier (born c.1725), of Prince George's County, Md., lived at Notley Hall, nearly opposite Alexandria (BROWNE, 309; BRUMBAUGH, 1:85). The previous spring he had advertised in the *Maryland Gazette:* "YOUNG TRAVELLER, now in the Possession of Mr. *Henry Rozer,* in *Prince-George's* County, Covers Mares at Two Guineas. He is Five Years old, full Sixteen Hands and an Inch high, was bred by Col. *Tasker,* got by Mr. *Moreton's* TRAVELLER in *Virginia,* and came out of MISS COLVILL" (2 April 1761).

30.   Chesnut Mare covered by Alexrs. H[orse] Countis & blk. refused.

Roan Mare & old black coverd by McCartys horse.

Capt. Daniel McCarty (d. 1791) of Mount Air charged GW £3 for "the use of your Horse to 4 Mares" (LEDGER A, 82).

31.   White Mare & Rankin covered by Do.

June

1.   Guy Sick and did no Work.

2. Good Season at D[ogue] Run Quartr. planted abt. there.

4. Jno. Askew came to Work.

In 1759 GW hired John Askew (Askin), a local joiner, for £25 per year plus housing. In Oct. 1761 they changed the agreement, GW now paying Askew a per diem wage that amounted to the same £25-per-year rate. For a 5-day week with 11 holidays per year Askew's pay would come to 2s. per day. Hence, as Askew was paid per day, GW kept track of any absence or return to work by Askew.

7. Jno. Askew came to Work.

8. Roan Mare took McCartys Horse.
   Old black – took – Do. – Do.

9. Rankin's – took – Do. – Do.
   White – refused Do. – Do.
   English Mare refused Alexrs. Horse.

13. Recd. a Pipe of Wine.
    Hogs at Mill – viz.

6	Sows
13	large Shoats
9	Smaller Do.
6	Large Pigs
12	Small Do.
46	in all.

    Blaze Mare refused horse.

14. English Mare refused Do.

17. Began Mowing Meadow on C[ree]k side.
    Planted at Orchard point – Craiks and Cowpen my 5 sorts of Tobo. as follow
    At the point 100 hills of each sort in undunged gd. & 100 of dunged
    The 1st. Row next Tobo. bed Fred[eric]k & so on as they were sowed in March last then begg. with the same & so on alternately.
    The same Order observe at Craiks begg. next Creek & in the Cowpen next Wood.

Orchard Point was apparently a point of land on Clifton's Neck at the mouth of Little Hunting Creek (see "Observations" entry for 14 July 1768). On his

[300]

1766 map of River Farm, GW refers to a point of land across the creek from this as Old Orchard Point (*GW Atlas,* pl. 3).

19.   Finished Mowing 2 Meadows—& Makg. Hay. Note 5 hands can easily cut both in two days.
   Rankin Covered by McCarty's horse.
   2 Steers & Cow & Calf from Dogue Run.

20.   Roan Mare & old black took horse.

22.   Hay in both Meadows Cured & stacked.

25.   Began clearing at Rivr. Side Quarter.

27.   Rankin covered by McCartys horse.

28.   Corn planted in Tobo. Grd. at Muddy hole R[ive]r[side Quarter]. Will George & Ned went to Work at Bells.

29.   Replanted Tobo.—poor Season—corn replanted just coming up. Much hurt by B⟨   ⟩.

30.   Good Season—planted best part of Tobo. gd.

[July]

1st.   Roan Mare took McCartys horse.
   Black Do. Do.   Do.   Do.

3.   Recd. 494 bushls. Oyster Shells.

4.   My Mares came from Mr. Rozers.
MY MARES: the mares sent to Rozer's to be bred (see entry for 28 May 1762).

7.   Broached pipe of Wine.

8.   Finished plantg. & replantg. at all Qrs.

9. ⎫Cut my wheat at R[iverside] Qr. & Ck. Do. Also finished
10. ⎭first cuttg. of Hay.

12.   Finished plowg. gd. behind Garden.
   Carpenters went to Reapg. at Poseys.

13.   Mares brot. from Mr. Digges's.

GW brought back his English bay and black mares which had been sent to William Digges's plantation to be bred (see entry for 28 May 1762).

14.   Counted my Sheep as follows—
              6 Rams at Johnson's
            12 Ewes at Do.
            94 Do. runng. at large
              1 Do. put into Oats
            13 Weathers put into Do.
            16 rung. in pasture
          142 old Sheep, besides one at Colo. F[airfa]xs
            12 Ram lambs put into Oats
              8 Weather Do. in grass gd.
            38 Ewe Ditto—in Ditto
          200—in all & this day parted Ewes & L[am]bs
      Puttg. the followg. Cattle for fattg. upon Oats
          2 old Steers from D[ogue] Run ⎫
          1 old Cow from Do.   ⎬ —formerly
          2 old Steers from there to day.   ⎭
          1 old Cow from Muddy hole
          2 old Oxen Home Ho[use]
          1 old Cow Do. Do.—wch. came formly. from R[ive]r[side Quarter]
          9—in all.

15.   Nancy Gist left this.

Nancy Gist, daughter of Christopher and Sarah Howard Gist, had gone to live with William Fairfax's family at Belvoir in 1757 while her father was on the frontier, first as a captain with the Virginia Regiment, then as deputy to Edmund Atkins, superintendent for Indian affairs in the southern colonies (William Fairfax to GW, 17 July 1757, DLC:GW; GW to Sally Fairfax, 25 Sept. 1758, WRITINGS, 2:292–94; TRIMBLE, 145–47). She never married and after her father's death in 1759 went to live with one of her brothers.

19.   Will, George, Sam, & Mike went to Bells agn.

20.   Recd. my Goods from the Unity—Captn. Robson.
      Bot. Frederick & Judy of Mr. Lewis.
      Began grubg. my Meadow. Note sometimes 4, & sometimes 6 hands at Wk.

Capt. William Robson of the *Unity* carried a large shipment of goods which GW had ordered from Robert Cary & Co. on behalf of himself and the two

A typical tobacconist's trade card. (Trustees of the British Museum)

Custis children. The complete order amounted to £463 15s. 8d. and included such items as a new still, clothing, china, food, farm equipment, and books (invoices of goods shipped to GW, 1754–66, DLC:GW). GW wrote Cary & Co. on 18 Sept. 1762 that everything had arrived except some shoes. "There must likewise have been a mistake in Shipping the Plows, for many of the most material parts being wanting, the rest, according to the Bill of Parcells, is entirely useless, and lye upon my hands a dead charge" (DLC:GW).

FREDERICK & JUDY: On this date GW paid £115 to Col. Fielding Lewis for two Negroes (LEDGER A, 146).

26.   Sowed a little of each kind of Seed that came in, in the Garden to try their goodns.

Opened a Cask bottled Porter contg. as follows

6.	1	full bottles		29.6	full Bs.
3.	4	pieces	also 3 Casks	1	Piece
1.11		empty	Dorsets. Beer	2.1	broken
	9	broke	as follows	31.8	in all
12.1		in all			

27.   Crump went over to Bells to work.

29.   Tom also went over.

31.   Guy finished the 3 sides of Garden all to Capp[in]g Pill[a]r. B. Mitchell went away.

Burgess Mitchell of Maryland had been employed 1 May 1762 by GW as overseer of the Home House plantation, the farm on which the mansion house was located. He was to work until the end of October, for which GW was to pay him £6 plus his levy and tax and to provide him with laundry services, lodging, and food. According to the terms of the agreement, if Mitchell did not fulfill his obligations satisfactorily he could be "turned of at any season between this" and the last of October and would forfeit his wages (agreement of Mitchell with GW, 1 May 1762, DLC:GW). He left before the six months were up.

[August]

2.   Philip Fletcher came to making Bricks.

Sowed a Bushel of Buckwheat in Sandy grd. at Ch[arle]s C[rai]ks.

Philip Fletcher was paid £14 10s. for making 78,000 nine-inch bricks, 2,125 tiles for the garden wall, and 1,080 nine-inch-square flooring tiles (LEDGER A, 130).

After this early trial of *Fagopyrum esculentum*, buckwheat, GW appears to have neglected it as a crop for many years. He next begins to experiment with it when he receives 50 bushels from Levin Powell of Loudoun County, as he notes in his entry of 1 Dec. 1786. When Powell sent him several more bushels in April 1787, he included a letter advising GW on raising the crop and explaining that it was fed to cows and horses as a meal mixed with straw or chaff. GW planned to use it both as livestock feed and as green manure to be plowed under. Seven years later he was still learning how to raise the crop. When the Whiskey Rebellion called him into rural Pennsylvania in 1794, he paused at Reading to write William Pearce at Mount Vernon some observations he had made on the methods used by Pennsylvania farmers. Eventually he gave up buckwheat completely, believing that it depleted as much as it enriched the soil.

3.   Inspected 11 hogsheads—Tobo. H[untin]g C[ree]k Warehouse.

5.   Sowed Turnip Seed.

12.   Sowed Rye & Hop Trefoil behind Garden.

RYE: *Secale cereale,* important to GW in sheep husbandry and in his overall plan when in later years he had developed a seven-year crop rotation. He usually grazed sheep on the young rye, withdrawing them in time to produce a grain crop.

16.   Began Sowing Wheat at River Quarter.

20.   Began beating Cyder at Ditto.
    Recd. 1 hhd. Molasses qty. 120 Gals. & 1 Barl. Sugar wt. 254 lb. of Colo. Walke.
    Also recd. of Mr. Thos. Thompson leathr. as follows Viz.

> 10 Sides Sole leathr.—wt. 200 lbs.
> 17 Sides upper Do. & ⎫
> 2 hides Do.   Do.   ⎬ wt. 100 lbs.

Col. Anthony Walke (1692–1768), of Fairfield, Princess Anne County, was a merchant based in Norfolk who imported rum and sugar from the West Indies. By 1762 his son Anthony Walke (1726–1782) had become a partner in the business. In his LEDGER A, 118, GW records Thompson's first name as William.

21.   Recd. 70 Bags of Salt—abt. 280 Bushels.

25.   Began Sowing Wheat at Creek Quartr.

30.   Began Sowing wheat at Muddy hole.
    Began cutting Creek Meadow.

31. Winney came from Mountain Quarter.
Agreed with Nelson Kelly to Overlook Gists &ca.

MOUNTAIN QUARTER: Bullskin plantation. Winney may be the slave of the
same name who was a house servant at Mount Vernon from 1766 until some
time after 1773 (Toner Transcripts, DLC).
  According to articles of agreement signed the following day, Kelly, described as a "Planter," was to oversee the next year's tobacco and corn crops
at GW's "quarters on Doegs Run known by the names of Gists and Ashfords"
and in return he was to receive a part of the crops, some meat provisions,
and a cash bonus on the tobacco (DLC:GW).

[September]

8. Carried the last of my Tobo. to H[untin]g C[ree]k W[are-
house].
Finished sowing Wheat at Muddy hole 15 [   ].

13. Began getting Fodder at Muddy hole.

[October]

4. Put up 4 Hogs for forwd. Bacon at R[iver] Side.

GW had left Mount Vernon for Frederick County 3 Oct. and did not return
until eight days later (GW to George W. Fairfax, 30 Oct. 1762, PHi: Dreer
Collection).

12.
13. } Sowed Rye at Muddy hole.

18. Planted 4 Nuts of the Medateranean Pine in Garden close
by the Brick Ho[use].

23. At Night set fire to brick Kiln.

26. Put up at Muddy hole   21 hogs
             at Doag Run   9
             at Ditto from Mill   16
             at Creek Qr.   6
             at Rivr. Side   4
                                   ——
                                   56

27.   Stopd Kiln holes about 2 oclock.

Ned Violette moved off for Frederick & John Alton to Muddy hole.

30.   Sowed 3 pints of Timothy Seed below my Meadow at Ashfords.

Note—A small part on the So. West Side not broke up, but very light notwithstanding.

[November]

4.   Killed four hogs from Rivr. sid[e] Quarter. Nett wt . . . 435 lbs.

10.   Set of for Williamsburg & returnd Decr. 1st.

GW apparently repeated his practice of visiting the Custis plantations on his way to Williamsburg and probably arrived in that city on 15 Nov., when he took his seat in the House of Burgesses. The fourth session of the 1761–65 assembly had begun on 2 Nov. 1762 and was a busy one, passing 44 acts before its prorogation on 23 Dec. As the assembly tended to do most of its major work in the middle half of a session, GW was present for consideration of most of the major bills, including some which must have had particular interest for him. Among the bills passed were four that concerned military affairs; one for encouraging local manufactures; one for enlarging the growing town of Alexandria; and one for enlarging the boundaries of Truro Parish, to whose vestry he had just been elected in October. While in Williamsburg, GW stayed at Christiana Campbell's tavern on Duke of Gloucester Street near the Capitol. He also tended to some personal and financial concerns: he paid Anthony Walke for the sugar and rum delivered the previous August, collected some of his burgess's allowances which, under the new act, allowed him 15s. per diem plus £7 10s. travel expenses per session, and visited his barber.

29.   28 hogs & 2 Beeves come from Bullskin.

30.   Killed the above Hogs & 6 from Mudy. hol[e] & 10 from Doeg Run—wt. Nett.

from Frederick—3663
Doegs Run—1028
Muddy hole— 621
—————
5312 lbs.

[December]

4.   Finished Measg. & Lofting Corn.

6.   94 Barrls. Corn in great Corn Ho[use] at Muddy hole—when they began to use it.
   Mr. Adams 8 Sheep from Mudy. hole.

GW records this delivery to Robert Adam of Alexandria in his LEDGER A, 133, as "8 Fat Sheep."

15.   8 Ditto from Doeg Run.
   Killed 28 Hogs viz.

from Muddy hole	11	weighg.	1012
from Doeg Run	11		1056
from Riverside	2		196
from Creek	4		471
			2,735

Whereof 16 were sold	1535
4 To Overs[ee]rs	315
8 for Family	885
	2,735

To that there has been for the Family this Year   435
                                                      5312
                                                       885
                                       In all   6,632

GW made the above entries in *The Virginia Almanack* for the current year, as was his custom. The 1762 edition, like many eighteenth-century almanacs, contained a printed section of proverbs and anecdotes, appearing in this case near the end of the volume. Of the 100 items there, GW marked 15 with an X, apparently indicating that he found them especially interesting or amusing.

Plantation Records

1763

[March]

Brought to D. Run Plantn. 3 of my Stray Steers.

2. Seven young Pigs at R[iver] Side Qr.

6. Eight Do. at Muddy hole.

9. By this lost 3 of my Sheep viz. a Ram & two young Ewes.

10. Brot. a strayed Heifer of mine to Rivr. Side Qr.

April 24, 1763

At my Plantation in King William

15 Negroe Sharers
2 Overseer
——
17 in all
——
126 head of Cattle besides Calves—9 of this spring
——
52 head of sheep besides Lambs—13
——
8 Sows for Breeding
16 for Porkers at the Fall
18—of 6 Months old
32—of 6 Weeks Ditto
28 young Pigs
——
102 in all
——
M 190 Corn holes good Tale.
M 170 Tobo. Hills Do. Do.

M 190 CORN HOLES: That is, 190,000 corn holes. GW frequently used the roman numeral M to indicate one thousand.

[May]

At Bridge Quarter

Overseer—Cluning
9 Negroe Sharers
——
10 in all
——

100,000 holes of Corn $\left\{\begin{array}{l}110,000 \\ 106,100\end{array}\right\}$ lately countd
120,000 Tobo. Hills

7 Work steers
56 head Cattle
13 old Sheep
12 Lambs
2 Sows
5 Barrows
15 Pigs – 6 Weeks old

At Ship Landing

Willm. Jackson
7 Negroe Sharers
8 in all
70,000 Corn holes $\left\{\begin{array}{l}77,056 \\ 81,158\end{array}\right\}$ Countd
80,000 Tobo. Hills
45 Head Cattle
1 Boar
10 young hogs
15 Six Weeks old
5 One Week Ditto

May 13.   Told my sheep & cut & Marked Lambs as follows – viz.

Ewes in all here	119	Ewe Lambs at H.	27
At Rivr. Side	1	R. Lambs for Killg.	13
At Creek	5	Weather Lms.	13
Weathrs. at home	18	At Creek Qr.	7
at Creek Qr.	4	At Rr. Side	1
Rams at home	7		61
at Creek Qr.	3		
	157		

Tobo. Ground belonging to Muddy hole

at the Mill	13,100
Cowpen by Gate	4,200
By Muddy hole Swamp	5,800
By Lane & Road at Hannahs	4,200
Slipe below Hill near Do.	6,350
Joing. Rye & Woods	8,700
In all	42,350

[June]

24.   Began to cut Timothy at Ashfords.

30.   Finished Do. – 2 days Rain in the time.

On 3 June 1763, GW attended the initial meeting, probably at Stafford Court House, of a group of Potomac valley men who were interested in developing western lands. This meeting followed by only four months the Treaty of Paris, in which France renounced all claim to lands west of the Appalachian Mountains, thus opening these lands to settlement by the American colonists. To this end colonial land companies began forming, and one of the first was the Mississippi Company, organized at this meeting. The regulations agreed upon provided for a limit of 50 members (there were never more than 40), each of whom was to get 50,000 acres, and none of whom could transfer his interest without approval of the company, thus protecting the company from infiltration by members of rival land companies. Assessments were to be provided for as needed. The company would be run by a ten-member executive committee, which was to execute the decisions of the annual meeting of the full company (Mississippi Company regulations, 3 June 1763, DLC:GW; CARTER [1], 109).

[July]

1st.   Began to cut Rye by Garden.

5.
6.
7. } Cut and secured all my Wheat (by Stacking) at River & Creek Quarters – abt. 60 Acres. Carpenters, Smiths, & home Gang employd.
8.
9.

Writing to Burwell Bassett 5 July, GW reported that his wheat crop was largely destroyed by rust and other defects, "and our Crops of Indian Corn and Tobacco in a manner lost in Weeds and Grass, occasioned by continual and excessive Rains" (WRITINGS, 2:401).

11.   Cut & Stacked wheat at Mudy. hole & Cut Rye there.

12. }
13. } Cut & Stackd Do. at Dogue Run & Stackd Rye at Muddy hole.

14.
15. }
16. & } Cut & made Hay of Clover at River Quarter with part of the hands – the Rest Workg. at D[ogue] R[un].
18.

[311]

19.
20. } Cutg. Hay at Hell hole.

21.
22. } Makg. Do.—Rainy.

23. People doing Jobs.

25.
26. } Cutting & makg. Hay at Sein Landg.
27.

28.
29. } Cut Timothy Seed at Ashfords & new topd. the stack there.
Note. This seed was cut too soon & did not stand long enough in the field wch. occasioned gt. loss.

30. Doing Jobs.

[August]

1.
2.
3.
4. } Cutting curing and Stackg. Hay from Creek Meadow.
5.
6.
Note. Too late cutting Hay for first Crop this year.

15. Sowed Turnips at Muddy hole.

16. Sowed Do. at Rivr. Quartr.
  Do. at home in Peach Orchard—English seed from Clifton & Posey.
17. Sowed Do. below Garden. Seed from England.

18. Ditto in Apple Orchard. Some English seed & some Country Do.
  Sowed likewise at Creek Qr. & Doeg Run—Country Seed.
Note. No Rain upon them until the ⟨   ⟩ Inst.

20. Counted sheep pr. List Inclosd.

26.   Sowed a little English cloverseed at Quince tree in Garden to see if it was good.

QUINCE TREE: *Cydonia oblonga,* an unimportant fruit in GW's orchard scheme.

29.   Began sowing Wheat at Muddy hole.

31.   In Turnips below garden and Peach Orchard sowed about a Peck of Spelts in Drills—also abt. a Hat ful in Apple Orchard lower corner.

Spelt is *Triticum aestivum* var. *spelta* or any other variety of wheat in which the chaff adheres to the grain. It therefore cannot be threshed like other wheats but must be milled. GW raised white and black varieties.

[September]

1st.   Observed that my yg. Corn was just beginning to show, occasioned by Rains falling abt. the 25th. Quere has it time to make or Ripen.

2.   Sowed a Bushel & half of Winter Barley on an Acre of Ground in Apple Orchard.

3. ⎫
4. ⎭ Sowed Rye in Ditto & began Stilling Cyder.

8.   Agreed with Thomas Nichols a farmer to Overlook my People at Home & work wt. them for £20.

9.   Began to sow wheat at C[ree]k Qrs.

On this day GW attended the first annual meeting of the Mississippi Company, held at Thomas Ludwell Lee's home, Belleview, on the south side of Potomac Creek in Stafford County. At the meeting the company agreed upon a formal memorial to the crown, appointed William Lee treasurer-secretary, and chose its ten-member executive committee, which was to meet semi-annually at Westmoreland Court House. GW was not one of the ten, probably because the members were chosen on the basis of their proximity to the meeting place; John Augustine Washington, who lived in Westmoreland County, was on the committee. GW paid his company quota of £8 5s. for hiring an agent in England who was to prosecute the memorial and also invite into the company not more than nine English members "of such influence and fortune as may be likely to promote its success" (CARTER [1], 170). The meeting also authorized special meetings of the full company.

Four weeks after this meeting the crown promulgated the Proclamation

Line of 1763, which prohibited any settlement west of the Appalachian Mountains. Although GW later observed to William Crawford (21 Sept. 1767, DLC:GW) that he could "never look upon that Proclamation in any other light . . . than as a temporary expedient to quiet the Minds of the Indians and must fall of course in a few years," the presence of the Line, coupled with the instability of British ministries during the 1760s and the claims of competing land companies, caused the Mississippi Company's petition to remain dormant for the next four years.

10.   Began to sow Do. at Rivr. Qr.

12.   Began to sow Do. at Doag Run.
   Finished sowing Do. at Muddy hole 25 ⟨Bls.⟩

15.   Planted in 11 holes on the West side of the Garden 22 English Walnuts.

17.   Began to sow Rye at Muddy hole.

19.   Began getting fodder at Do.

21.   Frost bit Tobacco at D[ogue] Run.

22.   Frost bit Do. at Do. and at Muddy hole also bit Fodder very much.
   Began to get fodder at Creek Quarter.

[October]

1st.   Finished sowing 7 Bushels of Spelts in 7 Acres of Corn Ground at Muddy hole—the Sowing of which was began the day before.

Novembr.

4.   Finished sowing Wheat at Doeg Run—viz. 33 Bushls. in the large Cut 24 in the next adjoining 4½ by the Gate & 3 in the other Tobo. Ground. In all 64½ Bushels.

5.   Finished Sowing Wheat at C[ree]k Qr. in all 32½ Bushls.
   Finished sowing Do. at River Qr. in all 47½ Bushels.

7.   Put up 10 Hogs to fatten at River Quarter.

8.   Put up 15 to fatten at Mudy. Hole.

9.   Put up 24 to fatten at Doeg Run.
    Got done Sowing Wheat at the Mill & home House viz. 32 at
the first and 4½ at the last.

15.   Put up 10 Hogs at Doeg Run from the Mill.

18.   Killed 5 Hogs from Creek Quartr. nett wt.—590 lbs.

Memorandoms—March 21st.

21.   Grafted 40 Cherrys—viz.
        12 Bullock Hearts (a large black May Cherry)
        18 Very fine early May Cherry
        10 Cornation—Cherry—& planted them as followeth—
        the Bullock Hearts in the first Row next the Quarter
        beginning at the furthest part thereof & ending at a
        stick.
        The early may next to them in the same Row & ending
        at another stick.
        The Cornation finishing the said Row.
    Grafted 12 Magnum Bonum Plums beginning at the further
part of the Second Row.
    Planted 4 Nuts of the Mediterranean Pine in the Pen where
the Chesnut grows—sticks by each.
Note the Cherrys & Plums came from Collo. Mason's—Nuts from
Mr. Gr[een].
    Set out 55 cuttings of the Madeira Grape—viz.—31 in finishing
the 2d. row where the Plums are and 24 in the next beginning at
the hither end—these from Mr. Greens.

GRAFTED 40 CHERRYS: All the cherries mentioned here and elsewhere origi-
nated in England; the sweet varieties are *Prunus avium*, the sour *P. cerasus*,
and the duke cherries *P. avium regalis*. Here GW is grafting the Bullock, or
Ox Heart, a dark red cherry with large, heart-shaped fruit which ripened in
July; one of several varieties of May cherries, and the Carnation, a large
and handsome light red cherry highly esteemed for making brandy and
preserves (DOWNING, 194). The Magnum Bonum plum was also known as the
egg plum in American gardens, occurring in both white and yellow forms.
    MEDITERRANEAN PINE: probably *Pinus pinea*, the Italian stone pine, native
to Italy and southern Europe and often cultivated for its edible kernels.
Nurseryman Bernard McMahon listed it as a desirable planting in his
CALENDAR [1], 273, and it still is a popular landscaping tree in the South, but
not hardy in Virginia. Peter Collinson sent seeds of this species to John

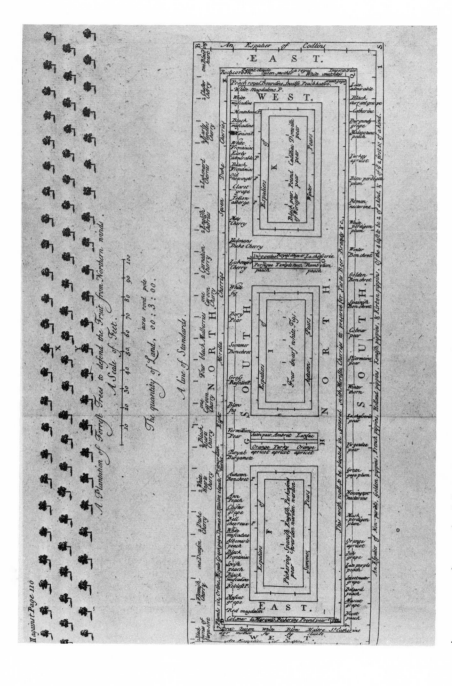

Arrangement of an orchard from Batty Langley, *New Principles of Gardening*, London, 1728. (Beinecke Rare Book and Manuscript Library, Yale University)

Custis, Williamsburg, from England, but in 1738 Custis reported that he had been unable to save the seedlings he produced (SWEM, 69, 74).

COLLO. MASON: George Mason (1725–1792), one of GW's neighbors, lived at Gunston Hall, located about 16 miles south of Alexandria on Pohick Bay. Mason was an enthusiastic farmer and he and GW frequently exchanged views on agriculture as well as on political events. Mason was a trustee of Alexandria, a member of the Truro Parish vestry, a justice of Fairfax County, and treasurer of the Ohio Company. Although he disliked holding public office, he served briefly in the House of Burgesses and for a number of years in the House of Delegates and exerted considerable influence on the political thought of his Virginia contemporaries.

22.   Transplanted to the Corner of the Borders by Garden House a Cherry Graft—from the Cherry tree at the other Corner of the said Bord⟨er⟩ by the first Fall.

26.   Grafted 12 Quinces on Pear and Apple Stocks and planted them next the vines in Bd. [Border] Row in Nurs⟨ery⟩.

Also grafted 10 of a pretty little early (June) Pear from Collo. Mason's and planted them at the end of the Quinces except 3 wch. begins the 4th. Row at the other end.

Transplanted about 350 hundd. young Crab Scions from Creek Quarter into the Nursery.

30.   Grafted, & planted as followeth.
viz.
12 Spanish pairs from Collo. Masons. They hang till November & are a very valuable Fruit—these stand next the little early pair in the 4 Row beging. with the 4th. Tree in the said Row.

Also grafted 12 Butter pears from Collo. Masons—these esteemed among the finest pears, & stand next the Spanish pears.

Grafted 10 black Pear of Worcester from Collo. Mason's next the Butter Pear—these are a large course fruit for baking.

Grafted 10 of the Winter Boon Chrns.—from Collo. Masons—who had them from Collo. Fairfx. who praises them much—these begin the 5th Row next Grass Ground.

Grafted 8 of the Summer Boon Chrns. next these. From Do. who had them from Do. &ca.

Grafted 10 of the Bergamy Pears from Collo. Masons next the Sumr. Boon. These are a very fine Fruit but Co⟨arser⟩ than most other English Pears.

Grafted 10 of the New Town Pippin from Collo. Masons who had them from Mr. Presidt. Blair.

Grafted 43 of the Maryland Red Strick—had the Grafts from Mr. Wm. Digges—these are the whole of the 6th. Row.

George Mason, Washington's neighbor at Gunston Hall. (Mr. S. Cooper Dawson, Jr.)

WINTER BOON: GW means Bon Chrétien pears. There are several varieties, summer, fall, and winter.

The Newtown Pippin apple was developed on Long Island, proved most popular, and is now called the Albemarle Pippin because of its association with the orchards of Albemarle County, Va. When he writes "Strick," GW means "Streak." Downing describes a "Red Streak" variety and calls it a good cider apple. An English Redstreak was offered for sale by nurseryman Philip Walten of Baltimore in 1788. George Mason used the Redstreak for cider and sent GW a quantity of it 5 April 1785, cautioning him that it would not be ready for drinking until May. Mason suggested that if GW decided to drink some while it was still sweet, he ought to grate a little ginger into it to make it "much more grateful to the Stomach" (Mason to GW, 5 April 1785, DLC:GW).

John Blair (1687–1771), of Williamsburg, became a member of the council in Virginia in 1745. Upon Governor Dinwiddie's return to England in Dec. 1757, Blair took the oaths as president of the council and served as acting governor until the arrival of Gov. Francis Fauquier in June 1758. During that period GW, as commander of the Virginia Regiment, reported to Blair.

To the Great Dismal Swamp

15 October 1763

EDITORIAL NOTE. The following entry, recording details of GW's visit to the Dismal Swamp, appears faintly in pencil on the front of the 1763 diary and is repeated, in ink, in the diary for 1764. Variations between the two texts are minor. Although the entry is dated 15 Oct., it covers his first visit to the swamp in May, while he was attending meetings of the General Assembly in Williamsburg. The notes apparently were prompted by his second visit to the area in October, during which he did not enter the swamp.

The Dismal Swamp, in southeast Virginia and northeast North Carolina, is a coastal swamp about twenty miles long which at one time extended over some two thousand square miles. It is geologically unusual in that it is higher than the surrounding land, and water drains out of it rather than into it. At its center is Lake Drummond, about three miles across, which GW calls "the Pond" (see main entry for 28 Oct. 1768).

In 1763 GW and several partners including Fielding Lewis and Burwell Bassett formed a company, "Adventurers for Draining the Dismal Swamp," and the General Assembly of Virginia empowered them to construct canals and causeways through private land without being subject to suits for damages (HENING, 8:18). The purpose of the undertaking was to harvest lumber while the swamp was draining and to farm the land once it became dry. Early developers including Washington showed little interest in the digging of a canal for boat traffic between Chesapeake Bay and Albemarle Sound, a project which was accomplished a generation later. Although GW acquired land in the area and helped to finance some draining, his interest waned about twenty years after the following memorandum was written. His Dismal Swamp activities will be dealt with more fully in notes accompanying his correspondence on the subject.

Here GW documents a trip from Suffolk, down the west side of the swamp, across the Perquimans River to a site near present-day Elizabeth City, N.C., then back along the eastern side of the

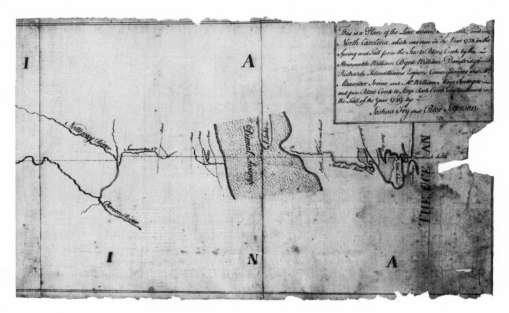

The Dismal Swamp is shown in this detail from a manuscript map of 1749 by Joshua Fry and Peter Jefferson. (Manuscripts Department, University of Virginia Library)

swamp to Suffolk. Among the landowners named by GW were some from the prominent Nansemond County families of Riddick, Sumner, and Norfleet. Willis Riddick, from whom GW later bought land, was a member of the House of Burgesses for many years.

Memm. From Suffolk to Pocoson Swamp is reckoned about 6 Miles, and something better than 4 perhaps 5 Miles from Collo. Reddicks Mill run (where the Road x's it). The land within this distance especially after passing Willis Reddicks is Level & not bad. The banks down to this (Pocoson) Swamp declines gradually, and the Swamp appears to be near 75 yds. over, but no Water in it at present. Note—Mills Riddicks Plantn. seems to be a good one the land being level and stiff. So does Henry Riddicks above.

From Pocoson Swamp to Cyprus Swamp (which conducts more Water into the great Dismal than any one of the many that leads into it) is about 2½ Miles. This also is dry at present, but appears to be 60 or 65 yards across in the wettest part.

The next Swamp to this is called Mossey Swamp and distant about 3 Miles. Near this place lives Jno. Reddick on good Land, but hitherto from Pocoson Swamp, the land lyes flat, wet, & poor. This Swamp is 60 yards over and dry.

Between Cyprus Swamp, and the last mentioned one, we went on horse back not less than ½ a Mile into the great Swamp (Dismal) without any sort of difficulty, the horse not sinking over the fetlocks—the first quarter however abounding in Pine and Gallbury bushes, the soil being much intermixed with Sand but afterwards it grew blacker and richer with many young Reeds & few pines and this it may be observed here is the nature of the Swamp in general.

From Mossey Swamp to a branch and a large one it is, of Oropeak (not less than 80 yards over) is reckoned 4 Miles—two Miles short of which is a large Plantation belonging to one Brindle near to which (on the South side) passes the Carolina line.

The Main Swamp of Oropeak is about ½ a Mile onwards from this, where stands the Widow Norflets Mi⟨ll⟩ & luke Sumners Plantations. This Sw⟨amp⟩ cannot be less than 200 yards across but does not nevertheless discharge as much Water as Cyprus Swamp.

At the Mouth of this Swamp is a very large Meadow of 2 or 3000 Acr⟨es⟩ held by Sumner, Widow Norflet, Marmaduke Nor-flet, Powel & others & valuable ground it is.

From Oropeak Swamp to loosing Swamp is about 2 Miles, and this 70 yards across.

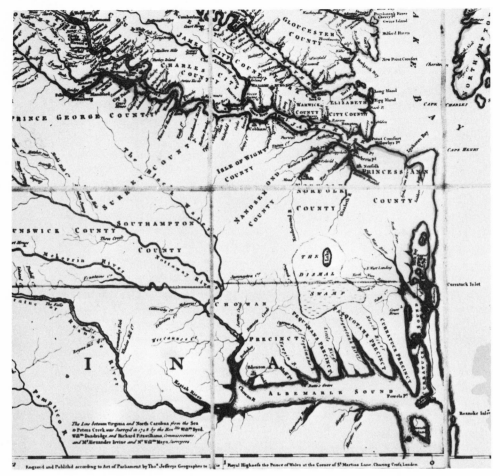

Extent of the Dismal Swamp is seen in this section of the Fry-Jefferson map of 1751, showing portions of Virginia and North Carolina. (Tracy W. McGregor Library, University of Virginia)

From hence again to Bassey Swamp the lower Road may be allowed 2 Miles More but this Swamp seems trifling.

And from Bassey Swamp to Horse Pool (which is the last, & including Swamp running into the Dismal) is about 2 Miles more & 35 yards across only.

The whole Land from Pocoson Swamp to this place and indeed all the way to Pequemen Bridge is in a manner a dead level— wet & cold in some places—sandy in others and generally poor.

This last named Swamp—viz. the Horse pool, is called 9 Miles from the upper Bridge on Pequemin River; within a Mile of which lives one Elias Stallens, and within 5 Miles is the lower Bridge—from whence to the bridge, or Ferry over little River is 15 measured Miles the course nearly due South as it likewise is from Suffolk to the said Bridge the Dismal running that course from that place.

From little River Bridge (or Ferry) to Ralphs Ferry on Paspetank is (I think we were told) abt. 16 Miles, the course East or No. East; and from thence if the ferry is not crossed along up the West Side of the River to the Rivr. Bridge of the said Paspetank is reckoned ———— Miles and about a No. Wt. course the Dismal bordering close upon the left all the way.

Note—the above Acct. is from Information only, for instead of taking that Rout, we crossed from Elias Stallens (one Miles above the upper bridge on Pequemin) across to a set of People which Inhabit a small slipe of Land between the said River Pequemen & the Dismal Swamp and from thence along a new cut path through the Main Swamp a Northerly course for 5 Miles to the Inhabitants of what they call new found land which is thick settled, very rich Land, and about 6 Miles from the aforesaid River Bridge of Paspetank. The Arm of the Dismal which we passed through to get to this New land (as it is called) is $3\frac{1}{4}$ Miles Measured—Little or no timber in it, but very full of Reeds & excessive Rich. Thro. this we carried horses—without any great difficulty.

This Land was formerly esteemed part of the Dismal but being higher tho' full of Reeds People ventured to settle upon it and as it became more open, it became more dry & is now prodigeous fine land but subject to wets & unhealthiness.

It is to be observed here that the tide, or still Water that comes out of the Sound up Pequemen River flows up as high as Stallens, and the River does not widen much untill it passes the lower Bridge some little distance. At Ralphs ferry upon Paspetank the River is said to be 2 Miles over, and decreases in width gradually to the bridge called River bridge, where it is about 30 yards across and affords sufficient Water for New England Vessels to come up and Load.

From what observations we were capable of making it appeared, as if the swamp had very little fall (I mean the Waters out of the great Swp.) into the heads of these Rivers which seems to be a demonstration that the Swamp is much lower on the South & East Sides because it is well known that there is a pretty considerable

Stylized artist's view of the Dismal Swamp. (Library of Congress)

fall on the West side through all the drains that make into Nansemond River & the Western Branch of Elizabeth at the North End of the Dismal.

From the River Bridge of Paspetank to an Arm of the Dismal at a place called 2 Miles Bridge is reckoned 7 Miles, & a branch of Paspetank twice crossed in the distance.

This Arm of the Dismal is equally good & Rich like the rest & runs (as we were informed) 15 or 20 Miles Easterly, and has an outlet (as some say) into Curratuck Inlet by No. West River, or Tulls C[ree]k but these accts. were given so indistinctly as not to be relied upon. However it is certain I believe that the Water does drain of at the East end somewhere, in which case a common causay through at the crossing place woud most certainly lay all that Arm dry.

From this place wch. is 2 Miles over to the Carolina line is about 4 Miles, and from thence to No. West landing on No. West Rivr. a branch of Curratuck, is 3 Miles more.

Note—the Carolina line crosses the Swamp in a West direction, and is 15 Miles from the place where it enters to its coming out of the same near Brindles Plantation. Flats and small Craft load at No. West landing.

To the great Bridge from No. West landing is accounted 12 Miles the Lands good, as they are on all this (East) side and highly esteemed valued in general according to the Propretors own Accts. from 20/. to £3. pr. acre but we were told they were to be had for less. This gt. Bridge is upon the South Branch of Elizabeth River & abt. 10 Miles from Norfolk and heads in the Dismal as does likewise No. West River Paspetank little River & Pequemen.

From the Great Bridge to Collo. Tuckers Mills is about 8 Miles within which distance several small Creeks making out of South Rivr. head up in the Dismal.

Farleys Plantation at the Forks of the Road is reckoned 5 Miles from the aforesaid Mills near to which the dismal runs.

From hence to Roberts's Ord[inar]y is 6 Miles and from thence to Suffolk 10 more. The lands from the Great bridge to within a

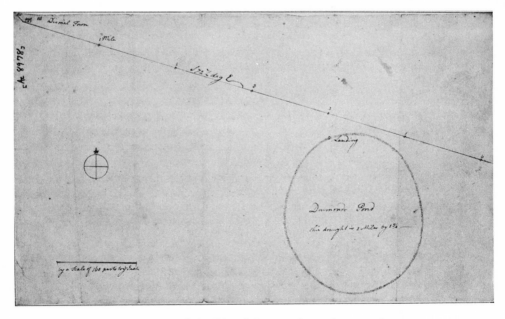

Lake Drummond, in the center of the Dismal Swamp, shown in an early survey. (Library of Congress)

Mile or two of Roberts's is generally sandy & indifferent. From hence to Cowpers Mill they are good & from thence to Collo. Reddicks Mean again.

Note—from the River B. on Paspetank to the Great Bridge on South River the Road runs nearly North and from thence to Farleys Plantation it seems to be about West from this again to Collo. Reddicks (or Suffolk) So. Wt. and from thence to Pequemen B. & little Rivr. South as beforemend. the Swamp bordering near to the Road all the way round—in some place close adjoining & in others 2 and 3 Miles distant.

Cherries, Plums, Apples, and Pears

1764

March

29.   Grafted as follows viz.

8 Bullock Heart Cherry's: these are a fine large bla: Cherry, ripe in May, but not early. They begin the first Row in the Nursery next the Quarter—& at that end next to the Ray Grass Field. Between these and the rest a Stake is drove. Then—

8 of the finest early May Cherry—ending at another Stick. Then—

6 of the large Duke Cherry, ending at a stick likewise all in the same Row. These three Cherrys from Collo. Mason's. From hence to the end of the Row are Cherry Scions for Grafting upon another year.

Grafted also—12 Magnum Bonum Plumbs beginning the 2d. Row at the end next Ray Grass, & ending at a stake. From hence to the end of the Row are Plumb Scions for grafting upon—another year. Note the Magnum Bonum Plumb from Collo. Mason's.

In the 3d. Row (beging. next Ray Grass) the 1st. 4. & 5th. trees are of a pritty little early (June) pair from Collo. Masons.

The 2, 3, 6th. and to the 15th. tree Inclusive (at the end of which a stake is drove) are the bla: Pear of Worcester—from Collo. Mason—a large course Pear for Baking.

Then 10 Bergamy Pears from Ditto, ending at a Stake. These are a very fine fruit but Cou⟨rser⟩ than most other English Pears.

Grafted also—the 3d. Row aforesd. continued.

Then—after the 10 Bergamy Pears—one of the Summer Boon Chrn. [bon Chrétien pear]. This from Collo. Mason who had them from Collo. Fairfax—who praises them much.

From hence to the end of the Row are apple Scions to Graft upon.

4th. Row all apple Scions to continue Pear Grafts upon next year.

5th. Row—beginning at the end next to Cherry Walk are first 15 New Town Pippins from Collo. Mason—who had them from Mr. President Blair. These end at a Stake & the Remainder of the Row & all the

6th. Row are Maryland red Stricks—68 in number.

VIII.   A U G U S T.   31 Days.

IF youth be wild, then for to cure the fame,
  Marriage and mouldy cheefe will make them tame;
If they be lazy, then the whip apply,
There's no difeafe but has a remedy.

Full ● 1ft, at 2 Morn.	New ☽ 16th, at Noon.
Laft Qr. 8th, at 9 Morn.	Firft Qr. 23d, at 6 Aftern.
	Full ● 30th, at 11 Morn.

1	thu	Lamm. Day.	♒ 15	5 0	7 0	Rife	Now men that have good fweet-hearts got,
2	fri	Settled	♓ 0	5 1	6 59	A	Although the weather's very hot,
3	fat.	clear	14	5 2	6 58	8 39	
4	F.	9 p. Trinity.	28	5 3	6 57	9 2	Yet if he have a mind to have her,
5	mo	weather,	♈ 11	5 4	6 56	9 24	
6	tue	and	24	5 5	6 55	9 47	He'd better marry now than never;
7	we	very warm,	♉ 6	5 6	6 54	10 7	
8	thu	with	18	5 7	6 53	10 37	But if fhe is a fcolding flut,
9	fri	heavy	♊ 0	5 8	6 52	11 15	And one that has no money got,
10	fat.	dews.	12	5 9	6 51	11 56	Confidering all 'tis ten to one,
11	F.	10 p. Trinity.	24	5 11	6 49	Morn	She had be better let alone.
12	mo		♋ 6	5 12	6 48	1 48	
13	tue	Now expect	18	5 13	6 47	2 48	
14	we	a good	♌ 0	5 15	6 45	Moon	
15	thu	Affu. V. M.	12	5 16	6 44	Set	
16	fri	⊙ Eclip. inv.	24	5 17	6 43	A	
17	fat.	deal of falling	♍ 7	5 18	6 42	7 50	If one fhould come to thee that is of no worth,
18	F.	11 p. Trinity.	20	5 19	6 41	8 12	
19	mo	weather,	♎ 3	5 20	6 40	8 34	
20	tue	with	16	5 21	6 39	9 1	And afk thee to be bound for him, and fo forth,
21	we	intervening	♏ 0	5 22	6 38	9 32	
22	thu	fun-fhine.	13	5 23	6 37	10 12	
23	fri		27	5 24	6 36	11 0	In all fuch things as that be thou a flow man,
24	fat.	St. Barthol.	♐ 11	5 26	6 34	12 0	
25	F.	12 p. Trinity.	25	5 27	6 33	Morn	Tell him thou wilt to prifon go for no man,
26	mo	Fine	♑ 10	5 28	6 32	1 18	
27	tue	growing	24	5 29	6 31	2 34	
28	we	weather,	♒ 9	5 31	6 29	Moon	
29	thu	as can be	24	5 32	6 28	Rife	
30	fri	☽ Eclip. inv.	♓ 8	5 33	6 27	A	
31	fat.	defired.	22				

In the almanacs that he used for his diaries, Washington often used symbols which are discussed on p. 329. (Library of Congress)

Note the last years Grafts from Mr. Digges—this Collo. Mason. Grafted also—In the 7 Row, 43 Gloucester White Apple. 8 Row beginning next Ray Grass 7 more of Do. (in all 50) endg. at a Stake. Note these from Collo. Mason.

In the border just above the 2 Fall in the Garden Grafted one of the fine early May Cherry—Collo. Mason.

Note this is the 2d. Graff in the Border & stands nearest the middle walk.

All the old standard varieties of pear were derived from *Pyrus communis,* the European species. In the first catalogue of fruits published in America, gardener William Prince advertised the "black pear of Worcester, or Parkinson's warden." It is "dirty brown in color" and does best against a wall (HITT, 344). A horticulturist writing in 1950 reported that trees of this variety are said to be more than 200 years old (HEDRICK, 35). There were several kinds of Bergamot, and the Autumn Bergamot may have been raised in England in the time of the Caesars. GW is following English custom in calling it a "Bergamy."

The Gloucester White apple does not appear to be a common variety; GW may simply be describing it on the basis of where he got it. A Gloucester Cheese variety is named in WATSON [1], 296–97.

[June]

5.   Got one load of Hay from Peach Orchard weight   1483 lbs.
6.   Got the rest in viz.   1979
                                                          ————
                                                          3462

7 & 8.   Dug up abt. [   ] load of Marle to spread over Wheat Land—for experiment.

8.   Sowed Lucerne again in the missing places below Garden.

11.   Finishd (with two Plows) the Gd. behind the Garden wch. was begun the 4th.

12.   Began to cut Meadow (Greek).

13.   Meazured of 64 Gallons & put undr. Bishops care for Harvest &ca.

This month GW began to make various notations—words, names, abbreviations, letters, numerals, symbols, and other marks—in the margins of the monthly astronomical calendars printed in his almanacs. There are few substantial clues to the meaning of these casual jottings. Varying greatly in form and seldom having any apparent relation to corresponding diary or almanac entries, they appear at random over two widely separated periods: June 1764–Nov. 1775 and Feb. 1795–Dec. 1798. In most cases the editors can make no sense of them, but some can be understood. During the summer of 1770 GW used the calendar pages for a health record, counting his stepdaughter Martha Parke Custis's recurring epileptic attacks for a period of about three months (see main entry for 31 July 1770). During 1772 and 1774 the calendar notations served on several occasions to remind him of future obligations. The abbreviation "Fred" next to 15 Sept. and 23 Nov. 1772 meant that he had business in Fredericksburg on those days, and another notation next to 18 Sept. 1772 apparently told him that he must return to Mount Vernon by that date for a court-ordered survey and division of land that involved him. Several days in Nov. 1774 were similarly designated for the sale of a friend's lands (see main entries for 20–27 Nov. 1774). As aids to

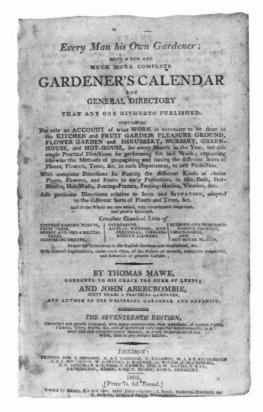

Every Man his Own Gardener;

BEING A NEW AND

MUCH MORE COMPLETE

GARDENER'S CALENDAR

AND

GENERAL DIRECTORY

THAN ANY ONE HITHERTO PUBLISHED.

An earlier edition of this work on gardening
was owned and used by Washington. (Mount
Vernon Ladies' Association of the Union)

memory and measurement, GW's notations in each of these cases served the
same general purposes that the other parts of his diaries did, but without
duplicating the exact functions of those other parts (see illus., p. 328).

[August]

1 & 2.   Sowed Turnips—behind Garden.

10.   Sowed Spelts—behind Ditto.

14.   Cut Timothy Seed at Doeg Run.

Allowing for artistic license, this engraving from Mawe and Abercrombie's *Gardener's Calendar*, London, 1803, might have been sketched in the Mount Vernon gardens. (Mount Vernon Ladies' Association of the Union)

[331]

15.   Onwards getting Apples for Cyder.

17 & 18.   Brought Oats from Ashfords. Note they were good Oats & a bushl. of them when well cleand weighd 30 lbs. & a bushl. of Spelts—weighd 28.

22.   Trimmed up 52 heads of Tobo. at Creek Quarter for Sweet-scented Seed.
    Began to cut Meadow on Creek.

23.   Peaches require to be gatherd for B[rand]y.

24.   Began to sow Wheat at Muddy hole.

27.   Began to sow Do. at Riverside Qr.

28.   Began———Do. at Creek.

30.   Began———Do. at Doeg Run.

31.   Finished curing & Stacking Hay.

[September]

8.   Sowed a few Oats to see if they woud stand the Winter (at Doeg Run).

15.   Finished Sowing Wheat at Riverside Quarter 50 Bushels.

20.   Sowed Wheat as far as Ransoms Houses at Muddy hole 55 Bushels.

Elizabeth Ransom, a widow, had rented a farm from GW from 1757 to 1760.

21.   Began to cut Tops at Muddy H. & R. Qrs.

The practice in GW's day was to remove the tops and blades from the corn-stalks during the fall, leaving the bare stalks standing while the ears ripened. The tops and blades, and later the harvested stalks, became fodder for live-stock.

22.   Finishd Sowing the Wheat in Corn Ground on this side the Run at Doeg Run Qr. Wint[er] (Wheat) from home 36 Bls. thrashed at the Quartr. 38 Bls. in all 74 Busl.

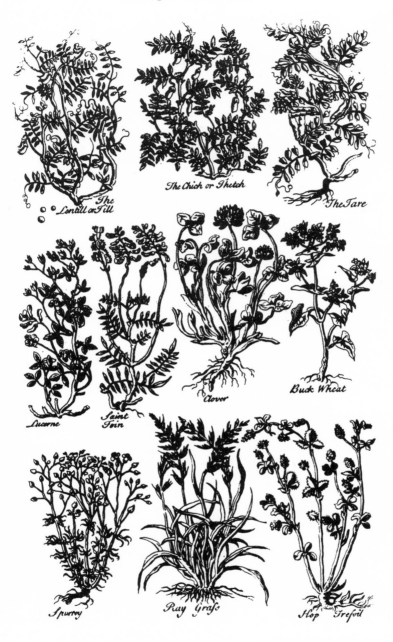

Washington raised nearly all the crops shown in this illustration from Hale's *Husbandry*, London, 1758. (Mount Vernon Ladies' Association of the Union)

Finishd plan[tin]g. Turnips behind Garden wch. was begun 20th.

27.   A Negro & Apprentice of Robt. Wrights began to Work upon my Mill.

Transplanted Lucerne below Garden & Sowed [   ] Rows of St. Foine.

GW tried doggedly to raise sainfoin (*Onobrychis vicioefolia*), also called esparcet, a crop now in very limited cultivation in the United States. It does not adapt well in areas where red clover and alfalfa will do much better, as Arthur Young knew when GW asked him for seed of the English strain in 1786. Young replied 2 Feb. 1787 that he was sending only a small quantity of seed, "for I cannot conceive that it will succeed at all with you" (DLC:GW). Young was correct. GW wrote Samuel Powel 15 Sept. 1788 that his fall planting in 1787 died by frost and his spring 1788 crop failed to come up at all (ViMtV). Still, GW continued to plant small quantities of it, hoping to accumulate enough seed for a full crop. Despite the dissatisfaction with the plant, it was still being advertised in the *American Farmer*, 1 (1820), 376, for sale in Baltimore. The advertisement referred to it also as "Hundred Year's Clover."

[October]

1st.   Robert Wright began to Work at my Mill.

Gathered Apples for Cyder.

Robert Wright, a local millwright, finished repairing GW's mill by 20 Oct.

2.   Sowed 7 Bushels of Spelts by the Orchard.

Morris & George went to Work at Mill along with the Mill wright.

13.   Finishd getting & securing Fodder at Muddy hole & Creek.

15.   Finishd Do. Do. at Doeg Run.

Finishd Sowing Wheat at Muddy hole & began to Sow Spelts.

18.   Finishd securing fodder at Riv. Side.

Hemp as a Fiber Crop

1765

January

1st.   Had at the Home House 78 sheep besides the 11 which are up

fattening	78
At the River Plantation there are	60
At Muddy hole	28
At Doeg Run	
Cattle at Home House — viz. —	
Work Steers	6
Fatting Do. & 3 Cows	8
1 Bull	1
Cows	
Yearlings	
At Rivr. Plantn. in the whole	
At Muddy hole Do.	
At Doeg Run Do.	
Hogs at Home house besides }	3
Pigs in a Pen — 2 Sows & a boar	

Riverside	Grown
	Shoats
	Pigs
Muddy hole	Grown
	Shoats
	Pigs
Doeg Run	Grown
	Shoats
	Pigs
Mill	Grown
	Shoats
	Pigs

[March]

5th. March 1765.   Grafted 15 English Mulberrys on wild Mulberry Stocks on the side of the Hill near the Spring Path. Note the Stocks were very Milkey.

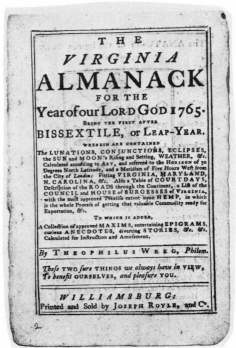

Many of Washington's diaries were kept in interleaved copies of the *Virginia Almanack*. (Library of Congress)

There is no species known as the English mulberry, but *Morus nigra,* black mulberry, was commonly grown in England for its edible fruits. It was known to eighteenth-century Virginia planters as the English mulberry. While feeding silkworms on mulberry leaves and making paper from the bark were much discussed and attempted in GW's day, there is no evidence that he raised the trees for anything but ornamentation and fruit. *M. alba multicaulis,* the white mulberry used in silkworm culture, is not mentioned in any of the Mount Vernon documents. GW purchased four young paper mulberry trees, *Broussonetia papyrifera,* from William Hamilton in Mar. 1792.

6th.   Grafted 10 Cornation Cherrys on growing Stocks in the Garden—viz. 5 of them in and about the Mint Bed, 3 under the Marella Cherry tree 1 on a Stock in the middle of the border of the East square, and just above the 2d. fall (note this Graff is on the Northernmost fork of Do. On the Westernmost one is a Bullock Heart & on the Easternmost one is a May Cherry out of the Cherry Walk) 1 other on a Stock just above the 2d. gate—note this is on the Northernmost prong. The other Graff on the said stock is of the May Cherry in the Cherry Walk.

15.   Grafted 6 Early May duke Cherrys in the Nursery, beginng. at that end of the first Row next to the Lane—the Row next the Quarter is meant—at the end of this a stake drove in.

Also Grafted joining to these in the same Row 6 of the latter May dukes—which are all the Cherrys in the Row.

Also Grafted 7 Bullock Heart Cherrys in the last Row.

30.   Grafted 48 Pears which stand as follows viz. in the 3d. Row beging. at the end next the Cherry Walk are 12 Spanish Pears. Next to these are 8 Early June Pears then 10 latter Burgamy— then 8 Black Pear of Worcester—and lastly 10 Early Burgamy. Note all these Pears came from Colo. Masons & between each sort a stick is drove down. The Rows are counted from the end of the Quarter.

This day also I grafted 39 New Town Pippins, which compleat the 5th. Row and which Row are all of this kind of Fruit now.

The 6th. Row is compleated w. Grafts of the Maryland Red Streck, which are all of this sort of Fruit and contains [   ] trees so is the 8th. Row of this Apple. Also 54, in number and 20 in the 9th. Row beginning next the Cherry Walk.

The 7th. Row has 25 Graffs of the Gloucester white Apple which compleats this Row with that sort of Fruit.

[May]

12.   Finish Sowing Oats at Muddy hole.

12. ⎫
13. ⎭ Sowed Hemp at Muddy hole by Swamp.
Sowed Do. above the Meadow at Doeg Run.

15.   Sowed Do. at head of the Swamp Muddy H.

16.   Sowed Hemp at the head of the Meadow at Doeg Run & about Southwards Houses with the Barrel.

GW had rented some land on Dogue Run from Benjamin Southward in 1761.

18.   Began to Sow the old Gd. next the Orchard at Muddy hole with the Drill & finish'd 25 Rows & then stopd it sowing two fast.

20.   Sowed 14 Rows more—the drill beg. altered with 1 Bushel of seed.

Sowed two pices more at Doeg Run — viz. the two Orchards.

Sowed Lucern — also 4 Rows adjoining with St. Foin — & [   ]
other Rows with Fenugreek Seed.

Trigonella foenum-graecum, fenugreek, is an annual trefoil grown as forage
and bearing a seed with a strong, bitter taste; it was often used as an emol-
lient in poultices. GW does not appear to have gone very seriously into its
production.

30.   Peter Green came to me a Gardener.

Apparently Peter Green was on a yearly wage contract of £5. He appears on
GW's tithable lists only for July 1765 and left his position in June 1766. In
1771 GW was trying to find a good "Kitchen Gardener" on a four- or five-
year indenture at a moderate wage, and even inquired in Scotland. He hired
David Cowan, "late of Fredericksburg," as a gardener for the year 1773.
According to the articles of agreement signed 11 Jan. 1773, Cowan agreed to
serve "in the capacity of a Gardener; & that he will work duely & truely,
during that time, at the business; and also when need be, or when thereunto
required, employ himself in Grafting, Budding, & pruning of Fruit Trees and
Vines — likewise in Saving, at proper Seasons, and due order, Seeds of all
kinds" (DLC:GW). His salary was £25, plus lodging and food for his family.

31.   Cut my Clover for Hay.

The diary entries for the month of May are taken from a loose sheet in the
Dreer Collection, PHi.

[June]

8.   Sowed Turnips for forward use.

17.   Began to cut my Meadow by the Sein Landing, and on the
24th. finished securing all my Hay at the Home House out of the
three Meadows and on the [   ].

25th.   Began to cut my Timothy Meadows on Doeg Run &
finished making & securing the Hay on the 2d. of July. Rain
falling the 28th. otherwise the whole might have been compleated
by the 30th.

27.   Began my Harvest at the River Plantn.

[July]

22.   Began to Sow Wheat at Rivr. Plantn.

23.   Began to sow Do. at Muddy hole.

25.   Began to Sow Do. at the Mill.

A DESCRIPTION OF THE ROADS.

From CHARLES-TOWN *in* SOUTH-CAROLINA, *to* WILLIAMSBURG *in* VIRGINIA, *thus accounted.*

	Miles.		Miles.
FROM Charles-Town To Goose-Creek Bridge	16	To Grave's Ferry on News-River	20
To Cooper River Ferry	10	To Bath-Town on Pamplico River	32
To Jenderoon's on Santee	24	To Bell's Ferry on Chowan-Sound	45
To Lewis John's on Winea	35	Over the Sound to Edenton	3
To the Westermost End of Long Bay	30	To Bennet's-Creek Bridge	30
To the Eastermost End of Long Bay	25	To Nansemond Court-House in VIRGINIA	30
To Shallot River	22	To Isle of Wight Court-House	20
To Lockwood's Folly	8	To Hog-Island Ferry on James River	18
To New Town on Cape-Fear River	15	To Williamsburg.	7
To New-River Ferry	45		In all 470
To Whittock River.	30		

From WILLIAMSBURG to ANNAPOLIS.

	Miles.		Miles.
FROM Williamsburg To Doncastle's	16	To Hooe's Ferry	15
To Claiborne's Ferry	12	To Charles-Town, commonly called Port-Tobacco	10
To King William C. House	12	To Upper Marlborough	30
To Todd's Bridge	12	To Queen Anne's	9
To Snead's Ordinary	20	To London Town Ferry	9
To Port Royal	12	To Annapolis	4
			In all 161

From ANNAPOLIS in MARYLAND to PHILADELPHIA.

	Miles.		Miles.
FROM Annapolis To Patapsco Ferry	30	To Newcastle	17
		To Christeen Ferry	5
To Gun Powder Ferry	20	To Brandy-Wine Ferry	1
To Susquehanna Ferry	15	To Naaman's Creek	9
To Principio Iron Works	3	To Chester,	5
To North-East	6	To Derby	9
To Elk River	7	To Philadelphia	8
			In all 145

18

His use of the almanac as a diary gave Washington convenient data on roads, lunar changes, holidays, and other well-known almanac fare. (Library of Congress)

[August]

3.   Began to sow Turneps behind the Garden—the upper part of which, & down to a stake is the Norfolk Turnep. From thence to the bottom Naper Turnep.

5.   Finishd sowing Do. & a good shower fell thereon the same day.

GW wrote to Burwell Bassett 2 Aug. that the weather had rendered the prospects of a good crop "truely melancholy." "I lost most of my wheat by the rust, so that I shall undergo the loss of a compleat crop here, and am informed that my expectations from below [in York County] are not much better" (WRITINGS, 2:424).

6.   Sowed Turneps where the Drilld Wheat was, behind the Garden. These of old Seed.
   Finish'd Sowing Wheat at Muddy hole.

7.   Began to seperate the Male from the Female hemp at Do.— rather too late.

HEMP: *Cannabis sativa,* a highly profitable fiber crop, providing work in the off-season. After the 1720–22 sessions, the General Assembly offered a bounty of 4s. for every "gross hundred" of hemp, water-rotted, bright, and clean, to encourage production (HENING, 4:96–97). GW speaks of separating the male and female plants. "This may arise from their [the male] being coarser, and the stalks larger" (CALENDAR [1], 457). In the 1790s he experimented with a variety from India.

9.   Abt. 6 Oclock put some Hemp in the Rivr. to Rot.

10.   Seperated my Ewes & Rams but I beleive it was full late— many of the Ewes having taken Ram.

13.   Finish'd Sowing Wheat at the Rivr. Plantn. i.e. in the corn ground. 123 Bushels it took to do it.

15.   The English Hemp i.e. the Hemp from the English Seed was pickd at Muddy hole this day & was ripe.
   Began to seperate Hemp in the neck.

17.   Finishd Sowing Wheat in the Corn field, which lyes over the Run at the Mill 27 Bushl.

22.   Put some Hemp into the Water about 6 Oclock in the Afternoon—note this Hemp had been pulld the 8th. Instt. & was well dryed, & took it out again the 26th.

[September]

4.   Began to Pull the Seed Hemp but it was not sufficiently ripe.

5.
6.
⎫
⎬   Sowed Turneps behind the Garden.
⎭
7.
9.

Getting of Fodder at Mill & Muddy H.

15.   To this date my Carpenters had in all worked 82 days on **my Schooner.**

The schooner, apparently built at Mount Vernon, was finished and rigged by Dec. 1765 and launched the following February.

22.   This Week they workd 22 days upon her.

Here GW means man-days. Hence, if four of the six slave carpenters GW had in 1765 worked a 5½-day workweek they would have put in 22 man-days for that week.

23.   Began to sow Wheat from Colo. Colvils in Peach Orchard, & finishd 24th.—4 Bushls.
   Began to cut my Meadows at Hell hole & Creek.

Col. Thomas Colvill (d. 1766), of Cecil County, Md., had inherited Cleesh, on the south side of Great Hunting Creek, from his brother John (d. 1756).

24.   Took up Flax which had been in Water since the 12th. viz. 12 days.

FLAX: *Linum usitatissimum.* Arthur Young chided GW 19 May 1789 for wasting his time with flax. "What in the name of wonder can you do with flax? Not make linnen I hope; buy from England, from France, from Russia, anywhere rather than employ a soul in fabrics while wastes surround you by millions" (DLC:GW).

25.   Hempseed seems to be in good order for getting—that is of a proper ripeness—but oblige to desist to pull my fodder.

26.   Began to get fodder at Doegs Run & River Plantn.—rather too dry.

28.   This Week my Carpenters workd 22 day's upon my Schooner. And John Askew 3 days upon her.

GW revised his contract with his joiner Askew in April 1764, now paying him per diem at the rate of £4 per month. In Dec. 1765 Askew agreed to supervise GW's slave carpenters for an annual salary of £35 per year plus some provisions and to pay GW £7 10s. per year for rent. Askew's employment ended in the spring of 1767.

[October]

5.   This Week my Carpenters workd 24 days upon the Schooner & John Askew 4 Do.

7.   Finish'd gettg. & securing my fodder at Doeg Run.

8.   Do.—Do. at Rivr. Plantation—too dry.

10.   Finishd pulling Seed Hemp at River Plantation.

12.   Finishd pullg. Do. Do. at Doeg Run. Not much, if any, too late for the Seed.

The Virginia General Assembly offered a bounty for raising hemp of high quality. From "Agriculture," in Diderot's *Encyclopédie*, Paris, 1780. (Mount Vernon Ladies' Association of the Union)

This Week my Carpenters workd 22 days upon my Schooner & J. Askew 3 Do.

19.   This Week the Carpenters workd 18 days which makes in all 190 days & 10 of Jno. Askew.

21.   Began to sow Wheat in Hemp Gd. at Rr. Plantn.

22.   Began to sow Wheat at Doeg Run, on the Corn field on this side.

25.   Began to sow wheat in the Corn field on this side the Run at the Mill.
    Sowed three Pecks of Wheat (had from Colo. Lewis, of a sort, which he says is early and of an extraordinary Increase, also very large graind) behind the Garden in drills. Note it begins next the ditch & ends at a stake.

26.   Sowed the Remaining part of the Turneps in drills with an early Wheat also abt. 3 Bushels more broad[cast] in the same Ground & the residue thereof in spelts – 6 Bushels.

28.   Sowd. the residue of P. Orch. with spelts. [   ] B.

31.   Finishd sowing Wheat in Hemp Ground at Rivr. Plantn. & plowd in a good deal of shattered Hemp Seed – 27 Bushls. in all 152 [   ].

[November]

1st.   Sent 1 Bull 18 Cows & 5 Calves to Doeg Run in all – 24 head branded on the left Buttock GW.
    Sent 3 Cows, & 20 Yearlings & Calves to the Mill, wch. with 4 there makes 27 head in all viz. 5 Cows & 22 Calves & Yearlgs. branded on the Right shoulder GW.
    Out of the Frederick Cattle made the Stock in the Neck up 100 head – these branded on the Right Buttock GW.
    Muddy hole Cattle in all [   ] head branded on the left shoulder GW.

6.   Finishd sowing Wheat at the Mill – viz. 19 Bushls. in the large cut within the Post & Rail fence & 6 B. in the small cut wch. with 27 Bushl. sowed the other side makes in all 52 B.

13.   Finishd sowing Wheat at Doeg Run,
viz.—on the other side—find. in Sepr   38 Bushl.
    Corn Gd. & Do. in one adjg. this   108
    Early wheat in Tobo. Gd. &ca   5½
    large white Do. in Orchd.   ½
            In all at Doeg R.   152
            Do. in the Neck   152
            Do. at Mudy. hole   75
            Do. at the Mill   52
            Do. at home   9
The whole years Sowg.   440
Finishd getting Corn at the Mill.

Repository Symbols

Bibliography

Index

Repository Symbols

BDA	Barbados Department of Archives
CSmH	Henry Huntington Library, San Marino, Calif.
DLC	Library of Congress
DLC:GW	George Washington Papers, Library of Congress
ICHi	Chicago Historical Society
MHi	Massachusetts Historical Society, Boston
MWA	American Antiquarian Society, Worcester, Mass.
NBLiHi	Long Island Historical Society, Brooklyn, N.Y.
NjMoNP	Washington Headquarters Library, Morristown, N.J.
NjWoG	Gloucester County Historical Society, Woodbury, N.J.
NN	New York Public Library
PHi	Historical Society of Pennsylvania, Philadelphia
PPiU	University of Pittsburgh
PPL	Library Company of Philadelphia
PPRF	Rosenbach Foundation, Philadelphia
P.R.O.	Public Record Office, London
PU	University of Pennsylvania, Philadelphia
Vi	Virginia State Library, Richmond
ViHi	Virginia Historical Society, Richmond
ViMtV	Mount Vernon Ladies' Association of the Union
ViU	University of Virginia, Charlottesville

Bibliography

ANNALS   Arthur Young, ed. *Annals of Agriculture & Other Useful Arts.* 46 vols. London: various publishers, 1784–1815.

BAILEY [1]   L. H. Bailey. *Manual of Cultivated Plants.* New York: Macmillan Co., 1925.

BAILEY [2]   L. H. Bailey and Ethel Zoe Bailey. *Hortus, a Concise Dictionary of Gardening, General Horticulture, and Cultivated Plants in North America.* New York: Macmillan Co., 1934.

BAILEY [3]   Kenneth P. Bailey. *The Ohio Company of Virginia and the Westward Movement, 1748–1792: A Chapter in the History of the Colonial Frontier.* Glendale, Calif.: Arthur H. Clark Co., 1939.

BD. OF TRADE JL.   *Journal of the Commissioners for Trade and Plantations . . . Preserved in the Public Record Office.* 14 vols. Reprint. Nendeln/Liechtenstein: Kraus Reprint, 1969–70.

BELAIR STUD   Fairfax Harrison. *The Belair Stud, 1747–1761.* Richmond: Old Dominion Press, 1929.

BETTS [1]   Edwin M. Betts, ed. *Thomas Jefferson's Farm Book.* Princeton, N.J.: Princeton University Press, for the American Philosophical Society, 1953.

BETTS [2]   Edwin M. Betts, ed. *Thomas Jefferson's Garden Book, 1766–1824.* Philadelphia: American Philosophical Society, 1944.

BINING   Arthur Cecil Bining. *Pennsylvania Iron Manufacture in the Eighteenth Century.* Publications of the Pennsylvania Historical Commission, vol. 4. Harrisburg: Pennsylvania Historical Commission, 1938.

BLACK [1]   R. Alonzo Brock, ed. "Journal of William Black, 1744." *Pennsylvania Magazine of History and Biography,* 1 (1877), 233–49, 404–19; 2 (1878), 40–49.

Bibliography

BLACK [2] Henry Campbell Black. *Black's Law Dictionary.* 4th ed., rev. St. Paul: West Publishing Co., 1968.

BROCKETT Franklin Longdon Brockett. *The Lodge of Washington: A History of the Alexandria Washington Lodge, No. 22, A.F. and A.M. of Alexandria, Va.* Alexandria, Va.: George E. French, 1876.

BROWN Stuart E. Brown, Jr. *Virginia Baron: The Story of Thomas 6th Lord Fairfax.* Berryville, Va.: Chesapeake Book Co., 1965.

BROWNE Fairfax Harrison, ed. "With Braddock's Army: Mrs. Browne's Diary in Virginia and Maryland." *Virginia Magazine of History and Biography,* 32 (1924), 305–20.

BRUMBAUGH Gaius Marcus Brumbaugh. *Maryland Records: Colonial, Revolutionary, County, and Church from Original Sources.* Vol. 1. Baltimore: Williams & Wilkins Co., 1915.

BURNABY Rufus Rockwell Wilson, ed. *Burnaby's Travels through North America.* Reprint. New York: A. Wessels Co., 1904.

BUTTERFIELD [1] Consul Willshire Butterfield. *The Washington-Crawford Letters, Being the Correspondence between George Washington and William Crawford, from 1767 to 1781, concerning Western Lands.* Cincinnati: Robert Clarke & Co., 1877.

BUTTERFIELD [2] Lyman H. Butterfield. "Worthington Chauncey Ford, Editor." Massachusetts Historical Society, *Proceedings,* 83 (1971), 46–82.

BYRD Louis B. Wright, ed. *The Prose Works of William Byrd of Westover: Narratives of a Colonial Virginian.* Cambridge, Mass.: Harvard University Press, 1966.

CALENDAR [1] Bernard McMahon. *American Gardener's Calendar; Adapted to the Climates and Seasons of the United States. Containing a Complete Account of All the Work Necessary to be Done . . . for Every Month in the Year; with Ample Practical Directions for Performing the Same.* Philadelphia: B. Graves, 1806.

CALENDAR [2] Leon de Valinger, Jr., comp. *Calendar of Kent County, Delaware Probate Records, 1680–*

1800. Dover, Del.: Public Archives Commission, 1944.

CAMPBELL [1]   Thomas Elliott Campbell. *Colonial Caroline: A History of Caroline County, Virginia*. Richmond: Dietz Press, 1954.

CAMPBELL [2]   Charles A. Campbell. "Rochambeau's Headquarters in Westchester County, N.Y., 1781." *Magazine of American History*, 4 (1880), 46–48.

CARROLL   Charles Carroll of Annapolis and Charles Carroll of Carrollton. "Extracts from the Carroll Papers." *Maryland Historical Magazine*, vols. 10–16 (1915–21).

CARTER [1]   Clarence E. Carter. *Great Britain and the Illinois Country, 1763–74*. Washington, D.C.: American Historical Association, 1910.

CARTER [2]   Clarence E. Carter. "Documents Relating to the Mississippi Land Company, 1763–69." *American Historical Review*, 16 (1910–11), 311–36.

CARTER [3]   Jack P. Greene, ed. *The Diary of Colonel Landon Carter of Sabine Hall, 1752–1778*. 2 vols. Charlottesville: University Press of Virginia, 1965.

CARTMELL   Thomas Kemp Cartmell. *Shenandoah Valley Pioneers and Their Descendants: A History of Frederick County, Virginia*. Winchester, Va.: Eddy Press Corp., 1909.

CÉLORON   Mary C. Darlington, ed. "Journal of Captain Céleron." In *Fort Pitt and Letters from the Frontier*. Pittsburgh: J. R. Weldin & Co., 1892.

CHAPPELEAR [1]   Curtis Chappelear. "Early Grants of the Site of Berryville and Its Northern Vicinity." *Proceedings of the Clarke County Historical Association*, 8 (1948), 17–38.

CHAPPELEAR [2]   Curtis Chappelear. "A Map of the Original Grants and Early Landmarks in Clarke County, Virginia and Vicinity." *Proceedings of the Clarke County Historical Association*, 2 (1942), facing p. 56.

CLELAND   Hugh Cleland. *George Washington in the Ohio Valley*. Pittsburgh: University of Pittsburgh Press, 1955.

Bibliography

CONTRECOEUR DIARY   Donald H. Kent, ed. *Contrecoeur's Copy of George Washington's Journal for 1754.* Harrisburg: Pennsylvania Historical and Museum Commission, 1952.

COUNCIL   "Journals of the Council of Virginia in Executive Sessions, 1737–1763." *Virginia Magazine of History and Biography,* 14 (1906–7), 225–45.

CRAIK [1]   David Craik. *The Practical American Millwright and Miller: Comprising the Elementary Principles of Mechanics, Mechanism, and Motive Power, Hydraulics, and Hydraulic Motors, Mill Dams, Saw-Mills, Grist-Mills, the Oat-Meal Mill, the Barley Mill, Wool Carding and Cloth Fulling and Dressing, Windmills, Steam Power, etc.* Philadelphia: Henry Carey Baird, Industrial Publisher, 1870.

CRAIK [2]   James Craik. "Boyhood Memories of Dr. James Craik, D.D., L.L.D." *Virginia Magazine of History and Biography,* 46 (1938), 135–45.

CRESSWELL   Lincoln MacVeagh, ed. *The Journal of Nicholas Cresswell, 1774–1777.* New York: Dial Press, 1924.

CROZIER [1]   William Armstrong Crozier, ed. *Virginia Colonial Militia, 1651–1776.* Baltimore: Southern Book Co., 1954.

CROZIER [2]   William Armstrong Crozier, ed. *Spotsylvania County Records, 1721–1800.* Baltimore: Southern Book Co., 1955.

DARLINGTON   Mary Carson Darlington, ed. *History of Colonel Henry Bouquet and the Western Frontiers of Pennsylvania, 1747–1764.* N.p.: privately printed, 1920.

DIARIES   John C. Fitzpatrick, ed. *The Diaries of George Washington, 1748–1799.* 4 vols. Boston and New York: Houghton Mifflin Co., 1925.

DICKINSON [1]   Josiah Look Dickinson. "The Manor of Greenway Court." *Proceedings of the Clarke County Historical Association,* 8 (1948), 44–55.

DICKINSON [2]   Josiah Look Dickinson. *The Fairfax Proprietary: The Northern Neck, the Fairfax Manors, and Beginnings of Warren County in Virginia.* Front Royal, Va.: Warren Press, 1959.

DINWIDDIE   R. A. Brock, ed. *The Official Records of Robert Dinwiddie, Lieutenant-Governor of the Colony of Virginia, 1751–1758, Now First Printed from the Manuscript in the Collections of the Virginia Historical Society*. 2 vols. Richmond: Virginia Historical Society, 1883–84.

DNB   *Dictionary of National Biography*. Reprint. 22 vols. London: Oxford University Press, 1968.

DONEHOO   George P. Donehoo. *A History of the Indian Villages and Place Names in Pennsylvania*. Harrisburg, Pa.: Telegraph Press, 1928.

DOWNING   Andrew Jackson Downing. *The Fruits and Fruit Trees of America*. New York: Wiley & Putnam, 1845.

FAŸ   Bernard Faÿ. *George Washington, Republican Aristocrat*. Boston and New York: Houghton Mifflin Co., 1931.

FISHER   "Narrative of George Fisher." *William and Mary Quarterly*, 1st ser., 17 (1908–9), 100–139, 147–76.

FITHIAN   Hunter Dickinson Farish, ed. *Journal & Letters of Philip Vickers Fithian, 1773–1774: A Plantation Tutor of the Old Dominion*. Williamsburg, Va.: Colonial Williamsburg, Inc., 1943.

FORD [1]   Worthington Chauncey Ford. "Washington's Map of the Ohio." Massachusetts Historical Society *Proceedings*, 61 (1927–28), 71–79.

FORD [2]   Worthington Chauncey Ford, ed. *The Writings of George Washington*. 14 vols. New York: G. P. Putnam's Sons, 1889–93.

FRANKLIN   Julian Boyd, ed. *Indian Treaties Printed by Benjamin Franklin, 1736–1762*. Philadelphia: Historical Society of Pennsylvania, 1938.

FREEMAN   Douglas Southall Freeman. *George Washington*. 7 vols. New York: Charles Scribner's Sons, 1949–57.

GIST   William M. Darlington, ed. *Christopher Gist's Journals with Historical, Geographical, and Ethnological Notes and Biographies of His Contemporaries*. Cleveland: Arthur H. Clark Co., 1893.

GRAY [1]   Arthur P. Gray. "Washington's Burgess

Route." *Virginia Magazine of History and Biography*, 46 (1938), 299–315.

GRAY [2]   Lewis C. Gray. *History of Agriculture in the Southern United States to 1860*. 2 vols. Washington, D.C.: Carnegie Institution, 1933.

GREENE [1]   Jack P. Greene. "The Case of the Pistole Fee." *Virginia Magazine of History and Biography*, 66 (1958), 399–422.

GREENE [2]   Evarts B. Greene and Virginia D. Harrington, eds. *American Population before the Federal Census of 1790*. New York: Columbia University Press, 1932.

HAMILTON [1]   Stanislaus Murray Hamilton, ed. *Letters to Washington and Accompanying Papers*. 5 vols. Boston and New York: Houghton Mifflin Co., 1898–1902.

HAMILTON [2]   Harold C. Syrett, ed. *The Papers of Alexander Hamilton*. New York: Columbia University Press, 1961–.

HANNA   Charles A. Hanna. *The Wilderness Trail, or The Ventures and Adventures of the Pennsylvania Traders on the Allegheny Path*. 2 vols. New York: G. P. Putnam's Sons, 1911.

HARDEN   William Harden. "James Mackay, of Strathy Hall, Comrade in Arms of George Washington." *Georgia Historical Quarterly*, 1 (1917), 77–98.

HARRISON [1]   Fairfax Harrison. *Landmarks of Old Prince William*. Reprint. Berryville, Va.: Chesapeake Book Co., 1964.

HARRISON [2]   Fairfax Harrison. *The Proprietors of the Northern Neck*. Richmond: Old Dominion Press, 1926.

HAYDEN   Horace Edwin Hayden. *Virginia Genealogies: A Genealogy of the Glassell Family of Scotland and Virginia*. 1891. Reprint, Baltimore: Genealogical Publishing Co., 1973.

H.B.J.   H. R. McIlwaine and John Pendleton Kennedy, eds. *Journals of the House of Burgesses of Virginia*. 13 vols. Richmond: Virginia State Library, 1905–15.

HEDRICK   U. P. Hedrick. *A History of Horticulture in America to 1860*. New York: Oxford University Press, 1950.

HENING   William Waller Hening, ed. *The Statutes at*

Large; Being a Collection of All the Laws of Virginia from the First Session of the Legislature, in the Year 1619. 13 vols. New York, Philadelphia, Richmond: various publishers, 1819–23.

HITT   Thomas Hitt. *A Treatise of Fruit-Trees.* London: printed for the author, 1755.

HODGE   Frederick Webb Hodge, ed. *Handbook of American Indians North of Mexico.* 2 vols. Washington, D.C.: Government Printing Office, 1907–10.

HOPPIN   Charles Arthur Hoppin. *The Washington Ancestry.* Greenfield, Ohio: privately printed, 1932.

HUGHES   Griffith Hughes. *The Natural History of Barbados in Ten Books. London,* 1750.

INDIAN WARS   "Indian Wars in Augusta County, Virginia." *Virginia Magazine of History and Biography,* 2 (1894–95), 397–404.

IRVING   Washington Irving. *Life of George Washington.* 5 vols. New York: G. P. Putnam & Co., 1857–59.

JAMES   Alfred Procter James. *George Mercer of the Ohio Company: A Study in Frustration.* Pittsburgh: University of Pittsburgh Press, 1963.

KENT   Donald H. Kent. *The French Invasion of Western Pennsylvania, 1753.* Harrisburg: Pennsylvania Historical and Museum Commission, 1954.

KLAPTHOR   Margaret Brown Klapthor and Paul Dennis Brown. *The History of Charles County, Maryland.* La Plata, Md.: Charles County Tercentenary, Inc., 1958.

LATROBE   Benjamin Henry Latrobe. *The Journal of Latrobe.* Introduction by J. H. B. Latrobe. New York: D. Appleton & Co., 1905.

LEDGER A   Manuscript Ledger in George Washington Papers, Library of Congress.

LEDGER B   Manuscript Ledger in George Washington Papers, Library of Congress.

LEDUC   Gilbert F. Leduc. *Washington and "The Murder of Jumonville."* Boston: La Société Historique Franco-Américaine, 1943.

Bibliography

LEWIS

John W. Wayland, ed. *The Fairfax Line, Thomas Lewis's Journal of 1746.* New Market, Va.: Henkel Press, 1925.

LOGSTOWN

"The Treaty of Logg's Town, 1752." *Virginia Magazine of History and Biography,* 13 (1905–6), 143–74.

MCDONALD

Cornelia McDonald. *A Diary with Reminiscences of the War and Refugee Life in the Shenandoah Valley, 1860–1865.* Nashville: Cullom & Ghertner Co., 1935.

MAIN

Jackson Turner Main. "The One Hundred." *William and Mary Quarterly,* 3d ser., 11 (1954), 354–84.

MAYS

David John Mays. *Edmund Pendleton, 1721–1803: A Biography.* 2 vols. Cambridge, Mass.: Harvard University Press, 1952.

MEADE [1]

William Meade. *Old Churches, Ministers, and Families of Virginia.* 2 vols. Philadelphia: J. B. Lippincott Co., 1910.

MEADE [2]

Everard Kidder Meade. "Frederick Parish, Virginia, 1744–1780: Its Churches, Chapels, and Ministers." *Proceedings of the Clarke County Historical Association,* 5 (1945), 18–38.

MEMOIR

A Memorial Containing a Summary View of Facts, with Their Authorities. In Answer to the Observations Sent by the English Ministry to the Courts of Europe (Translated from the French). New York: H. Gaine, 1757.

MIDDLETON [1]

W. E. Knowles Middleton. *A History of the Thermometer and Its Use in Meteorology.* Baltimore: Johns Hopkins University Press, 1966.

MIDDLETON [2]

Arthur Pierce Middleton. *Tobacco Coast: A Maritime History of the Chesapeake Bay in the Colonial Era.* Newport News, Va.: Mariners' Museum, 1953.

MULKEARN

Lois Mulkearn, ed. *George Mercer Papers Relating to the Ohio Company of Virginia.* Pittsburgh: University of Pittsburgh Press, 1954.

MULLIN

Gerald W. Mullin. *Flight and Rebellion: Slave Resistance in Eighteenth-Century Virginia.* New York: Oxford University Press, 1972.

Bibliography

NEWMAN

Harry Wright Newman. *The Maryland Dents: A Genealogical History of the Descendants of Judge Thomas Dent and Captain John Dent Who Settled Early in the Province of Maryland.* Richmond: Dietz Press, 1963.

NORRIS [1]

J. E. Norris, ed. *History of the Lower Shenandoah Valley.* Chicago: A. Warner & Co., 1890.

NORRIS [2]

Walter B. Norris. *Annapolis: Its Colonial and Naval History.* New York: Thomas Y. Crowell Co., 1925.

N.Y. COL. DOCS.

E. B. O'Callaghan and Berthold Fernow, eds. *Documents Relative to the Colonial History of the State of New-York.* 15 vols. Albany, 1853–87.

PA. ARCH.

Samuel Hazard, et al., eds. *Pennsylvania Archives.* 9 ser., 138 vols. Philadelphia and Harrisburg: various publishers, 1852–1949.

PA. ARCH., COL. REC.

Colonial Records of Pennsylvania, 1683–1800. 16 vols. Philadelphia: various publishers, 1852–53.

PAPIERS CONTRECOEUR

Fernand Grenier, ed. *Papiers Contrecoeur et autres documents concernant le conflit anglo-français sur l'Ohio de 1745 à 1756.* Quebec: Les Presses Universitaires Laval, 1952.

PARKINSON

Richard Parkinson. *A Tour in America, in 1798, 1799, and 1800. Exhibiting . . . a Particular Account of the American System of Agriculture, with Its Recent Improvements.* 2 vols. London: T. Davison, 1805.

PRICHARD

Armstead M. Prichard, comp. *Abstracts from the County Court Minute Book of Culpeper County, Virginia, 1763–1764.* Dayton, Va.: Joseph K. Ruebush Co., 1930.

RILEY [1]

Edward Miles Riley, ed. *The Journal of John Harrower.* Williamsburg, Va.: Colonial Williamsburg, Inc., 1963.

RILEY [2]

Elihu Samuel Riley. *Riley's Historic Map of Annapolis.* Annapolis: Arundel Press, 1909.

ROBITAILLE

Georges Robitaille. *Washington et Jumonville.* Montreal: Le Devoir, 1933.

SARGENT [1]

Winthrop Sargent, ed. *The History of an Expedition against Fort Du Quesne in 1755 under Major-General Edward Braddock.* Philadelphia: J. B. Lippincott & Co., 1856.

[357]

SARGENT [2]   Charles Sprague Sargent. *The Trees at Mount Vernon.* Reprinted from the *Annual Report* for 1926 of the Mount Vernon Ladies' Association of the Union. N.p., 1927.

S.C. IND. AFF. DOCS.   William L. McDowell, Jr., ed. *Colonial Records of South Carolina: Documents Relating to Indian Affairs.* Columbia, S.C.: Archives Department, 1958–70.

SHERIDAN   Richard B. Sheridan. "Letters from a Sugar Plantation in Antigua, 1739–1758." *Agricultural History,* 31 (1957), 3–23.

SHILSTONE   Eustace M. Shilstone. "The Washingtons and Their Doctors in Barbados." *Journal of the Barbados Museum and Historical Society,* 20 (1943), 3–10.

SHRYOCK [1]   Richard H. Shryock. "Eighteenth Century Medicine in America." American Antiquarian Society *Proceedings,* 59 (1949), 275–92.

SHRYOCK [2]   Richard H. Shryock. *Medicine and Society in America, 1660–1860.* Ithaca, N.Y.: Cornell University Press, 1960.

SINGLETON   W. Ralph Singleton. "Agricultural Plants." *Agricultural History,* 46 (1972), 71–79.

SIPE   C. Hale Sipe. *The Indian Chiefs of Pennsylvania.* Butler, Pa.: Ziegler Printing Co., 1927.

SLAUGHTER [1]   Philip Slaughter. *The History of Truro Parish in Virginia.* Philadelphia: G. W. Jacobs & Co., 1908.

SLAUGHTER [2]   Philip Slaughter. *A History of St. Mark's Parish, Culpeper County, Virginia, with Notes of Old Churches and Old Families and Illustrations of the Manners and Customs of the Olden Time.* Baltimore: Innes & Co., 1877.

SPARKS   Jared Sparks, ed. *The Writings of George Washington: Being His Correspondence, Addresses, Messages, and Other Papers, Official and Private, Selected and Published from the Original Manuscripts.* 12 vols. Boston: John B. Russell, 1833–37.

STEVENS [1]   William Oliver Stevens. *Annapolis: Anne Arundel's Town.* New York: Dodd, Mead & Co., 1937.

STEVENS [2]   Sylvester K. Stevens and Donald H. Kent, eds. *Wilderness Chronicles of Northwestern Penn-*

Bibliography

sylvania. Harrisburg: Pennsylvania Historical Commission, 1941.

SWEM   E. G. Swem. "Brothers of the Spade: Correspondence of Peter Collinson, of London, and of John Custis, of Williamsburg, Virginia 1734–1746." *American Antiquarian Society Proceedings,* 58 (1948), 17–190.

TONER [1]   Joseph M. Toner, ed. *Journal of My Journey over the Mountains by George Washington, While Surveying for Lord Thomas Fairfax, Baron of Cameron in the Northern Neck of Virginia beyond the Blue Ridge in 1747–8.* Albany: Joel Munsell's Sons, 1892.

TONER [2]   Joseph M. Toner, ed. *The Daily Journal of Major George Washington in 1751–2.* Albany: Joel Munsell's Sons, 1892.

TONER [3]   Joseph M. Toner, ed. *Journal of Colonel George Washington Commanding a Detachment of Virginia Troops.* Albany: Joel Munsell's Sons, 1893.

TRIMBLE   David B. Trimble. "Christopher Gist and the Indian Service in Virginia, 1757–1759." *Virginia Magazine of History and Biography,* 64 (1956), 143–65.

VA. EXEC. JLS.   H. R. McIlwaine, Wilmer L. Hall, and Benjamin Hillman, eds. *Executive Journals of the Council of Colonial Virginia.* 6 vols. Richmond: Virginia State Library, 1925–66.

VA. TROOPS   "Virginia Troops in French and Indian Wars." *Virginia Magazine of History and Biography,* 1 (1893–94), 278–87, 378–90.

VIRKUS   Frederick Adams Virkus, ed. *The Compendium of American Genealogy: The Standard Genealogical Encyclopedia of the First Families of America.* 7 vols. Chicago: various publishers, 1925–42.

VOYAGE   "Narrative of a Voyage to Maryland, 1705–1706." *American Historical Review,* 12 (1906–7), 327–40.

WAINWRIGHT   Nicholas B. Wainwright. *George Croghan, Wilderness Diplomat.* Chapel Hill: University of North Carolina Press, 1959.

WALLACE   Paul A. W. Wallace. *Conrad Weiser, 1696–1760, Friend of Colonist and Mohawk.* Phila-

[359]

delphia: University of Pennsylvania Press, 1945.

WALPOLE   Horace Walpole. *Memoirs of the Reign of King George the Second*. 3 vols. London: H. Colburn, 1847.

WATERMAN   Thomas Tileston Waterman. *The Mansions of Virginia, 1706–1776*. Chapel Hill: University of North Carolina Press, 1946.

WATSON [1]   Alexander Watson. *The American Home Garden*. New York: Harper & Brothers, 1859.

WATSON [2]   Winslow C. Watson, ed. *Men and Times of the Revolution or Memoirs of Elkanah Watson*. New York: Dana and Co., 1856.

WESSEL   G. A. Wessel and S. Leacock. *Barbados and George Washington*. Barbados: Advocate Co., 1958.

WINFREE   Waverly K. Winfree, comp. *The Laws of Virginia, Being a Supplement to Hening's* The Statutes at Large, *1700–1750*. Richmond: Virginia State Library, 1971.

W.P.A. [1]   W.P.A. Writers' Project. *Prince William: The Story of Its People and Its Places*. Manassas, Va.: Bethlehem Good Housekeeping Club, 1941.

W.P.A. [2]   W.P.A. Writers' Project. *Maryland: A Guide to the Old Line State*. New York: Oxford University Press, 1940.

WRITINGS   John C. Fitzpatrick, ed. *The Writings of George Washington from the Original Manuscript Sources, 1745–1799*. 39 vols. Washington, D.C.: Government Printing Office, 1931–44.

Index

The index in the final volume of the *Diaries* will be complete and extensive. Preliminary indexes, such as the one that follows, consist primarily of references to persons. The abbreviation "id." is used for "identification."

Index